For current pricing information,
or to learn more about this or any Nextext title,
call us toll-free at **1-800-323-5435**
or visit our web site at www.nextext.com.

A NEXTEXT COURSEBOOK

INTRODUCTION TO

Journalism

Authors

John Reque Susan Hathaway Tantillo Judy Babb

Melissa McIntosh Bryan Denham

Author Affiliates

John Reque, Northwestern University, Evanston, Illinois.

Susan Hathaway Tantillo, Wheeling High School, Wheeling, Illinois.

Judy Babb, Southern Methodist University, Dallas, Texas.

Melissa McIntosh, formerly of Jeffersonville High School, Jeffersonville, Indiana. She is currently with KA.net Internet Services, Louisville, Kentucky.

Bryan Denham, Clemson University, Clemson, South Carolina.

Cover and interior illustrations: Eric Larsen

Printed in the United States of America

ISBN 0-618-00377-0

2 3 4 5 6 7 — QKT — 06 05 04 03 02 01 00

Table of Contents

Word Choice
Clarity and Brevity
Fighting Redundancy
Clichés
Modifiers
Action Verbs and Active Sentences

FEATURES

Example

CHAPTER 1

The Challenge of Journalism

In this chapter, you will learn:

- about the role of journalism in our society
- how high school journalism serves its audience
- about the importance of teamwork in journalism
- how to connect high school journalism and professional practice

As the journalism profession enters the 21st century, it faces major challenges. For one thing, the technology of journalism is changing so fast we aren't quite sure from one year to the next just how the news will be delivered. The traditional newspaper is still with us, but even in 1997 only 50 percent of adults said they'd read a daily paper the previous day, while in 1965, 71 percent had. Magazines proliferate; in 1992, 679 new magazines entered the marketplace, although half of them never made it to a second year of publication. Radio and television now bring us news around the clock, much faster than print can. But we're finding that the Internet can do it even faster, and who knows what form of news delivery is just around the corner. What's in store for future journalists?

Defining Journalism

Traditionally, **journalism** is defined as bringing the news of the day—material of current interest or importance—to an audience. Yet this definition of journalism has blurred, at least in the eyes and ears of consumers, who aren't too sure just who's a journalist and who isn't. As the technology of journalism has diversified, the lines between journalism and gossip, between journalism and entertainment, have narrowed.

At the high school level, journalism is still best approached as the process of reporting and writing the news and packaging it as a product for an audience. Whatever the technology, news is information that must be collected and presented to a consumer. News—or journalism—is only one part of what is called media. Journalism is not the movies, book publishing, public relations, corporate communications, television sitcoms, radio talk shows, Web sites, or any of the other subdivisions of mass communications. This book focuses only on journalism, with its chief emphasis on high school journalism.

Because journalism results in a product, it can be studied as a discipline. And while the discipline has its own key values and ethics and best practices, it can't be studied as an abstract concept. This text regularly applies the discussion of journalism to the specific task of putting out a school newspaper, yearbook, magazine, or news broadcast. A journalism class is a laboratory in which the goal is production by a team, just as it is in the professional press. Let's begin by looking at the purposes of the journalism product.

Roles for a Publication

If you were in charge of a high school newspaper, yearbook, magazine, or news broadcast, what would be your priorities in ranking the **ten** roles for a publication listed below?

1. **News reporting.** To what degree will you report what goes on in the school—the good, the bad, the past, present, and future? What do you consider to be news? Should you produce anything but news?

2. **Entertainment.** How important is giving your audience an emotionally rewarding break from academic life, including a focus on the humorous, light side of themselves? If it isn't serious, can you call it news?

3. **Matter of record.** To what extent will you report all events during the school year so there will be a record of the year for others to look back on? What details are important? To what extent are you producing history? Is journalism history on the run?

4. **School spirit.** How responsible are you for stressing the positive and for helping readers see the good side of the school year? Are you a cheerleader, obliged to publicize and promote school life?

5. **Community image.** Is the community beyond your high school campus part of your audience? How important is it to give community residents a positive image of school events? Does it matter what they, as parents and citizens, think about your school?

6. **Educational skills.** How important is it for you to learn and practice the professional standards of journalism as a foundation for your own journalism education? Should the commercial press be your model? Is high school journalism the first step in a career?

7. **Reader culture.** How far should you go in giving your readers and viewers what they want, no matter what it is?

Should your journalistic judgment supersede theirs? Will they buy your product if it does?

8. **Leadership.** To what extent will you show your audience what alternatives and choices might exist to resolve problems and conflicts at your school? To what extent will you try to control or influence their decisions?

9. **Public forum.** How much opportunity will you provide for your audience to express their views, to sound off on whatever they want? Are all topics open to public discussion?

10. **Interpretation.** To what degree will you try to explain how events, issues, and personalities are tied together and affect student life at your school?

Setting Priorities with Teamwork

While all of the 10 goals above have validity, a publication or broadcast staff must generate some *agreement* on which ones are most important if it's to develop a consistent product. Otherwise, you'll confuse your readers.

The way to set priorities is through staff discussion. Journalism is a group effort from beginning to end. In the commercial press, journalism requires specialists whose work blends together as the publication or broadcast is produced. At the high school level, journalism is more likely to be the work of generalists, beginners who do a little bit of everything because that's the best way to learn. So these goals need to be argued about on a regular basis—they form the foundation of what you're going to learn to do.

As you ponder their priority for yourself, your journalism team, and your school, here are a few thoughts about each of the 10 primary roles.

Primary Roles

❶ News Reporting

Reporting news is a higher priority for a newspaper or news broadcast and a lower priority for a yearbook or magazine. The difficulty with this goal is determining what is news. As a journalist you are a **gatekeeper**—you, not the audience, decide what news items will be presented. Once you forfeit your right to control access, you stop being a journalist. News choices will be discussed in detail in Chapter 3, *Defining the News.*

❷ Entertainment

This function has evolved as a strong priority for most forms of journalism—to the dismay of traditionalists who see information and truth as journalism's most noble goal. Yet news and entertainment have long coincided in the same journalistic medium. The question here is one of balance. Teenagers have a reputation for preferring entertainment to all else. But do you, really? Many adults have the same reputation. Which comes first, a diet of entertainment or the preference for it? The storytelling approach to journalistic writing (as Chapter 6, *The News Story,* discusses) is one result of the entertainment priority. Another result is the growth of entertainment pages in high school newspapers.

❸ Matter of Record

This journalistic purpose takes highest priority in publication of the yearbook, which by definition records the year. Professional newspapers do this, too—notice the detail recorded in the stock market report, score boxes on the sports page, or the weather page. Chapter 18, *Working on the Yearbook,* touches on how broadcast and the matter-of-record function meet up in the video yearbook, which has begun to replace the printed version at many high schools. Magazines, especially those published for a **niche audience**, can be detail-obsessed, as Chapter 19, *Magazines,* explains. Broadcasts need to record the details of the news visually. (See Chapter 20, *Broadcast Journalism.*)

④ School Spirit

Journalism and promotion aren't the same thing, so this priority may be low. You might run into conflict with school officials who would like you to present the school only positively. Other students may see your job as publicity agent for their activities. Don't simply dismiss this goal—learn to understand its importance to others and to your school environment. You should also get used to the **blaming the messenger** element in journalism, in which you get criticized for what you print—and what you don't print.

⑤ Community Image

This goal deals with public relations, implying that because adults outside the school may read the newspaper, it should be written with them in mind. You need to prioritize your audience here. Is it students? adults within the school? adults beyond the school, especially parents? Answering this question will help you develop a realistic attitude about the community image role of a newspaper.

⑥ Educational Skills

While your journalism teacher might well make this the top priority, you probably would not. Yet a journalism class, like any other course offered by a school, ought to develop useful skills in those who take it, especially if students are considering journalism as a profession. That's a strong argument for developing as professional an approach as possible to what you're learning.

⑦ Reader Culture

This is a tempting priority fraught with risks. If you're sure your audience is homogeneous, it's easy to address their tastes, but you might end up with a cross-word puzzle magazine or a comic book. While the high school audience is narrower than many—students within a four- or five-year age range who live in the same community and spend their workday in the same place—you still can't be sure they agree on what they want to read or watch. Some awareness of their needs is fine, but realize that these needs will conflict quickly with the other goals on this list.

⑧ Leadership

It's quite easy for the newspaper to have influence in certain areas or on specific issues, but journalists disagree on the importance of this goal. Traditional journalists argue that the press should report the news in a neutral manner and not try to influence decisions. Yet the more active leadership role of the press in influencing public behavior has been a clear preference for quite some time.

⑨ Public Forum

This purpose has legal implications as well as journalistic ones. Getting agreement from the school administration that your publication is, indeed, a public forum is the best way to avoid censorship in the high school press. (See the policy discussion in Chapter 2, *Law, Ethics, and Policy,* for the legal background of the school newspaper as a forum.) The forum role does not include unlimited access by non-staff members, but it does suggest using a formal process of selecting guest writers and letters to the editor, and careful monitoring of diversity in getting opinion quotes from readers or listeners.

⑩ Interpretation

This function deserves a high priority in all forms of student journalism because it takes the audience beyond the superficial and tries to explain the environment in which they spend much of their time. But consistent interpretation through journalism is difficult to develop for **two** reasons:

1. It is a complex process.
2. It requires substantial amounts of valuable publication space or air time. Chapter 8, *In-Depth Reporting,* covers interpretation in detail.

Other Roles of Journalism

Paying your way. A primary goal in the commercial press is profit. Journalism is a business, goes the argument, so your first task is to make money because you can't survive without doing so. While that's true in the professional world, it raises the question of whether the high school press should be financed by the school or expected to earn its own way. Schools vary widely in this regard. If your school's athletes, musicians, and actors don't have to raise money to pay for their activities, should journalists? If you have to sell your newspaper, will that affect how you treat reader culture?

Honors. Some adults see the purpose of any extracurricular activity in a school as winning prizes. Beware of the seduction of competition because it will overtake all the other roles of the school press. Contests are fine, but they're not why you're in this activity.

Showcase. Providing creative students with an outlet for publication or broadcast can be seen as a role only if you put the audience first. Do we support orchestras, school plays, and athletic teams in high schools just because they entertain an audience? Yet where would these activities be without an audience? Or are their roles more subtle—more educational—than that?

Journalism Goes to the Movies

Journalism has been the focus of many films over the years. Here's a list of 10 journalism movies from Jon Roe, former public journalism editor of The Wichita Eagle, *and the questions they raise about the press.*

Citizen Kane director: Orson Welles, 1941. Often regarded as the greatest film of all time, *Citizen Kane* is based on the life of publisher William Randolph Hearst. We all go into journalism to do good, but watch how Kane sets out to give readers what they need and deserve by using only his own judgment. How easy is it to move from servant to savior? *Kane* profiles a journalist who is seduced by his own power of the press.

Meet John Doe director: Frank Capra, 1941. Has a columnist ever made up a letter in the column? Barbara Stanwyck does so to tweak her newspaper's new bottom-line owner, and all heck breaks loose. The press and the politicians in Capra's brave post-Depression, pre-World War II movie get as intertwined as possible as Stanwyck dupes Gary Cooper into being a hero to average Americans. But all the while industrialist Edward Arnold is using Cooper as a front man for a third-party run at the presidency. Cooper then decides to commit suicide. Capra shot several different endings—see if he used the right one.

Lonelyhearts director: Vincent Donehue, 1958. Robert Ryan is the cynical editor of a big city daily who breaks in cub reporter Montgomery Clift by assigning him to write the advice column. Clift wrestles with whether he really should help the unhappy people who write him with their problems. Or should he use them as entertainment?

La Dolce Vita director: Federico Fellini, 1961. The good life in Rome is sucking all the meaning from life, and tabloid reporter Marcello Mastroianni reports on the death throes of society as he lives them. He knows something is wrong, but he thinks it's just him. Fellini's classic work asks how, and if, the reporter can see and report the story without becoming part of it.

The Man Who Shot Liberty Valance director: John Ford, 1962. Ford's most intellectual film asks what the press's duty is in a democracy. Is telling the truth enough? Lawyer James Stewart uses the local newspaper as a textbook when he teaches the citizens of Shinbone, Texas, about democracy. But who's using whom when he becomes a U.S. senator on the strength of a lie? How often do we follow the editor of the *Shinbone Star,* who tells Stewart, "When the truth becomes myth, print the myth"?

Network director: Sidney Lumet, 1976. Paddy Cheyevsky's script was a warning then. It's a reality now. Does the news

continues ▶

quality matter if the entertainment value is good enough? If I'm a TV anchor who tells you I'm going to commit suicide on the air, and you watch, am I not just giving the audience what it wants?

The China Syndrome director: James Bridges, 1979. Should you shoot tape when your source has expressly forbidden it? To whom does the tape belong? Your TV station, right? But what if the tape films a nuclear accident at a power plant, and the plant management convinces the TV bigshots to lock it up? Should you steal the tape?

Absence of Malice director: Sydney Pollack, 1981. If you print just the truth, how can harm come from that? Is it your fault if someone gets hurt along the way? How about if someone gets killed? Miami reporter Sally Field stumbles her way among a conniving federal

agent, a smarmy lawyer, and a nagging editor, all of whom just want to do the right thing.

Broadcast News director: James Brooks, 1987. "You totally crossed the line," TV producer Holly Hunter tells anchor William Hurt. He replies, "I tried not to cross it. They keep moving the little sucker, don't they?" He's on the way up in an industry that has replaced ethics with cathode rays. Hunter seems to be fighting a losing battle against Hurt's carefree approach to the news.

Up Close and Personal director: Jon Avnet, 1996. "If it bleeds, it leads," snaps news director Robert Redford, running a local TV station after his fall from the network. He's mentoring reporter Michelle Pfeiffer, who's on her way up to the networks, in a film that asks: "Can anyone do anything worthwhile and get it on the TV news?"

Decisions, Decisions: Journalistic Models

Journalism is full of questions, ones journalists ask themselves besides the ones they ask their sources. The role of the press in a democracy has evolved from the **three** general models of how journalism serves its audience, according to Michael Schudson, in *The Idea of Public Journalism*.

❶ Advocacy Model

In this model, journalism provides news from the perspective of a political party. This was journalism's role until the beginning of the 20th century, but it faded as political parties lost much of their power and mass-circulation newspapers developed. It still exists in newspapers that serve ethnic groups, magazines for special-interest organizations, and newsletters.

❷ Market Model

This model provides whatever kind of journalism the audience demands because what is newsworthy is determined by advertising. It still drives much of local television news as well as supermarket tabloids and other publications that cater to a consumer-driven audience. Journalistic content is selected here only to make money.

❸ Trustee Model

In this case, the journalist operates as a professional expert who determines what the audience needs to know and delivers it accordingly. Its premise is that the reader or viewer hasn't the time or skill to find out everything that is happening himself or herself and consequently turns over that task to experts.

The trustee model would seem the most effective for high school journalism. It avoids the narrow advocacy role by serving the entire student audience, not just a clique. It doesn't need to make a profit, so the demands of consumer advertising are minimal. It can be modified through **public journalism**, an offshoot of the trustee model that developed in the 1990s. Trustee journalism requires a staff trained in the skills of journalism, who operate as a team of experts in how to report, write, and produce the news, which is what you will learn about in this book.

Sidebar

The Six News Audiences

"Mainstream" audience (20 percent) skips the highbrow stuff, reads a local newspaper, watches both network and cable news, is interested in sports and crime but not in foreign news.

"Basically Broadcast" audience (17 percent) gets most news from local TV and networks such as prime-time "magazines," rarely watches cable news; enjoys health, community, and crime news.

"Very Occasional" audience (18 percent) tunes in only when something big is happening, tends to be lower income, and is heavily male.

"Constant" audience (13 percent) watches, listens to, and reads almost everything, somewhat indiscriminately; likes all topics and uses the clicker.

"Serious News" audience (12 percent) relies heavily on National Public Radio, the NewsHour with Jim Lehrer, the *Wall Street Journal*, the *New York Times*; likes news and business magazines.

"Tabloid" audience (14 percent) rejects traditional broadcast news; favors the *National Enquirer*, tabloid TV, and tell-all talk shows.

Source: Reported in *Warp Speed: The Age of Mixed Media*, Bill Kovach and Tom Rosenstiel, Century Foundation Press, 1999, p. 74.

Patricia Callahan, Beat Reporter

"The morning of the Columbine tragedy I was working on a follow-up story to my 'Dangerous Dining' investigation, when I heard a commotion at the city desk halfway across the room," says Patricia Callahan, 28, beat reporter for the *Denver Post*. "I heard the words 'guns,' 'grenades,' 'school,' and went to the desk and said I could help."

That began a marathon of coverage of the Columbine shootings for Callahan and the *Post* staff, and it led to Callahan's assignment to a Columbine beat through the first anniversary of the tragedy in April 2000. "The *Post* put together a Columbine team to cover the issues that came out of the school shooting," Callahan explains. "This was the biggest story of the year, and it was clear that it wasn't going to go away."

On the day of the shootings, April 20, 1999, Callahan jumped in her car and went to Leawood Elementary School, where she interviewed students who'd survived the shootings as they were being reunited with their parents. "I've covered tragedies before—murders, fires, floods, accidents— but nothing prepared me for how emotionally wrenching the Columbine assignment was," she says. "Students were describing how they saw their classmates get shot, how they ran for their lives, how they watched a teacher die."

Parents came up to Callahan in a panic and demanded information. But she didn't have it to give them. As busloads of rescued students arrived, there were tearful reunions. "And after the last student stepped off the bus, there were parents left standing at the fence," she recalls. "That was the most difficult part of covering Columbine, watching the faces of the parents left on the fence and realizing that they probably wouldn't ever see their kids again."

The following day Callahan wrote an 80-inch narrative of what happened April 20, starting with kids gossiping about the prom and ending with families realizing their children weren't coming home. While she continues to do occasional daily stories about Columbine developments, most of her pieces are long-form Sunday stories.

Before her Columbine assignment, Callahan was an urban affairs reporter at the *Post*, where she's worked since 1996. She started as a general assignment reporter working 3 p.m. to midnight. "On slow nights I did enterprise reporting," she says. An investigative series she wrote about public mistrust of investigations following shootings by the police led to her assignment on an urban affairs beat, which covered police misconduct, poverty, public housing, urban neighborhoods, and other social issues.

"I loved the variety," says Callahan. "One day I'd profile a wacky neighborhood character. The next day I'd be digging up documents to prove that a baby died after county caseworkers refused to heed hospital workers' warnings about her teenage mother's inability to care for her extremely premature baby."

Before joining the *Post*, Callahan pursued a journalism career that began in high school, when she worked as a sports stringer for a suburban weekly in her home town of Park Ridge, Ill. She was also co-editor of the literary magazine. "I didn't have any formal journalism classes in high school, but I spent a lot of time working on essays, poems, and fiction," she says. "While high school newspapers can be a good experience, I think creative writing can be just as helpful for young writers."

Callahan majored in journalism at Northwestern University, where she was a campus stringer for the *New York Times.* Her first internships were writing profiles for "Trib News," the *Chicago Tribune's* in-house newspaper, and *American Nurseryman* magazine, where "I had to edit the 'Pest Control' column," she says.

Subsequent internships during college included the *Sun-Sentinel* in Ft. Lauderdale, Fla., the *State-Journal-Register* in Springfield, Ill., and "CBS This Morning" in New York. "While that was a good experience, I decided that summer I liked newspapers best," Callahan says.

After graduating a quarter early in 1993, Callahan did three-month internships at the *Chicago Tribune* and the *Los Angeles Times* and then spent a year in Bangkok, Thailand, as a Henry Luce Scholar. She worked mostly for the wire service Reuters, writing about environmental, social, and political issues and working on an investigative piece about the trafficking of children for prostitution. "I would encourage high school students to consider studying or working abroad either during or after college," she says. "English-language newspapers overseas often are looking for young, eager writers."

When Callahan returned to the United States, she worked for a year for the *Chicago Tribune,* covering courts in Lake County, Ill. Then she took the *Post* job. Looking back at her Columbine assignment, she says, "The upside is that it's exciting to be competing with the national press on a story. The downside is that it can be very draining to be continually writing about murdered children."

Besides pursuing creative writing, Callahan encourages young journalists to read good writers constantly. "When you find a style you like, pay attention to how the sentences are structured," she says. "And volunteer or freelance for small, home-town newspapers. It's a great experience, and it can give you clips to send out when you get to college and start looking for internships."

Public Journalism

Public journalism, also called civic journalism, has evolved as a response to **three** key criticisms of the press:

1. It no longer speaks to its audience's needs and interests.
2. It sensationalizes and trivializes the news.
3. It throws information endlessly at us without telling us what it means.

Public journalism is an effort to bring the reader or viewer more directly into the journalism process.

* It doesn't turn over decisions about the news to the audience; rather, it consults its audience, listening to them both formally and casually about their ideas for stories and approaches to the news.
* It plays a role in organizing community projects, in serving community needs.
* It goes past the objective, neutral stance of journalists who simply report the news as it occurs.
* It acknowledges that the public and the journalist should work toward improving civic life.

If you choose to learn more about public journalism and how a high school staff might adapt it to the school it serves, remember a few suggestions.

Journalism's job is to help ensure that the democratic process works. You need to be objective but not detached. You need to frame issues through the lens of the students, not administrators, teachers, parents, or your own staff.

Tomorrow's news is happening today at the neighborhood level. Listen, understand what people are discussing and are concerned about, and report it.

People don't demand "good" news, but they do demand a sense that the problems you present can be solved and that they can solve them.

You must present choices to solve a problem, choices that force people to confront the real tradeoffs, to understand others' beliefs and examine their own.

Don't try to find people on the far ends of an issue to argue a point; they don't represent the readers. Interview the people in the middle—the ones with the same problems as your readers.

Your editorial voice shouldn't preach to readers but should be one in a chorus of voices, all dealing with the problems and how to solve them. Your job is not to hand down solutions but to further deliberation and discussion of them.

Write about faith and values. Students have them; they're part of the way people approach problems.

Always give empowering information in the story—someone to call, something to do or attend, watch for, read, hear, view, think about.

Provide your audience with easy ways to contact you and share ideas.

Tell your readers or viewers what you're investigating. They'll put up with a lot if you share what's happening with them.

Despite the technological changes that are revolutionizing how we get our news, journalism remains the art and craft of reporting, writing, and presenting the news. But our definition of journalism keeps changing as well. Neither producers of news nor its consumers are in agreement on exactly what the term journalism ought to mean. As you read this book, you will gain practical knowledge on how to report the news and write it, edit it, and deliver it to an audience. Your own definition of journalism will evolve as you pick up real journalistic skills. Your thoughts may be different from your fellow students' definitions, from those of your teacher, or from those of your editors when you work on school publications or broadcast shows. If you enter journalism as a career, you'll continue to fine-tune your definition. That is as it should be, for journalism has a protean quality. It changes with the culture it serves.

Journalism WORDS TO KNOW

blaming the messenger—a term taken from Greek tragedy, the habit of holding the press responsible for the information it conveys, even though it is simply transmitting a report, not causing an event.

gatekeeper—a traditional role for the press, which has the power to decide which information to publish and which information to ignore.

journalism—the process of presenting current information of importance and interest to an audience.

niche audience—an audience for journalism with specialized interests; for example, a political viewpoint, a common religion, an occupation, a hobby, a preference for a certain kind of music.

public journalism—an approach to journalism that emphasizes service to an audience and a concern for readers' and viewers' roles in the information process.

Laws, Ethics, and Policy

In this chapter, you will learn:

- how laws relate to journalism
- about the ethical standards of journalism
- how to form a consistent policy for your publication
- about landmark legal cases in high school journalism

Is there freedom of the press today? Yes, in the United States, there is—mostly. Despite the guaranteed freedom of the First Amendment, restrictions on the press do exist.

This country has certain laws that allow journalists to be sued—brought into court, tried, and slapped with a fine if convicted. Who sues journalists? People who feel damaged in print or broadcast are especially likely to bring lawsuits.

Of the laws that affect journalists, libel laws seem to be applied most often, but invasion of privacy laws also permit journalists to be sued and punished with fines. Laws also permit the members of the press to be sued for violation of obscenity standards. We'll get into and define the terms laws, ethics, and policy as we go along.

What Are Laws, Ethics, and Policy?

Laws

Laws are about what we have to do. Ethics are about what we should do. It doesn't take a rocket scientist to figure out that there are some similarities and some differences. Here, we will talk about three areas of law—libel, invasion of privacy, and obscenity.

Ethics

What are **ethics**? In journalism, standards of ethics provide a kind of self-discipline for reporters, writers, and publishers. In the past 25 years or so, ethical issues have become a major factor in the way members of the media conduct themselves. So much has gone on in this country between Watergate in 1972 and now that the press has become a more and more vocal critic of our government and society.

Policy

To understand the legal restraints on journalism and ethical issues that affect the field—and how these together influence the profession—you need to understand exactly what reporters and editors can or cannot, and should or should not, publish or broadcast. If you are going to work on a **publication**, you need to know what sort of consistent **policy** that publication has. A policy is a statement that announces a publication's rights and privileges and spells out its acknowledgment of limitations on

what will be published. If your publication is brand new or has no policy, it is a good idea to get together with other students and set one. Your instructor or adviser will help you work through this task.

A high school staff should work as a team to formulate and revise its policy. Its readers and viewers must be regularly informed of policy matters. For example, readers need to know whether you will print letters to the editor, how long they should be, and whether or not they must be signed or anonymous. Some tension between the press and its audience is bound to happen, but that tension will be healthy if each group understands the basics of the journalism process. For example, if your policy specifies that unsigned editorials have been voted on by the editorial board and thus represent staff opinion, readers are less likely to jump on an individual editor for what has been written.

Legal Restrictions on the Press

This chapter will outline everything you've always wanted to know about legal restrictions on the press—and do it as briefly as possible. Entire college courses and textbooks deal with just the first legal topic—**libel**—so this coursebook will present only an overview. But no journalist should begin the practice of this craft without a decent introduction to the law.

What Is Libel?

Libel may be defined as publication of a false statement that injures someone's reputation. "Publication" in this case includes broadcast and other electronic journalism. But what if it's true? No problem. The truth isn't libelous. How can you be sure of the difference? That's the issue.

What Is Slander?

Originally, slander was libel that was spoken rather than written. It can be said to be the "oral form of libel." It's become too complicated to separate slander from libel, so the slander definition has been absorbed into the libel definition. (They're the same thing, in other words.)

What's Libel in Your State?

Although federal libel laws do exist, most cases come under state laws, so journalists must be familiar with the libel laws of the state in which they work.

Libel Is a Civil Complaint.

You can't go to jail for libel; the punishment is normally a fine, and libel damages have gone as high as $20 million in recent years.

How Is Libel Proved?

Lawsuits against high school publications are rare. Even then, most libel suits are settled out of court, meaning that an agreement is reached before a full trial begins. On top of that, the odds in a libel suit favor the publication because the plaintiff—the one who claims libel—has the burden of proof. Still, the aggravation of even a threat to sue for libel can paralyze a newspaper staff, which must marshal valuable time and energy to fight a lawsuit. To sue for libel and win, the plaintiff must demonstrate a convincing combination of the following **five** points.

❶ Defamation

Defamation is spreading false reports about someone that injures that person's reputation. Standards of defamation, or what really is nasty, change within the culture. Calling someone a Communist 40 years ago probably would have been libelous, but now it might not be.

Defamation depends on the belief that the plaintiff has been damaged in the eyes of society by untruthful remarks. While what society regards as damaging is dynamic, not static, some standards do exist. Truly libelous accusations can lower someone's reputation in the community. Here are some instances that are at particular risk in libel cases:

* Accusing someone of criminal behavior.
* Attacking someone's character or ethics, such as accusations of business failure, drunkenness, cheating, lying, or using drugs.
* Accusing someone of being a traitor or spy or advocating a cause generally disapproved of by society, such as being a skinhead or a member of the Ku Klux Klan.
* Accusing someone of immoral conduct or of spreading something, such as AIDS or venereal diseases.
* Suggesting occupational incompetence or lack of integrity.

But, you say, there are a lot of stories in the press about crimes and bad behavior. When information about a person's criminal activities and so on appear safely in the press, it occurs because an official government source, such as the police, has provided the information. In this case, the journalist has what we call **privilege**—the right to report fully, fairly, and accurately on the contents of official government records or the words of official government spokespersons. Sources of such information are vital to protecting the staff from a lawsuit.

❷ Identification

The plaintiff must show **identification**, or that he or she is clearly the person that the publication is "saying bad things" about—the person being defamed.

That seems easy when someone's name is used, but what if it isn't? A "physics teacher," "sophomore cheerleader," or "third-floor security guard" might be quite enough for identification if some readers could identify the person. A name isn't always required.

Large groups (usually more than 25 people) cannot sue, so it's pretty hard to libel "the faculty." But a smaller group, such as "the basketball team," can sue.

Someone who is dead cannot be libeled.

A government body, such as a school district, cannot sue, but individual officials, such as school board members, may bring a libel suit.

❸ Publication

The defamatory material must be shared with a third party, or have **publication**.

A private letter that defames the addressee isn't libelous.

Generally, the damages, or monetary awards given in libel suits, hinge on the size of the audience who would read or hear the material.

❹ Fault

The plaintiff must prove that the publication or broadcast station was at fault in one of two ways:

* A private figure has only to prove **negligence**—that the report was published or broadcast without reasonable care. For example, reporters not on tight deadlines—such as high school journalists—have plenty of time to verify facts and seek additional sources (and would have no defense against real negligence). The more likely the remarks are to be hurtful, the more the reporter should check them out.

* A public figure or **public official**, however, must meet the **actual malice or reckless disregard** standard. That means the reporter knew the information was false but went ahead to publish it anyway, or that the reporter published or broadcast information that was so improbable only a reckless journalist would have done so. It's harder for public officials and public figures to sue for libel, because in their public role they have forfeited some privacy and they have an easier time of rebuttal than the private figure. The "contest" with the press is more equal; hence it is harder to sue.

❺ Damages

When the plaintiff demonstrates injury to reputation (not character), which is defined as others' feelings about you, and wins a lawsuit, damages mean money. A jury may award both *compensatory* and *punitive* damages. That is, the jury may order the defendant to compensate the plaintiff for any real injury, such as loss of business, and they may order more damages as a form of punishment to the libeler as well.

As we said, few libel cases go to trial because they are usually settled out of court, but of those that do, the media lose an estimated 70 to 80 percent. In 1996, the average libel judgment was $4.5 million. In other words, if a publication is taken all the way to court in a libel suit, there is a good chance it is going to pay up.

Definitions

Who's a Public Figure? A public figure is someone who has assumed special prominence—celebrity status of any sort— or who has come to the forefront of a public issue and has therefore some access to the media.

Who's a Public Official? A public official is someone elected to office who has substantial policy-making authority, as well as some access to the news media. School board members and administrators are probably public officials. So might be coaches. Teachers are less likely to be so defined.

How to Avoid Libel

Mindy Trossman, a Chicago media lawyer and professor, recommends the following:

* Check your sources. Corroborate anything risky. Beware the one-source story.
* Understand criminal procedure and terminology.
* Edit carefully. A sensitive story should be edited by several people, including the faculty adviser, who functions as the publication's legal expert. If you see a real risk, ask a lawyer to read the story.
* Have a notes policy, and either save all of your notes or destroy them. This policy should be applied staffwide.
* Realize that notes could be subpoenaed— avoid confidential content and editorial comments in your notes.
* Keep a log of your efforts to check out the story.

Libel Defenses

There are **three** main libel defenses a journalist can take to court.

1. **Truth.** This sounds obvious, but the truth may be harder to prove than you think. How do you prove someone is an alcoholic, of questionable character, or incompetent? For that reason, beware the single-source story.

2. **Privilege.** You are protected from a libel suit if you fully, fairly, and accurately quote a public official on official business or if you fully, fairly, and accurately quote from a public document, such as a police report. Such material may be incorrect, but you are protected because you did not know that.

3. **Fair Comment and Opinion.** If material is clearly labeled as opinion, such as in an editorial or a review, it is protected from libel. But the facts used to construct or support the opinion must be true. Fair comment assumes the journalist's right to criticize public events, such as a school play, or commercial enterprises, such as a restaurant. But be careful about the facts within the opinion. You can say that Juliet gave a poor performance, but cannot credit it to her partying all night before.

* Always seek comment, reaction, or rebuttal from those you're writing about. If you get a "no comment," include that in the story.

* Behave professionally by identifying yourself as a reporter.

* Avoid using general file photos or other material that could create mistaken identity. Realize that many people share the same name.

* Realize that correctly quoting a source about the person you're writing about does not shift the blame away from you. Accuracy and truth are not the same thing.

* Understand you can be sued for submitted material, such as letters to the editor.

* When someone becomes angry and threatens libel about a story, listen patiently. People often threaten libel without knowing what it is. You may wish to publish a correction or clarification, not so much because you have really libeled someone but because it will defuse the anger. Serious problems rarely get as far as court, but they often require full discussion to be fair. Your editor and adviser will become involved at this point, often to a greater extent than you as the writer.

Invasion of Privacy

Although it is much less common than libel in journalism, **invasion of privacy** is a legal matter in most states. As with libel, the plaintiff carries the burden of proof, and the penalty is usually a fine. Below are **four** privacy issues journalists must be careful to recognize.

❶ Intrusion

Intrusion involves a reporter's behavior while gathering the news. It does not require publication or broadcast, and the question of truth is irrelevant. It includes:

* Misrepresentation—pretending to be someone you're not.
* Trespass.
* Surreptitious use of a camera or tape recorder.

How to avoid it: Since consent of the source is about the only defense against intrusion, get permission if you intend to go onto private property.

❷ Public Disclosure

The idea of **public disclosure** involves publication of accurate information regarded as private, such as a crime victim's name, a sensitive illness, or someone's old criminal record. The issue centers on:

* Does the information concern the private, as opposed to the public, life of the individual?
* Is the information newsworthy?
* Is it "highly offensive" to a reasonable person?
* As with intrusion, the truth is not relevant here. Defense focuses on consent— if a teacher agrees to discuss his or her AIDS, then OK. If the material can be

Legal Troubles Serious problems rarely get as far as court. But, when they do, the media lose an estimated 70 to 80 percent of the time. ▶

found in a public document, you'd be protected if your account is full, fair, and accurate. One potentially serious problem is records from juvenile courts. Most are confidential, but if you acquire them legally, you should be safe.

How to avoid it: Be sure that the story is newsworthy and that your reporting is accurate.

❸ False Light

False light is defined as portraying someone inaccurately to the point that he or she is embarrassed and a reasonable person would be offended. For example, if you use a photo of students eating lunch in the cafeteria to illustrate a story on food fights, you might be implying that the pictured students engage in food fights, which could potentially embarrass them.

How to avoid it: If the material is false, then truth is the best defense. Consent is a key defense, too: if you get the students' permission to use their picture with the food fight story, then you aren't in trouble.

❹ Appropriation

Most often a problem in advertising, **appropriation** involves commercial exploitation of someone's name or image. It includes unwanted publicity, such as using an old photo of a student being written up in a story on school discipline.

How to avoid it: If you use student names and photographs in advertising copy, always get prior written permission from those students.

AT ISSUE

The Copyright Box

Copyright law protects those who have created original works, such as articles, photographs, or graphics, from having their work reproduced without permission. It benefits you as a high school journalist because it protects your work. You, in turn, however, must be wary of using material from other sources without giving credit. That means not lifting photos and art that might violate copyright for use in your newspaper. An exception to this rule—also known as "fair use"—occurs when material is reviewed or used for educational purposes. To get an understanding of the complexities of the 1976 Copyright Act, see Chapter 7 of *The Law of the Student Press*, published by Student Press Law Center, 1815 N. Fort Myer Drive, Suite 900, Arlington, Va. 22209-1817.

Obscenity

Like libel, **obscenity** is a word tossed around by readers or viewers who may not really understand it. It is not the same as vulgarity, profanity, or bad taste, all of which are protected in the press and yet are frequently the targets of high school press criticism.

True obscenity rarely occurs in high school journalism—no legal cases involving it are on record. But staffs need to be able to defend themselves from being accused of it. Although obscenity does not enjoy First Amendment protection, defining it remains difficult. Supreme Court Justice Potter Stewart said in a 1964 case that obscenity "may be indefinable, but I know it when I see it." Three factors are commonly used in identifying obscenity.

The Line Between Crude and Obscene

Bethel School District vs. Fraser (1986) is one of the three best-known court cases that affect high school journalism today. (See pages 30–31 for a discussion of the other two important cases.) In Bethel, the court upheld the suspension of a high school debater who used sexual innuendo in an assembly speech to support a student council candidate.

Implicit sexual references and vulgar language or imagery are commonplace in print and broadcast journalism. But the courts frown on them in the high school press because schools have the right to control student exposure to such material. Therefore, a high school staff needs to be sensitive to just how far it can or should go in such matters. Trying to avoid all possible accusations of poor taste would make a publication too bland, and taste is subjective. On the other hand, seeking out vulgarity and lewdness, while not quite courting the obscenity definition, will produce a raunchy publication that loses credibility because readers are persuaded it exists only to tease.

The balance lies somewhere in between and depends heavily on the standards of your community. A state university town or a big city might be more used to relaxed language and graphic suggestiveness than a small community. Location influences standards. If you prefer a liberal approach, be aware that you may lose the respect of many readers. Recognize that charges of poor taste are inherent in journalism, and get used to defending your material from chronic complainers who may not always understand the logic of your decisions.

1. Whether a reasonable person applying community standards would find that the item appeals to prurient (sexual) interest.
2. Whether the material depicts or describes in an obviously offensive (gross, graphic, or sleazy) way, sexual conduct specifically defined as obscene under state law.
3. Whether the material lacks literary, artistic, political, or scientific value.

In short, material of an explicit sexual nature may be offensive yet not obscene. Offended readers may want to apply censorship anyway. At least one Supreme Court decision has upheld censorship of vulgar language in high school.

Journalism Ethics

Unlike questions of law, in matters of journalism ethics the debate is more important than the outcome. That is because ethics is open-ended—it focuses on the *moral elements of journalistic behavior*. Ethical premises may well include honesty and truth, but each ethics decision is a new one, not strictly tied to earlier situations or evidence that drives the law. Because there are no absolute rules, each ethical circumstance must be examined individually, and that requires constant staff discussion.

To simplify ethical issues, many professions develop codes of ethics, and journalism is no exception. The best known may be that of the Society of Professional Journalists.

Three Ethical Principles

The Poynter Institute of Media Studies in St. Petersburg, Fla., compacts ethical standards in journalism into **three** strong statements.

1. Seek the truth and report it as fully as possible.
2. Act independently.
3. Minimize harm.

But any ethical standards are guidelines, not rules. Unlike most professionals, journalists cannot be licensed in the United States. You can be fired for unethical behavior at one newspaper and get a job at another that sees nothing wrong with what you did because it has different ethical standards.

Ethics is ultimately a personal choice about right and wrong. It emanates from and contributes to your individual character. But, as part of a publication's staff, your ethical decisions affect the group, and they must be made with an awareness of your publication's ethical code.

Ethical Examples, Ethical Issues

Let's look at **six** ethics situations, all based on real circumstances. Ask yourself what ethical issues each illustrates. Each numbered example, or case, is followed by an examination of the issues at stake and the questions raised.

The Principal and the Bomb Threat

Your principal admits there have been several phoned-in bomb threats when you ask after hearing a rumor to that effect. But the principal asks you not to print a story, feeling confident the threats are fake and wanting not to close down the school for the day to have it searched. Will you comply?

This case relates to the journalist's relationship to the source of the information. Is the school in potential danger here? Will publication of the threats encourage copycat threats? What makes the principal so sure the threats are fake? Are the rumors going to increase if nothing is published? How would you feel if a bomb did go off?

Remember that no firm answer exists here about what you should do. But reporters have an ethical obligation to make sure that sources understand what they do with information. If the principal does not tell you this information is off the record (see Chapter 3) before supplying it, a reporter may use it. The reporter may later have to deal with an angry source—the principal—who may not cooperate the next time. When a source is a regular one in the newspaper, it is important to maintain good relations. That does not mean to give in to any request from the source. Which is more important here—the readers' possible danger or the principal's need to avoid disrupting the school day?

Minority Representation

A group of minority students demands that your all-white staff accept anything submitted by a minority student and aim at least 20 percent of the newspaper's content to minority interests. Minority students comprise 20 percent of the student body. What needs to be weighed in this decision?

One issue in this case is diversity. Another is access. What obligation do you have to cover that part of your audience not represented on your staff? How will you do this? Some high school journalism staffs are run by notorious cliques interested only in their own lives. While no one is likely to support a quota demand, is that really the issue in this instance? It is more likely that these minority students are making a valid point. Newspapers do not provide automatic access to their pages from non-staff. But they do welcome letters and guest columns from outsiders. If you believe in the forum role of the publication (see p. 3), a newspaper needs to work with these students without giving up the inherent right to choose what is published.

Teacher with AIDS

A teacher in your school is rumored to have AIDS, not pneumonia as announced. Do you try to do a story? Suppose the teacher with AIDS later dies. Do you mention the illness in the obituary? Does the newspaper even write an obituary?

Privacy can be both a legal matter and an ethical one. Is there a need for your readers to know about this disease? Isn't it highly unlikely, however, that anyone is at risk, given what we know today about how this disease is communicated? Is there a need for readers to know about anyone's private health matters? Can you respect the school's efforts to keep it quiet?

What is the teacher's wish? He or she may feel that students' awareness could be educational, putting a human face on a serious worldwide epidemic. He or she may feel that others' knowledge of the illness is neutral—it is what it is—or that it is simply no one's business. Remember the teacher is not a public figure, unlike Arthur Ashe, the tennis player whose AIDS was announced by the press shortly before his death in 1993. What if this teacher dies? In obituaries, the cause of death can be routinely mentioned. Would there be repercussions if a newspaper did so?

Case 4
Questionable Ads

A condom advertiser offers you a $400 contract for several ads, pointing out that the college newspaper in your community accepts the ads. High school students can legally purchase condoms. Will you accept such ads?

In this case, a conflict of interest occurs between the need for the advertising money and the reactions from readers, especially adults who are uncomfortable with teenage sexuality. Is the newspaper appearing to take sides in the premarital sex issue? How do you respond to charges of poor taste? Your school's sex education policy supports abstinence but provides birth control information. Are you violating the school or the newspaper policy here?

Case 5
The Writer and the Burglary Ring

Using fake names, your best feature writer turns in a story on two students who operate a successful burglary ring. The reporter refuses to tell the real names of the sources. Should the editor use the story?

Credibility or accuracy is an issue here. How do you know the whole story has not been faked? Can you expect readers to believe this story? On the other hand, would the sources have confided in the reporter if the newspaper intended to use their names? Won't the police want to know who the members of this burglary ring are?

Case 6
Fake IDs

A nearby store is selling fake ID cards, according to a reporter who shows you one. The reporter wants to go undercover with a tape recorder to buy a card so the newspaper can get the story. Is this OK?

Deception is the problem in this case. Does the value of the story outweigh the means proposed to get it? If fake ID cards are being sold, will you have a lot of angry readers who cannot buy them because the store will have to stop the practice when the story is published? Should you consult the police before you do the story? Would two wrongs make a right? The reporter probably has other ways of telling this story and getting at the truth without using deception.

More Ethical Areas

At least **three** more areas in journalism give rise to ethical issues. Some of these probably sound familiar to you.

1. **Plagiarism**—lifting material from elsewhere without credit. Most students are alert to this problem. The issue is the distinction between writing about similar ideas, which is permissible, and borrowing someone's language, which is not. Think of how you would feel if someone else stole a story you spent time on and went as far as actually putting his or her name on it.

2. **Fairness**—equal treatment of the various sides of a story. All stories have more than one side. Do proponents of hate crimes merit equal attention with those who oppose them?

3. **Photojournalism**—where truth or misrepresentation is seen in an image. Ethics in this area deals with the good taste question of showing extreme violence or suffering; the ability of digital photography to manipulate and thus distort details; the problem of exposing the private behavior of those who happen to get photographed in a public place.

Making Decisions

Because ethics decisions in journalism often need to be made quickly under deadline, reporters and editors benefit from experience and previous ethical problems. Not all ethical problems can be anticipated, but the more they can be categorized, the smoother the decision process will become. Development of a set of ethics guidelines should be a staff goal.

Ethical Hypotheticals

In a group, discuss each situation below as if you were on the editorial board of your school newspaper.

* The new principal plans to contribute a column to the opinion page this year. Will you accept it?
* The news editor plans to run for the current vacancy on the student council because it will look good on college admissions applications. Is this OK?
* A speaker uses the phrase "bureaucratic B.S." (in its full glory) in remarks at a rally protesting student parking fees. The newspaper adviser suggests the phrase be edited out of the story. Does the newspaper comply?
* A food review story about six hot dog stands warns about serious health hazards at one restaurant that spends $600 a year in advertising. What will you do?

What's the Policy?

Legal and ethical standards form the base of press policy, but other factors influence it as well. Policy is a statement that defines a publication. Policy serves **two** purposes:

1. Policy tells the audience the ground rules for operation of the publication because the policy is published on the

editorial page—sometimes in each issue, sometimes less often, such as in the first issue of the school year. Abbreviated policy statements are acceptable.

2. Policy sets standards for staff operation, providing a framework for troubleshooting management problems and consistent guidance for the publishing process. As staffs change personnel, the policy provides a foundation from which to work. This type of material is not published for the newspaper's audience but remains on file for staff access.

If your publication already has a policy statement or manual, you have achieved a major goal. If it does not, you need to develop one—*but slowly*. This is a staff project. To function productively, it requires input or approval from those who have a stake in journalism operations at your school. That includes the faculty adviser, the school administration, and the school board. Unless they agree on policy content, the guidelines will be toothless.

What takes time in developing policy is getting agreement on content and approach. In some schools, adults and students see eye to eye on how publications should be run; in others, they disagree. Setting up policy in schools without agreement between faculty and students may be difficult because the process raises issues that can irritate some adults if they feel forced into such discussion. So proceed carefully. Try to understand the attitudes of people before you begin.

Checklist

Contents of a Good Policy Statement

A policy document available to readers or viewers should include:

☑ Ownership, or literally, who owns the publication?

☑ Basic purposes of the publication, especially the forum definition.

☑ Access—determination of content, including staff editorials, guest editorials, letters.

☑ Accuracy—how corrections are to be handled.

☑ Editorial board and its makeup and duties.

☑ Legal limitations on publication advertising acceptance.

Policy that affects staff only, not readers, should include:

☑ Financing the publication.

☑ Staff appointment and removal.

☑ Staff duties or job descriptions.

☑ Staff responsibilities, such as checking quotes.

☑ Postal regulations.

☑ Ethics matters.

Model

High School Newspaper Policy Statement

The Times of Lakewood High School, Lakewood, Ohio, publishes a complete policy statement in each issue:

As preservers of democracy, our schools shall protect, encourage and enhance free speech and positive exchange of ideas as a means of protecting our American way of life. The official newspaper of Lakewood High School has been established as a forum for student expression and as a voice in an uninhibited, free, and open discussion of issues.

Content of *The Times*, therefore, represents only the views of the student staff and not school officials.

The Times and its staff are protected by, and bound to, the principles of the First Amendment and other protections and limitations afforded by the Constitution and the various court decisions implementing those principles.

Online media like that produced in the Online Journalism course, may be used by students to educate, to inform, and to entertain both the school and the wider community and are entitled to the same protections and subject to the same freedoms and responsibilities as all other student media as outlined in this policy.

Online media are forums for expressive activity and are similar to traditional media in their freedoms, responsibilities, and professional obligations. As such they will not be subject to prior review or restraint.

Student journalists may use online media to report news and information, to communicate with other students and individuals, to ask questions of and consult with experts, and to locate material to meet their newsgathering and research needs.

As a forum for student expression, *The Times* will not be reviewed or restrained prior to publication.

The Times staff will strive to not publish any material determined by student editors or the student editorial board to be unprotected, that is, material that is libelous, obscene, materially disruptive of the school process, an unwarranted invasion of privacy, a violation of copyright or electronic manipulations changing the essential truth of the photo or illustration.

Specific definitions for these instances of unprotected speech can be found in Law of the Student Press.

With this in mind, student journalists have sole right to determine content of official student publications. By not interfering with *Times* or other publications content, school officials are therefore not liable for, or responsible for, content.

The Times adviser will not act as a censor.

In case questions arise over specific copy as defined within this policy, the advice of a practicing communications attorney would be sought. The services of the attorney for the Student Press Law Center are recommended.

Complete definitions of protections, unprotected speech, and other obligations can be found in the LHS Student Rights and Responsibilities booklet available to each student.

The Times editorial board as a whole will be responsible for determining editorial opinions, which represent the opinions of a majority of the editorial board. No single member of *The Times* will be held responsible for editorial content decisions.

The Times is a tool in the learning process of journalism and operates as a learning laboratory. Any student may be a member of the staff, with or without prior journalism experience or enrollment on the staff for credit.

A forum for student expression, *The Times* will accept all letters to the editor, guest articles, and suggestions from any reader.

The Times publishes all letters to the editor, provided they are 300 words or less and contain the author's name, house, homeroom, and/or address.

We will publish letters using "name withheld" providing the *Times* editor, managing editor, or news editor knows the identity of the author.

We reserve the right to withhold a letter or column and return it for more information if we determine it contains items of unprotected speech as defined by this policy. Letters will be edited for spelling and grammar and checked for verification. Should a letter contain errors in fact, excessive grammatical errors or be too long, it will be returned to the author for resubmission.

Deadlines for letters and columns will be no later than two weeks before the next publication date.

The Times editorial board reserves the right to accept or reject any ad.

In cases involving political or issues advertising, efforts will be made to solicit all points of view. The ultimate decision for all advertising rests with the *Times* editorial board.

The Times may cover student, staff, faculty and alumnus deaths as the editorial board is made aware of them. We reserve the right to decide not to cover a death based on relevance, timeliness, and circumstances decided on by the editorial board.

Source: *The Times* of Lakewood (Ohio) High School

Landmark Legal Cases

Behind the development of policy statements are the legal decisions that have affected the high school press during the last 30 years. These include two Supreme Court cases, *Tinker vs. Des Moines (1969)* and *Hazelwood vs. Kuhlmeier (1988)*. They also include state and circuit court cases affecting limited areas of the country, which journalists in those areas need to become aware of.

Tinker: The Boundaries of Expression

The *Tinker* case established boundaries of student expression in public schools. The case developed over an issue from symbolic speech, not journalism. It originated with two students, Mary Beth and Christopher Tinker, who were disciplined because they wore black armbands to school to protest the Vietnam War in 1965. The court decision established the right of students to express themselves in school as long as they did not "cause a substantial disruption or a material interference with school activities." The decision also said students have the right to express unpopular opinions.

Looser Restrictions. This case is also credited with loosening restrictions on high school publications. *Tinker* established "substantial disruption of the school process" as a limit on student expression. That limitation, which remains in effect, prevents student expression from causing riots, boycotts, walkouts, or other activity that paralyzes normal school operations.

Public Forum Role. *Tinker* also led to the establishment of the public forum role of a school newspaper. Forum was defined as a publication that:

* Consists of published news, student editorials, and letters to the editor.
* Is distributed outside the classroom.

The forum definition became crucial nearly 20 years later when the Supreme Court took a more conservative view of student expression in another case.

Hazelwood: Prior Review

The only Supreme Court case to deal with high school journalism in particular, *Hazelwood* arose from a dispute in 1985 between editors of a St. Louis suburban high school newspaper and the school administration over censorship of stories about teenage pregnancy and children of divorced parents. The Supreme Court determined the newspaper was not a public forum and thus not protected by the protections established in the earlier *Tinker* case. Rather, it said the paper was school-sponsored, thus permitting control of content by school officials, just as they would control content of the rest of the school curriculum.

School-Sponsored Paper. The Supreme Court determined the newspaper was school-sponsored because:

* It was under faculty supervision.
* Its purpose was to teach skills or knowledge to students.
* It used the school's name and resources.

The *Hazelwood* decision permitted censorship but did not require it, and many high schools have shown no interest in pursuing censorship. If a school wishes to censor, the censorship "must reasonably relate to pedagogical concerns," the Court said, citing some examples of material that could be censored:

* Material that is ungrammatical, poorly written, inadequately researched, biased or prejudiced, vulgar or profane, unsuitable for immature audiences.
* Such topics as "the existence of Santa Claus in an elementary school setting, the particulars of teen-age sexual activity in a high school setting, speech that might reasonably be perceived to advocate drug use or alcohol use, irresponsible sex, or conduct otherwise inconsistent with the shared values of a civilized social order."
* Material that would "associate the school with anything other than neutrality on matters of public controversy."

Prior Review. Most importantly, perhaps, through *Hazelwood* the Supreme Court permitted school administrators to review publications before going to press. This **prior review** clause is the major source of conflict in journalism after the *Hazelwood* decision. Those who support it often use an analogy that labels the school principal as the newspaper's publisher. In the commercial press, the publisher as agent of the owners certainly does have the right to determine content. Most journalists thus work for someone who can tell them what to print or broadcast.

Those who oppose prior review call this analogy false. The principal is not an owner's agent, they argue, because no one owns a public school—it is government supported. Further, they worry that censorship has increased since *Hazelwood* because school officials use different criteria than trained journalists would about what should be published. The prior review process delays publication because it represents an intrusion on the schedule by someone who does not understand the deadlines. It may also have a chilling effect, provoking self-censorship by nervous staffs who fear the school administrators and hesitate to challenge them.

Hazelwood has been superseded in several states that have established scholastic press laws along the line of *Tinker:* California, Massachusetts, Colorado, Iowa, Kansas, and Arkansas. Efforts in other states to circumvent *Hazelwood* are underway. The best recourse for publications susceptible to prior review, meanwhile, is a policy that establishes the publication as a forum and determines the newspaper adviser as the only adult in charge.

Effective journalism requires that you understand the rights and responsibilities of the press. Some of these involve the law. Libel, invasion of privacy, and obscenity are the three main legal areas in journalism. Others involve ethics, or a journalist's moral sense of right and wrong. Both legal and ethical issues need a framework of consistency spelled out in a policy statement that serves as a publication guideline. A policy ideally should be the result of cooperation by a publication's staff and school officials. Once in place, it notifies readers and viewers of what to expect.

Journalism WORDS TO KNOW

actual malice or reckless disregard— standards in libel required from public officials or public figures in order to sue.

appropriation—using someone's name or image for commercial purposes without permission.

defamation—in libel, untruthful accusations that lower someone's reputation in the community.

ethics—subjective standards that relate to moral elements of journalistic behavior.

fair comment or opinion—in libel, protection of the journalist if the opinion is clearly labeled as such.

false light—portraying someone in an embarrassing role that would offend a typical reader.

identification—in libel, the plaintiff's need to show that he or she is clearly the target of defamation.

intrusion—in media law, limits on how a reporter obtains information for a story.

invasion of privacy—in media law, claim by a plaintiff that private information has been improperly used by the press.

libel—the publication of a false statement that injures someone's reputation.

negligence—in libel, publishing defamatory material without reasonable care.

obscenity—published material that offends local community standards, portrays sexual conduct specifically described as obscene by state law and lacks serious artistic value.

policy—statement that announces a publication's rights and privileges and spells out its acknowledgment of limitations of what will be published.

prior review—permitting officials outside a publication's staff to examine and edit content before it is published.

privilege—in libel, protection of the journalist who is quoting a public official or from a public document.

publication—in libel, sharing defamatory material with a third party.

public disclosure—limits on how newsworthy facts about an individual must be if they are to be published.

public official—someone elected to office and/or having substantial policy-making authority.

Defining the News

In this chapter, you will learn:

- about the main qualities and elements of news
- how news judgment and other factors influence news choice
- how to generate story ideas

If you look at today's high school press, can you define news? Is news a new state law about carrying handguns? a debate team victory? a soccer defeat? an analysis of dating trends? a proposal for block scheduling? the school budget? record reviews? Yes, yes—and yes.

Defining the News

Today, news can be nearly anything that an audience finds (1) accurate, (2) informative, and (3) interesting. There are dozens of definitions of news, but they all share common ground in **three** areas.

1. Factual information is still the basis of news. *Accuracy* is what the press has to sell. Without it, the product is fiction, and that isn't news.

2. Readers and viewers differ in what *information* they value. The more the news personally affects the audience, the better. Whoever said "all news is local" understood that an audience wants to identify with the information it receives.

3. Bombarded with information, the news audience likes its facts to be *interesting*. People don't want to study the news because they're busy eating lunch, riding to work, or trying to pay attention in class. News is concise and easy to read.

Hard and Soft News

* **Hard news** is what you need to know, in the judgment of editors. Hard news is important.

* **Soft news** is what the editors think you'd *enjoy* knowing. Soft news is interesting.

A news story can both inform and interest you, of course, and that's surely a goal of journalism. Knowing that both goals are legitimate should help you find news and turn it into a **story**.

Story is journalism jargon for article.

Reporters' stories are fact, not fantasy. They narrate, describe, and explain, as fiction does—but they tell the truth, what really happened.

Qualities of News

Many press critics insist all news stories be objective—just the facts, covered from all sides. While **objectivity** is an admirable quality in journalism, it remains more of an ideal than a reality. Journalism as a discipline aspires to be neutral, but it's created by people who bring a point of view to their work. Human experience affects the pure objectivity of the journalist. Still, objectivity remains a quality to work toward.

Like objectivity, **balance** in the news means presenting a mix of information that matches the mix of the audience. The more diverse the readership or viewership, the broader the mix of stories. Knowing who your audience is affects the news you offer. A high school audience is relatively narrow—limited in age range and sharing a small community. Students are the target audience. Should adult readers such as faculty, staff, and parents be considered as well?

News Judgment

Several elements help explain **news judgment**, the process of deciding what's news. These **twelve** elements guide editors' news choices.

I. Timeliness. Historically, newspapers provided information the reader didn't already know but was willing to pay for. Although electronic journalism has sped up the process, this is effectively still true. Radio and television news reaches us much faster than print. The Internet delivers news even more quickly. (The Internet provides a huge challenge to news accuracy today. Read more about this in Chapter 4.)

High school news has a major timeliness deficit. Most papers appear monthly; even those few that publish weekly can't bring stories to readers who don't already know something about them. The "gee whiz" quality of news—its surprise element—is hard to develop in the high school press.

2. Conflict. Controversy drives news, just as opposing characters and forces make interesting fiction. Conflict develops the narrative quality of the story, supplying an interest level that supports the facts. Conflict may be physical, emotional, intellectual, or psychological. Or it may parallel literary conflict: person vs. self, person vs. person, person vs. nature, person vs. society.

3. Proximity. The more we relate as readers or viewers to the story, the more attention we pay. The high school press covers its own community for this reason, not events in the state capital or in Asia. Occasionally, events elsewhere have a **local angle**, justifying their development in the school publication.

4. Impact. Consequence, the effect of the story on the readers, draws them into the news. Readers are self-centered. Their personal concerns attract their attention. Sometimes journalism has to show readers how a story affects them by explaining its impact. For example, a story on activity fee increases will tell the student just how much more he or she will pay for the yearbook, athletic contests, concerts and plays, and social events.

5. Prominence. Why do celebrity stories seem to be everywhere in the news? Probably because the cliché that names make news is true. Some people make the news because they're important, others because they're interesting. News, after all, nearly always reports human behavior, and audiences like well-known humans. High school news is not as driven by prominence as the commercial press, where name recognition often sells papers. Still, a story about a famous person to whom student readers can relate can be a hit.

6. **Oddity.** News reports the unusual, not the routine. That's why crime and accident news stories are important and interesting. Most "everyday" facts are just too ordinary to become news, especially at school, where an uninterrupted routine is important to get work done.

7. **Drama.** News stories can dramatize events by developing character, action, and sometimes even suspense and climax. Of course, news events are much more ragged and uneven than the tightly controlled sequences of fiction. The facts cannot be made up just to slow down the telling of the story. Yet the dramatic elements of news and fiction reveal many similarities. Journalism is good storytelling.

8. **Space and time.** The number of pages in the newspaper or magazine or the length of the broadcast will affect what gets reported. It's normal for editors to collect more stories than they need, then drop some when breaking news pushes them aside.

◀ **Decisions** Journalist tries to balance the many factors that make a story newsworthy.

9. **Audience.** Journalism is sensitive to what readers want, yet it also supplies what readers need. The comic strip will be there, but so will a budget analysis.

10. **Policy.** Your newspaper staff may decide to give more space to teenage crime in the belief that the community faces a serious problem. You may omit the obituary of a retired teacher because policy specifies who merits an obituary. (See Chapter 2 for a complete explanation of policy.)

11. **Competition.** The high school press is regularly scooped on major stories because the commercial press publishes every day. Another paper's **scoop** can kill some stories and force editors to develop a different angle on others. There's not much point in writing about a two-week-old event as if it just happened. You have to **update** it, or add fresh information to the story.

12. **Presentation.** Television thrives on pictures. It's at its best when it covers live action, such as sports. When it tries to analyze a rise in inflation, TV often resorts to film of consumers pushing grocery carts. Print journalism is more flexible. The reader supplies some imagination and can skip from story to story; accompanying photos or illustrations can be action packed.

Generating Story Ideas

News, then, becomes a staff project to which everyone contributes every day. In professional newsrooms, the possible stories for each edition are discussed at an editorial or staff meeting (sometimes called a **budget meeting**), at which section editors present their ideas for their colleagues' reactions. These meetings are essential at the high school level as well. In an editorial meeting:

* Discussion is open and frank. Editors help each other with ideas and in the process avoid duplication.
* Unpredictability must be dealt with regardless of deadlines. Breaking news can alter the best planning, of course.
* The entire staff might participate, or perhaps just the editorial board may meet. This group effort is the first major step in planning an issue or broadcast.
* The meeting results in a **tally**, a list of stories to be assigned.

But where do these story ideas come from? They do not merely fall out of the sky. They need to be developed. The next section covers the ways to develop and uncover news stories.

The Beat System

A **beat system** divides the community into logical areas that produce news. Reporters assigned to a beat make regular contact with the sources of possible news to find out what's worth writing about.

Beats on a city newspaper include city government, police, education, hospitals, and public transportation. On a school newspaper, beats might include administrators, the school board, department chairs, student government, organization leaders, and such officials as the head librarian, director of food services, and director of building operations.

As a reporter assigned to one or more of these beats, you are expected to contact your sources regularly to learn what news might be developing. You then write a brief description of the news item and turn it in to the news editor. If the editor decides it's worth a story, you'll get the assignment.

Beat systems are not foolproof ways of producing news.

* ***Pros:*** They tend to provide routine news efficiently. Stories about awards, upcoming concerts and plays, new courses, and policy changes grow out of this system quite easily.
* ***Cons:*** The reporter who seeks more than the routine cannot just walk into a source's office and say, "Got any news?" Often the source doesn't realize that what's going on in that department could be news. For example, a librarian has just determined that 200 books have disappeared this semester and is upset. She may not realize, however,

that your readers would be upset too if they knew about it.

Sometimes a source is reluctant to reveal the news. The principal who knows SAT scores have gone down this year may not volunteer that information but would discuss it if the reporter brought up the topic.

You'll find that practical psychology—the kind you've used for years on your parents and teachers—must occasionally be used on news sources. Sometimes you can charm the information out of the source. Other times, it takes a lot of extra listening before you get to the real news. Once in awhile, a source is just not cooperating and must be circumvented. In that case, getting the information elsewhere and then confirming it may work.

Reporters need to know as much about their beats as possible. This can take years for professionals who specialize in a beat such as the White House. A high school reporter needs to learn quickly the personnel in an office and how the program operates. If you cover vocational arts, you need to know the faculty and the department secretary, what courses are offered, plans for new programs, and general developments in vocational education.

The beat system produces most of the material that goes into the **newsbrief column**, a collection of shorter stories, rarely over three paragraphs each, that are designed as a unit on the page. Routine items, such as National Merit semifinalists, award winners, concerts, and career night programs, fit in well here.

Newsbrief Column

2
Sept. 21
1998

New faces in classrooms

Teachers bring fresh ideas

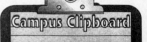

by Anja Kern

Walking into school the first day, students noticed construction workers, lost freshmen, and new teachers, some maybe looking a little lost themselves. Here are some facts about a few of these new faces at Westside. *More teachers will be highlighted next issue.*

David Bushnell
Age: 49
Experience: 12 years teaching Biology at Arbor Heights. 12 years at Westside Middle School.
Duties: Biology, Biocom, coaches cross-country
First Impression of Westside: "The most interesting thing I noticed was seeing all the faces I knew from the middle school last year in a new situation."

John Hiffernan
Age: 28
Education: BA in history from UNL, BS in secondary education from UNO, currently working on masters in public administration at UNO.
Experience: first year
Duties: AP U.S. History, World History, coaching wrestling
First Impression of Westside:
"The modular scheduling system is really different. I kind of feel like I'm a freshman. When you have to prepare for large groups it's a different feeling, too, because you have to prepare to speak in front of 350 people."

Doran Johnson
Age: 33
Education: University of Northern Iowa at Cedar Falls
Experience: Grundy Center (6-12th grade) in Iowa.
Duties: Freshmen Choir, Concert Choir, Warrior Choir, Warrior Express, Simply Irresistible, and Varsity Show Choir.
First Impression of Westside: "I see the district as a whole as a very professional district. But, kids are kids no matter where you are."

Mary Welch
Age: 23
Education: University of Iowa, post graduate education at Creighton
Experience: coached debate in Iowa City, Iowa
Duties: American Literature, Debate, Advanced Debate, Speech and Debate
First Impression of Westside: "I attended Westside five years ago, so the weirdest thing was teaching with teachers I once had to call Mr. and Mrs."

Eric Smith
Age: 25
Education: Graduated from Westside in 91, UNL
Experience: first year
Duties: Geometry, Discrete Mathematics, Algebra
First Impression of Westside: "I feel like I am really part of the math department and that everyone has welcomed me really well."

PEPSI
New contract unveils changes for next generation of students

Lance

by Natalie Shanks & Kathleen Massara

Is this true that if someone has a Coke shirt he'll have to turn it inside out? Will a student get suspended if he drinks a Coke product with his lunch?

Rumors are going wild due to the 1.3 million dollar contract with the Pepsi Company.

Freshman Rachel Stastny said, "What will they do next- tell us what food to eat?"

Rest assured that you didn't sell your soul to the devil, or sign away your civil rights along with the "Responsibility Rules" pamphlet that will be understood and signed by every Westside student.

It's true that a person can't bring any Coke products into the building, but it is also true that a person can't bring any beverages at all. The concern, according to Principal Phyllis Uchtman, is bringing spiked drinks into the school. Also, littering is a problem, with spilled drinks and pop bottles being dropped along the corridors.

The original reason for the Pepsi deal is that the Coke deal expired with the 1997-98 school year. As a result, school administrators sought to make new deals with other companies that were interested. The front-runners were Mid-Continent Bottlers, the Coca-Cola Company, and PepsiCo.

"We chose the overall best proposal," said Al Inzerello, assistant superintendent of Westside school district 66, "The school will receive $1.3 million over a seven-year period; the profits will go to a variety of activities for all of the district's schools, including the elementaries, and Westside Middle School."

Many students believe "Westside has sold out to corporate sponsorship." But according to Dr. Uchtman, Westside has had partnerships all along, one example being the janitorial partnership with ServiceMaster.

"It is not unusual for schools to make corporate partnerships," Uchtman said.

"There are lots of advantages to partnerships. In return for a long-range relationship, [the companies] support our programs."

Administration message loud and clear

Tardy, hazing policies emphasized

Campus Clipboard

Rockbrook hosts art fair

The Rockbrook Art Fair has always been a fun way to spend some time on the weekend. It was held at Rockbrook Village at 108th and West Center Road. This year was the 27th year of the fair.

The fair ran from 10 a.m. to 8 p.m. Saturday, Sept. 12, and from 10 a.m. to 6 p.m. Sunday, Sept. 13.

Rockbrook Art Fair has had good success as many people enjoyed walking around the village to look at art, jewelry and other items from over 150 artists, who represented all 50 states. Many artists are regulars every year, some were new to the art fair this year.

Along with the finest from these artists, there was plenty of food and refreshments. Also many of the stores in Rockbrook Village had sales.

"The art fair always seems to be a fun time and there is a huge turnout every year," an employee at the Garden Cafe said.

Volunteer Fair Day held

Volunteer Fair Day will be held Tuesday, Oct. 6 in the Loge.

From 9 a.m. to 1 p.m. there will be a variety of agencies represented. From the University of Nebraska-Omaha Medical Center to the Humane Society, there will be plenty of opportunities for service learning.

A reminder about Volunteer Fair Day will be put in the announcements.

Any questions can be directed to Miss Palmesano at the Service Learning desk in the front office. This is a great opportunity to find service learning hours.

Auditorium suffers theft

Between Thursday, Aug. 14, and Sunday, Aug. 16, roughly $10,000-15,000 worth of audio equipment was stolen from the auditorium. A VCR and a CD player were taken as well.

The administration turned over all the information, including several names, to the police.

The equipment will be replaced, but the administration is taking additional precautions to prevent further incidents.

The administration is also reviewing current security, and is considering keyless touchpads and keycards.

They also plan to monitor access to expensive equipment so that other incidents will not arise.

Forum elects officers

The purpose of Forum is to represent the student body on a smaller scale so agreements can be made between the school and the students.

Source: *The Lance*, Westside High School, Omaha, Neb.

Tips from Readers

Ideas from readers can result in many good stories, but you have to consider the trivial with the valuable. Think about these **four** things:

1. Readers generally don't understand journalism judgments, and their ideas can be too narrowly focused, vague, or just not interesting enough to be useful.
2. Frequently, tips from readers are requests for publicity for a favorite event.
3. While the staff must protect its right to decide what news it prints, listening patiently to all ideas will produce a few good items.
4. When a reader's idea won't work, explain why as pleasantly as you can. Never turn off readers from bringing in ideas—you never know when a good one will show up.

Brainstorming

Brainstorming is an excellent way to develop soft news—stories that interest readers yet don't depend on specific events of importance. (It's not so effective for hard news stories.) **Brainstorming** is a small-group process that works on the premise that one word or idea leads to the next and can often be developed into a story topic. It proceeds *deductively*—from broad ideas to specific information. It works best in a group because students give each other ideas as they articulate them.

Other Media Sources

You don't steal stories in journalism; that's plagiarism. But you do borrow ideas. Any story topic from another newspaper, magazine, or broadcast is fair game for you, *provided you borrow just the idea and develop your own version of the story.* Write the story to fit your school community and angle it to suit your own purposes. Don't feel guilty about this. It's normal in the media. Here are **three** tips:

1. **Localize your stories.** The commercial press is a strong source of story ideas. Court decisions and city council or state legislature proposals often affect teenagers. Localize the story for your school. Your staff should be monitoring the newspaper and TV broadcasts every day for story possibilities it can adapt.
2. **Check out back issues.** Back issues of your own newspaper may provide ideas. Much news is cyclical. History does repeat itself. It may seem obvious that you cover Homecoming and teacher retirements every year, but reading back issues may also lead you to check whether cafeteria prices are up again and what's been spent on building repairs over the past summer.
3. **Take advantage of exchange issues.** Copies of other high school newspapers that you receive in exchange for your paper are called **exchange issues**, and they provide a wealth of story ideas. Again, borrow only the topic, not the story itself. You'll need to do completely new research to angle the story to your

school, and the thrust of the story may turn out completely opposite from the idea you borrowed. Getting as many exchange papers from other schools therefore can be quite useful.

Know What's Happening at School

Curiosity, or a "nose for news," may be a cliché, but it is a cliché with merit. A genuine "nose for news" is hard to implant in a school reporter. It's partly a real interest in school operations and the people who carry them out. A certain skepticism about what sources have to say also helps. Here are some ideas:

* Sharpen your curiosity by carefully looking over routine documents, such as the minutes of the school board, the school budget, dress code, or freedom of expression rules, and see what ideas for stories you can pull from them.

* Try interviewing someone you wouldn't normally think would provide a story, such as the phone repair technician. Ask her, "Do you come here often?" "About once a week to fix the pay phones," she says. That sounds like the beginning of a story.

* Simply pay attention to your own routine day. A change in bus fare, a new sport in gym class, a classmate's unusual history project, the removal of milkshakes from the lunch menu, a Chess Club deficit can all happen in one day at school. And any of them could be the genesis for a good story.

Wrap-up

News is factual, informative, and interesting. It's aimed at a specific audience, but that audience might be broad or narrow, and the content of the news will adjust accordingly. News is developed and produced by editors who understand its qualities and elements. Editors are the gatekeepers for news, the people who decide what is published or broadcast. They may disagree with one another in their decisions, of course, but the news product, whether print or electronic, is the result of regular staff discussion and decision about news ideas that will soon be turned into stories.

Journalism — WORDS TO KNOW

balance—the goal of covering all sides of a journalistic story as fairly as possible.

beat system—divides the community into logical areas that produce news.

brainstorming—a small-group, idea-generating process that works on the premise that one word or idea leads to the next and can often be developed into a story topic.

budget meeting—a story planning session for a specific edition or broadcast during which editors present story ideas and compete for space; a major part of the teamwork process in journalism.

exchange issues—copies of newspapers from other schools received in exchange for copies of your school's newspaper.

hard news—news that's important, that readers need to know.

local angle—the part of a story that focuses on your readers' interests.

newsbrief column—a collection of shorter stories, rarely over three paragraphs each, that appears as a unit on the page.

news judgment—the process of deciding what's news.

objectivity—being neutral and focusing on facts, not opinions, in journalism.

scoop—an exclusive story that the other media don't have.

soft news—news that's interesting, that entertains readers.

story—any article in a journalism publication or broadcast. A story in this case is fact, not fiction.

tally—a list of story assignments for a specific edition or broadcast citing the topic, reporter, and editor, and estimating length.

update—adding fresh information to a story as events continue to develop.

Sources for News

In this chapter, you will learn:

- about the key role of human sources
- how to find and use physical sources in the staff room and the library
- how to access public records
- about the role of computer databases and the Internet as sources
- about some good electronic sources to access

When scholastic journalism teachers ask their students, "Why did you sign up for journalism class?" the most frequent response is "I like to write." And that's terrific. However, journalists do not write in a vacuum off the tops of their heads. They must dig for information before they can even begin to do their job well. The job of any reporter is to represent his or her readers, to take them where they cannot go, to give them information they cannot get without a great deal of trouble. Fulfilling this job means that the journalist not only needs to develop a "nose for news" but also a love of research. These research tools are the subject of this chapter.

Consulting Human Sources

People are the most frequently used sources for any journalist. There are **four** types of human sources:

1. <u>Primary sources</u> are the main players in the story. For a school-related story, they can be anyone from the most important officials in the school district—the board of education and the superintendent— to the students who are affected by the outcome of a decision made by those most important officials.

2. <u>Secondary sources</u> are those people who are not key to the story but whose point of view enhances other information.

3. <u>Professional sources</u> are adult experts who have information about a topic related to the story but who may not have specific knowledge about the topic as it relates to your school. When interviewing any of these sources, it is a good idea to ask if they have suggestions about other people you can talk to as well.

4. <u>Person-on-the-street sources</u> are random individuals who can offer an opinion about a topic but who are not personally involved in the specifics of the story. Such opinions can be included in the story itself or used as a photo opinion or quote collection sidebar to the story. One caution to student journalists about person-on-the-street sources: Do not interview your friends or other journalism students. Use this as an opportunity to quote students in your publication who wouldn't be quoted otherwise. Strive for a balance between girls and boys, across cultures, among differing viewpoints represented in your school, and through grade levels. Student staffs that are concerned about quoting as many different students as possible throughout the year keep a used sources list so they can avoid duplication whenever possible.

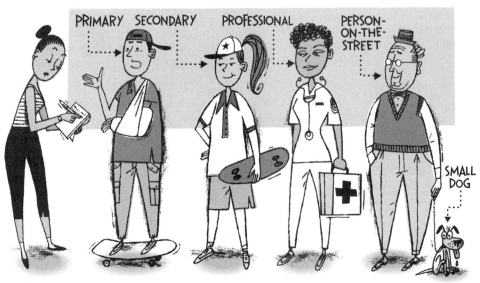

PRIMARY SECONDARY PROFESSIONAL PERSON-ON-THE-STREET

SMALL DOG

Types of Sources

To understand how different types of sources work in a specific story, let's look at an example. Imagine you are writing a story about "body fat tests." The physical education department conducts body composition tests each quarter as a part of the fit-for-life component of the curriculum and includes the test results in the student's grade. Most teachers make no attempt to hide the test results. In fact, some teachers use student helpers to perform the tests and record the results. Others announce test results for all to hear. In addition, students are grouped for activities based on the results of these tests. Students have grumbled about this practice for years. One girl and her parents have even gone so far as to write a formal letter of complaint to the board of education. What human sources will you use?

* Primary sources: the girl, her parents, her PE teacher, the PE division chairman at her school, the president of the board of education, anyone else?
* Secondary sources: other PE teachers, other students in the PE class, the principal, anyone else?
* Professional sources: psychologist or social worker, physical fitness expert, anyone else?
* Person-on-the-street sources: random students—striving for balance across grade levels, cultures, viewpoints, and sexes—anyone else?

Depending on what the board of education decides to do about the letter, you may end up with a series of stories on this topic. How might the sources change for a story written after this family's concerns are discussed at a public meeting? How might the sources change if the district policy about body composition testing is reaffirmed? How might the sources change if the district policy about this testing is changed?

Relationships with Human Sources

Having a good relationship with a source is usually critical to obtaining helpful information. Since reporters never know from whom they may need information in the future, it is best to treat everyone as a potential source. Don't make enemies or undermine your credibility with anyone who is a potential source for a story.

In some cases, you may need to have a fellow staff member, your adviser, or someone else introduce you to a source who has been reluctant to talk to you. This is called **sponsorship**; the person making the introduction is someone known and trusted by both you and the source. The **sponsor** helps facilitate your interview by making the introduction.

Decisions on Using Information

Once an interview has taken place (see Chapter 5 for specifics), you will be faced with decisions about how or whether to use information from your source. Unless a source specifically tells you ahead of time that his or her information is off-the-record, then you should be able to use any information you get during the interview. Begin any interview by reminding sources who you are and that your purpose is to gather information for a story that will be published in your student newspaper or yearbook.

The day-to-day position of a student journalist is different from that of a professional journalist in that students have all sorts of interactions with adults and peers when they are clearly not operating in their journalistic role. This raises the ethical question of whether it is appropriate to quote something someone tells you when the setting is not a formal interview.

Do your friends have to fear they may find themselves quoted in the newspaper or yearbook, even when they say something outside of a formal interview? If they do, you probably won't have many friends for long. However, you should always be thinking of potential stories, and you may get ideas from something you overhear. The good journalist will pursue the ideas formally to obtain a full story.

Chapter 5 discusses the four levels of attribution: on-the-record, off-the-record, on background, and on deep background.

Should You Use Anonymous Sources?

What will you do if your source agrees to talk only if you agree to keep him or her anonymous, or unnamed? Some professional newspapers, such as *USA Today*, have a policy about not using **anonymous sources**. Others are extremely reluctant to publish anonymous sources. The Society of Professional Journalists' Code of Ethics advises, under the heading "Seek Truth and Report It," "Identify sources whenever feasible. The public is entitled to as much information as possible on sources' reliability" and "Always question sources' motives before promising anonymity."

This is most likely a good policy for student publications staffs to adopt, especially for hard news stories. However, for stories on certain topics, especially features, you will want to protect the identity of a source to avoid his or her embarrassment or revealing sensitive facts about a specific individual. Teen pregnancy, runaways, and rehabilitation are of interest and importance to teens, but a primary source may not want to be identified.

When using a **pseudonym**, or assumed name, for such sources, be sure to make clear to readers that this is not the source's real name. Also check the student list and a local telephone directory to be sure you are not inadvertently using the name of a real person in your area.

Wise student publications staffs discuss the use of these types of information ahead of time, so they are not forced to make a decision under pressure of deadline.

Jimmy: Not Even a Pseudonym

Perhaps the most significant ethical instance involving unnamed sources in recent years occurred at the *Washington Post*. A reporter at the *Post* named Janet Cooke wrote a compelling front-page story, "Jimmy's World," about an eight-year-old heroin addict, his mother, and her boyfriend. The story, published in 1980, was so compelling with its realistic descriptions of Jimmy, his mother, her boyfriend, and their lives that Cooke won a Pulitzer Prize in 1981.

However, Cooke was forced to return the prize and resign from the *Post* later that year when it became clear that Jimmy did not exist. Some accounts say suspicion was aroused when the police could not find Jimmy to help him. Others credit discrepancies in

Cooke's résumé discovered when profiles about her appeared in various newspapers. Investigation by the Pulitzer Board determined she had lied on her résumé, and an investigation by the *Washington Post* itself determined that Jimmy was not a pseudonym. The boy was not even a composite character. He did not exist in the real world at all.

This case served to alert all journalists to the dangers of dishonesty in reporting and in building their résumés. Many a professional editor has looked more carefully at stories and résumés as a result.

Sources Use anonymous sources as a last resort. The motives of the source and the journalist come into question when a source is anonymous. ▶

Consulting Physical Sources

<u>Physical sources</u> are printed materials that may be found in the professional publication's library or the high school publications staff room. Physical sources are also available at the public or school library and public agencies, such as the school district's central office or the state department of education. Like human sources, physical sources can be both primary and secondary. The advantage of physical sources over human sources is that they are usually available at any time and can be consulted again and again on the reporter's own timetable. However, a reporter cannot ask follow-up questions of physical sources nor are they likely to be as timely as a human source.

Despite the usefulness of printed sources (especially for background information or to make comparisons between a situation in your school and other schools), nothing brings a story closer to readers than direct quotes from real people they know. Therefore, do not substitute physical sources for human sources.

In the Staff Room

Professional print and broadcast media keep extensive libraries of their clipped published stories; historically, this library is known as the **morgue**. A typical first step for a reporter when she or he gets a story assignment is to check out the morgue on the topic. High school publications staffs can easily create their own file folder morgue by assigning one staff member to clip and file by topic all the stories in every issue for the entire year. Yearbook staffs can establish a morgue using photocopied stories from the finished book.

Here are **four** other tips for bringing sources into the staff room:

1. **School board.** Be sure to get on the list to receive agendas in advance and minutes following board of education meetings. If these meetings are not part of a staffer's beat, agendas and minutes can be a tremendous source of story ideas.

2. **Back issues.** A well-stocked staff room should also include bound volumes of the school newspaper and the yearbook dating back to the year the school began, the school's annual report, calendar, student handbook, faculty handbook, policy manuals, faculty and staff list with full names and telephone extensions, complete student list with year in school and home phone numbers, exchange newspapers and yearbooks, at least one quality daily newspaper, and one or more local daily or weekly newspapers. It might also be helpful to keep on hand local maps, the school budget, athletic information, and anything else produced by the school public information office. All of these resources can help to generate story ideas and can provide information to get started on a story.

3. **Wire services.** Professional media and many college newspapers subscribe to one or more **wire services**, such as Associated Press, United Press International, or Reuters. A wire service is a member organization that covers stories from all over the world and posts them for use by members. This is the way most local newspapers and broadcast outlets receive national and international news.

4. **Future book.** School newspaper staffs should also maintain a **future book** and **future files** designed to keep the staff organized about upcoming events. Early in the school year, one staff member should be assigned to list all the known upcoming events by month or publication date in a future book. Typically, one page is assigned to each month or each issue. The future file is a system of file folders with information relating to each idea in the future book. As additional events come up, they are entered in the future book. When an advance story is written about an event, this clip goes in the future file as well as in the morgue. Using this system of checks reduces the likelihood of the staff missing an important event. Yearbook staffs do this same type of advance planning when they determine their **ladder** for the book.

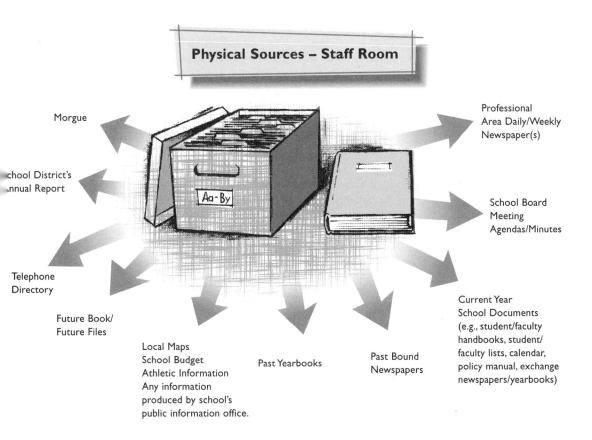

Physical Sources – Staff Room

Morgue

School District's Annual Report

Telephone Directory

Future Book/ Future Files

Local Maps
School Budget
Athletic Information
Any information produced by school's public information office.

Past Yearbooks

Past Bound Newspapers

Professional Area Daily/Weekly Newspaper(s)

School Board Meeting Agendas/Minutes

Current Year School Documents (e.g., student/faculty handbooks, student/ faculty lists, calendar, policy manual, exchange newspapers/yearbooks)

In the Library

Outside the high school staff room or professional media office, school and public libraries offer additional physical sources the enterprising journalist should explore. Browsing the reference section of a well-stocked school or public library will reveal a number of useful sources, depending on your topic. Don't overlook any of the following sources when attempting to find background, especially for a major story.

Encyclopedias. An encyclopedia, either general or specific, may help at the beginning of your research for a story; however, beware of dated material. General encyclopedias—such as *World Book, Encyclopedia Britannica,* or *Encyclopedia Americana*—can help with a more in-depth definition of a term than a standard dictionary or can give a general overview of a process.

Specialized encyclopedias can give more specific information as background for some topics. Examples of specialized encyclopedias that may be helpful to high school reporters at some time include *McGraw Hill's Encyclopedia of Science and Technology, The Encyclopedia of Drugs and Alcohol,* and the one-volume *Encyclopedia of Censorship.* Check your library shelves for others.

Facts on File World News Digest. This weekly publication indexes and summarizes news from around the world, including the United States. Categories of information include crime, deaths, people in the news, education, medicine, sports, religion, and science, along with leisure-time interests such as plays, films, and books. It can be consulted for specific background information or for world or national topics to localize.

Almanacs. Published annually, these hefty paperback reference books give brief factual information about an endless variety of people and events across the country and around the world. Consulting an almanac—such as *Information Please,* the *World Almanac,* or *Time Almanac*—may provide the perfect national or world tidbit of information to complete your story. Professional journalists often keep an almanac at their fingertips.

Guinness Book of World Records. Like almanacs, this treasure trove of unusual information is published annually. The 1999 volume has information in the following categories: Fame, Money and Big Business, Extraordinary People, Extraordinary Lives, The Body, The Natural World, The Material World, Hi-Tech, War and Disaster, Arts and Media, Music and Fashion, Sporting Heroes. Such information could be used to enhance an existing story, to generate story ideas, or as a starting point for polling your student body then using the Guinness list to compare results.

Other Fact Books

Even more unusual information to add to an existing story or to generate ideas may come from a number of other fact books. Once you locate one of these in your library, several others should surround it on the shelf.

The Book of Lists. This three-volume set was published by William Morrow and Co., Inc., in the late 1970s and early 1980s. Sample content: 16 Body Parts and What They Cost to Replace, 11 Famous Women Who Married Before the Age of 16, 11 Names of Things You Didn't Know Had Names, 15 Plays Most Produced by High School Theater Groups. Caution: Some information may be dated.

The Book of Lists: The 90s Edition. Published in 1993 by Little, Brown and Co., this updates the previous volumes, but may still be dated. Sample content: Stephen King's 6 Scariest Scenes Ever Captured on Film, 9 Recent Cases of TV Censorship, 15 Most Popular Ice Cream Flavors, 10 Foods You Should Never Eat, 9 Stupid Thieves, 10 Recent Cases of Book Censorship.

The Book of Firsts. Published by Bramhall House in 1982, "its purpose is to provide a wide range of 'firsts' that have contributed to life as we know it today, particularly those innovations that have altered society to some degree," according to its book jacket. It includes a chronology of events from 767 to 1974. Check on other "first" titles, such as *The Book of New York Firsts* (1995), *The Book of Tucson Firsts* (1998), *The Book of Women's Firsts: Breakthrough Achievements of Over 1000 American Women* (1992).

Incredible Facts: The Indispensable Collection of True Life Facts and Oddities. First compiled by Richard B. Manchester, this book was originally published in 1985,

with a new edition in 1994. The book jacket says, "A rare collection of colorful facts including amazing information about unusual people, wonders of nature, extraordinary athletic feats, strange places, bizarre achievements, oddities and superlatives."

Quote books. A wide variety of quote books exist, from the general to the most specific. They may be arranged by author or subject, chronologically or not. In some books, you can look up a familiar quote and find out who said it and under what circumstances. Titles include *Bartlett's Familiar Quotations*, *The Oxford Dictionary of Quotations*, *The New York Public Library Twentieth Century Quotations*, *The New Quotable Woman* (with quotes from 2,540 women), *Contemporary Quotations in Black*, *A Dictionary of Art Quotations*, *A Dictionary of Business Quotations*, and *A Dictionary of Musical Quotations*.

Directories

While every publications staff room should have a local telephone directory, other directories can also be helpful to the enterprising reporter. Even a careful look at the local telephone directory may reveal information you had no idea existed there.

Local telephone directory. You know about the white and yellow pages and how they differ. However, have you ever explored all the other information your local telephone directory contains? For example, local directories in some areas include a golf guide, stadium seating

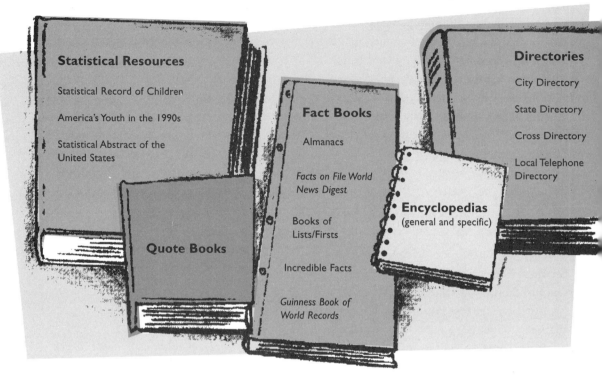

Statistical Resources

Statistical Record of Children

America's Youth in the 1990s

Statistical Abstract of the United States

Fact Books

Almanacs

Facts on File World News Digest

Books of Lists/Firsts

Incredible Facts

Guinness Book of World Records

Quote Books

Encyclopedias
(general and specific)

Directories

City Directory

State Directory

Cross Directory

Local Telephone Directory

---

guides, airport maps, coupons, ZIP codes for the entire state and a helpful listing of community services, and community street maps.

City directory. Published by private companies, this type of directory gives additional information about the community it serves, such as population, average income per household, news media, tax bases, transportation serving the community, and industrial sites. It also typically includes a telephone number directory along with the alphabetical listing of residents with addresses and phone numbers found in the local telephone directory.

Cross directory. Usually published by local realtors, this directory lists community residents by name, address, and phone number.

State directory. Also known as the blue book, this directory has listings and information for the executive, legislative, and judicial branch of your state government. It should also contain information on state schools—elementary, secondary, colleges, and universities. Some of this information may also be in your local telephone directory in a special government section.

Other directories. Again, browsing your school or public library shelves may reveal interesting resources. For example, the *National Directory of Nonprofit Organizations* lists information for all nonprofit organizations with incomes at or over $25,000. A quick survey on one visit to the public library also turned up information on the Athletic Directors Association, the Coalition Against the Death Penalty, and many other organizations.

Statistical Resources

When you want more complete statistical information than you have found anywhere else, consider using one of the following sources.

America's Youth in the 1990s. Published by the George H. Gallup International Institute in 1993, this volume is based on the annual Gallup Youth Survey and updates an earlier volume. It includes survey results on the "habits, hopes, fears and dreams of American youth. . . . In addition to exploring specific attitudes at a given time, the surveys delineate trends in teen thinking on more than 200 issues of continuing importance."

Statistical Record of Children. Published in 1994, this volume promises to be a collection "of easy-to-use statistical data. . . . gathered from a multitude of sources." It contains information about education, health, nutrition, medical care, teen pregnancy and abortions, child poverty, crime and violence with children both as victims and as perpetrators, juvenile delinquency, sports, and recreation.

Statistical Abstract of the United States. Published annually by Hoovers, Inc., this is the "standard summary of statistics on the social, political, and economic organization of the United States." In addition, it is a great source for postal and Web addresses and phone numbers of 33 federal agencies, ranging from the Department of Education's Office of Information Services to the Department of Health and Human Services' National Center for Health Statistics.

Accessing Public Records

Beyond the library, look to local, state, and federal agencies for documents that may be useful in specific situations.

Freedom of Information Act

Reporters have access to such documents under the **Freedom of Information Act**, also known as FOIA, written in 1966 and amended in 1996.

FOIA is a federal law that requires the government to make available to the public on request all federal documents except those dealing with national security or foreign policy; those related to confidential financial data, personnel issues, or internal matters of federal agencies; or those related to some law enforcement investigations.

An automatic letter generator is available at The Reporter's Committee for Freedom of the Press (RCFP) Web site at www.rcfp.org.

State Open Records Laws

As of June 1996 the **Student Press Law Center (SPLC)**, an advocacy group for the student press, reports all 50 states and Washington, D.C., have **state open records laws**. These laws allow public access to records and documents from state agencies, including public schools.

The idea behind these laws is that the public has the right to know what government agencies are doing.

Both the information available and how cooperative officials are in releasing it varies from state to state. As with the FOIA, states may make exceptions about releasing some information, especially when it would violate an individual's right to privacy. "An informal request for the relevant records should be enough to get the information you want," the SPLC writes in its packet *Access to High School Records*. "Just asking the appropriate school or government official politely should be all that it takes. However, if your informal request is not successful, you may be forced to invoke the power of your state's open records law by making a formal request in writing."

An automatic letter generator is available at the Student Press Law Center's Web site at www.splc.org.

Federal agencies are required to respond to a written request within 20 working days, but state laws vary. Many require a response in three to ten working days, but others only specify a "reasonable" time. Delays are not uncommon, so plan ahead when writing a story that requires this level of research.

While private schools do not have to comply with state open records laws as far as information related only to the private school, such as a school budget report, information held by federal, state, or county agencies, such as school bus inspection records, will be available.

Computer Searching and Internet Sources

Over the past decade, school and public libraries have abandoned their traditional worlds of card catalogs and bookshelves filled with volumes of the *Reader's Guide to Periodical Literature*. They have moved into the world of the computerized database and the Internet. In some cases, libraries don't even have back copies of magazines and newspapers on the shelves. Instead, they have CD-ROM versions of the *New York Times* or the *Chicago Tribune* or *Time* magazine. When you want to research a topic, you sit down at the appropriate computer and query away, printing out the parts you need or taking notes from the screen.

When was the last time you used your school library to research an oral report or a major paper? Were you overwhelmed by the new technology available? With nearly unlimited access to a world, literally, of information as close as the nearest keyboard, the student and professional journalist's life should be much simpler. However, keeping up with the changes your school and public libraries make in their databases from month to month can be a challenge.

Assuming you can navigate all this technology with ease, you'll no doubt discover that it all yields too much information to look at, much less understand and evaluate.

Even so, computer research, including the Internet, is a wonderful tool that scientists, researchers, and university professors—not to mention high school and college students across the country—use successfully.

The Computer Search

For the story on body composition testing (see page 45), we might want to search our library's databases of recent newspaper and magazine articles. Perhaps we will find more background information, reports about another high school where such testing has become an issue, or an article that supports body composition testing as "the solution" to increasing students' desire to be fit. On the other hand, we may find nothing.

In addition, we will want to do a World Wide Web search on the Internet. Here, in addition to the above ideas, we might find articles in other high school papers on the same topic. New Web sites appear daily, so you don't really know what you might find until you try.

To perform a search, you need to use a **search tool**, or **search engine**, a means for accessing the information you want. These are divided into **two** types:

1. **Subject-directory search tools**, which work like telephone directory yellow pages to give you categories and then subcategories and sites.

2. **Text-indexing search tools**, which scan documents for specific terms.

Experts suggest using a subject directory when you want to find out what the Internet contains about a broad topic and using a text index when you want to find out what Internet sites contain a specific word or phrase.

Yahoo!, found at www.yahoo.com, is a popular subject-directory search tool. Using Yahoo! to search for "body composition test" in one test resulted in references to 39 Web pages. The same search using AltaVista, a popular text-indexing search tool found at www.altavista.com, yielded 140 Web page references.

Some searches will result in many more **hits**, items matching your request. For example, searching for "high school journalism" using AltaVista resulted in 1,644 hits in one test. Searching for these words without using quotation marks yielded 694,811 hits. It is important to make your search as specific as possible to eliminate unrelated sites and be sure to enclose your search term in quotes. Otherwise, the search tool will give results for each word individually.

Subject-Directory Search Tools
The Argus Clearinghouse www.clearinghouse.net
Inter-Links alabanza.com/kabacoff/Inter-Links
The Internet Public Library www.ipl.org
Library of Congress World Wide Web Home Page lcweb.loc.gov
The WWW Virtual Library vlib.org/overview.html
Yahoo! www.yahoo.com

Text-Indexing Search Tools
All-in-One Search Page www.AllOneSearch.com
AltaVista www.altavista.com
Excite www.excite.com
Infoseek Guide infoseek.go.com
Lycos www.lycos.com
Magellan magellan.excite.com
Metacrawler www.go2net.com/search.html
Savvy Search www.savysearch.com
Search.com www.search.cnet.com
WebCrawler www.webcrawler.com

Source: Andrew Harnack and Eugene Kleppinger, *Online! A Reference Guide to Using Internet Sources*, St. Martins Press, 1998.

Evaluating Internet Sources

While it's easy to find multiple sources through an Internet search, it is not so easy to evaluate them.

* *Usefulness.* You will need to skim through potential sources to determine their usefulness, just as you would magazine or newspaper articles you find through a database or *The Reader's Guide to Periodical Literature.*

* *Reliability.* Once you have found a source with potential for your article, you need to evaluate its reliability. Remember that almost anyone can create a page on the Internet and say just about anything, true or not. As a reporter with credibility, you don't want to get caught referring to a source with no credibility or with a specific bias about a topic—or worse yet, libeling someone because you used information from an unreliable source.

To evaluate information, try to determine its author and what his or her qualifications—or biases—are for the topic you are researching. Then answer these questions:

* Is there a homepage link to find out more about the author? Is there an e-mail address to contact the author?
* Is the article reproduced from another publication? If so, it may have more credibility.
* Is there a date of publication or one indicating an update of the site? Are there links to other sites with some measure of credibility?

Some Helpful Guides

Your source evaluation skills will improve as you use them.

In *Online! A Reference Guide to Using Internet Sources,* Andrew Harnack and Eugene Kleppinger suggest several Web sites to consult for help:

* "Evaluation of Information Sources" by Alastair Smith at www.vuw.ac.nz/~agsmith/evaln. This page contains links to documents that can help in source evaluation.
* "Evaluating Information Found on the Internet" at the Eisenhower Library at Johns Hopkins University includes Elizabeth Kirk's discussion of **six** major criteria for evaluation:

1. authorship
2. point of view or bias
3. referral to other sources
4. publishing group or body
5. currency
6. verifiability

Collect, Save, and Attribute

When you do find information you want to use, make a copy, cut and paste it into a word processing program to save to a disk or to your personal file folder, or take notes before you leave the site. Unfortunately, one quirk of the Internet is that sites you find today may not be there tomorrow or may have moved. Therefore, get all the important information on your first visit, including as many of the following as apply: author's name, title of document, title of work, site description (such as homepage), date of publication or last revision, date of access, and the site's Web address, or **URL (uniform resource locator)**.

Of course, as with any source, you must give credit in your article to anything you use from the Internet. Besides more traditional types of credit, such as author's name and qualifications, you may wish to include the site's URL in your article so that readers can visit it.

Internet Security

Using the Internet to access information put there by others should not cause you any security problems. Just be sure when you put information on the Internet that you do not post anything you don't want the whole world to know, especially personal information. Schools and other locations offering public access to the Internet most likely have rules against using e-mail, entering chat rooms, gambling, surfing "inappropriate sites," and other such activities. These rules are for your safety, and you should respect them or risk losing your Internet privileges.

Some Good Electronic Sources to Access

Sites high school journalists and their advisers will find useful include:

Computer/Internet Sites

Search Engines

Helpful Web Sites

High school newspaper online editions

Scholastic press organizations

Pulitzer prizes

Newspapers and Magazines

Other journalism related sites

The Journalism Education Association, Inc.
www.jea.org. This is the only independent national scholastic journalism organization for teachers and advisers. The organization has much to offer those interested in journalism education. This site contains information about membership, conventions, contests, certification, its bookstore, scholarships and awards, curriculum aids, student press rights, and online high school publications, along with a membership directory.

National Scholastic Press Association.
The online home of the NSPA, this site (www.studentpress.org/nspa.) includes information on membership, upcoming workshops, conferences and conventions, competition opportunities, excerpts from the quarterly member publication *Trends in the High School Media*, a list of online member publications, a member database, and a list of publications.

NSPA Sourcebook. From this part of the NSPA site, you're just a click away from hundreds of organizations and resources that can help student journalists and journalism teachers do their jobs better. The site (www.studentpress.org/sourcebook.) includes links under many headings: Legal Issues/First Amendment/Freedom of Information, Student Media Membership Organizations, State/Regional Press Associations, and so forth.

Student Press Law Center. The SPLC is a nonprofit organization dedicated to providing legal help and information to the student media and journalism educators. This site (www.splc.org.) contains an online legal clinic, SPLC news flashes, the online SPLC Report, and information about Law of the Student Press, (SPLC's comprehensive guidebook to student press law) and SPLC membership.

National Elementary Schools Press Association. The National Elementary Schools Press Association is an organization dedicated to helping elementary and middle schools start and improve existing class and school newspapers. This site (www.nespa.org.) contains information on membership and the NESPA rating and review program; a bookstore; tips for teachers and students; and links to related sites, such as the country's top 100 professional newspapers.

Columbia Scholastic Press Association.
The CSPA functions as an educational press organization providing services to student newspapers, magazines, and yearbooks in schools and colleges that are members of the CSPA. This site (www.columbia.edu/cu/cspa.) includes information on membership, awards, conventions, a bookstore, and issues of the bi-monthly *The Student Press Review* for downloading.

Quill and Scroll. The Quill and Scroll Society was organized in 1926 by a group of high school advisers to encourage and recognize individual student achievement in journalism and scholastic publication. Since its founding, charters have been granted to more than 13,780 high schools in all 50 states and 41 countries. This site (www.uiowa.edu/~quill-sc/index.html) includes information on membership, publications, contests, and scholarships. It features a downloadable order form for pins and certificates.

Associated Student Press and Highwired.Net. These sites (www.aspwire.net) and (highwired.net) offer student access to the Internet for their publications.

The Pulitzer Prize. This site (www.pulitzer. org) documents 80 years of American intellectual and artistic excellence in journalism, letters, drama, and music. It includes an interactive timeline listing the names of all winners of the Pulitzer Prize since 1917 and an archive of all Pulitzer Prize-winning works from the past three years, including photos, editorial cartoons, music clips, and the full text of all winning articles.

Wrap-up

To do his or her job well, the journalist—whether professional or student—relies on reporting what sources have to say to take readers or viewers where they cannot go on their own. Cultivating human sources is the key to writing a successful journalistic piece. For the scholastic journalist, this means getting out of the staff room and talking to lots of fellow students. The number one priority of scholastic journalists should be to represent their entire student audience. This means making sure they interview different sources throughout the year and making sure those sources are representative of all the grade levels, genders, cultures, and viewpoints found in their school.

Besides heavy reliance on human sources for the primary development of the story, journalists also need to know how to do effective research in the staff room, the library, and even through government agencies using different types of physical sources. These range from the simplicity of a local telephone directory to the vast complexity of the World Wide Web. With practice and natural curiosity, enterprising journalists will develop research skills rivaling those of the best detectives—and will feel a tremendous amount of satisfaction when they write that award-winning story as a result.

anonymous source—unnamed source.

Freedom of Information Act of 1966 (FOIA)—federal law that requires the government to make available to the public on request all federal documents except those dealing with national security or foreign policy; those related to confidential financial data, personnel issues, or internal matters of federal agencies; those related to some law enforcement investigations.

future book—list of known upcoming events, organized by date, that the publication should cover.

future file—system of file folders containing information relating to each idea in the future book.

hit—item matching a request in an Internet search; visit to a Web site.

ladder—order of pages or articles to be included in an issue.

morgue—traditional newspaper term for a clipping library.

person-on-the-street sources—random individuals who can offer an opinion about a topic but who are not involved enough to be primary or secondary sources. Use of these should be balanced among and representative of all grade levels, genders, cultures, and viewpoints represented in the student body.

physical sources—printed materials used to research an article.

primary sources—those people interviewed who are key to the story.

professional sources—adult experts who have information about a topic related to the story that may not be specific to your school.

pseudonym—assumed name for a source.

search tool (search engine)—a means for accessing information on the World Wide Web.

secondary sources—those people interviewed who are not key to the story but whose point of view adds to other information.

sponsor—the mutual friend who introduces a reporter to a source.

sponsorship—using a mutual friend to make an introduction to a source.

state open records laws—state laws that allow the public access to records and documents from state agencies, including public schools. States may make exceptions about releasing some information, especially when it would violate an individual's right to privacy.

Student Press Law Center (SPLC)—an advocacy group for the student press.

subject-directory search tool—way of searching the World Wide Web. Like telephone directory yellow pages, it gives information in categories and sub-categories, generally used to find information about a broad topic.

continues ▶

text-indexing search tool—way of scanning documents on the World Wide Web for specific terms. Use to find Internet sites that contain a specific word or phrase.

URL (uniform resource locator)—a Web address. Each page of information on the World Wide Web has its own unique URL.

Web address—see URL; the location of a site on the World Wide Web.

wire services—a membership organization that covers stories from all over the world and posts them for use by members. Wire services include the Associated Press, United Press International, and Reuters.

Interviewing

In this chapter, you will learn:

- why the interview is the fundamental form of gathering information in journalism
- how to prepare in advance for an interview
- how to manage a productive interview session
- how to write different types of interview stories

Most journalism starts with interviews. Although eyewitness observation is helpful in spot news reporting, and consulting printed sources can be valuable in research, journalists rely most on talking to people as sources of news information. Nearly all journalism is local, and your job as a reporter is to find people who have the information you need for your story and to interview them—in person, on the phone, or even by e-mail. Throughout a career as a journalist, you will spend a large amount of time talking to strangers, sources who have the facts that complete your report and form the basis of your story. Interviewing, the systematic way a reporter relies on human sources, is the subject of this chapter.

The Challenge of Interviewing

Skillful interviewing is a psychological process. Sometimes it's even a contest. You may find yourself trying to get information from someone who doesn't really want to give it to you, or someone who wants to give you something else. Whether you know it or not, you're already well equipped for the more formal process of the journalistic **interview**. You've been interviewing people casually since you first learned to talk.

While nearly any piece of journalism includes some interviewing, many stories, especially features, are almost purely based on the interview. Often you'll conduct an interview with a single person, but sometimes you'll need to do an interview with several people. An interview can focus on a source's information, opinions, or personality.

Types of Interviews

The **informative interview** reports details that the source can provide because of his or her expertise. The source may hold an official position in the school or community or simply be a prominent person. Or the source may have the knowledge or experience that supports the topic you're writing about.

Sidebar

Why People May Not Want to Be Interviewed

1. **Time.** Public figures will give this answer more than private citizens. Sometimes you are competing for a share of an already crowded day.

2. **Guilt.** People understand the dynamics of conversation enough to know that they may say something they didn't expect to say.

3. **Anxiety.** A shy person may be afraid of the actual experience of being interviewed.

4. **Protection.** A person may be shielding a loved one or someone who is guilty of wrongdoing. An interviewee also may be afraid of being connected with an incident or a comment that will embarrass or condemn someone else.

5. **Ignorance.** An interviewee may not want to admit that he or she knows very little about the subject you want to discuss.

6. **Embarrassment.** A person may feel that the experience you want to discuss is humiliating, tasteless, or too intimate.

7. **Tragedy.** A distraught person often does not want to share a personal catastrophe with the public.

Source: Shirley Biagi, *Interviews That Work*, 2nd edition, Wadsworth Publishing Co., Belmont, Calif., 1992, pp. 58–59.

The **opinion interview** reveals attitudes or viewpoints that are significant because they come from prominent people or authorities or that are interesting because they're unusual or well phrased. Articulate people are most likely to show up in opinion interviews, as television news demonstrates.

The **personality interview** tries to bring out the essence of an individual by looking at the facets of his or her life. Such an interview creates a sensory image, allowing readers or viewers to see and hear the person in action. The personality interview creates a snapshot or sketch—or even a whole album. It is an effort to get the reader to comprehend an abstract personality through concrete observation. Film does it best, but writing can do it well, too.

Many interviews are a mix of these three types. Nevertheless, the reporter needs to be sensitive to the details that define each category. When you interview the principal about block scheduling, you don't report what shade of lipstick she's wearing or ask about her dog, details that might come up in a personality interview. You must know the exact purpose of the interview before the process begins. Are you going after information from the head of the juvenile crime unit about teenage crime rates? Then you might inquire about his views on the need for a tighter curfew, but you don't bring up the baseball season.

Preparing for the Interview

Nearly all interviews require advance preparation. The following **six** steps should guide that process.

1. **Choose someone to interview.** In many cases, the story topic determines whom you'll interview because you need to talk to experts. In other cases, you have flexibility because you need sources who illustrate your story topic, such as students who work for minimum wage jobs when you've been assigned to cover the proposed minimum wage increase. Accessibility of sources and your ability to persuade them to talk to you affect your choices.

2. **Set up an appointment.** Deadlines will affect the process here, but don't assume you can get an interview on the spur of the moment. When you can, it may come as a surprise; many unprepared reporters have to improvise when a source becomes immediately available. But try to work ahead.

3. **Identify yourself.** When you call for an appointment, be careful to explain who you are—a reporter for the Kelly School *Klarion*—what topic you want to discuss, and how much time you'll need. Most professional news interviews are done on the phone. But high school journalists should avoid phone interviews except when they need brief information. The face-to-face interview works better psychologically within the school; try the phone interview if you

must go off-campus. If you're doing a personality or feature interview, face-to-face contact is essential because your observation of the source's **body language** and environment may become part of the story.

4. **Research the source.** The more important your source, the more essential your background information becomes. You can't afford to waste time asking questions about trivia that you could have looked up. More importantly, you want to conduct the interview on an intelligent level. Otherwise, the source loses interest or begins to take advantage of your ignorance. Look into any school and community reference material before you interview public officials.

5. **Research the topic.** Know at least the basics of your story topic before you go to the interview. Read the school budget before you ask the finance administrator why the budget is being cut. Remember that sources can lose patience if you're uninformed.

6. **Prepare questions in advance.** Be sure of what you want to ask but also be ready to bring up other questions as they occur to you. You need a script, but you also must be ready to improvise. The prepared questions will come from your research. The improvised questions will occur as the source brings up unanticipated material.

Levels of Attribution

Four levels of __attribution__, or crediting, are possible in an interview:

1. **On-the-record.** When everything is on-the-record, whatever the source says may be used in the story, including as direct quotes. The source, who is identified by name and title, understands that he or she will be on-the-record before the interview begins. He or she also understands that the reporter controls how much of the interview will go into the story.

2. **Off-the-record.** When the source says something that he or she does not want to go into the story, this information is off-the-record. Both the source and the reporter understand this before the information is given, not afterwards. Some reporters will refuse to listen to an off-the-record statement; others will use it as background information or try to find someone else who will say it for attribution. At the high school level, off-the-record is often misunderstood by sources who think they can use it as an afterthought—"by the way, you can't print that." Your staff needs to develop a policy on this issue.

3. **On background.** When an interview is on background, the reporter may use the material but may not identify by name who said it. The attribution becomes, for example, "a government source." This attribution doesn't work too well at the high school level because of the difficulty of establishing credibility without revealing the source.

4. On deep background. When an interview is on deep background, the material may be used, but no indication may be given of where it came from. The attribution becomes something like "It has been learned. . . ." In this case, you need to do more research.

If the Source Asks to See the Quotes—or the Entire Story

First, your staff must have a policy about this problem, so be sure to consult your policy manual or set up one if need be. Generally reporters refuse to let sources review quotes before the story is published and certainly not the complete story. But, in the interest of accuracy, this policy has changed on some publications. The argument at the high school journalism level is that inexperienced students should be willing to check quotes to ensure accuracy. But the risk is great. Some sources will want to change quotes even though they were accurately quoted in the first place. Others will interfere even further, trying to control the entire story. Remember: It's your story. You are in charge. But accuracy is imperative, and in the case of an inexperienced reporter or a complex or sensitive story, some checking back may be a good idea.

The Interview Scene

High school journalists work from a slight disadvantage when they interview adults. Ideally, an interview is a conversation between equals; the journalist is the story expert, and the source is the information expert. But the adult source may not treat you as an equal because you're a student. Keep in mind **nine** tips that anticipate this problem:

1. **Be a bit formal.** Don't chew gum or pick up objects in the source's office. Don't sit down until you're invited to. Don't slouch in your chair.

2. **Dress conservatively.** Within your own school, you probably don't have to worry too much about dress (don't go out and buy a suit if no one can imagine you wearing one!), but do pay attention to dress if you're interviewing someone unused to teenage styles.

3. **Introduce yourself.** Even though you introduced yourself when you set up the appointment, again explain clearly who you are, the publication for which you're writing a story, and what you want to discuss.

4. **Ask permission to tape record.** Taping makes some sources nervous, so don't do it if they ask you not to. See To Tape or Not to Tape on page 71 for pros and cons of taping.

5. **Take notes conspicuously.** Even if you tape record, you must take notes in case the tape malfunctions. Sources are afraid of being misquoted or misunderstood, so make sure your notes are careful and

clear. Don't hesitate to ask the source to repeat information or to slow down. The more you demonstrate how hard you're trying to be accurate, the better.

6. **Take notes quickly.** Speed will come with practice. Develop a shorthand for note taking that you understand. Use a 4-x-8-inch hand-held reporter's notebook. Write out your notes more legibly as soon as the interview is completed.

7. **Observe the scene.** While this isn't so important in a news interview, if you're doing a personality interview you want to include details on body language, the source's appearance, and perhaps the setting. Record these details as you go along.

8. **Role play if you need to.** Adjust your questioning style to the source. This takes practice, and watching television interviews will give you some ideas of how professionals do it. You actually have plenty of experience at this. You know how to adjust your style to get information from different adults, don't you?

9. **Conclude with thanks.** As the interview ends, ask if you can come back or telephone if you need further information. It's embarrassing to forget something you should have asked about, but that should never stop you from doing it. You want to demonstrate your concern for producing an accurate, complete story.

Questioning Techniques

If you're going to control the interview to get the story you want, you must control the questions. Below is a list of questioning techniques.

Type of Question	Purpose	Examples
1. Factual	To get information To start the interview	Who? Where? What? Why? When? How?

2. Explanatory	To get reasons
	To broaden the discussion
	To add information
		In what way would you solve
		  this problem?
		Can you add evidence from
		  other sources?
		Just how would you do that?

3. Justifying or defending	To challenge ideas
	To develop new ideas
	To get thinking behind what
	  happened
		Why do you think so?
		How do you know that?
		Can you prove that?
		Doesn't Ms. X say the
		  opposite is true?

4. Leading	To introduce a new idea To advance other opinions To rephrase information into a quotable comment To change the subject	Will this remedy work? Could I ask you about this? Are you really saying that. . . ? Would this be an alternative?

5. Hypothetical	To develop new ideas
	To suggest another, possibly
	  unpopular opinion
	To change the course of the
	  discussion
		Suppose you did it this way
		  . . . what would happen?
		Another school does this . . .
		  is that feasible here?
		Suppose you had lost . . .
		  then what?

6. Alternative	To pin down a decision
	  between alternatives
		Which of these solutions is
		  better, A or B? Why?
		In your judgment, what is the
		  best way to do it?

7. Coordinating	To develop consensus	Is this the next step?
		Is there general agreement,
		  then, on this plan among
		  board members?

Tips for Productive Interviews

Pamela Cytrynbaum, visiting assistant professor of journalism at the University of Oregon and a former *Chicago Tribune* reporter, recommends the following:

1. **Be prepared.** The less your subject wants to talk, the more you should know about her or him. Before interviewing a public official or well-known person, read the clips on that person. If your source is not used to being interviewed, still read the clips about your story topic.

2. **Write everything down.** That includes details on casual comments, clothing, office objects, the brand of coffee in the paper cup. If a public official says, "I have absolutely no comment," use it. Everything a public official says is fair game.

3. **Start small.** Ask a few throwaway questions to give yourself time to judge your subject's demeanor. If you're dealing with grief, be gentle. If he or she doesn't want to talk, apologize and leave. If you see an opening, express your sympathy.

4. **Shut up.** The late *Chicago Tribune* columnist Mike Royko used to tell his assistants to "Let 'em talk." Shutting up, he'd say, is one of the best interviewing techniques. Often people start talking to fill the silence.

5. **Be flexible.** Of course you'll have a list of questions to work from, but don't be so wedded to them that you miss a great new line of inquiry. If the interview takes an interesting direction, chuck your angle for a new one.

6. **Get tough.** Most experts say you should save the tough questions for last, after you've developed a rapport. Others say that if it looks like the source won't talk to you anyway, put the tough questions up front and hope for a quote before the door slams. You be the judge.

7. **Be curious.** Wonder about everything. Anticipate. Stay focused. Don't get distracted. Listen.

8. **Be a good match.** Personality has way too much effect on an interview—your personality, that is. Be sensitive to the mood of the subject and adjust your approach accordingly. Especially for **profiles**, let the subject dictate the tone of the interview.

9. **Observe the basics.** Obviously the basic rules of polite behavior apply. Be early. Don't call adults by their first name unless they ask you to. Confirm the spelling of names and clarify all essential information.

10. **Be the grown-up.** No matter what you do, sometimes people will be mean, hostile, dishonest, petulant, absurd, and lots of other rotten things. Never lose your cool. No matter how difficult the person is, never get taken in. Get over it, move on. You represent "the media." Do us proud.

To Tape or Not to Tape

Reasons <u>to tape</u> record the interview:

* Quotes will be absolutely accurate, and the tape will provide a complete sense of context not available from your notes.
* Taping can relieve anxious sources about the accuracy of the interview.
* Taping allows you to hear the source a second, third, or fourth time.
* When the tape recorder is on, you can focus on developing a better rapport with the source because you can pay less attention to note-taking.

Reasons <u>not to tape</u> the interview:

* Taping can seduce you into not paying attention, and some of the positive tension of the dialogue can be lost.
* Tape recorders malfunction, leaving you without material. Even if you tape, be sure to take notes.
* Reviewing the tape can take hours— expect three or four times the length of the interview to write out a complete transcript.
* Awareness that the interview is being taped can stiffen the responses of some sources, even though they've agreed to be taped.

Writing an Interview

Write the interview story as soon as you can. Notes grow stale, and your overall impression of the conversation can fade if you delay. An interview can follow the **inverted pyramid** format if it's a news story, or it can use a **narrative** structure or perhaps a cause-effect approach if it's a feature story. (Chapter 6 covers journalistic writing in detail.) Let's look at several interviews from the high school press to see how they were put together.

Inquiring Reporter Interview

The simple **inquiring reporter's story** form is a good assignment for beginning journalists because they immediately have to talk to strangers about a topic and then organize a coherent story from several isolated interviews.

B Direct quotes alternate with paraphrased material. The standard attribution word is "said," with an occasional "explained."

Model

Get right outta Stoughton

by Emily A. Winecke

Sometimes the best way to deal with school on the weekends is to get as far away from it as possible.

Many students and teachers go away from Stoughton during the weekends. Some like to visit their families, others find it relaxing, and others just like the excitement of going away somewhere with their friends. This was the case earlier this year for seniors Kari Black and Marianne Manley.

Kari invited eight of her friends to see a Jars of Clay concert in LaCrosse. The nine students slept in a cramped apartment in LaCrosse the night before the concert. Both girls agreed that that weekend would be one that they wouldn't forget for a long time

"It was just an adventure," said Black. "I brought it up a week before hand."

"It was a nice getaway," added Manley.

Science teacher Jack Palmer owns a cabin in Eagle River. He tries to go there about one weekend a month. While up north, Palmer and his family enjoy hiking, snow shoeing and fishing.

A The lead sets up a general statement that anticipates the specific sources quoted in the body of the story. We know the topic right away, and we pick up an attitude about the topic not just from the first paragraph, but also from the headline.

C The writer moves logically from one source to the next, although we have no way of knowing whether she interviewed them in that order.

D **Transitions** link the sources' comments with one another. "Palmer and his family . . ." connects to earlier comments.

E "Foltz agreed with Kluge" compares the opinion of sources.

"It's refreshing to go to a place that's really different [from Stoughton], and my family likes to be outside," said Palmer.

Palmer and his family do not usually take the last-minute adventure approach to weekend getaways that Black and her friends used. They try to plan for their trip all month. However, it is still an outlet for relaxation and reflection for the family.

"It's important to enjoy it while you're there," said Palmer.

One of the most common ways for students to get away is for recreation like skiing. Sophomore Laura Kluge and her family often take weekend skiing trips in late winter. However, trips can pose problems, like having to actually be with your family.

"My brother gets on my nerves a lot . . . err!" Kluge said. "Actually, my sister annoys me more."

Even though she has to deal with her family and the cold of the Upper Peninsula of Michigan, Kluge still enjoys being outside and on vacation.

"It's nice to get away from the daily grind of school," she explained.

Sophomore Jessi Foltz also goes on weekend skiing trips. She has been doing this since she was three. Skiing is something that she has done all her life, and she looks forward to her skiing trips all winter long. She often skis with friends, but sometimes goes with her parents as well. Foltz agreed with Kluge that vacations are a great way to get away.

"It is really refreshing to be outside," she said. "And being away from Stoughton helps me recover from the stress of school."

Source: Stoughton High School, Stoughton, Wis., *Norse Star,* Jan. 29, 1999.

F A strong direct quote that summarizes the comments ends the story. Because she uses a quote from a source who seems to represent the entire group, the writer avoids direct **editorializing**.

Informative Interview

Factual details are the result of the interview that informs. We're interested in what's being said because the source is an authority and has expertise or experience.

Hsu scores 1600 on SAT

by Kris Fields

Any student who has ever taken the SAT knows that the chances of scoring a perfect 1600 are slim to none. Most shoot for the 1300-1400 range, sometimes even breaking that ominous 1500 mark; but some students shoot for that 1600 and hit it dead on.

One of the fortunate few is a CHS student. Standing 6'1" and playing varsity football and baseball, senior Ivan Hsu beat the odds and became only the second person in CHS history to score a perfect 1600 on his SAT. He has also maintained a flawless 4.0 GPA throughout high school.

Balancing four AP classes and playing on the varsity football team is quite a juggling act. So how does he do it? After coming home from practice around 5 p.m., he naps until 7 p.m. or so. Then the first thing he does after dinner is turn on a classic episode of "The Simpsons." Afterward, he hits the books until about midnight, all the time listening to KROQ to soothe his nerves and relax his mind.

Hsu only took one SAT prep course at the ACI Institute during the summer after his sophomore year and had only taken the test once before, scoring a 1490. "The main thing that classes help you do is to motivate you to practice. But if you already have a great will, then it comes more naturally to you to study," Hsu said.

A The lead is **deductive**; that is, it moves from a general statement about high SAT scores to a concrete example of a 1600 score in the second paragraph. It could just as well be **inductive**, moving from the specific example to its general significance.

B The story uses only three direct quotes, rather few for a story of this length. But there's no firm rule on how many quotes you should include. It will depend on how articulate the source is. Hsu seems modest, and the few quotes reflect that.

One might think it took a lot of studying to improve 110 points, but Hsu says that he didn't study all that much and had to play in a football game the night before the Oct. 10 test. "The test is a combination of luck and preparation. You prepare for what you can, and if it pops up on the test, then great," said Hsu.

Hsu learned about his score on Oct. 24 by calling in a week before the results would be sent home. He had known for a week about his score without telling anyone because he was trying to be modest about such an accomplishment.

When his results finally came in the mail on Oct. 30, his parents brought the letter to the football game to show Hsu.

He showed his coach, Trent Bordock and the coach's reaction was, "You got a 1600? Wow, now back to the game."

Hsu would like to go to Duke because he likes the campus. He's hoping to major in some type of medicine.

Even though Hsu doesn't read much beyond school assignments and "Rolling Stone," he believes that avid reading is the key to improving your vocabulary.

Probably the best attribute Hsu possesses is his self-motivation. In a world where parents are constantly pushing their kids to be better than the other, Hsu reveals his key to success by saying, "I push myself much more than my parents do. I'm not a perfectionist; I just expect the best from myself."

Source: Cerritos High School, Cerritos, Calif., *Informer*, Nov. 20, 1998.

Opinion Interview

This kind of interview emphasizes the opinions of the source, who is usually someone accomplished enough to make us pay attention. Information often shows up in the opinion interview, and personality is sometimes revealed indirectly.

A The story combines material from a speech, a **press conference**, and an interview. Press conferences tend to be disorganized. Watch how the article shifts quickly from topic to topic.

Model

Chicago Tribune editor raps "politically correct" news

by Justin Evenson

What's "politically correct" doesn't necessarily add up to good journalism, according to Howard Tyner, editor of the *Chicago Tribune*.

Tyner gave the opening remarks at a high school journalism workshop in Tribune Tower last week. Advisers and editors from nearly 100 Chicago area schools attended the *Tribune*-sponsored workshop, half the schools on Thursday and the other half on Friday.

"The business of journalism is under intense pressure," Tyner said. "Some of it is self-inflicted, the product of competition and hype that too often is unhealthy and destructive.

"Pressure also is coming from a politically correct world where the fear of offending is neutering our language, watering down our humor and making a minefield out of public discussion."

The *Tribune* editor explained that the world seems to be becoming a place where discourse too frequently has been replaced by shouting and where civilized disagreement seems to have become a thing of the past.

"'I respect your point of view, but think you are wrong and here's why' has given way to 'You're a bleeping idiot and I'm canceling my subscription until you write stories that conform exactly with what I think,'" Tyner explained.

He said that it would be easy for journalists to avoid the tough stories . . . to be intimidated . . . to concede to those who want only happy news.

"But then no one would win," Tyner said. "We'd have a public even less informed than it is already. We'd run the risk of governmental bodies running unchecked. After all, a press shackled by intimidation is no less effective than a press shackled by government decree."

The *Tribune* is keeping pace with the technological revolution by embarking on an innovative way to approach the news business. It is

B The story angle shows up in the lead and then expands during the private interview remarks in Tyner's office. It ranges over several subtopics, normal in a story of this length.

C The twelfth paragraph in the story is the bridge between the material from the speech and press conference and the private interview with Tyner.

D The story doesn't try to develop an ending that brings us back to the lead. It just stops, in inverted pyramid style.

based on the idea that newspapers, television, cable and the internet can and must work together to deliver information to the public.

Students took a tour of the *Tribune* newsroom and facilities and attended several seminars during the day. Seminar topics included "Newspapers and Careers," "Effective and Responsible Journalism," "Photography," "Successful Design and Layout Techniques," and "Getting Started or Revitalizing a Newspaper."

Later in the day, Tyner met in his office privately with JWN coeditor Justin Evenson and adviser Randy Swikle.

Tyner told the two that he is very passionate about "my company, my newspaper and my business." He said the job of balancing what the public wants to know with what the public should know can be very "tricky."

"I go after traditional areas that newspapers have always served: to provide a check on government and to serve as a device to help people make important decisions in their lives," Tyner said.

The editor said the *Tribune* prospers because it does not "pander to the lowest common denominator" as it presents news and information.

The editor also listened as Evenson talked about HB 154, the Illinois Student Publication Act, that the *Tribune* editorially opposed last year.

The bill, which overwhelmingly passed the House and Senate, defined the parameters within which students could control the content of their publication and beyond which school officials would have control.

Gov. Jim Edgar vetoed the bill, and although the House overrode the veto, it was withdrawn in the Senate because senators wanted to wait for a court case involving a liability question to be resolved. The bill will be reintroduced next year.

Tyner invited Evenson to speak to the *Tribune's* editorial board when the bill surfaces.

Source: Johnsburg High School, Johnsburg, Ill., *Johnsburg Weekly News*, Dec. 18, 1998.

Q & A Interview

A This interview uses a **Q & A** format, reading like a transcript of the interview's questions and answers. It may seem easy to write, but a good Q & A story is deceptively well edited. The Q & A format should be used sparingly because it's harder to read and works well only with an articulate source.

Example

Leaving it behind
Senior Jonathan Fenton

By Juliette Wallack

Minutes OF Fame

With his final year of high school beginning, senior Jonathan Fenton has much to look forward to. Last spring, however, Fenton had little to anticipate but days of physical therapy and recovery after being stricken with a serious complication of a common viral infection.

Last year you missed several weeks of school; what happened?

I got mononucleosis, and there were complications that one half out of one percent of those who get mono develop. It's called myelitis, which is inflammation of the spinal cord. What happens is the spinal cord gets infected, and I couldn't feel below my waistline. I ended up at Riverview Hospital for a week. I thought I would be better, so I went home for a couple of days, but I wasn't improving at all; instead I just got worse and worse. They brought me back to the hospital; I had lost tons of weight, and so they had to put me on IVs to feed me.

I was in Riverview for another week, but I still couldn't move. So they brought me to Rehabilitation Hospital of Indianapolis (RHI), and that's where I stayed for another week and a half. They started physical therapy. I had to get up every day and just do all kinds of therapy. It was boring, but the feeling eventually came back.

How did you feel about missing the end of the boys' track season because of your illness?

That hurt me. The four by eight relay team, which is what I was on, had a really good chance. They went to Regional, but they didn't make State. I think they were maybe just a second off. I would have really loved to run in the four by eight in Sectional, Regional and maybe State.

You missed a lot of school; how did that affect you?

It was definitely difficult when I came back. I'd missed three and a half weeks of school. So, when I came back I had to go to all of my teachers and get the homework. I was lucky; I only had to make up the tests, and I didn't have to make up the homework. But, I still had eleven tests to make up. It took me two weeks to do it. But, I finished all of it. Being absent for so long didn't really hurt my grades, either. They pretty much stayed the same.

FENTON FACTS

Favorite food: Steak

Most embarrassing moment: One cold day during second grade, he managed to get his tongue stuck to the flagpole. When he pulled it off, it was bleeding, and a trip to the nurse was necessary.

Always wanted to: Sky dive

Scariest thing that's ever

Source: Carmel High School, Carmel, Ind., *HiLite,* Aug. 18, 1998.

B Note the display devices that enhance the story: pull quotes, the head summary, and the facts box.

C The questions here require long answers, which is essential if the format is to avoid a jerky, incomplete effect.

E The tone here is positive. We identify with the subject because we can imagine our own feelings in his situation. This adds to reader interest.

F The final quote is effective because it leaves us with something to think about.

Scariest thing that's ever happened to him:
Not knowing if he'd be able to walk again.

Favorite place:
Hilton Head, SC

Favorite band:
Dave Matthews

Jonathan's
QUOTE OF THE ISSUE

《 "Victory" 》
belongs to the most persevering.
NAPOLEON BONAPARTE

HiLite
8.18.98

A complication resulting from mononucleosis, a common viral disease, took the ability to walk away from senior Jonathan Fenton. Now fully recovered, Fenton said the support of those around him helped immensely to bring him through the ordeal.

work. But, I still had eleven tests to make up. It took me two weeks to do it. But, I finished all of it. Being absent for so long didn't really hurt my grades, either. They pretty much stayed the same.

How did being sick change your outlook on life?

It definitely changed my outlook. The thing that got me through this was all the prayers; people would send me cards; I got at least 20 cards from my friends and family friends, and my church group prayed for me a lot. My faith in God really helped out and brought me through. It really kept me in high spirits, and I could have been really down, just lying there in a hospital bed.

At a couple of points I got really down. But, when I was in really low spirits, I'd just look at the cards people sent me and that would cheer me up. It also helped that a good friend came in to talk to me.

Being sick definitely improved my faith. Now I have a knowledge of how well prayers work. I think this whole ordeal showed me that whatever line of work I go into later in life, I need to enjoy it. I can't go into it simply for the money. I have to do it for a good reason.

Now that you've recovered, are you finding that your relationships have differed with those who helped you pull through this ordeal?

I got a lot closer to my parents because they were there for me. My mom took off two weeks of work just to come into RHI everyday and watch me do physical therapy. That was really, boring for her I'm sure because when I could barely walk all I'd do was get a walker, and then the therapists would just watch my feet. My mom was always there in the hospital room with me, and she

Sending a tennis ball whizzing over the net, senior Jonathan Fenton devotes much of his time to sports. After spending weeks in a wheelchair without the ability to play, Fenton said he has a new appreciation for his physical abilities.

was my friend for the two weeks. Both she and my dad were great.

My sister Kristin was at IU at the time, and she came up on weekends. Since she's gone most of the time, our relationship isn't that close. In general though, as we've grown older, we've grown closer, probably since we don't fight as much. When we're apart we realize that our relationship is pretty important to us. We deal with each other a lot easier than when we were little. We're friends now.

Also, I learned that all of my friends really back me. They're great people to be able to call friends. They came in a couple of times after school to see how I was doing and talk to me. It really cheered me up that they cared for me so much that they could make a special trip out of their way to see me.

You were forced to use a wheelchair when you returned to school after recovering somewhat from your illness; how did this affect you?

Well, I was in a wheelchair for two weeks after leaving the hospital. I can't imagine being in a wheelchair for the rest of my life. You get weird looks from the people who don't know you. The people who knew me were fine, but the people you don't know look at you differently than if you were walking beside them.

I have a completely new respect for those in wheelchairs, whether temporarily or permanently. When I was at RHI, I was the only patient under 20 there. I became really good friends with some ladies and men who were in wheelchairs. We'd just sit in front of the television and talk after we were done with therapies. I have a total new respect for them, because I got lucky. I was able to leave my wheelchair behind after being in it for a few weeks, but some of those people are never going to recover.

> **"My faith in God really helped out and brought me through.**
> SENIOR
> JONATHAN FENTON

D Most of the questions use a "how" focus. The information is the bulk of the story, but through it we get a good sense of Fenton's personality.

G We have no way of knowing whether the material has been rearranged from the interview itself, but in most Q & A interviews, that's what happens.

Interviewing 79

Interviewing underlies nearly all journalistic writing. The successful interview requires a reporter who knows what the story should be about and who has prepared intelligent questions that cover the topic. But interviews have a psychological side, too. Persuading someone to give you information or opinions, and to reveal personality in the process, can be difficult. The more you watch and read interviews, the better you will become at asking sensitive questions.

Journalism

attribution—process of crediting sources within the text of the story. This "who said so" gives the story credibility.

body language—nonverbal gestures and mannerisms that reveal attitudes such as boredom, fear, amusement.

deductive—approaching a topic with a general statement followed by specific examples.

editorializing—expressing opinion in a story when objectivity is preferred. Avoided in news stories, less so in features; see Chapter 6.

inductive—approaching a topic with specific examples followed by a general statement.

informative interview—reports details that the source can provide because of his or her expertise.

inquiring reporter story—a person-on-the street interview in which several people, often chosen randomly, are asked what they think about a topic.

interview—dialogue between a journalist and one or more sources for the specific purpose of gathering information for a news or feature story.

inverted pyramid—news story structure that puts the most important points first and concludes with the least important; see Chapter 6.

narrative—telling a journalistic story in chronological form with a distinct beginning, middle, and end; see also Chapter 6.

opinion interview—reveals attitudes or viewpoints that are significant because they come from prominent people or authorities, or that are interesting because they're unusual or well phrased.

personality interview—an interview that tries to bring out the essence of an individual by looking at details that make up an image of that person.

press conference—meeting at which the press is invited to ask questions of a source, who may begin with a specific announcement.

profile—an interview that goes beyond talking just to the subject by including information from others about him or her.

Q & A—interview story in the question-answer format; an edited version of the interview transcript.

transition—writing device that links topics or ideas in a story to each other.

The News Story

In this chapter, you will learn:

- **how to organize your thoughts to start writing**
- **about the importance of your lead**
- **different options for your lead**
- **how to organize and write your final story**
- **about writing special types of news stories**

You collected the information—now what? Returning to the newspaper or yearbook staff room after completing the final interview for your story, you find a free computer and sit down to contemplate the random screensaver patterns. "What do I do now?" you ask yourself. You have a notebook full of information, but no plan. Advice about how to develop and carry out a plan is found in this chapter. To create a successful story, you'll need to have an overall idea of where that story should go. You'll need to produce an irresistible lead to pull the busy reader into your story. Then you'll need to write a well-organized story that flows honestly from your lead and keeps your audience reading to the very end.

Getting to the Heart of Your Story

While experts differ on the specific approach reporters should take to news stories today, all agree you must be able to identify the main point of your story before you can write it. Use **two** steps to do this:

1. Ask yourself "So what?" or "What's this about?" or "What's my point?" while considering the information you have gathered.

2. Type the answer or answers to these questions in one sentence at the top of your computer screen or write them at the top of a blank piece of paper. This one sentence will guide you as you write.

Once you have identified your main point, you can consider what approach you will take to the overall story. Is this a serious story, or **hard news**? Or, is it soft news? Does it need a direct lead or an indirect lead? Will you follow traditional inverted pyramid story organization or some other type?

Fry's Writing Process

In their book *Coaching Writers: Editors and Reporters Working Together* (1992), Don Fry and Roy Peter Clark of the Poynter Institute for Media Studies illustrate the use of questions to guide you to your main point. Their diagram traces the process through time from start to finish. However, remember that no real writing is done in such a linear way. .

Idea
Start with an idea.
Report
Gather information from sources.
Organize
Decide what you want to say: "What's this about?" "What's my point for my reader?" "What's the news here?" Answers = one-sentence Point Statement. Discard anything that doesn't go with the Point Statement. List parts of story in order, and use your own code words = Road map. Plan ending and include in Road map.
Draft
Write a first draft as quickly as possible.
Revise
Read whole piece aloud once without making any changes. Reread making corrections. If there's a major problem with the piece, move back one step and repeat.

Source: Adapted from Roy Peter Clark and Don Fry, *Coaching Writers: Editors and Reporters Working Together*, St. Martin's Press, N.Y., 1992.

FORK Method

Carole Rich, a University of Kansas journalism professor, calls Fry's process the Focus step, the first in her FORK method of organizing a story.

F = Focus
Lead or **nut graf**
To find your focus, try writing a headline for your story. What would you say about it if you had only a few words?
How would you describe your story to a friend?
Answer in a sentence or two: "What's it about?"

O = Order
Decide what you will include from your notes. Code your notes so you know what information you will use in the story.
Consider organizing according to main topics, what you would put in a highlights box, what you would ask if you were giving a test on this information, question/answer format, chronological order.
Decide how you will end the story.

R = Repetition
Repetition refers to repeating key words to provide smooth transitions from one idea or paragraph to another, but don't overdo word-for-word repetition.

K = Kiss-off
Organize blocks of information by source or main idea, especially when there are three or more in the story. Finish with one source or idea and then "kiss it off" and move on to the next. This is less confusing for the reader than intertwining multiple sources or ideas throughout the story.

Source: Adapted from Carole Rich, *Writing and Reporting News: A Coaching Method*, Wadsworth Publishing Co., Belmont, Calif., 1994.

Writing Your Lead

The **lead** is the opening of any piece of journalistic writing. Except for the headline, the lead is the writer's only chance to hook the reader into continuing with the story. Readers spend about three seconds deciding whether to stay with one story or skip to another. An interesting lead hinging on carefully chosen opening words is critical to the success of any story. But this does not mean reporters can trick readers with a dishonest lead. Think of the lead as a contract between you and your readers. What you promise in the opening paragraph you must deliver in the story.

Direct News Lead

The hard news story traditionally begins with a **direct news lead** or summary lead. This is also known as an AP summary lead since the Associated Press (AP) stresses it. A direct or summary lead consists of a one- or two-sentence opening paragraph that contains the most important elements of the story and does not exceed about 35 words. Important elements in a news story include the 5Ws and 1 H. These are the time-honored journalistic questions: Who?, What?, When?, Where?, Why?, How? A smoothly flowing lead probably cannot include all six of these ideas, so the writer must decide which is the most important one to emphasize by placing it first and which of the others to include in that opening paragraph. The others can be used later in the story, perhaps as early as the second paragraph.

Direct Leads Through 5Ws and 1H

In writing a summary lead for a fee increase story, the reporter must consider which of the following facts is the most important to student readers. To do this, it will help to recall the questions posed earlier: "So what?" "What's this about?" "What's my point?" If you were actually writing this story from the few facts listed here, what one-sentence answer would you write to one of these questions?

* **Who?** District 214 Board of Education; Students
* **What?** Increased fees for 1999-00 for all six district schools: parking permit fee up $10 to $60; book rental fee up $5 to $95; driver ed fee up $50 to $150
* **When?** April 29 for the 1999–00 school year
* **Where?** At its regular meeting in the Board Room at Forest View Education Center
* **Why?** To continue philosophy of students paying more of the cost of programs
* **How?** By 7-0 vote

In theory, the summary lead could start with any of these facts. The writer must decide which one will attract more readers to the story. The following are ways to experiment with writing leads across the 5Ws and 1H spectrum. In light of your sentence, which lead presented here do you think is the most effective, if any? Why? Can you rewrite it to make it even better? If none of these leads works for the main idea sentence you wrote, write a lead that does.

Who?

The District 214 Board of Education voted 7-0 on April 29 to increase student fees for 1999–00 for driver education, parking permits, and book rental.

This lead contains 27 words, but does it put the emphasis on a *Who* of interest to student readers? No, it probably does not. Consider the following rewrite:

Students in District 214 will pay higher fees for driver education, parking permits, and book rental next year as a result of a 7-0 Board of Education vote on April 29.

This lead is 32 words long and may attract more reader interest by opening with "Students in District 214." However, sentences are easier to understand if they are no longer than 16 or 17 words. Consider the following rewrite:

Students in District 214 will pay higher fees for driver education, parking permits, and book rental next year. The Board of Education voted 7-0 to approve the increases on April 29.

This lead is still 32 words long, but it is easier to understand when broken into two sentences.

What?

Fee increases will face District 214 students for driver education, parking permits, and books when they register for 1999–00. The Board of Education approved the hikes at its April 29 meeting.

Again, this lead is 32 words and two sentences. Other *What* elements could be emphasized in different leads. For example, if the reporter wants to attract the attention of those students who will be paying the higher driver education fee, the lead could be written like this:

Driver education fees for 1999–00 will increase by $50 as a result of a Board of Education vote April 29. Fees for parking tags and books will also increase.

This is a 30-word, two-sentence lead. If the reporter wants to highlight the fee increase that will affect every student, the lead could be written like this:

Book fees will increase by $5 for the 1999–00 school year in District 214, bringing the cost of book rental to $95 for every student. Driver education and parking permit fees will also rise.

This 35-word, two-sentence lead includes more specific information about one aspect of the fees but omits who increased the fees and when they were increased. Are these ideas important enough to include in the lead? Or can they wait until later in the story?

When?

On April 29, the District 214 Board of Education voted to increase student fees for 1999–00. Increases will occur in fees for book rental, driver education class, and parking permits.

What are the strengths and weaknesses of this 31-word, two-sentence lead? Compare it to the *Who* and *What* leads above.

Another *When* lead might feature the time when the fee increases go into effect:

For the 1999–00 school year, some District 214 student fees will increase. At its regular meeting on April 29, the Board of Education voted 7-0 to hike fees for book rental, parking permits, and driver education.

This 38-word lead is a bit long for the guidelines established (35-word maximum), although some editors would say it is OK as long as it doesn't go over 40 words.

How effective is this lead with the emphasis on the following school year as the *When?* So far, which lead do you think is the best? Why?

Where?

At its regular meeting in the Board Room of Forest View Education Center on April 29, the Board of Education voted 7-0 to increase student fees by $65 for next year.

At 32 words and one sentence, this lead is hard to follow. Another weakness is its delay in getting to anything of interest to readers. Nothing in the first 24 words is likely to catch the busy student reader's attention enough to finish reading the lead paragraph, let alone the whole story. Is the $65 figure misleading? Why or why not?

Why?

To put more of the cost on students, fees for driver education, parking permits, and book rentals will increase for 1999–00 across District 214. The Board of Education approved the hikes on April 29.

This lead contains 35 words in two sentences. It is likely to attract reader attention and explains why the Board took the action it did. Compare it to earlier leads for clarity and depth of information. Which lead do you like best now? Why?

How?

By a vote of 7-0, District 214's Board of Education voted on April 29 to increase student fees for driver education, parking permits, and book rentals for the 1999–00 school year. With 33 words in one sentence, this lead is hard to understand, and it repeats "vote" and "voted." Reword it into two sentences, keeping the *How* element at the beginning. What are its strengths and weaknesses? How does it compare with the others in terms of effectiveness?

While no two professional reporters may come up with identical leads from the same set of facts, most often they will begin their hard news summary leads with the *Who* or *What* element. Occasionally, they may begin with the *Why* or *How* aspect. Only in very unusual circumstances, when the time or place of an event is newsworthy in itself, would the professionals start with the *When* or *Where* elements.

In the case of the student fee increase story, the school newspaper reporter might begin with the *Why* element. Remember—most student newspapers are published every two weeks or less frequently. Student readers are likely to know about the fee increase by the time the story is published. The new aspect for them may be the reason behind the increase. This will be true of many news stories printed in high school newspapers regardless of what topics they cover. For this reason, student journalists will need to dig past the most obvious facts to get at reasons for the news item.

Impact Lead

Since timeliness is nearly impossible to achieve in high school papers, much of the news covered by the high school press is written in a "featurized" way. This does not diminish the importance of the news story. Rather, it challenges student journalists to consider the *How* and *Why* functions of the

journalistic questions more carefully. As a journalist, you'll want to analyze the specific effect of news events on the audience—your fellow students.

An **impact lead** starts to answer the "So what?" question. It makes absolutely clear what effect this news event will have on the reader. An effective impact lead for the fee increase story might go as follows.

All District 214 students will pay higher book rental fees next year. But students taking driver ed and those who park in school lots will pay even more for these privileges.

This 31-word, two-sentence lead makes clear exactly who will feel the impact of the fee increase. The other information about the hikes, including specific amounts, will be developed in the story's next paragraphs. Can you revise this lead to make it more effective?

Quote Lead

The **quote lead** does just what it says: starts the story with a compelling quote that sums up its main point. Compelling quotes are rare. In news stories, the lead a reporter creates is usually more effective in getting across the whole idea of the story than any comment from an individual. In general, it's best to avoid starting with a quote as the lead paragraph. However, a partial quote or a quote as the second sentence in the lead can create an effective lead.

Fees for book rental, parking permits, and driver ed classes will go up in District 214 next year. "The Board wants students to cover a greater share of the cost for these services," Rick Henrickson, District 214 controller, said.

This 39-word, two-sentence lead explains the *Why* element. But does it work better than the earlier leads? Why or why not? What information had to be removed to make room for the quote and attribution? Could this quote be used just as effectively later in the story?

Question Lead

The **question lead** is simply a lead paragraph phrased as a question. Like the quote lead, these leads do not give the reader solid information about the story, so it's best to avoid them most of the time. Beginning journalists might rely on the question lead because it can be an easy way to get started. However, all too often their questions can be answered yes or no by the reader. And when readers answer no, they're ready to move on. You don't want to take this chance. A good rule for a high school newspaper staff is to allow no more than one question lead in an issue, if any, and do not use it on a news story. In addition, be certain no other lead would be better.

Do you know why the Board of Education raised the fees for book rental, driver ed and parking permits for 1999–00 at its last meeting?

Indirect Lead

Today journalists are not limited to using the direct or summary lead to begin their news stories. Creativity has become increasingly important to newspaper journalists as consumers get more of their immediate news from 24-hour news services, such as Cable News Network (CNN), Headline News, and the Internet.

The **indirect lead**, or **soft lead**, draws the reader into the story in some way other than directly with a summary of the facts. Because it delays getting to the main point of the story, this is also known as a **feature lead**, or a **delayed lead**. Before it gets to the specifics of the news event, it may:

* Set a scene
* Introduce a character
* Introduce a situation
* Relate a story or anecdote

Leads that relate a story are also known as **storytelling leads**. A **teaser lead** is an opening paragraph containing a one-sentence reference to something in the story that will pique the reader's interest. The "something" is then explained more fully in the second paragraph. Any of these openings can be used on hard or soft news stories as well as feature stories, opinion stories, and sports stories. (See Chapters 10 through 13 for more about these types of writing.)

By their very nature, feature leads may take more than one paragraph to develop. Most experts agree the indirect lead should take no more than four paragraphs. No later than the fifth paragraph, the reader should encounter the nut graf, the paragraph that explains the focus of the story and that may be very much like the summary or direct lead discussed earlier. The most successful creative leads are those that flow naturally from the content of the story itself.

Professionals Experiment with Leads, Too

By now you may think there's no way you can ever write an effective lead for a story. Don't despair. You're right to realize the great responsibility the lead carries—to grab your reader's attention in three seconds, in the first few words, and to compel that reader to continue. But don't think you have to come up with the perfect lead—the one that tells the story best—with the first sentence you write or even that you have to write the lead first. Professional journalists approach lead writing in as many different ways as there are Pulitzer Prize winners.

Donald Murray, writing coach for the *Boston Globe*, uses experimental lead writing to find the focus of his stories. He suggests you "write as many leads . . . as you can as quickly as possible. Twenty, thirty, forty, sixty leads. Sixty is about normal for me on an article. I may use the third one, but after sixty I know the third one is good," he says. "These . . . shouldn't be written carefully. They should take about three minutes each. They play off each other. Many are silly, and most won't work. But each will trigger other leads . . . other ways to get hold of the subject."

In contrast, Don Fry says he starts writing from his point statement or nut graf. Once he has finished the rest of the story, he writes his lead.

Ultimately, you will decide what method suits you best.

Sidebar

Lead Openings No One Wants to Read

* All-City High will once again . . .
* Once again . . .
* Every year . . .
* All-City High . . . (assuming this is the name of your school)
* Recently . . . As years go by . . . As many of you may know . . . As the year winds down . . .
* Over the summer . . .
* Most students . . . Some students
* That time of year again when . . .
* Well . . .
* Oh my!
* As most of the student body has already realized . . . Lately, things . . . There are . . .
* Imagine . . . According to . . .
* Leads beginning with the time or date unless this is the unique feature of the story.
* Leads beginning with *a, an,* or *the.* If you can, figure out any other way to begin.

Sources: Donald Murray, *Writing for Your Readers,* The Globe Pequot Press, Chester, Conn., 1983. Roy Peter Clark and Don Fry, *Coaching Writers: Editors and Reporters Working Together,* St. Martin's Press, New York, 1992.

Organizing Your Story

You have your lead, or at least your nut graf, and you're ready to continue building your story in the most effective way to keep your readers' interest and to get across the main ideas related to the news event. As with writing a lead, you have more than one choice in organizing your story.

Inverted Pyramid Style

The inverted pyramid, or upside-down triangle, is the traditional pattern for a hard news story (see model on pages 90–91). At least **four** reasons exist for using this format:

1. **It benefits hurried readers.** Even if the reporter hooks readers with a great lead, they may not have time to finish the story. The inverted pyramid style ensures readers will get the most important facts first.
2. **It benefits beginning journalists.** The inexperienced reporter can be overwhelmed by all the options available for writing a lead and organizing the body of the story. The inverted pyramid formula gives that beginner a specific model to follow. It is a good pattern for briefs or short news stories, which beginners usually write first.
3. **It benefits the headline writer.** In most professional newsrooms, the story writer and the headline writer are different people. The inverted pyramid style gives the headline writer the most important facts and saves the time it would take to read the entire story.
4. **It benefits the page layout editor.** Again, in most professional newsrooms, once the writer completes a story, he or she gives up control of that story to others, such as the layout editor. The inverted pyramid style allows the layout editor to cut the story from the bottom to fit without losing valuable time finding and consulting with the writer about what can be cut.

A fifth reason may also exist: The inverted pyramid style is often a natural way to tell a story, although experts disagree on this point.

Example

Inverted Pyramid

LEAD

MOST
Important Details

Less Important Details

least
important
details

Inverted Pyramid

A The model story features a 29-word, one-sentence direct lead beginning with the **Who** element. The opening paragraph also includes **What** (learned to educate elementary school kids about the dangers of smoking), **How** (in a full-day Teens Against Tobacco Use workshop), **When** (Monday, Feb. 22), **Where** (in the library).

B The second paragraph expands on the **How** aspect.

D By the fourth paragraph, the reader knows why the volunteers got the training. If the writer had stopped at the end of paragraph four, she would have had an informative news brief.

Model

Student group to spearhead anti-tobacco use campaign

by Jill Rosenberg, News/Feature Staff

Sixty freshmen learned to educate elementary school kids about the dangers of smoking in a full-day Teens Against Tobacco Use (TATU) workshop on Monday, Feb. 22 in the library.

Through activities and discussion, representatives from the American Lung Association and Humana, a health insurance provider, trained students to teach elementary school kids about tobacco awareness.

"They taught us to talk to kids," said freshman Laura Brinkman. "Before I went into it, I wouldn't have known."

Students will go to Hatch Elementary School next Tuesday afternoon to present their own workshops on the problems students face when confronted with tobacco use. Through the rest of the year, the TATU mentors will visit Oak Park and River Forest elementary schools and speak with the students.

The 60 students volunteered to participate in the program for various reasons. Freshman Vernicia Elie believes smoking awareness is important because "little kids look up to high school kids, but they [high school students] set a bad example."

Brinkman chose to get involved because she has a lot of friends who smoke and "it's really gross." She hopes to increase elementary kids' awareness and prevent them from picking up the habit later in life.

C In the third paragraph, the writer includes her first quote, which tells **Why** the student volunteers needed the workshop. It is also good journalistic writing style to include the first quote no later than the third paragraph.

E Paragraphs five and six give more information about why two specific students volunteered for the program. Both paragraphs include partial quotes. The writer could have interviewed more of the 60 volunteers and added those comments to this section.

F Paragraphs seven and eight tell details about the full-day workshop. Readers could stop after either of these paragraphs.

H Notice how the final paragraph gives interesting, but nonessential, information. It does not end with a summary of the workshop, a summary of the story as a whole, or with any evaluative comment from the writer. This is another strength of this story. The traditional inverted pyramid story ends with the least important information.

At the training sessions, students brainstormed their ideas about the pressures facing fourth through sixth graders, discussed lies and misleading images in tobacco advertising, witnessed several demonstrations about the amounts of tar in cigarettes and watched a video that showed graphic examples of the harm done by tobacco use.

In the afternoon, participants broke into teams of three or four, made posters and created their own presentations geared towards elementary school kids. The groups will present to other freshmen in Freshman Seminar as well as visiting elementary schools in Oak Park and River Forest.

Brinkman's presentation entails a discussion with the class about how many people smoke and whether or not it is "cool." It also features activities, including one where kids run in place for a minute and breathe through a straw to show the feeling of emphysema. Another activity uses empty pop bottles to demonstrate the amount of tar in a cigarette.

TATU is a national organization, part of the American Lung Association, that "helps young people ages 14–17 teach 9–12-year-old children to avoid tobacco," according to a handout from the organization.

Source: Oak Park-River Forest High School, Oak Park, Ill., *Trapeze*, March 12, 1999, Volume 88, No. 10, p. 1.

G Paragraph nine tells details about Brinkman's presentation. Readers could stop after this paragraph.

Answer: The layout editor has five places where she or he could cut without losing essential information. The editor could easily remove the final paragraph, the ninth paragraph, the eighth paragraph, or the seventh paragraph to make the story fit into the available space. Because the fifth and sixth paragraphs are linked in showing two reasons for volunteering, the editor should not cut the sixth without also cutting the fifth.

Storytelling Pattern

As established earlier, the inverted pyramid is not the only organizational pattern available for the journalist. Perhaps it should not even be the one used most frequently by more experienced writers who have developed confidence in their ability to organize information.

The narrative, or **storytelling pattern**, uses an indirect lead to capture the reader's interest. Following the lead, the nut graf gives the main point of the story. Then the writer develops the details of the event as they happened—with a beginning, a middle, and an end—in the middle, or body, of the story. This portion of the story uses **narrative techniques** such as dialogue (quotes or conversation) and description. At the end, the writer plants a **clincher**, also called a **kicker**, which gives the reader something to remember without repeating previous information. When the kicker returns to the opening paragraph idea, it is called a **circle kicker**. For a visual representation of the storytelling pattern, see the example on the next page.

The Crop Test

Once you have written your story, you can apply what journalists call the **crop test**, or cutoff test, to be sure it is written in true inverted pyramid style. To do this, follow **two** steps:

1. Analyze your story beginning with the final paragraph to be sure nothing important is lost if that paragraph is cut.

2. Continue checking from the end of the story to be sure the information in each paragraph is more important.

Question: How would you apply the crop test to the model on the anti-smoking campaign on the previous page?

Planning an ending for any story not written in the inverted pyramid style helps journalists avoid the moral they often want to tack onto the end. This planned ending might contain the natural climax to the story, might tie back to the opening, or might use a compelling quote, but it should not preach to readers in the reporter's own words. The models in this chapter illustrate the idea of planned endings that do not result in writers expressing their own opinions.

Basic Techniques for Storytelling

In her book *Writing and Reporting News: A Coaching Method* (1994), Carole Rich recommends the following:

- ✓ Use concrete details rather than vague adjectives.

- ✓ Use dialogue when possible and appropriate.

- ✓ Set a scene.

- ✓ Use action verbs.

- ✓ Observe or ask questions involving all your senses.

- ✓ Use show-in-action description.

- ✓ Tell a story like a plot, with a beginning, middle, and climax. Get a chronology or sequence of events. You may want to use the chronology in all or part of your story. Even if you don't use chronological order, you need to understand the sequence.

- ✓ Follow Mark Twain's advice: "Don't say the old lady screamed—bring her on and let her scream."

Example

Circle Kicker

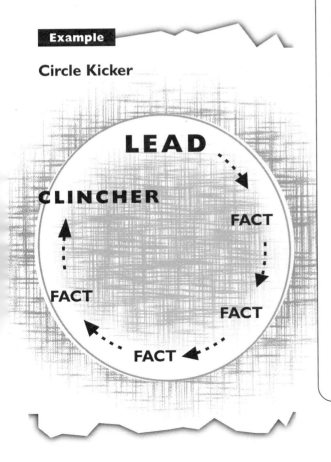

Storytelling Pattern with Natural Climax Kicker

A The story starts with an indirect lead.

Stolen 'chariot' returned

by Michael Ritter, Sports Editor

It was 10 p.m., and Andrew Kahn ('99) and a friend were out driving to a party. He was driving south on Barrington, when all of a sudden he saw two kids swerving in and out of the crosswalk, at the intersection with Olympic Boulevard, in a yellow golf cart.

"Wait, that's our cart!" yelled Kahn, as he swerved across the street, chasing and cutting off the yellow cart in a 7-11 convenience store parking lot. Kahn jumped out of his car to interrogate the two teenage boys.

"I wasn't scared of the two boys because they didn't look like the type that would pull a gun out on me. I do admit that it was stupid, but I was more intimidating than them," said Kahn.

The two boys, who were between the ages of 15 and 19, were dressed in army clothes, according to Kahn. The older one told Kahn that the cart was on the VA property and that he was old enough to drive it. Kahn responded by telling the two boys, "Actually the cart was stolen from my school."

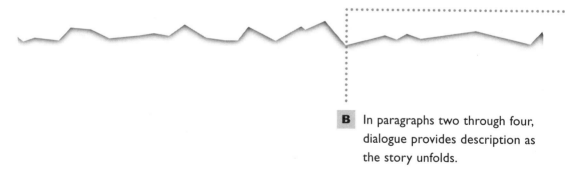

B In paragraphs two through four, dialogue provides description as the story unfolds.

The yellow golf cart, which is referred to as the "Batmobile" by Mike Estrada, the varsity baseball coach, has a top speed that is estimated to be at approximately 5 miles per hour.

The cart, property of Brentwood School, is used by the maintenance crew and the coaches who transport equipment to the VA field.

The cart was stolen the night before from its parking space next to the baseball field on the VA property. It was suspected that whoever stole the vehicle had unscrewed the locked gates from their hinges and completely torn them down.

Kahn, who had no idea what to do with the cart after the two thieves had left the scene, called Estrada for guidance. Estrada, who was asleep at the time, told Kahn to call the police to ask for help.

While Kahn was calling the police to report the stolen cart, a group of kids, who Kahn described as "punks," began flirting with his friend.

"They turned out to be pretty cool guys," said Kahn, as he proceeded to wait two hours for the police to come.

Once the police came, according to Kahn, they had bad attitudes and lectured him for wasting their time, because the police said that the yellow cart did not count as a stolen vehicle.

Eventually two more cops arrived and took the cart away, which was returned to school two days later.

Source: Brentwood School, Los Angeles, Calif., *Flyer*, March 17, 1999.

Storytelling Pattern with Compelling Quote Kicker

A The story begins with an indirect storytelling lead.

C This paragraph contains the story's first nut graf.

Model

Explosion leads to expulsion

by Kate Tresley, Staff Writer

Ambulances, fire trucks, and some 2,000 students stood outside Hinsdale Central on the morning of Nov. 13 after a canister of pepper spray exploded in the foreign language stairwell.

According to Myles Laffey, English dept., it was 7:57 a.m. when he heard the explosion. Mr. Laffey knew immediately that an explosion had occurred. "I could tell that this sound wasn't just a firecracker or a smoke bomb," he said.

Terry Meyers, Foreign Language dept., not only heard the explosion before her French 5 class, but felt its effects as well. "The students in the room and I were paralyzed at the sound," she said.

Marina Fennessy, Foreign Language dept., went into the affected stairwell to ensure that no one was hurt. "No matter what the large boom was, my main concern was for the students and making sure that no one was severely injured," said Ms. Fennessy.

After coming in contact with the pepper spray, Ms. Fennessy felt the explosion's effects. "I was having trouble breathing, and my throat and eyes were burning," she said. Ms. Fennessy was treated for burnt corneas at Hinsdale Hospital for approximately three hours.

Following the incident, extensive investigation prompted school administrators to take serious disciplinary action against the suspected students.

According to James Ferguson, principal, the duration of a particular expulsion trial varies from case to case; the proceedings, however, are generally the same.

The Illinois School Code states that any "gross or disobedient" behavior warrants an immediate expulsion. Dr. Ferguson acknowledges that virtually any violation of the school code can result in expulsion.

B Details about the pepper spray incident follow in these paragraphs.

D These paragraphs provide background on student discipline policies.

F Here we return to storytelling.

"For example, if a student is late to every class every day, he is obviously thumbing his nose at the school. Eventually, [the administration] says 'That's it. This student obviously does not want to be a productive member of this environment,'" said Dr. Ferguson.

Once a student has behaved in a "gross or disobedient" way, a meeting is scheduled with Dave Franson, asst. principal, and Dr. Ferguson. Then, Dr. Ferguson makes the decision whether or not to proceed with a formal expulsion. If a trial is decided upon, Dr. Ferguson's involvement ends here. "After [the decision is made], I only provide the student files," he said. The case is then reviewed by the School Board members, who make the final decision.

At the School Board's Dec. 14 meeting, a 7-0 ruling was made to expel three male students for their involvement in the incident. The two seniors were expelled until June 10, 1999. The third student, a junior, has withdrawn from Central. If the student decides to return, he cannot do so before Jan. 22, 1999, as he is expelled until then.

With the help of the student body and others, the administration was able to solve the pepper spray mystery. "As principal, I take my responsibility seriously to protect the rights of kids. [Central] is an honorable and ethical place," said Dr. Ferguson.

"The unfortunate thing is when students put themselves in a position where expulsion is a possibility," he said. "The kids want to focus on finding the loophole rather than improving their behavior. People want to know how to get out of the [situation] rather than focusing on how they got into it."

According to Dr. Ferguson, regardless of the particular case, one thing is for sure: "[The administration] also regrets being put in a position to [expel someone]."

Source: Hinsdale Central High School, Hinsdale, Ill., *The Devil's Advocate*, Jan. 25, 1999.

E Paragraph 11 is the story's second nut graf.

G The compelling quote ends the story.

Chronological Order Pattern

The <u>chronological order pattern</u> uses time in some way to organize the story in a 1-2-3 sort of way. Yes, it is an element in the narrative storytelling pattern, but depending on the story it may also be useful in its own right. Chronological order may be used successfully to relive the crucial final minutes of a major sports contest, to preview the events planned for Homecoming Week, to highlight the significant events of the year in an end-of-year retrospective. Need more visualization of a chronological pattern? See the graphic below.

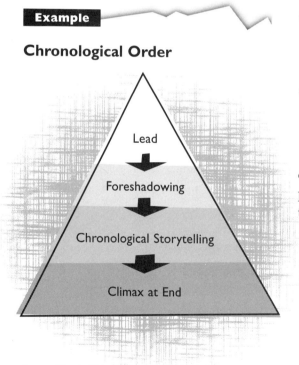

Example

Chronological Order

Lead

Foreshadowing

Chronological Storytelling

Climax at End

Source: Carole Rich, *Writing and Reporting News: A Coaching Method*, Wadsworth Publishing Co., Belmont, Calif., 1994.

Combination Pattern

Most likely, reporters will want to experiment with a combination of styles, especially once they get past writing four-paragraph newsbriefs. Often the content of the story itself will suggest an appropriate organization. Here's an example:

* A story about new construction at your school begins with a three-paragraph sights and sounds description of an overcrowded classroom.
* The nut graf following this scene gives the most important 5Ws and H about the upcoming construction.
* The next paragraph quotes an adult or student about construction plans.
* The following paragraphs develop the construction details in inverted pyramid style, alternating quote paragraphs with fact paragraphs.
* The final paragraph contains a clincher that returns the reader to the original classroom scene.

This story combines the techniques of the indirect lead, nut graf, inverted pyramid style, and clincher storytelling technique.

Combination Pattern: Storytelling/ Chronological

A The storytelling approach begins with an indirect lead.

Model

Disability: Junior has opportunity to experience handicaps

by Kelly Tibbert, Lifestyles Staff

Next time Marianne Smith '00 is tempted to park in a handicapped space, she said she will think again. Smith had the opportunity last Wednesday to go downtown to experience what it would be like to spend a day as a disabled person.

As a member of Generation of Promise, Smith was given this opportunity when she chose to further explore being physically disabled. The group's purpose is to expose members to diverse situations. In order to become a member, Smith had to submit an application for review.

Other topics to explore included teen sexuality, crime and punishment, crisis and poverty and homelessness.

C Chronological order begins. The story unfolds as the day progresses.

7:00 a.m.

Waiting for her ride, Smith prepares to travel to Southfield Lathrup Senior High School.

She arrives at the school an hour later to breakfast and a group of 30 females and 15 males. Varsity jackets from Warren Fitzgerald, Allen Park, Livonia Franklin, Lake Orion attest to the diversity of the group.

8:20 a.m.

Group discussions begin as the mass divides to areas designated by topic.

Discussion includes the Americans with Disabilities Act, which entitles facilities to be handicap accessible and outlaws discrimination due to disability. Despite this law, group members realize some of the challenges facing disabled people include buildings with stairs and small doorways, plane trips and being limited to certain fields of work.

continues ▶

B The nut graf follows quickly in the second paragraph.

D Time of day and details about activities continue throughout the story.

Combination Pattern:
Storytelling/Chronological

(continued)

9:45 a.m.

Arriving at the Department of Veterans Medical Center, the group meets Chief of Prosthetics and Sensory Aids Dave Thomas, a wheelchair-bound Vietnam veteran. He describes the public's reaction to people with disabilities.

"You have to overcome the disability in the other person's mind," Thomas said. "When people look at people with disabilities, they see themselves. You're looking at me right now and thinking 'that could be me.'"

When people see others who are disabled, they have a tendency to stare, Thomas said. It is important to try to minimize feelings which cause you to discriminate either intentionally or unintentionally, he said. Although staring is a bad habit, some have to find a polite way to overcome it.

Children are usually open and curious, while adults stare out of fear or ignorance, Thomas said. If a disabled person has accepted their situation, they are generally willing to talk about it. After all, he said, part of their duty is to educate others.

"The disability should not change you. It changes how you do things, but it should not change you," Thomas said. "Be careful as to holding them [handicapped people] up as role models; true, they have overcome a significant challenge, but you would do the same in that situation."

After passing around goggles which simulate blindness, it is time for the group to receive their disabilities. Group members rush to the bathroom as they take their last free steps.

On the way to lunch at the Majestic Cafe, several blocks away, six members of the group are wheelchair bound, three are blind, two cannot use one hand, and the rest assist the others. Smith chooses to be blind.

12:30 p.m.

Finally arriving at the restaurant 30 minutes after leaving the Medical Center, the group members stumble and wheel their way to special tables as they await their lunch. Stares encountered from passersby are nothing compared to the difficulty Smith will face as she tries to eat the artichoke hearts she ordered.

E The ending quote ties back to the opening paragraph.

"It was hard because I wanted food and I couldn't get at it. I knew I was getting it all over the place," Smith said. "You almost feel like a baby."

Smith said this part of the day taught her to value her independence. It was really frustrating when her cane got caught in the cracks in the sidewalk. Trying to hold conversations was not easy.

An hour later, Smith traded the gift of sight for a wheelchair as they went back to the Medical Center.

2:10 p.m.

Ascending the hill to the center is very painful and challenging, Smith said. An unexpected difficulty she encounters is the slope of the sidewalks. They gently tilt towards the street, forcing the disabled person to push harder with one arm to avoid the street.

"Now I have a better understanding of how it is to be in a wheelchair," Smith said. "I guess you would get used to it if you were actually in that situation, but it hurt so bad,

even afterwards. I ended up being pushed most of the way."

Upon the group's return, full health is restored as they receive a quick overview of how technology has increased the quality and efficiency of prosthetic limb production.

2:30 p.m.

Although it still feels early, the group thanks Thomas before leaving. Smith said the day's experiences were beyond her expectations. The activities forced her to take a second look at her life and learn about another lifestyle.

"People tend to look at disabled people and say, 'Wow, that's so great,' but if you put yourself in that place, you would do the same thing," Smith said. "So don't put them up on a pedestal, just treat them like normal people who have overcome difficult circumstances."

Source: Grosse Pointe South High School, Grosse Pointe Farms, Mich., *Tower*, March 10, 1999.

News Story Essentials

Unfortunately, it's not enough to write the world's greatest lead and execute an award-winning organizational pattern. Those two ingredients are critical to a successful story, no doubt. But there's more. Your story must also be accurate and objective, must usually be written from third-person point of view, and must be readable, with short sentences and paragraphs linked together with effective transitions.

Accuracy

Without accurate information and accurate presentation of that information, nothing else matters—not the lead and not the organizational pattern of your story. The best way to ensure accuracy of information is to check it with additional sources.

Legend has it that a sign in Chicago's old City News Bureau newsroom read, "If your mother says she loves you, check it out!" Perhaps you don't need to go quite that far, but a generally accepted standard in journalistic circles is to confirm something with two independent sources in addition to the original. This is particularly true for anything the least bit controversial.

Remember, your credibility and the credibility of your publication are on the line with every story you write, with every fact you include, with every person you quote, with every name you list. Legally and ethically, journalists are responsible for every word of their stories. Here are **three** tips:

1. Don't let sources take advantage of you. Check out any questionable information they have given you.
2. Don't assume you understand what a source told you if the information is fuzzy when you start to write. Go back to clarify.
3. Don't even assume you know the correct spelling of your source's name. Check it out!

Credibility is the most important characteristic you have as a journalist. Your readers have to be able to trust what you tell them. Once you lose that credibility, your job is nearly impossible because no one will talk to you on-the-record, if anyone will talk to you at all.

Objectivity

Like accuracy, objectivity contributes to your credibility as a reporter. Of course, absolute objectivity is humanly impossible. Choosing what stories to cover, what sources to interview, and what order to present information in all require decisions. Objectivity and ethical behavior require that reporters recognize their biases and work to overcome them in making these decisions. Above all, reporters must remember they report facts and the stated opinions of other people. They do not include their own opinions in stories unless they are writing an opinion story, such as an editorial, a column, or a review. (See Chapters 11 and 12 for more about opinion writing.)

Word Choice

"Unless such words as 'interesting', 'important', 'tragic', or 'beautiful' are attributed," warns Helen Smith in *Scholastic Newspaper Fundamentals*, "they indicate the writer is drawing conclusions." Such conclusion drawing should be avoided.

Sidebar

Resist the Temptation to Conclude Your News Story Like This:

* It goes to show you . . .
* So in the end . . .
* In the end . . .
* As this year comes slowly to a halt . . .
* Most importantly, however . . .
* Not only are the standards useful in preparing for college, but they will be helpful to students in their lives after college.
* She looks forward to the obstacles and tasks that she has yet to face, but whatever happens in the future, she'll be able to handle it.
* With class rank abolished, maybe college will begin taking New Year's resolution success rates into account instead. We might all be in deep trouble.
* Everyone seems to have an opinion about . . .
* We can only hope the administration agrees.

"Claims," "feels," "believes," and "thinks" are verbs to avoid using in place of "said" since they suggest a mind-reading capacity on the reporter's part. Colorful description must be based on observable fact, not the reporter's opinion. That's one reason beginning journalists will do well to stay with direct leads and inverted pyramid style, at least for a while, so they aren't tempted to editorialize, or include their own opinion, in a story.

Choice of Stories and Sources

Reporters can also ensure their objectivity by the types of stories they write and the sources they consult for stories. Consider these **three** tips:

1. Student reporters should not cover an event in which they play a key role. While it might seem easy for the star quarterback, who is also on the newspaper or yearbook staff, to cover football for the season or write the copy to accompany the football spread, doing so will jeopardize his objectivity and undermine his credibility with readers. Likewise, the girl who tries out for, but does not make, the swing choir should not cover it. Even though she might be perfectly objective in her own eyes, her readers could only wonder, and her credibility would be undermined.

2. When choosing sources for any story, reporters must interview students who represent a variety of viewpoints as well

as the ages, genders, and ethnic makeup of the student body. Avoid interviewing your friends or fellow journalism students unless they play a key role in the story. Don't interview just faculty members either.

3. Above all, when reporting on an issue or event with more than one side, you must dig for information to reflect all points of view fairly and completely.

Point of View

For most news stories, reporters write in **third-person point of view**, using such observer pronouns as "he," "she," "it," "they," "him," "her," or "them."

* Third-person point of view avoids all first-person references (*I, me, us, my, our*) and second-person references (*your*) unless they are in a source's direct quote.

* An exception to the "no second person" rule may be made for some indirect leads that invite the reader to participate in the story. To avoid overuse of these "imagine this" kinds of leads, staffs should discuss the use of second person in stories and make hard and fast rules. In general, writers should avoid the temptation to ask readers to "imagine this." However, if they do, the story should shift to third person once the indirect lead is complete.

Readability

An effective lead gets the reader to stop and read at least the first paragraph. After that, the writer wants to make sure the reader continues. Attention to **two** main things— short sentences and short paragraphs—has been part of the secret to the success of the national newspaper *USA Today* since 1982.

1. Short sentences, 16 to 17 words for the average reader, help keep the reader interested. Of course, not every sentence in every story has to be the same length, but longer sentences run the risk of losing readers. Likewise, sentences that begin with dependent clauses are harder for readers to follow than sentences that follow the direct subject-verb-object order. This does not mean writers should never vary their sentence structure. It does mean writers should make conscious decisions about varying sentence length and structure with the ease of readers in mind.

2. Like short sentences, short paragraphs also help readers. The white space introduced by frequent paragraph indents gives readers the illusion that a story is short. When word processing stories using standard margins of one inch on both sides, writers should take care that no paragraph runs longer than four typed lines, or about two sentences. This ensures paragraphs will not be overwhelmingly long when published in narrow columns of type.

Variety in sentence and paragraph beginnings also helps hold reader interest.

Transitions

Individual paragraphs of a story cannot stand alone. They must all be linked smoothly with transition words and phrases showing the relationships between ideas while providing a natural order and easy flow of ideas. Some transition words and phrases always perform this function in writing, while other transition ideas are unique to a specific story. Even quotes need to be linked smoothly, avoiding artificial transitional devices, such as "when asked."

Consider these **three** consecutive paragraphs:

1. Floor hockey team members received gold medals Feb. 1, <u>after</u> they earned the school's 12th Special Olympics state championship since 1993. <u>This</u> was <u>their</u> third straight state win in floor hockey.

2. <u>To prepare for state competition,</u> the team practiced throughout January. They <u>also</u> played in four scrimmage games against Hoffman Estates High School.

3. "<u>We</u> were really happy when we got <u>first place</u>," Maggie Berichon, senior team member, said.

Transition words are underlined in the example. Words such as *after, this, their,* and *also* are almost always transition words since they refer to something that came before. The transition idea unique to this specific story is the recurring idea of "state competition." The writer uses it in different forms throughout the story. "We" in the quote refers to team members, and "first place" in the quote continues the state championship-competition idea.

Five Categories

Common transitional words and phrases fall into **five** categories.

1. **Time** (*meanwhile, then, later, after, before, afterward, now, previously*)
2. **Location** (*by, near, here, there, at*)
3. **Logical relationships** (*therefore, so, because, consequently, thus, for example*)
4. **Comparison/contrast** (*however, on the other hand, in contrast, like, but, or*)
5. **Additions** (*and, also, another, next, additionally, besides, furthermore*)

The publications staff may want to create a complete list of transitional words and phrases to post in the staff room and include in the staff manual for reference.

A Final Check

Once you've written the best story you can, it's time to print it out and look it over with a critical eye. The *Check Sheet for Better News Stories* shown on the next page is designed to help you do that. This handy checklist summarizes the elements and techniques that should be found in any good news story. If you cannot honestly place a check in each blank, indicating that the element or technique is present in your story, you need to do some revision. Then give your story and the check sheet to a fellow staff member to find out if he or she agrees with your analysis of your story.

Check Sheet for Better News Stories

Name_____

(Complete and attach to top of story before handing it in for evaluation.)

✔ My lead starts with the key thought that is unique to my story in the first five words. If not, I have provided an indirect lead and a nut graf no later than paragraph five that makes the key idea clear.

✔ My opening paragraph has 35 words or fewer.

✔ I have used the full name of each source on first mention.

✔ I have correctly identified all sources on first mention.

✔ I have used the appropriate form of the source's name on second and later mention.

✔ I have attributed direct quotes in past tense.

✔ I have varied my paragraph beginnings.

✔ I have varied my sentence beginnings.

✔ I have used correct time, date, place, order if applicable to my story.

✔ When I have used a direct quote, it is at the beginning of a paragraph followed by appropriate attribution.

✔ I have avoided use of first (*I, we, us, me, our*) and second (*you*) person except in direct quotes.

✔ My paragraphs are limited to four typed lines.

✔ My story is logically organized. The organization I used is _____.

✔ I have tried to use alternating paragraphs of direct quotes and transitions. In other words, quotes are spread throughout my story. They are not all grouped together.

✔ I have used my first quote no later than the third paragraph.

✔ I have avoided expressing my own opinion in the story.

✔ I have spell-checked my story using the computer.

✔ I have made sure to follow appropriate style rules.

✔ I have had my story checked by another journalism student: _____.

One specific strength of this story is:

One specific suggestion for improvement of this story is:

Special Types of News Stories

There are many types of news stories. Below **eleven** types are described, but bear in mind that plenty of stories are a blend.

1. **Action story.** The action story focuses on an action-filled or action-based event that needs to be related in depth. At least part of a story that emphasizes action will be told in chronological order. The best action stories rely on vivid description, colorful verbs, and other storytelling techniques.

2. **Quote story.** The quote story, as its name suggests, relies heavily on quotes for its substance. It might be handled as a series of person-on-the-street interviews on one topic, such as "What were the first few days of school like for you on the new schedule?" Or it might be a series of quotes from students who attended the Homecoming dance, who heard the motivational speaker at the all-school assembly, or who have opinions about a controversial book, movie, or TV program. Quote stories gain strength when they include a variety of points of view from a representative cross-section of students and faculty, including diversity in gender, age, and culture.

3. **Surprise ending story.** A story nearly impossible to plan is the surprise ending story. They happen rarely but need special treatment when they do. Examples might be a boy who tries out for the musical only to appease his folks and winds up being cast in the lead role or the discovery that the star center on the league-championship basketball team attends your school illegally.

4. **Academic story.** One of the most obvious types of stories for a school publications staff to do is the academic story. Unfortunately, it is one of the most often overlooked categories of story. What's going on in all those classrooms hour after hour, day after day? Some story ideas must be lurking for the curious reporter to find.

5. **Personality story.** The best personality story has a reason for being, rather than consisting of a list of miscellaneous likes and dislikes. Get lots of quotes from the subject of the profile, but also talk to several secondary sources who know the person from the angle your story is taking. If the story is on the female state cross-country champion, talk to her in great depth, but also talk to her parents, her friends, her coach to add additional insight into your profile of her.

6. **Obituary.** An obituary—an account of a person's life and achievements as well as the fact and cause of death—is one of the most difficult of all stories to write in a student publication. A wise publications staff has a policy about how deaths of students and faculty will be covered. Without such a policy, publications staff members may become so caught up in the loss of a fellow student or teacher they cannot be objective in their reporting.

7. **Advance story.** Stories that feature the future—advance stories—are the best for high school newspapers whose publication schedules rarely allow reporters to break stories or tell readers information they don't already know. Use the future book to stay on top of coming events so that your staff can be the first to tell the student body what will be new about this year's annual events.

8. **Follow-up story.** In doing a follow-up story, instead of a rehash of details students already know, look for the unique angle—the *How* or the *Why* or the *What* element no professional reporter thought to follow. Try for a new advance angle in the lead or nut graf even when the story will focus on past events. This is known as featuring the future while reporting the past.

9. **Speech-report story.** When covering a speech and doing a speech-report story, remember that what the speaker says— not the fact that he or she spoke—is the idea to feature. Yes, the location, occasion, and date of the speech, along with the size of the audience, need to be mentioned somewhere, but these are not usually the key. Make note of audience reaction to important points. Try to research the speaker ahead of time so you can ask questions afterwards other than about the speech itself. This is a story that is likely to rely heavily on quotes. Try to obtain a copy of the speech, either in advance or at the conclusion.

10. **Meeting story.** For a meeting story, remember you are not a secretary taking and writing minutes. The fact that the meeting took place is not usually the key idea of the story, although your story should include the date and place of the meeting somewhere. Neither are details about roll call and minutes read. Listen for details about key issues affecting your readers. Feature results of discussions in your story, including the outcome of any votes taken. Try to obtain an agenda for the meeting ahead of time so you know what is expected to happen. But even if you do obtain an agenda, be prepared for changes.

11. **Survey results story.** What if you're doing a survey results story? Don't lead with the idea that a survey was taken. Look for a significant result instead. Somewhere early in the story, however, include when and where the survey was taken, by whom, and by how many so the reader can put the results in perspective. Supplement statistical data with lots of quotes.

Wrap-up

Keeping in mind you only have three seconds to grab your reader's attention, the lead paragraph is the key in writing the news story. But don't agonize over the lead and never get on with the story. Find the system that works best for you. Is it to write 60 leads so you know you have the best one you possibly can? Or should you write the creative lead last? Most likely, you will try a number of different approaches until you settle on your favorite.

Choose the pattern or combination of patterns for your story that seems natural for your topic. And remember—you can always fall back on the traditional inverted pyramid style if that seems natural for you. Don't be afraid to read your story aloud and don't be afraid to ask others for advice.

In choosing information to include and specific words to use in your story, always remember your credibility is on the line. Once a journalist loses her or his credibility, little else is left. Check facts, write balanced stories, use the objective third-person viewpoint, write sentences and paragraphs your reader can understand easily, and use transitions to guide your reader through your story.

Journalism

chronological order pattern—story uses time in some way to organize the story; may be a part of the storytelling pattern.

circle kicker—final paragraph that ties back to the opening paragraph.

clincher (kicker)—planned ending to a story, final paragraph; must not contain the writer's opinion.

crop test—a method for testing whether an article is written in true inverted pyramid style.

direct news lead—traditional opening paragraph for an inverted pyramid news story; includes as many of the 5Ws and H as practical (also known as summary lead or AP summary lead).

feature lead (delayed lead)—opening that delays getting to the main point of the story, beginning instead by setting the scene, introducing a character or situation, or relating a story or anecdote.

continues ▶

more Journalism Words to Know

hard news—urgent, timely stories about events or conflicts, usually topics such as crime, fire, meetings, protests, speeches, and court cases; has strong effect on readers; may emphasize events more than people.

impact lead—incorporates the "So what?" aspect into the opening paragraph of a story.

indirect lead (soft lead)—opening that draws the reader into the story in some way other than with a direct summary of facts; may consist of more than one paragraph.

lead—opening of any piece of journalistic writing.

narrative techniques—dialogue and description used as part of the story.

nut graf—paragraph that explains the focus of the story; should come no later than the fifth paragraph with a delayed lead.

question lead—lead beginning with or containing a question; not recommended for use on a regular basis, and especially not for news stories.

quote lead—opening that begins with or contains a compelling quote; not recommended for use on a regular basis.

storytelling lead—opening paragraph or paragraphs that relate a story.

storytelling pattern—organization that uses indirect lead, nut graf, and narrative techniques to relate the news.

teaser lead—opening paragraph of one sentence referring to something in the story that arouses reader interest but is not explained in that sentence; explained more fully in second paragraph.

third-person point of view—use of observer pronouns to tell the story (*he, she, it, they, him, her, them*).

The Right Way to Quote

In this chapter, you will learn:

- **about the basics of quotations and why you should add them to your stories**
- **how to get quotations right the first time**
- **how to attribute quotations correctly**
- **what makes a good quotation for your story**
- **how to effectively place and punctuate quotations in your stories**

A story without sources who speak directly to readers is like vanilla ice cream without hot fudge, nuts, whipped cream, and a cherry—a poor substitute for a fully satisfying experience. Quotes bring stories and sources to life for readers. Quotes give stories a feeling of immediacy and add authority, authenticity, and credibility. They allow opinions into stories that reporters can't interject on their own. Every story benefits from the addition of quotes. However, quotes need to be used effectively and not just inserted at will as a way to insert quotation marks into a story. This chapter provides guidance in the proper use of quotations to produce stories that satisfy your readers.

Sorting Out Quotations

Direct quotations, or **direct quotes**, are word-for-word replays of information from sources to provide insight into a story. They are placed in quotation marks so readers know they come from either human or printed sources. There are several types of quotes:

* Direct quotes may be full sentences or parts of sentences.
* Quote combinations consist of partial quotes and fragmentary quotes.
* A **partial quote** is more than a word or two but less than a full sentence taken directly from the source. It is used with a paraphrase and placed in quotation marks.
* A **fragmentary quote** is an exact word or two taken directly from the source and placed in quotation marks within a paraphrase. Partial and fragmentary quotes should be used sparingly and only when their use gives better insight into the story than the reader would gain from a paraphrase or full quote alone.
* In some cases, reporters choose to combine part of what a source says word-for-word with a **paraphrase**, or summary in the reporter's words, of the rest of what a source says. The word-for-word portion is placed in quotation marks while the paraphrase is not. A paraphrase is sometimes called an **indirect quote**.

Certainly you will want to use a mixture of full, direct quotes and paraphrases in your own stories since using only one or the other is almost as weak as quoting no sources at all.

Full, direct quotes are usually better than paraphrases at doing the following:

* Giving the story a feeling of immediacy
* Adding interest and importance to the story
* Lending authority, authenticity, or credibility to information in the story
* Recreating what was said during an event
* Taking the reader to the scene of the event
* Allowing voices into the story
* Helping readers feel they actually know the sources

Partial quotes are usually better than full, direct quotes when the source is extremely wordy or when the source has explained something extremely complex. Then the writer may help the reader understand better by stepping in with paraphrases.

Partial quotes are better than fragmentary quotes at letting readers hear sources speak. In fact, fragmentary quotes should be reserved for unusual circumstances. A story filled with fragmentary quotes calls undue attention to the quoted words themselves and suggests a reporter who needs more practice taking notes during the interview.

Warning: Paraphrase Carefully

Paraphrasing often causes problems for reporters who think they have accurately reworded what their source said only to

I.D.-a-Quote

Look at these **four** ways to express the same information:

1. Direct Quote

"We're all excited about the transition to the new library," Mary Ann Holbrock, head librarian, said. "However, the greatest challenge we face will be transporting the books from the old library to the new one and setting them in the proper order."

2. Partial Quote

Mary Ann Holbrock, head librarian, said the librarians are looking forward to the move to the new library. The biggest problem they see is "transporting the books from the old library to the new one and setting them in the proper order," she said.

3. Fragmentary Quote

Mary Ann Holbrock, head librarian, said the librarians are "excited about" opening the new library and predicted the "greatest challenge" will be moving and organizing the books.

4. Paraphrase

Getting ready to move into the new library, Mary Ann Holbrock, head librarian, said the librarians are looking forward to it even though shifting and organizing the books will be a big job.

All four paragraphs tell readers how the head librarian describes the anticipation her team of librarians is feeling about moving into the new library. All four paragraphs also mention what she sees as their biggest hurdle.

* Which one paragraph does it best?
* Which of these paragraphs do you think communicates best to the reader the ideas the librarian expressed?
* Which lets the reader hear how the head librarian talks?
* Which uses words most efficiently and which least efficiently?
* Do the paraphrases retain the ideas from the original accurately, or has the writer made inappropriate changes?
* If this were your story, which paragraph would you use? Why?
* Can you think of any other ways to present this information?

find out they misrepresented part of it. Also, avoid creating fragmentary or partial quotes that misrepresent the overall opinion of your source. Don't commit the sin motion picture ads sometimes do of quoting the one phrase that praises the movie out of a 10-paragraph review that, on the whole, criticizes it.

Balance

If a library story was a controversial one with a mixture of emotions about moving into the new library, or if there were disagreements about when the library should open or how the books should be moved or organized, then it would be important for the writer to gather comments representing all sides of the issue. Representing these various points of view through quoting different sources is known as **balance**. Presenting a balanced view is one way reporters gain objectivity in their stories.

Word-for-Word?

Just what does it mean to say the writer will represent the source's comments "word-for-word?"

Sidebar

Quotes on Quotes from AP

The Associated Press Stylebook and Libel Manual (1999), the standard reference book for journalists in the United States, says this about "quotations in the news":

"Never alter quotations even to correct minor grammatical errors or word usage. Casual minor tongue slips maybe removed by using ellipses [. . .] but even that should be done with extreme caution. If there is a question about a quote, either don't use it or ask the speaker to clarify.

"If a person is unavailable for comment, detail attempts to reach that person. (Smith was out of the country on business; Jones did not return phone messages left at the office.)

"Do not routinely use abnormal spellings such as *gonna* in attempts to convey regional dialects or mispronunciations. Such spellings are appropriate when relevant to help to convey a desired touch in a feature.

"FULL vs. PARTIAL QUOTES: In general, avoid fragmentary quotes. If a speaker's words are clear and concise, favor the full quote. If cumbersome language can be paraphrased fairly, use an indirect construction, reserving quotation marks for sensitive or controversial passages that must be identified specifically as coming from the speaker.

"CONTEXT: Remember that you can misquote someone by giving a startling remark without its modifying passage or qualifiers. The manner of delivery sometimes is part of the context. Reporting a smile or a deprecatory gesture may be as important as conveying the words themselves."

The AP *Stylebook* also gives this advice about "obscenities, profanities, vulgarities":

"Do not use them in stories unless they are part of direct quotations and there is a compelling reason for them."

Source: From *The Associated Press Stylebook and Libel Manual*, The Associated Press, New York, 1999.

On Profanity

Law of the Student Press (2nd ed.), 1994, gives this advice:

When editors believe the potentially offensive words are crucial to a story, many use a first letter and dashes or underlines (for example, f——) in their place. . . . Students should carefully weigh the benefits and costs of publishing language that readers might find offensive. Some issues to consider:

1. Is the language necessary to communicate the message of a story or to give a quote authenticity? Or will it divert attention from the article's primary focus?

2. Is the author simply using certain words for shock value?

3. Is there less offensive language that would communicate the same idea? High school students especially might want to consider whether the use of profane language warrants a possible confrontation with readers or school administrators, including possible long-term effects on the publication's credibility and autonomy.

A newspaper staff needs to consider such standards carefully. Then, whatever your staff decides, remember to carry it out equally with all sources. It's unethical to quote every slip of the tongue the principal makes but to correct similar errors students make.

---

* Does it mean you can reorganize the original comment to fit better with your story? No.

* Does it mean you can you take out a few of the words and insert an ellipsis (. . .) to show you omitted something? Yes, but only if that does not change the meaning of the original in any way. Professionals suggest using this technique only when you are faced with a lengthy excerpt from a speech, trial, or printed material.

Slip-Ups

Do you include every vocalized pause ("um," "well," "you know"), grammatical error, profanity, or obvious slip? The AP *Stylebook* directs reporters never to alter quotations, even to correct minor errors or word usage. In practice, however, even professional journalists usually edit out vocalized pauses (those "ums" and "ers") and correct minor grammatical errors in the interest of helping readers. Besides, it's just not a good idea to let someone look bad in print when the error is an innocent one.

Decisions about how much editing of direct quotes is allowed come under ethical guidelines adopted by the media. For those publications with a strict word-for-word standard, quoted material can be handled through a paraphrase. Most staffs decide to correct grammatical errors, to eliminate profanity, and to omit unnecessary words, such as vocalized pauses.

Get It Right the First Time

You certainly want to quote sources correctly for the sake of your own credibility as a reporter and for the sake of your publication's credibility. **Three** reasons to verify quotes are:

1. You want sources to remain open to being interviewed by you again. If you quote them incorrectly or twist what they tell you in some way, you are not likely to get cooperation in the future.

2. Verification is standard practice in publications with longer deadlines. While daily professional newspapers don't usually have the time to verify quotes, professional magazines often employ researchers who do just that. Depending on the frequency of your publication or the amount of time you have to do your interviewing and write your story, you may have time to verify quotes in every story you write.

3. Certainly you will want to verify quotes in controversial pieces or if you have been assigned to interview a source who has had problems with being quoted accurately by your publication in the past.

Tips for Fair and Accurate Quoting

Here are some tips to help you represent your sources fairly and accurately:

* Always use the same notebook so you're comfortable with note taking.
* Put quotation marks around your word-for-word notes at the time you take them.

* Don't be afraid to ask your source for clarification or to repeat something, especially something you think might make a good direct quote.
* If you wonder whether you heard the source correctly, ask for clarification at the time.
* At the time of the interview, read back quotes you think you might use.
* Don't be afraid to return later to verify information.
* You might use a tape recorder.

Permission to Quote?

The general answer is, no, you don't need permission to quote students or adults you interview. However, as Chapter 4 points out, you may need to educate your sources, especially students, about the source-journalist relationship.

* Make clear from the beginning of the interview that you are a reporter for your school's newspaper, yearbook, or radio or TV station, what the interview is about, and that you will be writing a story for publication as the result of the interview. Always being honest about when you are playing your role as student journalist will ease fears your friends might have about reading something in the school paper or yearbook that they said informally.
* If you do hear something that would make a good addition to your story but you are not in the formal relationship of reporter-source when you hear it, then you need to get permission.

Are You in Trouble?

In cases where you sense that printing certain comments may be troublesome, ethically or legally—to the writer, the speaker, or the publication as a whole—you'd be wise to question the quote with the source and with fellow publication staff members. This is not exactly the same idea as asking permission to use a quote, but it gives the speaker a chance to rephrase or rethink what he or she wants to say. This does not mean sources should be given a chance to change everything they say. It does mean when that little voice in your head or that queasy feeling in your stomach tells you "there may be a problem here," you should act on that feeling somehow. Go back to the source for confirmation or additional information. Talk it over with your fellow staff members and your adviser.

To avoid problems with sources who claim they have been misquoted, keep your notes. If you know you are interviewing a historically difficult source, you may want to have the quotes initialed by that source to protect yourself later.

Credit Where Credit Is Due

Attribution tells the reader the source of your information. (Levels of attribution were discussed in Chapter 5.) With human sources, readers need to know who said it and what the source's qualifications are so they can judge how credible the source is. If the principal or dean announces the school will have security cameras installed at all entrances and in all computer labs next year, readers will take the announcement much more seriously than if a student tells readers the same thing.

Sidebar

When to Attribute

How do you decide which information to attribute? One general principle is that information that is self-evident and indisputable does not need attribution, while you should give a source for any information that might be open to question. More specifically, you need to identify the source of:

* *Anything quoted or reprinted from a published source.* This is sometimes not just a matter of journalistic ethics, but a legal requirement. You must give credit to the original author of any quote you use in your article. This may be true of certain material you paraphrase as well.
* *Direct quotes of all kinds, whether from public documents, speeches, interviews, or any other source.* A direct quote means the use of someone's exact words. Virtually anything you put inside quotation marks should be attributed.

* *Any information whose source has a real bearing on its credibility.* This is particularly true of information provided by people or organizations with an ax to grind. If a spokesperson for a politician gives you favorable information about him or her, that is one thing. If the opponent gives you information that reflects poorly on the candidate, that is another thing. You should be wary of both kinds of information, and try to verify them from other, more objective sources. If you cannot, but still choose to use the information, you need to let the readers know where it came from.
* *Charges, accusations and criticism against individuals.* In general, you should give a source for any information whose publication will cast someone else in a bad light. . . . [T]his

continues ▶

kind of potentially damaging information is dangerous stuff and should be used with care. Its source is always relevant.

* *Any information received over the telephone or by fax.* And, now we would add e-mailed information.
* *Speculation.* Guesses and predictions are not appropriate to most stories. Still, some stories require conjecture about the possible causes of current events or what is likely to happen in the future. You should clearly label such information as the speculation it is and identify its source.

On the other hand, you do not need to give a source for:

* *Firsthand information.* As a reporter, it is your job to observe and report what you have seen. You do not need to name other sources for what you have seen yourself.
* *Matters of public record.* Government statistics and reports, court records, and so on, belong to the public and can be used without concern. In such cases, you may want to identify the source (to lend authority, for example), but you don't have to do so.

* *Common knowledge.* You do not have to name a source for facts that are well known and non-controversial. This includes historical information. The Marshall Plan helped Europe rebuild after World War II. . . . Richard Nixon resigned from the presidency because of the Watergate scandal. It also includes general knowledge about current events, such as that there is a high level of illegitimate births among young American women and a widespread fear of violent crime in the nation's cities. (If you choose to quantify such general information, however—"26 percent of births are to unmarried women," or "60 percent of American city-dwellers fear to walk the streets at night"—you should give the source of the figures.)
* *Any information already available from a large number of sources.* It would be silly, as well as unnecessary, to name a specific source for information that is available in any encyclopedia or that has recently been front-page news in every paper in the country.

Source: From Michael Kronenwetter, *How to Write a News Article,* Franklin Watts, N.Y., 1995.

How to Handle Attributions to Print Sources

With printed sources, readers also need enough information to evaluate the source's credibility. Consider these **four** points:

1. When was the source published? Last month or 10 years ago?
2. Who wrote the material? Name the organization so readers can judge whether the source might be biased.

3. If information is from an Internet site, give the Web address so that an interested reader can visit the site.

4. If information is from another media outlet, that outlet must be given appropriate credit.

Even when reporters paraphrase information, they must give credit to their sources—whether human or printed—or they are guilty of **plagiarism** (see Chapter 2). The best way to guard against plagiarism: When in doubt, attribute.

Attribution with Direct Quotes

Usually, what was said is more important than who said it. Therefore, the generally accepted rule is to begin a paragraph with a direct quote and follow it with the attribution. **Two** guidelines:

1. Generally, the first direct quote in a story should come no later than the third paragraph, and the quotation marks should begin the paragraph.

2. On occasion, however, the <u>Who</u> is more important than the <u>What</u>. In that case, begin the paragraph with the source. The writer must decide on the relative importance of the <u>Who</u> and the <u>What</u>.

Remember that what is at the beginning of a paragraph will attract the reader to your story or send her or him away to read another. Because quotation marks attract readers, it is usually better to begin a paragraph with the quote than to bury it.

Consider the following illustrations:

What is said is more important than who said it with a one-sentence quote. Place attribution at the end:

"Teachers should be more down to earth with students instead of degrading and demeaning them," Garrett Benedeck, senior, said.

"We have been learning how to work together better as a team," softball captain Sarah Strull said.

What is said is more important than who said it with a quote of more than one sentence. Place the attribution at the end of the first sentence only. More attribution in a single paragraph is redundant:

"We should review the later start because people in activities don't actually start doing homework until later," Jack Zoeller, freshman, said. "Why shouldn't we take that extra hour or so of sleep?"

"In 30 years of coaching, I have never had a stronger group of sophomores than we have now," debate coach Don Tantillo said. "As a result, I'm really excited about the next two years."

"I wasn't really expecting to win," said Ryan Croke, state champion Lincoln-Douglas debater. "I'm thrilled and excited. I can't just stop here, though. I have two more years of debate and hopefully two more years of success."

Who said it is more important than what is said. Place attribution at the beginning:

Dr. Jonas Whittington, principal, said, "We need the cameras to keep us safe and secure our property because we have millions of dollars worth of computers in this building."

Cobbling Together a Good Story

This story demonstrates how full, direct quotes and paraphrases from human and printed sources representing a number of different viewpoints can be combined effectively into a successful story. Seven adults and three students are used as sources, along with a professional newspaper.

A A close reading of the story reveals use of "said" as the attributive verb in all but two cases. What are the two exceptions?

C Evaluate the writer's use of "according to" in referring to the *St. Louis Post Dispatch.*

Model

VTS suspension rates fall below county average

by Kelley Lutzeier, News Writer

Walking counselor attempts to control conflicts by relating to students have kept student suspensions, including Voluntary Transfer Student (VTS) suspensions, below 10%, Dr. Deborah Holmes, assistant superintendent of schools, said.

Kirkwood's suspension rate of transfer students is lower than the county average of 17.4%.

"Walking counselors contribute to lower suspension rates, and may have a tremendous influence on the attitude at Kirkwood," Holmes said.

According to an article in the St. Louis Post Dispatch, in districts which employ a greater percentage of minority teachers and counselors there are lower suspension rates.

Five of the six walking counselors at Kirkwood are black.

Carl Hudson, sophomore grade level principal, said that is an insignificant figure because two of the walking counselors were new at the beginning of the year, and a third one joined the staff this semester.

"We had four [black] and two [white] earlier this year," Principal Franklin McCallie said. "We are trying to do three and three—three females and three males—three black and three white."

continues ▶

B Notice that the first direct quote in this story comes no later than the third paragraph. What function does this first direct quote perform?

Cobbling Together a Good Story *(continued)*

Although McCallie is striving for equal numbers of black and white walking counselors, he insists the reason the walking counselors help maintain low VTS suspensions is the same for resident students.

However, Assistant Principal Shepard Pittman acknowledges it is human nature to associate more closely to people of the same race.

"It is proven people gravitate to people like them, and kids have a gravitational pull to people of the same skin color," Pittman said.

Holmes said having black counselors gives the walking counselors more of an opportunity to relate to transfer students.

Bill Poole, walking counselor, said he sympathizes with desegregation students by drawing on his own personal experiences.

"I lived in the city, and I know what they [transfer students] feel," Poole said. "When kids know you come from the same background, they will open up to you because they know you relate to them."

However, Hudson said the walking counselors effectively relate to all students regardless of skin color.

Rachelle Jackson, resident junior, disagreed with Hudson.

"The majority of students—even white students—relate better to the black walking counselors," Jackson said. "They don't seem to be as judgmental."

Hudson said walking counselors handle disciplinary situations and maintain a reasonably safe and secure campus by acting friendly, trustworthy and approachable.

"Our relationship with the kids and the kids' relationship with us is the reason for lower suspensions," Greg Goessling, walking counselor, said. "We want to stop misunderstanding before it escalates into conflicts."

D Notice the mixing of paraphrasing and direct quotes.

E This paragraph contains paraphrased and attributed information.

F This paragraph contains full, direct quotes. Are paragraphs of full, direct quotes ever placed consecutively? When they are not placed consecutively, what separates them?

G Notice how quotes are used to begin paragraphs, followed by the attribution. In what order are information and attribution in the paraphrased paragraphs?

Hudson said students relate to walking counselors better not necessarily because of color but because of common interests and background.

Nevertheless, he said it is important to understand different cultural behaviors when assessing situations.

"Black students may have differences in behavior among Kirkwood students. I think sometimes African-American students may be louder," Hudson said. "Administrators must learn to tell if a particular behavior is simply 'loud' or a problem."

According to the St. Louis Post Dispatch, Anne Vieweg, Clayton counselor, said faculty members at Clayton have "learned to discern bad behavior from black behavior."

However, Audrey Thomas, resident senior, said there is no such thing as black behavior.

"There is a difference between bad behavior and ghetto behavior," Melissa Fleming, desegregation junior, said.

"By virtue of behavior being different it can be labeled as bad," Holmes said.

Sheila Helencamp, head walking counselor, said it is important to be "culturally sensitive" when evaluating behaviors.

Pittman said regardless of individual behaviors, discipline is based on quick, fast and fair punishment. He also said walking counselors work with grade-level principals and secretaries to bring out individual variables affecting student behavior.

"Walking counselors have keen eyes and ears. They get to know the kids, so they can pass on the background information about the student and know if there are extenuating circumstances," Holmes said.

Source: Kirkwood High School, Kirkwood, Mo., *Kirkwood Call*, Feb. 22, 1999.

H What quality does each full, direct quote add to this story?

I What is your overall evaluation of this story?

Partial Quotes or Paraphrases

Since partial quotes may not always begin a sentence and since paraphrases are not placed in quotation marks, whether the information or the source comes first is up to the reporter.

Partial quote:

Mario Cerdal, senior, said he got a tattoo on his 18th birthday because he was bored and "to prove I was strong enough to go through with it.

Getting a tattoo on his 18th birthday because he was bored, Mario Cerdal, senior, said he also did it "to prove I was strong enough to go through with it."

Paraphrase:

To explain the courage of those fleeing from the Nazis into Switzerland and Spain, guest speaker Walter Reed told about people who escaped successfully and people who were caught and executed by the Nazis.

Guest speaker Walter Reed explained the courage of those fleeing from the Nazis into Switzerland and Spain by telling about people who escaped successfully and people who were caught and executed by the Nazis.

He Said, She Said

Attributive verbs are those verbs used to link what was said with who said it. A simple "said" is best because it does not convey any additional meaning or imply any emotion. Other neutral words and phrases include "went on," "continued" and "added," as long as these are used in the proper context. Use of any word other than "said" often calls undue attention to itself—it "sticks out." When referring to printed sources, "according to" is a useful attributive phrase, but when applied to human sources it is too vague and should be avoided. (See Chapter 9 for more discussion about attributive verbs, especially the sidebar Be Wary of Synonyms for "Said.")

Choose It and Use It

How effectively quotations draw readers into a story depends on how good the quotes are. Just what is a "good quote"?

Good Quotes, Bad Quotes

Good quotes reveal something essential about the individual being quoted. They express an emotion succinctly, describe a moment precisely, present a unique perspective concisely. How good the quotes are is directly related to what kind of interview took place. When conducting their interviews, reporters must dig for emotional or uniquely informative quotes related specifically to each individual source.

Scholastic publications should be filled with good quotes. Don't discourage readership with a publication that looks dry and boring. With the possible exception of opinion pieces (staff editorials, columns, and reviews), all stories need a generous supply of good quotes. Don't stop at quoting only your primary source; use good quotes from secondary sources, too. And certainly don't limit quotes to adult experts. Let fellow students talk. They are often experts, too; and even when they aren't, they have legitimate opinions that readers want to hear.

Here are some sure-fire bad quotes:

* **So-what quotes.** Be sure all quotes contribute to the understanding or the atmosphere of the person or event. Avoid clichés or trite comments.

* **Ghostly quotes.** These are quotes that have not been attributed properly, so readers are left to wonder who said them. Be sure all quotes are clearly attributed.

* **Fact quotes.** These quotes state only facts. Let facts stand alone apart from quoted material.

Checklist

To Quote or Not to Quote?

Carole Rich offers these guidelines for deciding when to use quotes:

Use direct quotes

✓ When the quote is interesting and informative

✓ To back up the lead, the nut graf, or a supporting point in your story

✓ To reveal the source's opinions or feelings

✓ If the quote is very descriptive or dramatic

✓ To express strong reaction from a source

✓ To convey dramatic action

Avoid using direct quotes

✓ Just to prove you talked to the source

✓ When the source is boring or the information is factual and indisputable

✓ When the quote is not clearly worded

✓ When the quote does not relate directly to the focus and supporting points in your story

✓ When the quote is accusatory from a politician or a witness of a crime since quoting directly does not excuse a libel

To decide if it's quotable, ask yourself

✓ Can you remember the quote or the essence of it without looking at your notes?

✓ Does the quote move the story forward without repeating information?

✓ Is the quote emotional or controversial enough to add interest to the story? Will it work as a pulled quote?

✓ Can you state the information better in your own words?

✓ Are you including the quote for your source or for your readers? The answer should always be "for your readers."

Source: Adapted from Carole Rich, *Writing and Reporting News: A Coaching Method*, Wadsworth Publishing, Co., Belmont, Calif., 1994.

* **Something that could have been said by any one of several people.** Unless it's something unique to the source who said it, it's not a good quote.
* **Wooden quotes.** <u>Wooden quotes</u> are quotes that don't sound real, that seem stilted or artificial, or that are just weak. The problem of weak quotes can be solved by effective interviewing and digging for something meaningful or unusual from your source.

Good quotes come from interviews where actual conversations develop, not from a reporter sailing through a list of questions mindlessly jotting down answers and then rushing away. Never, never, never just walk up to a source and say, "Give me a quote about . . ." or "I need a quote about . . ." Reporters have the responsibility to ask good questions so that sources can give meaningful, personalized responses.

How to Place Quotes

Direct quotes should be liberally sprinkled throughout stories. There are **three** things to remember about placing quotes.

1. As Chapter 6 discusses, a direct quote may not be the best approach for a lead. Sources don't usually summarize the main point of a story perfectly in one all-encompassing quote. Again, staff should set a guideline of having the first direct quote no later than the third paragraph unless a creative lead requires an exception. This way even news briefs have at least one quote.

2. Especially for stories not written in inverted pyramid style, the concluding paragraph may be a perfect place for a compelling quote tied to a key point in your story. In fact, some writers choose this ending quote first to be certain they save it for the end. When ending your story with a quote, however, avoid putting the attribution last. You don't want the word "said" to be the final word your readers read.

3. As for the other paragraphs of your story, use a combination of direct quote, paraphrase, unattributed fact and <u>transition</u>. Transition paragraphs allow the reader to follow smoothly from one idea to another in your story. They can be used to put a direct quote in perspective or to signify the opinions of a different source coming up. A transition should not repeat information that will be in the quote. If it does, it makes the quote unnecessary.

Using Transitions

Weak use of a transitional paragraph:

"There's nothing magical about reading books on paper," said English teacher Jeff Lovell. "Right now I listen to books on tape, so I think electronic books could be a great invention."

Not everyone agrees, though. Senior Lindsey Hamilton cannot imagine curling up to read an electronic book.

"I think it's amazing the way technology is advancing, but I can't imagine curling up with some kind of computer to read an electronic book," Hamilton said.

Better use of a transitional paragraph:

"There's nothing magical about reading books on paper," said English teacher Jeff Lovell. "Right now I listen to books on tape, so I think electronic books could be a great invention."

Not everyone agrees, though. Senior Lindsey Hamilton doesn't see herself being a fan of these books any time soon.

"I think it's amazing the way technology is advancing, but I can't imagine curling up with some kind of computer to read an electronic book," Hamilton said.

A In this example, the second paragraph weakens the following quote because it repeats too much of what Lindsey has to say.

B This rewrite of the second paragraph lets the reader know that the next opinion is a different point of view without giving away Lindsey's key idea.

Here are additional guidelines for effective use of quotes in the body of the story:

* Use a new paragraph for each new quote.
* Avoid lengthy quotes; however, if you must use one, break it up. If one quote is longer than about 40 words—or four typed lines—divide it into more than one paragraph, attribute after the first sentence and then only as often as needed to clarify.
* Avoid using "when asked" as a transition into a quote or as part of the attribution.

Let the quote speak for itself and keep the reporter's presence on the sidelines.

* Avoid saying "said of" as a part of the attribution, as in ". . . Principal Harris said of the new security system." Make the context of the quote clear without using this crutch.
* Avoid stacking several quotes together unless you are creating a **quote collection** for a sidebar. Instead, use effective transitions among them. Putting too many direct quotes in a row creates a transcript, not a story.

* Avoid jumping back and forth among several different sources within the same story because this can confuse the reader. Usually finish all the information from one source and then move on to another after a clear transition.

* Never attribute a single quote to more than one individual (unless two or more individuals actually said something simultaneously—very rare, indeed!). You may need to attribute the quote to one person and then say another identified person agreed.

* Avoid attributing information to an inanimate object. If you do not know the exact speaker, do not say, "The school said . . ." Instead, say, "School officials said . . ." But remember it is much better journalism to identify the correct individual.

Ms. Tantillo's Handy Guide to Punctuating Quotes

Punctuating quotations in journalistic writing follows standard English rules of punctuation.

Use quotation marks to enclose the exact words of a source in your story. Use a comma to set off the attribution, placed last, first, or middle, appropriately:

"This year's celebration is going to be bigger and better than ever," said Hometown Celebration coordinator Michele Hirz.

Hometown Celebration coordinator Michele Hirz said, "This year's celebration is going to be bigger and better than ever."

"This year's celebration is going to be bigger and better than ever," said Hometown Celebration coordinator Michele Hirz, "because we have a record number of businesses participating."

"This year's celebration is going to be bigger and better than ever," said Hometown Celebration coordinator Michele Hirz. "Because of overwhelming support from the community, we have a record number of businesses participating."

Do not use quotation marks to enclose paraphrases. Punctuate the attribution appropriately depending on its placement.

This year's Hometown Celebration should be even bigger than last year's because of more community participation, Hirz said. (Place comma before attribution when it comes at the end of a paraphrase.)

Hirz said this year's Hometown Celebration should be even bigger than last year's because of more community participation. (Use no comma after attribution when it comes before a paraphrase.)

Commas and periods go inside quotation marks, as in the previous examples. Place other marks of punctuation according to the sense of their use. If a quote is a question, use only the single question mark.

Do not add a comma also when the attribution follows.

"When will the new library be open?" Joe Bates, senior, asked.

Joe Bates, senior, asked, "When will the new library be open?"

"No one expected us to win!" Gilda Crane, Special Olympics partner, shouted. "But we fooled them all and ran away with the state championship!" (Caution: use exclamation marks and the word "shouted" only if she actually did.)

When a single quote runs longer than one paragraph with the same speaker, omit the closing quotation marks until the speaker has finished. Attribute following the first sentence and then as often as necessary to clarify who is speaking.

"This new facility will give our students a chance to develop their creativity in a whole variety of new ways," said Linda Battle, business, technology and life studies division head. "Students will have the opportunity to create slide shows, presentations and design work in the new technology production lab.

"They will be able to come up with graphic shows similar to those used in business and industry rather than being limited to typical word-processed reports. This will make our students more competitive in the working world.

"It's a very exciting and challenging time in technology education," she said.

In truth, this three-paragraph quote would be more effectively presented in a combination of paraphrase and direct quote. However, this example shows proper punctuation and attribution for the multi-paragraph quote should you decide to use the technique.

When quoting something that already contains a quote, the inside quotation takes single quote marks while the outside quotation takes double quotation marks.

"We chose the musical 'Grease' because it has an overabundance of main roles and we have a marvelous group of super-talented seniors this year," Phil Stutz, director, said.

Getting It Together

With a partner, read this story carefully. Then label each paragraph of the story as full direct quote, partial/fragmentary direct quote, transition, fact or paraphrase.

B Note that the first direct quote in this story comes no later than the third paragraph. What function does this first direct quote perform?

Technology & education:
Girls type, boys program— Report reveals widening gap between genders in technology use

by **Andrea Haughton,** Editor in Chief

As the country is in the midst of a technological revolution, the American Association of University Women (AAUW) fears girls are being left behind in the high-tech realm.

The AAUW's new report, *Gender Gaps: Where Schools Still Fail Our Children*, identifies a growing gap: the disparity in use of technology by males and females.

"Girls have narrowed some significant gender gaps, but technology is now the new 'boys club' in our nation's public schools," said Janice Weinman, AAUW executive director. "While boys program and problem solve with computers, girls use computers for word processing, the 1990s version of typing."

The AAUW cites low enrollment in computer science courses, and the fact that only 17 percent of those who took the AP Computer Science exam in 1996 were female.

AP Computer Science is an occasional offering at the school, depending on interest. The course was offered last year and the enrollment was 10 boys and one girl.

Yearbook editor Ian Bergman ('99), himself a technologist, took the AP Computer Science course last year.

A The story begins with a strong lead. Attribution of the source follows immediately in the second paragraph.

C Make a list of the verbs used to attribute information to sources in this story. Compare the style of attribution used by this writer and the writer of the model on 121–123, "Cobbling Together a Good Story." Which is the more natural style? What about each paraphrase?

"I love computers, and I wanted to learn more about how they worked," said Bergman. "I wanted to know how to make them more productive for me."

Though Bergman noticed the discrepancy in enrollment, he wasn't surprised by it.

"It seems as though girls generally aren't interested in technology," said Bergman.

Data seems to validate Bergman's observation. A 1992 survey by the National Center for Educational Statistics found that while 28 percent of boys used a personal computer at least once a week, only 19 percent of girls do so.

According to *Gender Gaps*, "Girls tend to have a more circumscribed, limited, and cautious interaction with technology than boys."

Gender Gaps even suggests that for girls, technology means word processing, which is merely a new incarnation of typing.

"Anyone can be capable [with technology], but the guys in yearbook tend to want to know more about how to use the software in a more advanced way," said Bergman.

Even still, publication students at the school tend to be among those who use computers most for advanced projects. Quincy Campbell ('00), who joined the yearbook staff midway through the year, considered herself computer illiterate prior to yearbook. However, with the help of the entire staff, she has gained knowledge of Photoshop and PageMaker. Beforehand, Campbell could "barely type," as she put it.

continues ▶

D Make a list of all the sources used in this story. If you were writing this story, who else would you talk to?

E Does this story contain any buried quotes?

Getting It Together *(continued)*

"It's a lot easier once you get the hang of it," said Campbell.

Looking around the newsroom, Campbell sees girls and boys using technology and advanced applications.

"I just don't really see a gender gap [here]," said Campbell.

At work with PageMaker, Nick Brackney ('99) agrees with Campbell.

"It's so untrue that guys use technology to find things and fix things," said Brackney. "All I know is guys are the only ones I know who spend a bunch of time playing video games."

Despite publications students' optimism, the national statistics and the school's information support the concept of an emerging gap in the way the sexes use technology.

The emerging gap has already begun to influence the ability of boys to make more money than girls do.

According to "Turning to Teenagers for Tech Talent," by Eric Wee, *Washington Post*, March 1, 1998, employers are already turning to skilled teens to fill computer positions. Students can make as much as $50,000 a year by working three days a week.

Gender Gaps advises educators to incorporate gender equity into their technology teaching immediately, and to avoid overemphasizing technology before the nation's schools know how to encourage all students to be "power users."

Source: Charles Wright Academy, Tacoma, Wash., *The Academy Times*, March 30, 1999.

F What quality does each quote add to this story?

G What is your overall evaluation of this story?

Good quotes are essential to successful stories. Not only do they entice readers to keep on reading and bring stories and sources to life, they also give authority and authenticity to stories. To get good quotes, reporters must dig for them in interviews and learn to take good notes. Quotes in stories must reflect the comments of sources fairly and accurately or the publication's credibility will suffer. Publications staffs need to establish a policy about whether quotes can be altered and then apply the policy evenly to all sources. Reporters must know when to attribute information to their sources. Failure to do so when required results in plagiarism, a serious violation of ethical standards. The most successful stories contain good direct quotations, paraphrases, direct facts, and transitions intermingled to keep the reader moving through every paragraph from the lead to the end.

Journalism WORDS TO KNOW

attribution—telling the reader where information originated.

attributive verbs—verbs used to link what was said with who said it; neutral verbs, such as "said," are best.

balance—reporter's presentation of different points of view throughout a story so that all sides receive fair play

direct quotations (direct quotes)—word-for-word replays of information from sources; used to provide insight into a story; placed in quotation marks.

paraphrase (indirect quote)—summary in the reporter's own words of what a source says; not placed in quotation marks.

partial quote and fragmentary quote—less than a full sentence taken word-for-word from a source and placed in quotation marks; used in conjunction with paraphrase.

plagiarism—passing someone else's ideas and/or words off as your own.

quote collection—a group of quotes related to a single topic or from a single source; may be further enhanced with mug shot.

transitions—words that help the reader move smoothly through a story.

wooden quotes—quotes that sound unreal, stilted, or artificial; avoid them.

In-Depth Reporting

In this chapter, you will learn:

- what defines in-depth reporting and how it differs from other stories
- how to conceptualize, research, write, and format the in-depth story
- about types of in-depth stories, including investigative, interpretive or analytical, and trend stories

In television it's often called a special report or documentary. In print it's labeled news analysis, investigative reporting, focus, or even center spread. You've seen it in pieces about homelessness, bilingual education, and college admissions. Whatever its label, whatever its topic, **in-depth reporting** *both grabs your attention and stimulates your thinking. In-depth functions as a kind of fifth wheel to the four basics—news, features, sports, and opinion. You can get along without it, but it adds a colorful element. In-depth expands your deadline coverage to take a longer, more comprehensive look at topics in the news.*

Qualities of the In-Depth

The in-depth report entered high school journalism about 30 years ago as student journalists moved beyond the basics to longer, more thoroughly researched stories that explored hot topics of the 1960s and 1970s:

* Vietnam War protests, civil rights conflicts and issues, illicit drug use, and changing sexual attitudes
* Watergate, covered on page 143, which journalists consider the definitive in-depth story
* Changes in high school life—dress code relaxation, curriculum innovations such as team teaching, and "new" diseases such as mononucleosis

The well-known type of in-depth reporting embodied by Watergate is investigative journalism. Today's in-depth still investigates occasionally, but the genre is more often a magazine-type piece that reports a trend or interprets a complicated topic that needs extra time and space to develop. In-depth reporting is not a high school journalism requirement, but it does appear in high school newspapers nationwide, and you need to know about it.

The term *in-depth* implies length, but it has evolved to mean breadth of coverage as well. **Five** factors necessary for **in-depth reporting** are:

1. **Space.** If the topic needs it, adequate space must be made available. The in-depth story is not written to a line count.

2. **Deadline.** Few in-depths can be scheduled for a specific issue date. The research takes time. The story shouldn't be published until it's ready. An in-depth can take months to develop—and some in-depths never make it to print.

3. **Research.** The same research steps apply to in-depths as to other stories: observe, interview, and consult printed or electronic sources. But more sources may be required, and the information can be harder to come by.

4. **Staff.** In-depth writers can form a separate unit of the staff, supervised by an editor. More often they work for one of the four major sections of the paper and produce in-depths on the side.

5. **Planning.** Because the story isn't under immediate deadline, there's more time to plan and less excuse not to plan. The story evolves from a topic to a hypothesis to a first draft to a final draft to publication. Planning includes design, infographics, artwork, and photography. (See Chapters 14 and 15.)

Infographic

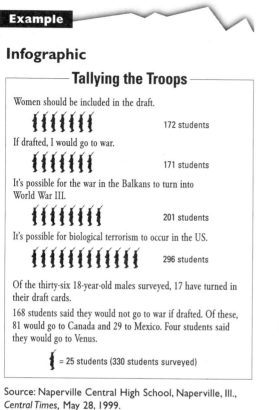

Tallying the Troops

Women should be included in the draft.

{{{{{{{   172 students

If drafted, I would go to war.

{{{{{{{   171 students

It's possible for the war in the Balkans to turn into World War III.

{{{{{{{{   201 students

It's possible for biological terrorism to occur in the US.

{{{{{{{{{{{{   296 students

Of the thirty-six 18-year-old males surveyed, 17 have turned in their draft cards.

168 students said they would not go to war if drafted. Of these, 81 would go to Canada and 29 to Mexico. Four students said they would go to Venus.

{ = 25 students (330 students surveyed)

Source: Naperville Central High School, Naperville, Ill., *Central Times*, May 28, 1999.

In-depth stories are frequently illustrated by infographics like the one above in which factual detail is reported via a chart, graph, or map.

Creating the In-Depth Story

Academically, you've probably already accomplished the equivalent of in-depth journalism. You've written a research paper—often the climactic assignment of a course—for which you chose a topic, narrowed or focused it to manageable size, researched it thoroughly to support your thesis, and wrote it out in patient detail. That's pretty much what happens in the in-depth story. But there are at least **four** differences:

1. Topic choice is based on readers' interests, not your personal interest. Your preference may get you started, but you must adjust it to benefit your audience. Unlike the term paper, the audience is far broader than a single teacher. To earn its space, the in-depth must reward a substantial number of readers or viewers with important and interesting information.

2. Research focuses far more on interview expertise than on library sources. What you locate in the library or on the Internet adds material that supports your local information, but it never dominates the story. Don't just transfer facts from one published source to another.

3. Writing style is journalistic, not academic. Paragraphs are short; vocabulary is direct. Footnotes and bibliography rarely appear; credit or attribution is usually given directly in the text.

4. Presentation is more than words on a page. Graphics, sidebars, boxes, artwork, and photographs are an inherent part of the in-depth.

Topic Choice

Most in-depth stories come from the news of the day. They grow from a **news peg**, an opportunity a journalist sees to tell audiences more about the topic than they

How to Develop In-Depth Story Ideas

☑ **Scrutinize national news.** Link up with a news peg.

☑ **Brainstorm.** A discussion of Thanksgiving leads to one about day-after shopping, which leads to an analysis of how much money students in your school have to spend and on what products. (See Chapter 3 for coverage of brainstorming.)

☑ **Pay attention to personal concerns.** What do students care about—or grouse about? Just be willing to reverse your thesis when your research proves your thesis wrong.

☑ **Get inspired by the school calendar.** Just what will the prom cost this year and how does that compare to previous years? Title IX turns 30 in 2002—how has your school equalized girls' sports?

☑ **Use beat reports.** The principal mentions an increase in the number of your school district's students being home-schooled. Is this worth more than just a news story? (See Chapter 3 for information on beat reports.)

☑ **Get some tips.** Can a disgruntled librarian's e-mail about book budget decline be expanded to a story on a shift in spending for research materials?

would get in an immediate news story. Editors may decide to localize a news item—to discuss its relevance for a group of readers narrower than a national audience. After the Columbine High School shootings in April 1999, hundreds of high school newspapers did in-depth <u>follow-ups</u> on whether that event could have happened at their school and what it implied about high school life. They didn't report Columbine as a news story; instead they used it as a news peg.

The millennium and Y2K are other national news topics recently localized by the high school press. Political campaigns, pop culture developments, health concerns, the minimum wage, and sexual issues have all shown up in high school in-depth coverage. Social security, airport noise, and gasoline prices have appeared, too, but these topics are much less obviously localized to a teenage audience.

Research

Although an in-depth may resemble a term paper in length, the story isn't the rephrasing of a topic into your words from a variety of miscellaneous library sources. That's not local enough for your readers or viewers, who aren't interchangeable with those of any other publication or video program. Your in-depth must serve your school; general rehash on anorexia, date anxiety, or college admissions won't do the job. Try localizing these topics like this:

* **Anorexia.** Collect statistics from eating disorder clinics in your city, talk to health experts who serve your school, and interview local students with the problem.
* **Date anxiety.** Examine several case studies, survey students about their experiences, and talk with counselors about the topic.
* **College admissions.** Narrow the topic to subdivisions such as the most popular choices among your seniors, what the waiting list really means, the hidden costs of college, and what college freshmen from your school wish they'd known a year ago.

Does that mean generic research doesn't belong in the in-depth? No, it means it is only the first step. Learning about the topic on-line or at the library and collecting facts that support your hypothesis will lay a foundation that the local interview material and your own observations will fill out.

Surveys and Polls

The **survey**, or poll, is an effective device for in-depth research. The results can run as a story or as a sidebar that confirms or supports the thesis of the in-depth report. Survey research is a highly technical process that drives marketing, politics, and other areas of American life today. Provided it's carried out scientifically, survey research can accurately predict group attitudes and behavior.

High school journalists are not well positioned to conduct super-accurate survey research, the kind that tells you who's going to win an election. The time involved and the technicalities of the research are overwhelming for a staff that's busy getting out a publication. Nevertheless, modest surveys, honestly reported, can support a story with factual evidence.

The worst way to conduct a survey is to interview your lunch table. That's where high school journalists tend to stumble. By definition, a survey polls strangers, not people you know. It proceeds randomly, meaning that those answering the poll should be as complete a cross-section of the student body as possible.

Tips for Surveys

Consider these **seven** tips for better poll taking:

1. Poll about 10 percent of the student body for a good sample.

2. Share the work with a beginning journalism class; just make sure everyone follows the same instructions. Polling is an excellent early assignment for getting students involved with the newspaper. A class of 20 can easily poll 200 people.

3. Create neutral questions that avoid nudging respondents away from the truth. Polls about sexual and other private behavior are susceptible to false answers. "Have you ever cheated on a test?" may push someone into rationalizing or being defensive. Instead, try:

"During a test have you ever: (A) copied from a neighbor (B) used a crib sheet (C) gotten the answers from someone who took it earlier (D) stayed out of class that day in hopes of getting an easier makeup test (E) other: _____." This approach defines cheating and doesn't let the respondent avoid answering.

4. Besides factual questions, ask a few that involve opinions—these provide good quotes to add to your story.

5. Decide whether you're polling anonymously, in which case you don't reveal respondents' identities, or by name. Be sure your "answerers" understand what you're doing and how the results will be published.

6. Simply wandering about the building to poll students here and there is not scientific, although it's the easiest way to conduct a survey. A better way is to obtain an alphabetized student list, pick a number at random (for example, 4), then phone that 4th person and every 10th person on the list after him or her. Doing it this way is much harder work, but this system gets you closer to the random quality of scientific polling.

7. When you publish the results, be sure to include how the poll was conducted: who did the polling, how many students were interviewed, and where the interviewing took place. Poll results have become persuasive in our culture, and you owe your readers a clear explanation of how you conducted the poll.

Writing the Story

As research proceeds, the in-depth story angle changes. The hypothesis you began with often doesn't quite fit as you keep learning new information. So be prepared to adjust the story when you sit down to write it. Consider these **three** steps:

1. *Examine the dimensions of the story.* Look at it from the viewpoints of everyone you talked with. What sources seem most valid? Is it because they're articulate, experienced, eager to promote their views, factually informed? Are there any information holes to fill in?

2. *Outline the story.* Do you have a thesis upfront—within the first few paragraphs—that the entire story flows from? Do you have logical subtopics supported by evidence from reliable sources? How will you end the story?

3. *Check the story for tone, balance, and fairness.* Never publish an incomplete in-depth. Everyone who worked on the story should be satisfied before it's ready for publication.

Three Options for Presentation

You have **three** choices for presentation, or packaging, your in-depth story. Remember that your goal is grabbing and holding readers.

1. **Run it as one long story.** This works well only if the piece is not of a super length. Given the nature of an in-depth, these are few and far between. Length often suggests that you need to consider the other two alternatives.

2. **Divide the story into a series published over several editions of the paper.** Because high school newspapers often appear just monthly, this is usually a weak approach. If you do develop a series, make sure readers don't have to remember much about the previous stories to understand the current one. The college admissions in-depth might be developed as a series because its parts aren't tightly dependent on each other. Students also take their time with the process of applying for colleges, so their interest may actually parallel the coverage. On the other hand, a piece on anorexia probably would not work so well as a series.

3. **Package the in-depth into a spread, several stories on two or four—or even more—pages of the same issue.** Usually a lead story introduces the others.

Of your three choices—a single story, a series, or a spread—the latter is by far the most popular in the high school press.

Perhaps that's because it allows teamwork to proceed so easily. The stories can be assigned to different staff members, and the editor can direct their work and coordinate it with design, art, and photography. Examples of spreads that have appeared in several high school publications follow.

The *Lion,* LaGrange (Illinois) Township High School, packaged a two-page in-depth on adoption into stories on parents' experiences in adopting a child, adopted children looking for birth parents, teenage girls who decide to let their children be adopted, and first-person columns by an adopted daughter and mother on their feelings about the adoption.

The *Excalibur,* McQueen High School, Reno, Nevada, covered the approaching millennium in two pages, with stories on Y2K, end-of-the-world predictions, party plans, a list of major events from 1000 to 1999, a sidebar on life in 999, and a "photopinion" that asked students what three trends or events they foresaw for the new millennium.

The *Little Hawk,* City High School, Iowa City, Iowa, discussed sexuality in a four-page special report introduced by a page-one article. Stories included interviews in which five students discussed their decisions about sexual activity, the media's unrealistic portrayal of teenage sex, and the contrast between sexual information in the 1950s and the 1990s. Infographics looked at types of birth control, a survey of teenage virginity, and views about teenage sex in other cultures.

The *Orange & Black*, Grand Junction (Colorado) High School, devoted an entire 20-page issue to a school board proposal to put the school on the same schedule as the other four high schools in the district. Stories approached the controversy from the viewpoints of students, teachers, technology, other schools, college students, counselors, administrators, and parents.

The *Lowell*, Lowell High School, San Francisco, California, published a 32-page edition to celebrate the newspaper's 100th birthday. Stories included alumni interviews, a chronology of news highlights, coverage of the World War II years, changes in racial makeup of the staff, and a feature showing newspaper design changes through the decades.

Sidebar

The Maestro System

Created by Buck Ryan, director of the journalism program at the University of Kentucky, the **maestro system** has evolved as a major approach to planning and packaging newspaper stories. Adaptable to newspapers of any size, it is especially effective for in-depth stories because of the longer time involved in the in-depth process.

The maestro system brings all members of the production team—reporter, copy editor, photographer, artist, designer—into the story at the beginning of the reporting process. It avoids the sequential structure whereby the story is completely written before anyone thinks about headlines or pictures.

The "maestro" could be the managing editor or a section editor—the in-depth editor in this case. Like an orchestra conductor, he or she coordinates the work of the various specialists on the team.

As soon as the story idea is firm and some preliminary reporting is done—but before the story is written—the team meets to plan the design, photography, and art for the story. Tentative sketches organize the spread. Photographers and artists discuss illustrations and begin to work. The infographics specialist comes up with an idea. Even the headlines are written in advance.

All of these preliminary plans can be changed, of course, as the nature of the story changes. But the process affords a smoother result, and all the participants feel they're more inherently a part of the spread than if they were just given directions once the story had been completed.

The in-depth section is an ideal place to experiment with the maestro system. If it works well there, it can be broadened to include other sections of the newspaper.

Alternative Journalist

At age 24, Sridhar Pappu is a staff writer for the Chicago Reader, *a 130,000-circulation alternative newsweekly, one of the most successful of its kind in the nation.*

"To be honest, talking about what it takes to be an 'alternative journalist' seems slightly precarious to me because the word 'alternative' is fraught with a kind of hipness for which I don't particularly care," he said. "I've always been preoccupied with writing about reality and not breaking news."

Pappu fell into journalism by accident. He didn't do it in high school, but after transferring from Miami University in his hometown of Oxford, Ohio, to Northwestern University, he earned both undergrad and graduate degrees in journalism. He had four internships in college, including the *Ann Arbor (Mich.) News,* the *Washington City Paper,* and *Harper's* magazine in New York City.

"The *Washington City Paper* introduced me to the form of the alternative weekly, in whose virtues—story telling, character development—I could believe," Pappu said. "At *Harper's* I got to work closely with some of the best story editors in the country and see the process that goes into great magazine writing up close."

At the *Reader,* Pappu's stories can range from 1,000 to 10,000 words, from a small, redeeming piece about a retired crime reporter who still keeps a clip file in his basement to a 9,500 word open letter to Chicago White Sox owner Jerry Reinsdorf, detailing the faults of his reign. "There's a lack of immediate gratification in the job, but what I like is that I can spend hours or days or weeks or months with a person and the same amount of time in the library until I have what I need," Pappu said.

Pappu sees his job as more like magazine journalism than that of the traditional newspaper form, with equal weight given to what the story is and the manner in which it's told. "For me it seems the correct beginning for a career that I hope will lead to writing books," he said.

Many of Pappu's stories are profiles. "The first piece I wrote of any length, 6,000 words, was about a man named Jim Hill, who had been a typesetter, an alcoholic, and a gambler, and whose body lay in the Washington morgue for nine months," he said. "I tried to retrace the last years of his life by going to the racetrack, to the boarding house where he died, and in so doing tried to explain what happens to a person when events overwhelm him. How—in the most practical sense—does someone get lost?"

continues ▶

Later, for the *Reader,* Pappu followed Chicago State basketball coach Phil Gary for four months. "I had access to everything—practices, team meetings, personal talks with players, after-game locker-room rants," he said. "Gary was given the impossible task to make a traditionally abysmal team better. Only he couldn't. My piece told both his story and that of the season, from its first optimistic tryouts and drills to mid-January, when both of us knew his end was near."

Every alternative paper is different. Some do mostly arts and entertainment stories while others compete with daily newspapers. "Internships are paramount for finding a staff job, as they are for trying to freelance your work," Pappu said. "Look at those summers not as vacations but opportunities in which to showcase your talent.

"And read. Books. Newspapers. Good magazines—the *New Yorker, Harper's*— breaking down the pieces for form and content, and most important, language."

Types of In-Depth Stories

In-depth stories explain and inform more than they entertain. Their message to the audience is: "We've got a story here that's worth extra space or time because it's important, and we're trying to make it interesting as well." In-depth categories include the investigative story, the trend story, and the interpretive or analytical story.

The Investigative Story

Watergate in 1972–74 established **investigative reporting** as the apex of U.S. journalism. When else have two newspaper reporters brought about the resignation of the president of the United States? Such in-depth investigative reporting has faded as costs have increased, but the approach remains a mainstay of such TV programs as *60 Minutes* and such magazines as *Mother Jones.*

Investigative reporter Rick Tulsky, who graduated from the University of Missouri in 1972, remembers how the success of Bob Woodward and Carl Bernstein's book *All the President's Men,* which tracked the investigation that led to President Nixon's resignation, stimulated journalism school enrollments and granted investigative reporters celebrity status. "All of us went out with high ideals that journalism could correct wrongs, could change life for the better," says Tulsky, who won a Pulitzer Prize for investigative reporting in 1987 while at the *Philadelphia Inquirer.*

But investigative reporting declined in the 1980s for three reasons, according to Tulsky: the high cost of paying reporters who didn't produce stories every day, an onslaught of libel cases, and abuse of the investigative process by a few reporters. Establishment of the Investigative Reporters and Editors organization in 1976 helped maintain standards and ethics. The Center for Investigative Reporting was set up to help freelance investigative journalists find funding for their projects.

Today investigative reporters are often freelancers who contract on specific projects and are funded by foundations. Less is being done in broadcast because of high costs, says Tulsky, but there is still plenty of investigative reporting in print journalism. "I'm pleasantly surprised when I judge contest entries to find so many journalists out there in obscure places working on their own," he says.

Taking Apart the Story

Structurally, the investigative story is much like any in-depth report. It grows from a thesis or nut graf (see Chapter 6), develops subtopics, and offers evidence from direct observation, interviews with local experts, and library or online research. Shown here is one example from the *Evanstonian,* Evanston (Illinois) Township High School.

The Investigative Story

What follows is an excerpt from a longer, more detailed story.

Model

Fire safety: no way out?

By Jeb Blount

A three-month-old *Evanstonian* survey of fire safety at ETHS has found the school to be in apparent violation of the city fire code in several areas. Other fire safety procedures cast doubt on the ability of the school to react properly in an emergency fire situation.

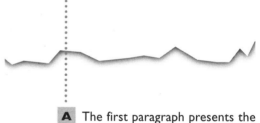

A The first paragraph presents the nut graf, which is also the lead.

B The second paragraph sets up the subtopics for the story (numbers added).

C The body of the story gives six paragraphs to subtopic 1, four paragraphs to subtopic 2, eight paragraphs to subtopic 3, and twelve paragraphs to subtopic 4.

E The concluding paragraph synthesizes the story material

1. The survey has found that many outside fire doors are kept chained much of the time.
2. The alarm system that notifies the Evanston Fire Dept. has malfunctioned.
3. There legally may not be enough fire drills each year; those that are scheduled raise questions as to their effectiveness.
4. Some staff members don't seem to recognize these problems and the Evanston Fire Dept. found no significant violations at a recent ETHS inspection.

Since the research for this story began last May, the areas of the school in which fire code violations have been cited have been checked more than 20 times. The violations have been repeatedly present. Security at a high school like ETHS, with its 65 exits and countless corridors, is difficult, and doubtless explains the presence of chains and locks. Still to be explained is what might happen should a real fire break out at ETHS.

Source: Evanston Township High School, Evanston, Ill., the *Evanstonian,* November 6, 1981.

D Sources include a fire department captain, the school security chief, the supervisor of custodians, the chair of boys' physical education, and several students who monitored fire drills and regularly checked locked doors and gates.

F The story ran as a full page of the newspaper, with two photos and one piece of art.

How Investigative Reports Differ

The distinction of the investigative piece among in-depth reports is its premise: Something is wrong. The reporter becomes a detective, looking for flaws that readers should know about. The story does not offer solutions. Rather, it points out injustice, dishonesty, hypocrisy, criminal behavior, or other legal and moral issues in the belief that readers or viewers will react if accurately informed. Publicity is used as a weapon to correct the wrong.

Investigative reports often attack government and other institutions on the premise that individuals are powerless to correct wrongs except in the glare of publicity. As major institutions in our culture, school administrations would seem to be an ideal target for investigation, offering students a built-in opportunity for vigilance. But will investigation work for you at your school? See the case studies for a discussion.

Investigating Investigation: A Problem-solving Approach

How do you decide whether to pursue an issue with an investigative story? Such a piece can take a lot of time and staff resources. How do you make sure it's worth it? Here are some strategies.

Case 1

Problem: *I don't have easy access to the information I need to do the story. The experts who have it don't want to give it to me. Now what?*

Solution: Find others who might. Sometimes disgruntled employees or others upset about something will supply information you can then confirm with authorities. Be familiar with the Freedom of Information Act at both federal and state levels. It allows citizens access to government information. For example, you have the right to know the salary of a public school employee.

Case 2

Problem: *I don't really understand the topic. The school budget is hundreds of pages. How am I supposed to find something wrong in it?*

Solution: You can learn. Once you have the budget—it's public information—you can seek help to interpret items that look suspicious. Ask your uncle the accountant for help.

Case 3

Problem: *How can I possibly investigate something when I'm a full-time student with an overload of activities?*

Solution: That's where teamwork helps. Most investigative pieces at the high school level are done by a team. Narrowing the topic helps as well. Don't investigate the whole budget when your real concern is how student activity money is being spent. Notice that the fire safety story took three months and required more than 20 inspections of gates and locks. To do the job properly, you must make time. If you can't, forget the story.

Case 4

Problem: *What about pressure? The principal says she'd be glad to write me a college recommendation. How can I ask her about her expense account when she goes to conventions?*

Solution: You may have to make some ethical decisions. Which is more important: irritating the principal with a valid story or getting a college recommendation from her? Investigative reporters can't have it both ways. (Besides, there's no harm in asking. Her expenses may all be valid.)

Case 5

Problem: *Well, what about the legal problems? Can't the threat of libel stop the investigation?*

Solution: It can. Certainly you must know the libel laws. You must also give anyone being criticized in the story the chance for rebuttal.

The Trend Story

During the past decade the **trend story** has become a hot, in-depth item in print and broadcast journalism. It reports a trend: a tendency, a direction, a topic that's dynamic, not static. Check out some examples from the professional press.

The *New York Times* recently reported that

* Biology, not just social pressures, is starting to explain why teenagers need to sleep in the morning.
* Technology is making it easier for students to buy term papers.
* Top colleges are filling more slots with early-admission applicants.

The *Christian Science Monitor* reported

* High-tech links are putting more families in touch with school information.
* Private colleges are increasing their marketing techniques to attract students.
* A growing number of students are taking a year off between high school and college.

The *Chicago Tribune* reported that

* Colleges are increasing the availability of housing where alcohol is forbidden.
* College fraternities are changing their image by emphasizing academics.

According to the *Wall Street Journal*

* College-educated, career-oriented women are marrying earlier than they did 10 years ago.
* Students on spring break are choosing more athletic challenges than just lying on the beach.

All of these examples state the nut graf, or thesis, of the story. It occurs within the first few paragraphs, condensing the story to a single statement. Like many trend stories, the following example by a high school senior uses a **Wall Street Journal lead**, in which a descriptive image or anecdote pulls the reader into the text. The nut graf follows in the third paragraph. The story localizes content by interviewing Orange County students and church officials. It balanced the topic in a sidebar interview with a student who has given up her Bible study group.

The Trend Story

Reading, writing, and religion

by **Dana Lenetz**/Special to the Times

Joyce Koo bows her head, a gold cross flirting with the collar of her white shirt. Her Bible, bound in a brown leather case, lies open in front of her, and her fingers sweep under each line. In an inspirational voice, Koo, 17, explains the meaning of prayer with a serene piety.

"I love to read the Bible and pray because it gives me insight into myself as both a person and a Christian," Koo said.

Koo is among the growing number of teen-agers across the nation who have turned in recent years to organized religion and Bible study. According to a Gallup youth poll, one-half of the nation's youth attended church weekly in 1993, up from 45% in 1992. A Gallup survey also showed that young adults are more likely (53%) to attend church than adults (40%).

Pastor Pat Follis of the Vineyard Christian Fellowship of Anaheim said she has noticed an increase in teen activity within her church in the past year.

"I have noticed more teen-age activity in Bible study, prayer and ministry with one another and with the community, and a greater attendance at Sunday services," Follis said. Some attribute a growing teen interest in religion to the deterioration of the family unit. Bible study and youth groups can offer a place of community and acceptance that some teens don't find at home, they say.

Senior Pastor George Munzing of Trinity United Presbyterian Church of Santa Ana says other social factors are at work, as well.

"Teen-agers look at the world we live in and recognize that many things are not satisfying," Munzing said. "Younger kids are seeing their older brothers and sisters being sent to Haiti and Kuwait; teen-agers are dying of AIDS and suicide, families are stricken with cancer. It seems that the circumstances in which we live are sobering. The church offers a moral stability we do not find in other places. Of course, it also offers love and good, healthy relationships that we all need."

Mirroring the growth in teen activity in churches is increased emphasis on religion in high schools–in campus clubs, in special events and in the debate over whether a constitutional amendment endorsing prayer in school should be adopted.

Christian clubs have been established on campus at many Orange County schools, with meetings held during lunch or before or after school. At Foothill High School in Santa Ana, Christian students created the Alternative Club, a Bible study/discussion group that meets every Wednesday during lunch.

The club has about 30 members, said member Tiffany Ang, but attendance varies from week to week, "depending on everyone's schedule."

Ang, who has gone to meetings regularly for more than a year, said the club "is a good way to support my personal beliefs.

"I am part of the Alternative Club because I am supporting others who share the same beliefs I do and to help those who don't know what we are about gain some insight."

For 17-year-old Sam of Santa Ana, who preferred that his real name not be used, the Christian club at his school became a lifeline. After years of abusing drugs and running with the "wrong crowd," Sam said he found help after a classmate invited him to a Christian club meeting.

"Before I discovered the club, I was so lost," Sam said. "My grades had fallen, my relationship with my parents was bad, people who I respected no longer respected me. I was heading toward self-destruction at such a quick pace. It scared me. Then I found the Lord."

As he plunged into his newfound spiritual world, Sam said, Christianity spurred him into overcoming his drug addiction.

"It was amazing," Sam said. "I made a new group of friends who knew exactly how I felt about the Lord, and I spent my sophomore year re-evaluating my life and reforming my goals.

"I cannot believe what a different person I have become and how much happier I am now."

Source: *Los Angeles Times* (Orange County Edition), December 23, 1994.

The Interpretive or Analytical Story

Analytical reporting explains the topic by breaking it into smaller sections and looking closely at them. That's the *analysis* part of the story. It may also *synthesize*—that is, it may try to tell you the significance of what you've read. The **synthesis** is the **interpretive** side of the story. In a term paper, the synthesis comes at the end. In an in-depth report, it may come in an editorial or an opinion column that's part of the package.

The *Lakewood Times,* from Lakewood (Ohio) High School, produced an in-depth spread on "cyberlove." The model here reproduces the story in four pages; the *Times*

also ran a front cover with it to announce the story and a back-page editorial cautioning students to approach online friendships carefully. The two-and-a-half page basic report consisted of stories that defined the topic, interviews with students about their experiences, and a development of lengthy comments by a local expert, a psychologist. Sidebars making up the rest of the in-depth included an explanation of the school's methods of blocking some Internet sites, plus a survey of other student uses of the Internet.

Note how the *Times* credited its Internet research sources—one way of providing fair credit and avoiding plagiarism.

The Interpretive or Analytical Story

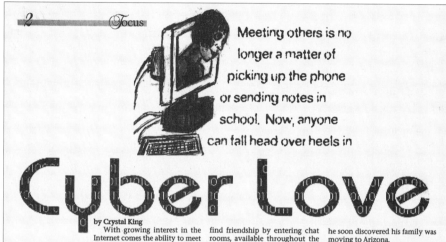

2 ___ *Focus*

Meeting others is no longer a matter of picking up the phone or sending notes in school. Now, anyone can fall head over heels in

Cyber Love

by Crystal King

With growing interest in the Internet comes the ability to meet new people via chat rooms and e-mail.

"The Internet is used, not only for information purposes, but also to socialize with people you find which have the same interests," a male sophomore explained why he used the Internet on a recent *Times* survey.

Unlike the early nineteenth and twentieth centuries, when meeting others was a matter of walking down the block or traveling within a city, the Internet has opened the world to teens - and others.

"I have quite a few pen pals [from] the net. To be safe, I use a P.O. Box. The one I talk to most is from Berlin," Michelle, a senior, said.

Another senior female wrote in her survey that she has met four girls and three guys.

"I still talk to all of them. We are all good friends," she said.

"I am currently talking to a girl from Canada," a male sophomore said.

Maggy Pietropaolas and Michelle Slysh reported on a Boston University website that their Yahoo search in April, 1996, found 62 Internet providers of cyberdating.

They also noted one cyberdating site, *www.cyberdating.com*, claimed to have 7500 "hits" on Sept. 30, 1997.

A hit is one person entering the site one time.

Some, staying away from the commercial sites for cyberdating,

find friendship by entering chat rooms, available throughout the Internet.

A senior female said she met someone at a chat table, and they wrote back and forth a lot. They eventually started talking on the phone and met twice in real life.

"I was chatting and met this girl. We said 'hi,' asked some questions and told each other about our interests. After that we started talking on the phone and stopped online chatting as much. Pretty soon, we met in person and started going out," 20-year-old Cleveland resident Patrick Steele said.

A Lakewood junior said on her survey she met someone in a chat room and they started writing back and forth everyday.

"Eventually," she said, "we started talking on the phone, and finally met in person."

A sophomore female said she hasn't met anyone online recently, but she met a kid from Akron and they called each other on the phone once or twice a week.

After about two months, she said, they arranged to meet at the mall. She said she doesn't really keep in touch with him now, though.

Nineteen-year-old Gustavo A. Rimola Jr., who lived in Cleveland but now lives in Arizona, said in an e-mail message he met a girl named Tracy online. They started chatting and e-mailing each other, and soon began phoning and writing. They started dating in person, but

he soon discovered his family was moving to Arizona.

"We have been boyfriend and girlfriend for one year already. If everything goes well for us we might get married after Tracy graduates from college. Even though I'm in Arizona now, I still love Tracy," Rimola added in his e-mail message.

Sophomore Cara Billey said she went in a chat room and was arguing with a guy about another girl in the chat room. Soon after, she said, they became friends.

"**We met and** went out in real life, which was better than talking online because you know the other person's emotions and you know who they are in real life," Billey said.

Some students, though, don't like the idea of meeting people through chat rooms or e-mail.

"I don't trust anyone on the web. You just don't know who they are," senior Adam Evanko said.

"You can't see who you're talking to or chatting with," a male sophomore wrote on the survey. "Someone could be saying, 'I'm a 15 year old who lives in Lakewood,' when in reality he or she is a 60 year old ex-con who lives in Canada after running from the police."

The sophomore did say, however, "It's easy to tell someone's age just by the way they act online, because a lot of times people who are younger act more immature and might say weird things."

Local clinical psychologist Ellen Casper said there are advantages and disadvantages of meeting people

> "I have quite a few pen pals [from] the net. To be safe, I use a P.O. Box. The one I talk to most is from Berlin."
> – Michelle, a senior

Times   *November 7, 1997*

online.

"It's a trend increasing in interest. A new way to meet people, and an interesting way to meet because you can take risks on the computer you couldn't take when meeting someone in person. You can be more open and honest," Casper said.

"With the Internet playing a larger and larger role in our lives, it's not surprising it has become an electronic matchmaker," Sara M. Carlstead said on her website called net.love.

"There are lots of places on the Internet set up for people to meet each other, often with romance in mind," Carlstead said.

After the initial meeting, net relationships usually go through a few stages to allow those involved to get to know each other better. Most relationships begin with casual, friendly e-mail a couple times a week. It escalates to a couple times a day, Carlstead said. Talking to each other in private chat is usually the next step. Then, it's talking on the phone, and eventually meeting in person, she added.

"From a practical viewpoint, Internet relationships let people communicate over long distances for a small price," Carlstead said. "The other practical appeal of net relationships is the wide variety of people you can meet with similar interests and compatible personalities."

The Internet allows people to get to know others without bas-

"There's no way to connect them to anything legitimate except what you've been told and your instincts." – **local clinical psychologist Ellen Casper**

ing their opinion of them on superficial things. It also provides the ability for people to communicate more openly, Carlstead said.

"You don't know who you're talking to, but it's better than meeting someone in real life because you look past just 'looks.' You go by personality, and you ask them things you wouldn't normally ask if you met them in person," Steele said.

"There are also some risks. One negative aspect is you don't know much about a person, except what

they're telling you, and you can't determine if they're being sincere. It's a risk for an individual to take," Casper said.

Some disadvantages to net relationships are the ease for people to lie, the difficulty of finding out the truth. Long distances relationships are hard to maintain, Carlstead said.

"People [meet others on the net] everyday and it's fine. But some people become addicted. I know some people get hooked on getting in the chat rooms every night and also meeting people and chatting privately. It can be as addictive as a drug," Bill Miller, assistant to local psychologist Donald J. Weinstein, said.

Not being able to speak directly with a person or to even sit next to him or her is a big disadvantage to cyber "dating," a web site maintained by Elizabeth A. Davis, *Daily*

CONTINUED ON PAGE 4

MICHELLE MURPHY '97

November 7, 1997

Times

Cyber Love

CONTINUED FROM PAGE 3

Beacon editor at the University of Tennessee, reported.

"People could just type in whatever they want. They could lie, and no one would ever see the smirk on their face or the lack of eye contact," Davis wrote.

"There's no way to connect them to anything legitimate except what you've been told, and your instincts," Casper said.

There is also another disadvantage to cyberdating, she added, that in most cases it lacks reality.

"Virtual" means lacking actuality and existing only in essence. So virtual love would mean something that resembles love but does not have all the attributes of real love, Davis said.

"There may be virtual "dates," but they are made up of typed words or maybe images," Davis said.

Casper said teenagers don't have enough experience. There are a number of examples where innocent teens are taken advantage of by older individuals.

Some ways a person can be more sure about someone they're about to meet is to gather personal information about the person. Make sure to ask them important questions like where they were born and their family life, Casper said.

Meet in a public place and go with a friend, Casper added.

"Even if a person sounds good on paper, you don't know what you're getting. The person is still a stranger. There is no connection except for words on a computer," Casper said.

"The world is growing and computers have increased our access to the world of information and the world of people," Casper said.

Miller said the value of the Internet is in its use.

"Like any other powerful technology, [online chatting] is good for the future, but it can be very bad. It depends on how it's used. People need to get away from their screens and meet face to face sometimes," Miller said.

There are pros and cons of meeting people online, Casper said. Proceed with caution.

INTERNET SOURCES USED FOR THIS STORY:

• http://beacon-www.asa.utk.edu/issues/v71/n23/cyber.23v.html
"Cyberspace provides only virtual romance," a site of the University of Tennessee's Daily Beacon reports.

• http://info.acm.org/crossroads/xrds1-4/netlove.html
"net.love" is a site posted by Sara M. Carlstead, a senior.

• http://www.korealink.com/public/sex/messages/248.htm
"Curious" posted a message on the internet that inquired about cyberdating, and people answered the question.

• http://web.bu.edu/SMGMIS/mba/is823/cyberdat/mainfile.htm#body
This Boston University site reports data on the number of cyberdating sites found by researchers.

CRITERIA UNDER WHICH BESS BLOCKS SITES :

• **Nudity:** The absence of clothing or exposing any and all parts of the human genitalia. Exceptions: "Classical" nudity (Michaelangelo), swimsuit models.
• **Adult Content:** Any material that has been publicly labeled as being strictly for adults.
• **Sex:** Description or depictions of all sexual acts and any erotic material.
• **Violence:** Graphic descriptions of all graphically violent acts including murder, rape, torture and/or serious injury.
• **Drug Use:** Usage or encouraging usage of any recreational drugs, including tobacco and alcohol advertising. Exceptions: material with valid educational use (e.g. drug abuse statistics).
• **Bad Language:** Crude or vulgar language or gestures.
• **Discrimination:** Denigration of others' race, religion, gender, nationality and/or sexual orientation.
• **Crime:** Encouragement, of, tools for, or advice on carrying out universally criminal acts. This includes lock-picking, bomb-making, and hacking information.
• **Tastelessness:** Excretory functions, tasteless humor, graphic medical photos outside of medical context and some extreme forms of body modification (cutting, branding, genital piercing).
• **Chat Sites:** Online chatting (might appear under the High Risk category as well).
• **High Risk:** Sites with lack of editorial control which then may fall into one of the other blockable categories.
Source: http://www.N2H2.com/

Filtering system installed to block objectionable sites

by Adam Humble

Bess, a filtering system, has been installed on the computers in the Lakewood schools to block certain Internet sites predetermined by its manufacturer.

The Bess filters reside on N2H2 servers and N2H2 Incorporated provides the Internet filtering service for Bess.

"N2H2 believes schools, libraries and organizations should not provide Internet access without filtering," Leslie Cleman, author of an explanation of the Bess system stated at that organization's website.

"Bess sets up a doorway at our Internet provider," coordinator of technology and communications Jim Marras said.

When the Internet browser tries to access a new site, Bess sorts out the pages and does not allow access to pages which have been established as non-academically oriented, Marras said.

LHS librarian Sandy Storey said Bess comes up when students access a non-educational site.

Lakewood's Acceptable Use Policy, approved by the board of education, states "The district will restrict, to the extent practicable or technically possible, access to certain information data sets or specific access types."

Cleman, writing at http://www.N2H2.com said Internet filtering is the process by which sites on the Internet are inspected and then allowed or denied based upon some set of "filtering" criteria.

"The most common use of filtering is to prevent access to Internet sites that would be unsuitable for viewing by children or employees," Cleman wrote.

Certain domains containing large amounts of inappropriate material are blocked completely, Cleman wrote.

Marras said there is no stopping a curricular aspect of the Internet.

"If a student working on a particular project. . .needs to get into a specific site, we can turn Bess off on that particular computer for the time they are working," Marras said. "It can be removed on a temporary basis from an individual station."

Cleman said people who work for Bess are constantly monitoring new sites and they choose which sites may be blocked.

Times

November 7, 1997

Online

Students make many uses of Internet

by Crystal King

Cyberdating isn't the only thing teens use the Internet for, a *Times* survey of 70 students showed.

Thirty-nine of the 70 said they use the Internet often, while 31 said they never or infrequently use it.

Usually students who go online said they do so for a great amount of time.

Junior Adam Evanko said he goes online about three times daily, sometimes up to 18 hours.

"I go online about once or twice a day," senior Travis Redding said.

"I use the Internet about two hours a day," sophomore Ryan Overman said.

Students say they use the Internet for a variety of reasons.

"It's incredible to be able to find out new things at the click of a mouse button," a senior male said.

Uses range from finding unique information, to be entertained and to keeping in touch with those who live far away.

"You can find information that you otherwise couldn't find," a sophomore female said.

Social studies teacher Tim Hinshaw supervises students in the LRC internet lab last year. Times file photo.

Michelle, a senior, said "It's something to do when I'm bored. I can learn info on my favorite things and I can meet tons of people from all over the world."

"It's a good way to keep in touch with people who don't live nearby," another senior female said.

"Going online is fun and it's a good way to enter-

tain you," a male sophomore said. "Some people use it as a way to entertain and baby-sit their kids, instead of the old TV method."

Others spoke of educational uses for the Internet.

"I use the Internet to get news, research stuff for school and to e-mail friends," a senior female wrote on her survey.

Evanko said he uses the Internet for "information, research, working on my web pages, building hyperlinks and hacking."

Michelle said "I use the Internet to help me on my college search, get info on my favorite bands, visit my favorite ghostly websites and to chat."

"I like going online because I get to talk to my friends who live in other states, and my sister at college," a junior female said.

Some said it brings the world to people's fingertips.

A sophomore male said he likes going online because "you can do almost anything you want on it."

"It opens you up to new thoughts and ideas and brings the world a lot closer," a senior female said.

Meeting new people, a variety of things to do and fun were other reasons given.

"It's fun to talk to people from all over the world," a senior female said.

A sophomore male said "there are many unique sites and things you can do."

"It's fun and easy, and it's cool to talk to people all over the country," senior Travis Redding said.

A senior female said "it's more convenient than going to the library, cheaper than the phone and faster than mail."

> *"I use the Internet to get news, research stuff for school and to e-mail friends."*
> **– a senior female**

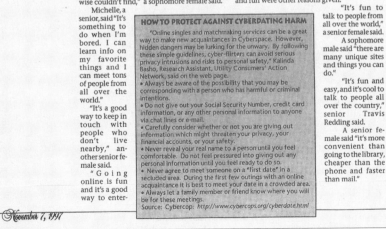

HOW TO PROTECT AGAINST CYBERDATING HARM

"Online singles and matchmaking services can be a great way to make new acquaintances in Cyberspace. However, hidden dangers may be lurking for the unwary. By following these simple guidelines, cyber-flirters can avoid serious privacy intrusions and risks to personal safety," Kalinda Basho, Research Assistant, Utility Consumers' Action Network, said on the web page.

• Always be aware of the possibility that you may be corresponding with a person who has harmful or criminal intentions.

• Do not give out your Social Security Number, credit card information, or any other personal information to anyone via chat lines or e-mail.

• Carefully consider whether or not you are giving out information which might threaten your privacy, your financial accounts, or your safety.

• Never reveal your real name to a person until you feel comfortable. Do not feel pressured into giving out any personal information until you feel ready to do so.

• Never agree to meet someone on a "first date" in a secluded area. During the first few outings with an online acquaintance it is best to meet your date in a crowded area.

• Always let a family member or friend know where you will be for these meetings.

Source: Cybercop: *http://www.cybercops.org/cyberdate.html*

The Interpretive or
Analytical Story *(continued)*

Here is the editorial that concluded the
four-page story spread.

24   The last word

Cyber Love
With online dating, anything is possible

Cyberlove is becoming more widespread in the search for finding one's true love.

Meeting people online without having to deal with the superficial factors of a relationship is a very efficient way to meet compatible people.

When meeting online, people don't have to worry about all the frustration of finding out if someone likes someone else.

One just needs to ask.

It's not as embarrassing as asking someone in person.

Online they don't have to worry about superficial things like namebrand clothing, height, weight or complexion.

None of those things matter.

With the good qualities of cyberdating also come problems.

When people meet each other online and describe themselves, a person has no idea who is telling the truth or who is lying.

A cyberdater can say she is a woman when he may really be a man. Anyone can say he or she is 16 when the person's real age is 65.

Any number of possibilities are likely when love is attempted online.

Cases exist where people have been raped and killed after meeting online "friends" in real life.

Those who meet online need to remember, they haven't actually met. They are still strangers.

People physically meeting someone for the first time should take precautions.

Some simple hints come to mind for those wanting to meet someone:

• meet the person in public and with friends, if possible.

• do not disclose any personal information to people met online. If the person does end up being someone bad, fewer problems exist if no personal information is ever disclosed.

Cyberlove is simply a different place to meet people.

Used wrong it could be deadly.

Use the Internet properly and be careful while meeting people online.

Source: Lakewood High School, Lakewood, Ohio, *Times,* November 7, 1997.

Wrap-up

In-depth reporting is the graduate work of high school journalism. You aren't ready for it until you've mastered the skills of the conventional news story as well as the feature story. Nor will you do it well unless you're a self-starter, because the in-depth doesn't lend itself well to deadlines. Remember that the in-depth is best produced by a team of reporters, writers, artists, and photographers and that it's an ideal assignment to practice teamwork in high school journalism. While a separate in-depth team may be a luxury on most high school staffs, in-depths can be produced by anyone with the time and determination to do something extra. Once you're prepared and motivated, you'll find the in-depth to be as rewarding a challenge and opportunity as that long paper you're doing for European History AP.

Journalism

analytical reporting—process of examining a news-related topic by breaking it into parts and looking at them closely.

follow-up—story that reports events that occur after the initial news event.

in-depth reporting—reporting that probes the topic in greater detail than the conventional deadline news story.

interpretive reporting—story that tries to explain the meaning of the news as well as report the event itself.

investigative reporting—reporting that reveals a problem of a legal or ethical nature that in the journalist's judgment the public needs to know about.

maestro system—organizing and planning system whereby the production staff (artist, copy editor, designer, infographic specialist, photographer) works closely with the reporter to present the story as a package.

news peg—news event from which stories grow that do not focus on the breaking news.

survey—process of polling a small sample of people about their behavior or attitudes in order to predict what the population in general will believe or do.

synthesis—establishment of significance or meaning from analytical results.

trend story—story that reports on the details that support a perceived change in newsworthy social behavior.

Wall Street Journal lead—lead that begins with an anecdote or description before announcing the nut graf of the story.

CHAPTER 9

Journalistic Style

In this chapter, you will learn:

- **what journalistic style is and why a style manual is important for consistency and credibility**
- **about specifics of scholastic style**
- **suggestions for what to include in a local stylebook**

When journalists talk about **style,** *they are really talking about two aspects of writing a story: first, the way a story is crafted for the print or broadcast media, and second, the specific rules journalists follow for their own publication or broadcast medium. The chapters that cover writing specific types of stories deal with the first aspect of style. This chapter addresses the second aspect in detail, discussing how writers carry out the style rules adopted by a specific print or broadcast medium. The role of copyeditors in maintaining consistent style will be covered in Chapter 17.*

Using a Style Manual

A reliable, consistent writing **style** gives a publication credibility. Using a style manual that specifies the style points that work best for your publication is a key way to set and maintain journalistic style for that publication.

Consistency and Credibility

First, let's look at how important consistency is for readers and, consequently, for writers. What would happen if every reporter writing for the *New York Times* or the *Chicago Tribune* made independent decisions about how to indicate the time and date of an event? Suppose an event will be taking place at 10 a.m. on August 6.

One reporter might choose to write it as 10 a.m. Aug. 6. However, other ways to phrase the same idea include the following: at 10 a.m. tomorrow, at 10:00 a.m. on Aug. 6, at 10 a.m. on August 6th, at 10 o'clock tomorrow morning. And those are only four of the alternatives.

While all of these styles no doubt communicate the time and date effectively, readers are more comfortable when they see a consistent pattern from story to story. Such consistency increases the credibility of the publication or broadcast medium for readers, viewers, or listeners since it communicates the idea that all the writers working for the organization are in agreement on some basic rules.

These rules are collected in a reference work called a **stylebook**, or **style manual.** This book contains all the decisions a particular staff has made about the rules it will follow for consistency in capitalization, spelling, punctuation, names, identifications, time, dates, usage, and even design.

AP Stylebook

Most professional newspapers across the United States have adopted the style of the Associated Press updated annually in *The Associated Press (AP) Stylebook and Libel Manual.* Because most professional newspapers in this country subscribe to the AP wire service and use stories provided by that service, their staff members find it easy to adopt AP style for the rest of the stories. This way, extensive editing does not have to be done to stories they use from the wire service. The two styles are already in sync.

However, nearly all media organizations have local situations not covered by the *AP Stylebook,* so they publish a supplement to it or create their own separate reference. In its bibliography, the 1999 *AP Stylebook* specifically mentions nine newspaper stylebooks, along with that of the U.S. Government Printing Office, which its creators consulted. See sidebar on the next page for complete list.

List of Stylebooks Consulted in Preparation of the Associated Press Stylebook

Boston Globe
Indianapolis News
Kansas City Star
Los Angeles Times
Miami Herald
Milwaukee Journal Sentinel
Newsday
New York Times
Wilmington (Del.) News-Journal
U.S. Government Printing Office

Source: Norm Goldstein, editor, *The Associated Press Stylebook and Libel Manual*. The Associated Press, N.Y., 1999.

Stylebook Contents

While the general style section of the *AP Stylebook* is lengthy, at 274 pages in the 1999 edition, it is the professional standard. This stylebook also includes:

* Supplementary sections devoted specifically to sports style and to business style.
* A 14-page Guide to Punctuation.
* A 40-page Libel Manual including information on right of privacy and guidelines about copyright.
* Proofreaders' marks.

Space-saving Style

The *AP Stylebook* directs the writer to the option that uses space most efficiently. Look at the earlier example on writing the time—"at 10:00 in the morning on August 6th." AP style would direct the writer to omit the colon and zeros when time is on the even hour; to use lowercase a.m. rather than uppercase, which takes more room; to omit "on" since it is not necessary for clear communication; to abbreviate August when used with a date; and to omit the "th" after the date. Result: 10 a.m. Aug. 6.

Other Resources

Other helpful style resources are available from **two** national scholastic journalism organizations:

1. Quill and Scroll Society at the University of Iowa publishes and sells the *Quill and Scroll Stylebook*.
2. Columbia Scholastic Press Association at Columbia University in New York City publishes and sells *The Official CSPA Stylebook*.

The Journalism Education Association's Bookstore also sells these stylebooks along with staff manuals/stylebooks from a few specific high school programs.

At least one of these books should be available for reference in every publication staff room. The Associated Press sells its stylebook through its New York City office, and it is also available through the Journalism Education Association Bookstore and various other bookstores.

Customizing a Stylebook

High school publications staffs should start with an existing stylebook and add a supplement containing their unique guidelines. Individual staffs will want to make local decisions about issues such as these:

* Whether to use courtesy titles (Mr., Mrs., Miss, Ms.) for adults.
* Whether to capitalize names of organizations or clubs at their school.
* Whether to capitalize the names of annual all-school events (Homecoming or homecoming, Prom or prom).

Every style decision, including those about design, needs to be written down for all staff members.

Sidebar

Another Reason to Know Style

The more familiar all writers on any staff—from school to professional media —are with style details, the easier the editor's task will be. This is why nearly all—if not all—professional media outlets give a basic grammar and style test as part of their job interviewing process. They are reluctant to hire journalistic writers who don't know how to recognize and use basic journalistic style rules.

Specifics of Style

Although each school publications staff will want to establish its own guidelines for its own unique situations, some style points are common to all journalistic writing. Guidelines for specific areas follow.

Gender-Neutral Language

Nonsexist language, according to Marilyn Schwartz in *Guidelines for Bias-Free Publishing*, "refers to language that avoids gender stereotyping." Journalistic writing should treat males and females equally by not only providing equal coverage of males and females and their school achievements—whether students or staff—but also in using **gender-neutral language**.

Titles

If your staff decides on courtesy titles for adult staff members at your school, then Mr. needs to be applied to men just as Miss, Mrs., or Ms. needs to be applied to women. To use a courtesy title with women and not with men, or vice versa, would be inequitable. Some staffs have avoided the problem of determining which courtesy title women prefer by using Ms. for all. Whatever your staff's decision, the guideline must become a part of your specific publication's stylebook.

Generalizations

When reporters write about students and their actions in general, using gender-neutral language is important. Consider the following sentence from a news story about grade-point averages:

The average student is worried about their grades.

Obviously, the writer has an agreement error: "student" is singular while "their" is plural. The age-old solution advocated by experts from all areas is to use the generic "he" to solve this problem. Thus, the solution was:

The average student is worried about his grades.

While this rewrite certainly solves the agreement problem, it creates another problem. Faced with this sentence, readers invariably picture a male, even though they may understand "he" to be used in a generic sense.

You may choose a number of alternatives to the generic use of "he" when applied to a singular antecedent of unknown or untold gender. One solution is to change the subject to plural:

Average students are worried about their grades.

So what's the problem? Rewriting in the plural may make the message fuzzy. This wording may suggest to the reader that only average students are worried about their grades and, further, that above-average and below-average students are not worried about their grades. Another solution must be found. One solution is to use the double pronoun:

The average student is worried about his or her grades.

The average student is worried about her/his grades.

Another solution is to remove the pronoun reference completely.

Students worry about grades.

In general, students worry about grades.

A complete rewriting of the troublesome sentence may be necessary:

When finally faced with college applications and the possibility of acceptance or rejection because of grade-point average, the average student worries about grades and how they will be viewed by someone making admissions decisions.

This rewrite omits the pronoun before "grades" and makes the next pronoun plural to refer to "grades."

Sometimes, although not usually in journalistic writing where first- and second-person references are usually avoided, a shift to first or second person may solve the problem:

We are often concerned about our grades.
You should be concerned about your grades.

These solutions may work for opinion pieces, such as columns or editorials, but they are not viable alternatives for most journalistic writing.

Likewise, the impersonal third-person use of "one" is usually too formal for journalistic writing:

If one is an average student, one worries about one's grades.

In some cases, "they" is viewed as singular, as it often is in spoken English. Marilyn Schwartz says, "Some linguists recommend this form within prescribed grammatical boundaries, such as to specify an indefinite pronoun or a 'multiple choice' antecedent: Everyone has to carry their own luggage." Our example about worrying over grades seems to fall into this "multiple choice" antecedent category. Thus, the following becomes an alternative:

Everyone worries about their grades.

Perhaps we have come full circle by now, or perhaps not. Did the writer of the original mean "everyone"? No, he didn't. The point is that writers should be acutely aware of appropriate word choice in their writing. Consider the following:

Everyone should bring his book to class.
Everyone should bring his or her book to class.
Everyone should bring their book to class.
All students should bring their books to class.
Students should bring their books to class.
Everyone should bring the appropriate textbook to class.

When might you choose to use one of these sentences over the others?

Roles at Work

Another key problem is reference to roles in the workplace. For example, "workman" would be better as "employee," "waitress" or "waiter" would be better as "server," and "chairman" should become "chair," "chairperson," "coordinator," "moderator," "presiding officer," or "head."

The Journalism Education Association (JEA), the national organization for secondary journalism teachers and publications advisers, has created a list of possible substitutions for such words. (See page 162.)

Again, careful writers are sensitive to gender issues and avoid gender descriptions not necessary to the context of the story. Even then, as suggested by JEA, writers should ask the sources what they prefer.

Possible Substitutes for Gender-Specific Terms

Not	*But*
airman	aviator, pilot
anchorman	news commentator, announcer, newscaster
businessman	entrepreneur, business executive
cameraman	camera operator, photographer
craftsman	artisan
enlisted man	enlistee, service member, recruit
fireman	firefighter, foreman, supervisor
housewife	homemaker
maid, janitor	house (office) cleaner, custodian
man (verb)	staff, operate
mankind	humans, humanity, people, human beings
man-made	artificial, manufactured
manpower	personnel, human resources, work force, labor
middleman	intermediary, wholesaler
paper boys, paper girls	paper carriers
policeman, policewoman	police officer
postman, mailman	mail carrier, postal worker
salesman, saleswoman	sales clerk, sales representative, seller
seaman	sailor
seamstress	dressmaker, tailor
serviceman	service member, member of the armed forces
spokesman	representative
steward, stewardess	flight attendant, attendant
watchman	guard
weatherman	weathercaster, weather reporter, meteorologist

Source: From Journalism Education Association, *JEA Stylebook*, 1998.

Race, Ethnicity, and Nationality

As a writer, you must be sensitive to the balance between recognizing diversity and not calling attention to the fact that people may be of different racial, ethnic, or national origins.

People are what they are, and in the context of a story, a description of a person's national, racial, or ethnic identity may be important. On the other hand, an individual should not be described as being "different" unless this identification is necessary. Think about the idea of "different"—different from whom or what?

When a description is necessary, you will need to know what term to use. Even accepted authorities disagree. For example, AP style prefers the use of "black" and "American Indian" or the specific name of an Indian tribe, such as "Navajo." But, other sources indicate the preferred terms are "African American" and "Native American." For the sake of consistency, your staff will need to decide which terms are best for your publication's audience, make a decision, and stick to it. Be sure to enter the decision in your local stylebook.

Word Choice

"The difference between the *almost right* word and the *right* word is really a large matter—'tis the difference between the lightning bug and lightning." Mark Twain is often cited as the originator of this famous observation on word choice in his essay "The Art of Composition" (1890). He couldn't have been more right, even though he said this more than 100 years ago.

When having a conversation face-to-face with another person or a group, facial expressions give instant feedback from listeners about whether they understand. Unfortunately, writers do not have the benefit of such instant feedback. Always remember the role of the journalist: to take readers where they cannot go on their own but not to color the event with biased presentation of the facts. Writers must be careful to choose the precise word, but not an emotionally charged word.

A Common Dilemma

Let's look at a word choice dilemma journalism students commonly face. Do you use "said" as an attributive word, or do you use something more descriptive? In reporting results of interviews, the best word to use for attribution is a simple "said." This word avoids any additional meaning conveyed by words such as "claimed," "stated," "exclaimed," "shouted," "confirmed," "declared," "remarked," and so on.

Be Wary of Synonyms for "Said"

The following words are just as neutral as "said" if they are used in the correct context:

went on   continued
added

These are descriptive, but may be useful under the proper circumstances:

insisted   maintained
complained   cautioned
explained   recalled
predicted

These are hazardous:

pointed out   noted
warned   charged
claimed

These are widely misused:

asserted   stated
declared   commented
observed   revealed

These are used often, regrettably:

avowed   opined
exclaimed   quipped
snapped

Adapted from Rene J. Cappon, *The Word: An Associated Press Guide to Good News Writing* (2nd Ed.), The Associated Press, New York, 1991.

Precise Meaning

Besides avoiding emotionally charged words, writers must be sure they have chosen the words they mean, even when emotion is not an issue. Unfortunately, the English language contains a large number of **homonyms,** words that sound alike but are spelled differently and have different meanings. These are especially troublesome for journalists.

Also, to be as precise as possible, writers should outlaw the following list of vague words from their stories: "many," "most," "few," "some" (instead, go for the specific number whenever possible), "stuff," "things," "rather," "very," "pretty" (as in "pretty good"). When interviewing sources, question them thoroughly so you don't find yourself using such less than helpful words even in quotations.

Clarity and Brevity

Writers achieve clarity by simplifying sentences and words; weeding out jargon, redundancies, clichés, and repetition; placing modifiers carefully; using action verbs; and writing active sentences.

Short Sentences

Sentences communicate best when they do not exceed 16 or 17 words and are written in subject-verb-object order. This does not mean every sentence should be this length or in this order. Remember **two** things:

1. When a sentence gets to be 25 or more words, it's definitely time to take a hard look at sentence structure.
2. Don't forget to mix in some shorter sentences for variety.

Minimal Punctuation

This sentence length guideline also helps the journalist cut down on punctuation. It minimizes use of colons and semicolons because they usually require complex sentences. Journalists even reduce the use of commas since AP style omits the comma before the "and" in a series. (This text does not follow AP style because it is a book, not a newspaper or periodical, and the series of books it is a part of has its own style.)

However, commas and semicolons are used to separate items and their description in a series. Example:

Class officers are Jamie Kaplan, president; Abbas Khan, vice president; Maria Steingoltz, secretary; Mike Nalepa, treasurer.

Quick Openings

Avoid sentence openings that don't get to the point. Specifically, avoid beginning sentences with "There are. . . ," "There is . . . ," "It is . . . ." Instead, rephrase the sentence to begin with the important idea. Instead of "There are five home football games this season," use

Five home football games will be played this season.

Varsity football will play five home games this season.

Short School Name

Avoid writing out the name of your school throughout your publication. In general, avoid reference to your own school's name. However, when it is necessary to refer to your school name, use the common abbreviation: All-City High School becomes ACHS. Of course, you will need to write out the names of other schools on first mention followed by the common abbreviation in parentheses. Then you can use the abbreviation throughout the rest of the story: Buffalo Grove High School (BGHS) on first mention and BGHS thereafter. Example:

All-City High School hosts Buffalo Grove High School in the first home football game of the season. Buffalo Grove is ranked fifth in the state in pre-season polls.

ACHS hosts Buffalo Grove High School (BGHS) in the first home football game of the season. BGHS is ranked fifth in the state in pre-season polls.

No Big Words

Don't use a big word when a simpler one will do just as well. Remember, your emphasis must be on communication, not on showing off your advanced vocabulary. As William Strunk and E. B. White advise in *The Elements of Style* (4th ed., 2000): "Avoid fancy words. Avoid the elaborate, the pretentious, the coy, and the cute. Do not be tempted by a twenty-dollar word when there is a ten-center handy, ready and able."

Twenty-Dollar Words

In *The Word: An Associated Press Guide to Good News Writing*, Rene J. Cappon provides a useful list of big words to avoid.

accommodations	rooms
ameliorate	improve
approximately	about
assistance	help
commence	begin
deactivate	close, shut off
endeavor	try
finalize	end, complete
implement	carry out
in consequence of	because
initiate	begin
methodology	method
motivation	motive
objective	aim, goal
peruse	read
prior to	before
proliferation	spread
purchase	buy
remuneration	pay
replicate	repeat
socialize	mingle, meet, make friends
substantial proportion	many, much
underprivileged	poor
utilize	use

No Jargon

<u>Jargon</u> is the inside vocabulary of a specific group. When you have to use these words, you need to translate them for the reader. Jargon is found in all professions, sports, institutions, hobbies, and corporations. As a high school reporter, you are likely to be faced with jargon from sources no matter what you are assigned to cover.

Here's an example of a golf story written by a reporter who either knows golf quite well or who doesn't know golf at all, but who was apparently afraid to ask for an explanation of the terms the source used.

In qualifying for the sectional golf meet, Cari Gaffke, senior, presented one of the few bright spots in an otherwise dismal season for girls golf. Gaffke posted an 85 on the Chevy Chase links Oct. 5 to qualify as an individual for the Schaumburg regional with a cut score of 86.

Key to the round was two pars on the treacherous water holes and an improbable birdie, eagle finish after hitting two OB on the 16th hole to card a quadruple bogey for her only snowman in the round.

"On the 15th hole my opponent tried to assess me a two-stroke penalty for carrying a rake into the sand trap," Gaffke said. "Although the rules committee didn't agree, I lost my composure on the 16th hole."

While several rewrites of this information would be acceptable, here's a suggestion that should make the story more easily understood:

After shooting 85 at the sectional golf meet Oct. 5 at Chevy Chase Country Club, Cari Gaffke, senior, qualified for the regional meet.

She is the only ACHS golfer to score lower than the 86 needed to make the cut and continue to the regional meet at Schaumburg Golf Club on Oct. 12.

"On the 15th hole my opponent tried to assess me a two-stroke penalty for carrying a rake into the sand trap," Gaffke said. "Although the rules committee didn't agree, I lost my composure on the 16th hole."

Gaffke said her two most important holes in the round were the 17th and 18th, where she scored one under par for a birdie and two under par for an eagle. Earlier, on the 16th hole, she had an 8, after hitting two balls out of bounds.

Here's another example from a reporter writing about the results of a debate tournament early in the season. If you were reading this story, what words would give you trouble? How would you suggest rewriting this information to communicate more effectively to most readers?

The first major debate tournament of the year took place Oct. 15-16 at Northern Illinois University. Fifty schools from across the state participated.

"We were happy to make octas in novice policy," So Yoon Oh, freshman debater, said. In the L/D division, Rich Ham, senior debater, and

Grant Dixton, junior debater, closed out finals.

Ten of the 20 entered by the Wildcats won speaker awards and five brought home team awards.

"Considering the size of the field, breaking to sextos in novice policy and L/D, and the full levels of competition, we were really pleased with the efforts of all involved," Jack Stanislaw, assistant coach, said.

Here's some good advice: Whenever you run into vocabulary unique to a specific group or activity, first be sure you understand what your sources are talking about. Never quote jargon blindly. Instead, ask clarifying questions until you understand the terms well enough to explain them to readers in your own words.

Fighting Redundancy

Redundancy is unnecessary repetition of an idea. Common examples are "8 p.m. tonight," "refer back," "personal feelings," or "honest truth."

One way to check for redundancy is to replace the modifier with its opposite. If the new idea is nonsense, then the modifier is likely an unnecessary one. Try these: "at 8 p.m. this morning," "refer ahead," "impersonal feelings," "dishonest truth." Under what circumstances, if any, are the original modifiers necessary? Check issues of your school publications or exchange publications to find redundancies.

Another type of redundancy continues an idea by including the obvious. Consider these phrases: "shrug his shoulders," "nod her head," "think to himself." What other body part does one shrug or nod? How else do we think except to ourselves? Thus, these are also examples of redundancy.

Common Redundancies

Test each of these redundancies by replacing the modifier with its opposite. Is the new idea nonsense? If so, the modifier is probably unnecessary.

absolutely conclusive
entirely absent
lifeless corpse
personal friend
agricultural crops
exact counterpart
meaningless gibberish
personal opinion
awkward dilemma
future plan
mutual cooperation
pragmatic realist
close proximity
general public

new record
present incumbent
complete monopoly
grateful thanks
old adage
sworn affidavit
completely full
hired mercenary
organic life
true facts
divisive quarrel
irreducible minimum
original founder
ultimate outcome
end result
lonely hermit
patently obvious
violent explosion

Source: From Rene J. Cappon, *The Word: An Associated Press Guide to Good News Writing* (2nd Ed.). The Associated Press, N.Y., 1991.

Stretching It

While redundancy weakens writing, fear of repetition can cause writers to consult a thesaurus and tempt them to use a less-than-exact synonym. See the sidebar "Is This Awkward" for an example of what can happen when you fight redundancy too vigorously.

Fear of repetition can also result in awkward, choppy sentences that have little or no relation to each other. Remember the discussion in Chapter 6 on transitions. Without good transitions, including some effective repetition of ideas and words, the opening paragraphs do not flow as smoothly as in the original. At the same time, be sure to vary sentence and paragraph beginnings for a smoother flow.

Original:

*Floor hockey team members received gold medals Feb. 1, **after** they earned the school's 12th Special Olympics state championship since 1993. **This** was **their** third straight state win in floor hockey.*

*   ***To prepare for state competition,** the team practiced throughout January. They also played in four scrimmage games against Hoffman Estates High School.*

Rewrite without effective repetition and transitions:

Floor hockey team members received gold medals Feb. 1. It is the school's 12th Special Olympics state championship since 1993. It was the third straight state win in floor hockey.

*   Floor hockey team members practiced throughout January. Floor hockey played in four scrimmage games against Hoffman Estates High School.*

The original version is more effective with appropriate repetition and smooth transitions.

Is This Awkward?

Suppose you are writing a story about journalism awards your newspaper has won. You want to avoid repeating the words *award* and *society* throughout your story, so you consult a thesaurus. The thesaurus gives you these choices for "award": "prize," "citation," "scholarship," "grant," "trophy," "medal," "decoration"; these choices for "society": "association," "brotherhood," "circle," "clique," "company," "fellowship," "fraternity," "organization." Because they do not carry the same meaning as "award," you reject "scholarship," "grant," "trophy," "medal." For "society," you reject "brotherhood," "circle," "clique," "company," "fellowship," "fraternity." If you had not rejected these choices, you might end up with a lead like this:

*The Spokesman staff received the George H. Gallup **Award** last month from the Quill and Scroll **Society** for issues published last year. **This grant** is the highest **decoration** given by the **fellowship.***

This awkward—and inaccurate—lead is the result of using a thesaurus without thinking. Here is another, somewhat better effort:

*The Spokesman staff received the George H. Gallup **Award** last month from Quill and Scroll **Society** for issues published last year. This **prize** is the highest **decoration** given by the **organization.***

Compare it to this one:

*The Spokesman staff received the George H. Gallup **Award** last month from Quill and Scroll **Society** for issues published last year. **It** is the highest **award** given by the **society.***

Which is more effective? Why?

Clichés

Phrases so overused they become meaningless are called <u>clichés.</u> We hear them every day, but that does not mean they communicate well. Often, high school journalists have not read widely enough to recognize an overworked phrase when they write one. The only solution is to read, read, read. When you do recognize a cliché, omit it entirely or substitute specific information to strengthen the sentence.

 Example

Types of Clichés

Some clichés are just moldy old proverbs:

* A penny saved is a penny earned.
* A stitch in time saves nine.
* The grass is always greener on the other side.
* He who pays the piper calls the tune.
* Variety is the spice of life.

Some are metaphors that have been overused:

* The cream of the crop
* Raining cats and dogs
* A slap in the face
* Burning the midnight oil
* Give the green light
* Hitting the nail on the head
* No holds barred
* A horse of a different color
* Dog tired
* Came out smelling like a rose

Some are just words—neither sayings nor metaphors—that have been used together so often that they seem inseparable:

* A sigh of relief
* Finishing touches
* The rules of the game
* Loud and clear
* Ups and downs
* Long holiday weekend
* In the final analysis
* Financial circles
* Goes without saying
* Tension is high
* Remains to be seen
* Speculation was rampant
* Nestled in the valley
* Leave in a huff
* Needless to say
* More of the same
* Powers that be
* Fueling speculation
* In no uncertain terms
* Fond farewell
* Breathless anticipation
* Sure thing

Source: From Gerald Lanson and Mitchell Stephens, *Writing & Reporting the News* (2nd Ed.). Harcourt Brace College Publishers, Fort Worth, Texas, 1994.

Modifiers

By definition, modifiers alter meanings of words. They make words more specific by adding additional information. When you use a modifier, you usually hope to create a more concrete picture in your reader's mind. However, if writers don't use modifiers carefully—and according to some rules—the concrete picture they hope to create can become comical. Consider these common errors in the use of modifiers.

Misplaced Modifiers

One of the most common errors in modifier placement occurs when modifiers are not placed as close as possible to the words they modify. Forgetting this rule results in sentences like these:

Muddled: The students listened attentively as English teacher Mike Smalley explained the characters of Pip and Estella munching their candy bars from the cheerleaders.

(Characters from a Dickens novel munched on candy bars from cheerleaders?)

Better: Munching their candy bars from the cheerleaders, the students listened attentively as English teacher Mike Smalley explained the characters of Pip and Estella.

Muddled: Sandra Smith, journalism teacher, wore the First Amendment design scarf around her shoulders which she had purchased at the Newseum in Washington, D.C.

(The journalism teacher purchased her shoulders at the Newseum in Washington D.C.?)

Better: Sandra Smith, journalism teacher, wore the First Amendment design scarf, which she had purchased at the Newseum in Washington, D.C., around her shoulders.

Muddled: The fans saw Jim Sabal, forward, make a free throw from the bleachers to win the league championship.

(Sabal shot a free throw from the bleachers?)

Better: The fans sitting in the bleachers saw Jim Sabal, forward, make a free throw to win the league championship.

Dangling Modifiers

Another type of modifier error occurs when the sentence contains no word for the phrase or clause to modify. These are called dangling modifiers. Forgetting this rule results in sentences like these:

Muddled: Listening attentively to English teacher Mike Smalley explain the roles of Pip and Estella, the shrill fire alarm made the students jump.

(The fire alarm could not be listening attentively.)

Better: Because they listened attentively to English teacher Mike Smalley explain the roles of Pip and Estella, the shrill fire alarm made the students jump.

Muddled: Running madly down the hall for her bus after school, senior Erika Kane's books fell and scattered everywhere.

(Erika's books could not be running down the hall madly.)

Better: Because she ran madly down the hall for her bus after school, senior Erika Kane dropped her books and they scattered everywhere.

Muddled: Having proofread the last story, the camera-ready pages were now ready for delivery to the printer.

(The camera-ready pages can't proofread.)

Better: Having proofread the last story, the editor was now ready to deliver the camera-ready pages to the printer.

Ambiguous Modifiers

A third type of modifier error occurs when a modifier can refer to more than one person or thing in the sentence. Careless sentences with this mistake always result in confusion—sometimes humorous.

Confusing: The coach told the substitutes after practice began to report to the locker room.

(Did the coach make the announcement after practice began or were the substitutes supposed to report after practice began?)

Clear: After practice began, the coach told the substitutes to report to the locker room.

Confusing: Lisa Espinosa, candidate for Student Council president, said in the interview her opponent spoke like a gentleman.

(Did Lisa make a comment in her interview that her opponent spoke like a gentleman, or did she say that her opponent, in a press interview that he gave, spoke like a gentleman?)

Clear: Lisa Espinosa, candidate for Student Council president, told the interviewer that her opponent spoke like a gentleman during the debates.

Clear: In his press interview, her opponent spoke like a gentleman, according to Lisa Espinosa, candidate for Student Council president.

Action Verbs and Active Sentences

Sentences written in active voice, rather than passive voice, make good use of action verbs and show subjects taking part in action, not being acted upon. Active voice sentences are more direct, more immediate for the reader and are often shorter than passive voice sentences. Whenever possible, write sentences using action verbs and in active voice.

Weak/Passive: Three cans of soda pop are consumed by the average teenage boy each day.

Stronger/Active: The average teenage boy drinks three cans of soda pop a day.

Weak/Passive: Audiences were entertained by the fall play, "A Company of Wayward Saints," Nov. 12-14 in the Little Theater.

Stronger/Active: The fall play, "A Company of Wayward Saints," entertained audiences Nov. 12-14 in the Little Theater.

Be Even More Specific

Once you have all the larger questions of journalistic style ironed out, it's time to consider the final details. In many cases of source identification, capitalization, abbreviations, numbers and when to use italics or quote marks, you can follow an established stylebook. However, in other cases, as this section points out, you will need to make decisions about how to handle cases that are unique to your school. Remember that being consistent and logical is the key. As always, add all the decisions you make about style to your local stylebook so everyone knows what they are.

Names and Identifications

AP style says sources are listed by their full names on first mention and then by last name only on second and subsequent mention. Here are **three** variations to consider:

1. In a personality feature you might refer to students by first name for second and subsequent mentions.

2. Identify sources on first mention, but identify them fully with their most pertinent mention in the story. Common sense takes precedence over consistency in this instance.

3. Students should be identified by their year in school—either with the year of their graduation ('03) or by their classification (senior). Your decision about this will go into your local style manual.

Titles of Courtesy

Likewise, your staff will need to decide whether to use courtesy titles (Mr., Mrs., Miss, Ms., Dr.) with the names of adults in your school.

IDs Before or After

Your staff will also need to decide whether you will place the identification before or after the name. Some publications adopt a guideline that says identifications up to two words are placed before the name while longer identifications are placed after the name. Some publications decide all identifications are placed after the name. When the source name is in the possessive form, the identification must come first to avoid an awkward sentence. What you decide about these additional style questions will go into your local style manual so that everyone on the staff knows the rules and can be consistent. Some examples follow.

Proper style for a publication that uses courtesy titles on second mention:

*Jason Witt, literary magazine adviser, announced the first meeting of the staff Nov. 3 in room 133. Experienced magazine staff members will help **Mr. Witt** decide the schedule of meetings for the rest of the year.*

Proper style for a publication that does not use courtesy titles:

*Jason Witt, literary magazine adviser, announced the first meeting of the staff Nov. 3 in room 133. Experienced magazine staff members will help **Witt** decide the schedule of meetings for the rest of the year.*

Proper style for a publication that does not use courtesy titles and that uses identifications of one or two words before the name with longer identifications after the name:

Patty Geppert, editor in chief of the literary magazine, announced the first meeting of the staff for 2 p.m. Nov. 3 in room 133. With other experienced magazine staff members, **Geppert** will help **faculty adviser Jason Witt** decide the schedule of meetings for the rest of the year.

Proper style for a publication that uses all identifications after the name:

Patty Geppert, **junior,** will be editor in chief of the literary magazine for 2001-02. She will lead a staff of 25, who will meet for the first time at 2 p.m. Nov. 3 in room 133.

Patty Geppert **'03** will be editor in chief of the literary magazine for 2001-02. She will lead a staff of 25, who will meet for the first time at 2 p.m. Nov. 3 in room 133.

Proper style when the name is in possessive form:

Editor Patty Geppert's first meeting of the literary magazine staff will be at 2 p.m. Nov. 3 in room 133. She will lead a staff of 25 to produce this year's publication.

Also note the consistent order of time, date, and place: "at 2 p.m. Nov. 3 in room 133." This is another element that needs to be consistent from story to story. Make a note of it in your local style manual.

Capitalization

Journalistic style follows standard English capitalization rules. However, you will want to decide how you will capitalize names of locations, organizations, and events specific to your school. Generally, minimize capitalization.

Offices or Rooms

With that in mind, it is a good idea not to capitalize name of offices or rooms unless they have a formal name: the theater, but the Robert E. Sang Theater.

Clubs and Organizations

Names of clubs and other formal organizations should be written out fully and capitalized on first mention. If you will be using an acronym on following mention, put it in parenthesis at the first mention: National Honor Society (NHS), NHS on subsequent mention; Student Council (SC) or (StuCo), SC or StuCo on subsequent mention. You will most likely not use an acronym for an organization such as Russian Club.

Sports and Teams

Names of sports teams should not be capitalized, nor should levels of competition: varsity football team, junior varsity soccer team.

What will you do about the debate team: Debate Team or debate team? What about Math Team (math team) or Scholastic Bowl (scholastic bowl)? These are local decisions and should follow some consistent logic. When you have decided, note the rules in your local stylebook.

Events

Will Homecoming Week be treated as a formal event and be capitalized? What about Homecoming Dance? Or will you only capitalize Homecoming in both instances or not capitalize homecoming at all? What about Prom? What about Winter Dance? Turnabout? Spring Fling? Winter Break? Spring Break? As each new problem in capitalization arises, the staff needs to make a decision and add it to your stylebook.

Abbreviations

Rules for using abbreviations fall into a couple of categories.

Months of the Year

According to AP style, months of the year are not abbreviated when they stand alone or are printed with a year and not a date. But when they are printed with a date, months of five letters or fewer are written out; the others are abbreviated. Examples: April 2003; November 2005; April 1, 2003; Nov. 25, 2005.

Acronyms

Acronyms generally do not take periods; however, exceptions include a.m. and p.m. with time and A.D. and B.C. with dates. Do not use acronyms without first writing out the complete title, as in the examples above. One exception is the name of your school. All-City High School becomes ACHS on every mention in your publication, but minimize the use of this. It should be clear to readers that you are writing about your school.

Numbers

Journalistic style for numbers is different from standard English manuscript rules. For journalistic style, numbers of two digits or more (10 and higher) are presented as numerals; zero through nine are written out. Exceptions:

* Always write out a number if it is the first word in the sentence.
* Always use numerals for dates, addresses, ages, amounts of money, temperatures, percentages, jersey numbers, sports scores and records, clock times.
* Omit the "th" at the end of a date: Aug. 10, not Aug. 10th.

Punctuation

Generally follow standard English guidelines for punctuation. However, when there is a conflict between AP style and standard guidelines, follow AP style, as in the omission of the comma before "and" in a series.

As noted earlier, this text does not follow AP style in this matter, because it is a book, not a newspaper, and the series of books to which it belongs has its own style rules.

Italics and Quotations

You'll also need to decide what to do about titles of movies, books, other newspapers and yearbooks, articles, TV shows, computer software, and so on. Will you follow standard English guidelines or AP style, or create your own style? Today's computers allow much more flexibility in these decisions than journalists had even 25 years ago. Just remember to write down what you decide so everyone on your staff knows what to do.

Italics

Because italics cannot be sent through Associated Press computers, AP style does not include use of italics. You may choose to follow AP style for titles or create your own style, using italics for some titles.

Quotations

In AP style, quotation marks go around titles of books, computer games (but not software), movies, operas, plays, poems, TV programs, lectures, speeches, and works of art. AP style does not place quotation marks around names of newspapers, magazines, the Bible, and books that are primarily for reference—catalogs, almanacs, directories, dictionaries, encyclopedias, gazetteers, handbooks.

Writers are responsible for making sure their stories are as accurate as possible both in terms of facts and in terms of the publication's style. However, once the writer has finished, the story goes to a copyeditor for further checking. The role of the copyeditor will be considered in Chapter 17. Your instructor may ask you to refer to parts of that chapter in preparing your stories for evaluation.

"Good writing is rewriting," said Truman Capote, author of In Cold Blood. *In these four words, Capote expresses the core advice for all writers. The techniques in this chapter— including principles of sensitivity, consistency, and good writing—give you a variety of tools to improve your own stories stylistically. The better each individual story in your publication is, the more credibility each staff member will have and the more credibility your publication will have overall. Memorizing specific style rules, knowing as much as you can about your school, and knowing as much as you can about effective written communication in general will go a long way toward achieving the goal of producing the best, most credible publication possible. After all, isn't that what it's all about?*

Journalism

clichés—phrases so overused they have become meaningless.

gender neutral language—point of view in writing that does not designate or suggest male or female roles unless relevant to the story's context.

homonyms—words that sound alike but are spelled differently and have different meanings.

jargon—inside vocabulary of a specific group; avoid using unless translated in the story.

nonsexist language—word choice that does not contain gender stereotyping.

redundancy—unnecessary repetition of an idea.

style—way a story is crafted for the print or broadcast media; the specific rules journalists follow generally for their own publication or broadcast medium for consistency in capitalization, spelling, punctuation, names, identifications, time, dates, usage, and even design.

stylebook (style manual)—collection of rules for a given staff to follow for consistency in capitalization, spelling, punctuation, names, identifications, time, dates, usage, and even design.

CHAPTER 10

Features

In this chapter, you will learn:

- how feature writing compares to newswriting and other aspects of journalism
- about the four types of feature stories
- how to organize your material to write a feature story

Many journalists thrive on the reporting end of their jobs, while many others thrive on the writing, or creative, aspects. Members of the "reporting club" love to be on the street, talking to people and gathering information. Those in the "creative club" enjoy taking that information and putting it into a tight, thoughtful article. Both aspects of journalism make important contributions to their news organizations, and both kinds of journalists are necessary for a newspaper to succeed. Of course, plenty of journalists love both reporting and writing. And what is one of the worthwhile results? Feature stories reflect the marriage of thorough reporting and good writing.

How Are Features Similar and Different?

Feature writers have more flexibility, and they are allotted more creativity than are hard-news reporters. However, accuracy and objectivity still apply.

Feature writing *is:*

* Interesting—and worth reading on its own merit.
* Well researched and reported.
* Professional—journalistic rules for language and style apply (see Chapter 9).

Feature writing is *not*:

* Promotion—especially if the feature concerns a profit-making enterprise.
* "Puff" or "softball"—readers grow suspicious when an article seems too soft and vague.

Types of Features

There are at least **four** types of feature stories: news, informative, profiles and human interest, and personal experience and accomplishment stories.

❶ News Features

Hard-news stories often lend themselves to related feature stories. When a feature writer pegs a story to a prominent news event, the writer may explore facets of the news story that otherwise would go unnoticed. (Read more about news pegs in Chapter 8.)

Say your town is seeing a rush of young soldiers off on a peacekeeping mission overseas. The hard news—the deployment of troops for a military action—may be accompanied by features indicating:

* How the mobilization will affect the families of soldiers
* What an individual soldier or family is experiencing
* What kind of training a typical soldier goes through
* How the army reserves are involved
* How local businesses often lose revenue when large numbers of people leave a community
* What kinds of technology assist the troops when they see combat

Hard-news events in national news routinely trigger features. Why, then, don't more features appear in newspapers? The answer is not because feature ideas have been exhausted but because newspapers lack the space to run such stories and writers lack the time to prepare them.

A good feature writer can consider a prominent news event and quickly come up with at least 10 possible feature stories. To evaluate each idea, consider these **four** criteria:

1. How important is the concept—will readers care?
2. How much time will be involved in researching and writing?
3. How much space will be available in the paper for it?
4. What kind of effect might the story have on readers or on the school?

Those features with the most impact are written first, followed by those containing other news values, such as proximity, timeliness, unusualness, currency, and prominence.

Sometimes, you may acquire information about a subject but do not have enough material to compose an entire article. In this case, you can create a brief sidebar to accompany a larger story. If the article is about how local businesses lose money when soldiers leave the base, a sidebar might address one merchant and how he or she is dealing with the deployment. (Chapter 8, *In-Depth Reporting*, covers sidebars in detail.) This book, too, uses sidebars to address relevant but slightly tangential topics.

❷ Informative Features

Informative features can focus on many subjects, from the latest in high school crime rates to identifying the best economy car. The key, of course, is *sound research*.

Make It Useful

When you pick up a newspaper, what common feature types do you notice? One major topic is health awareness; papers are saturated with stories about health risks, health maintenance, and trends in fitness. When well researched, these stories fulfill a key purpose of features—they *provide useful information* to readers who may not realize, for example, that prostate cancer in men has become pervasive or that AIDS continues to take thousands of lives despite the "drug cocktails" that have assisted those infected with HIV.

Newspaper readers seek information, and the best features present that information in an honest, efficient manner.

Some Traps to Avoid

Factual errors can lead to credibility problems and the omission of important information. What are some possible traps? Any feature discussing a consumer product should take as objective an approach as possible. Readers must not be led to view the article as an advertisement under the guise of a legitimate story. There are also plenty of legal and ethical questions. Libel can be a serious issue, so review the issues surrounding libel in Chapter 2 again.

Informative Feature

A Contrast lead in first sentence flows nicely into news peg in second sentence. Peg gives a logical reason for using the story in this edition.

B Explanation of the new club called Dimensions and its origins highlights story as an informative feature.

Model

New club works toward eliminating oppression and hate

by **Jen Hammer**, News and Features Editor

Diversity, intolerance and equality are not the typical topics of conversation among Pottsville high school students. Then again, attending a Ku Klux Klan rally on a Saturday afternoon at the county courthouse is not a very common occurrence either. The announcement by the KKK that the group would venture to Pottsville to rally on the courthouse steps Saturday, September 26 sparked community activists to schedule an onslaught of activities for a Schuylkill County Unity Day. The activities planned for the day were intended to steer citizens, especially the youth, away from the rally and towards events promoting positive racial beliefs.

The Unity Day festivities served as the first project for a new club at PAHS, Dimensions. Guidance counselor Ms. Ellen King, founder and adviser of the club, got the idea for the Dimensions Club from the success of a similar student group at North Pocono High School, the Rainbows. The National Educators Association newspaper also printed an article on diversity clubs, which helped to provide guidance for the creation of Dimensions.

Approximately 60 members of the student body attended the first meeting of Dimensions.

"I was impressed by the turnout, which shows that there is an interest to try to work towards positive and peaceful ways of dealing with intolerance," Ms. King said.

continues ▶

Informative Feature *(continued)*

C Body of the story develops more details about Dimensions' size, goals, and operations.

D Quotes support the information and add opinion about the club.

Model

Officers will be elected at next week's meeting, and the club is still accepting new members for anyone who is interested.

The goals of Dimensions include promoting diversity and equality in the student body and the community, and educating students about diversity. The concept of "zero tolerance" against violence, including fighting and all forms of harassment, is one of the key beliefs of the group. Sometime during the school year, the club hopes to sponsor a motivational speaker or a play for the entire student body promoting diversity.

"By creating a diversity club at PAHS, I think it will eliminate a lot of prejudicial and racial issues toward high school students, and help bring our school into the new millennium," senior Rory Reaves said.

First and foremost, the club's main task is to raise money to support its activities. A bake sale, possibly at a local mall, a Christmas card sale and a car wash are possibilities that have been discussed in the short time that the club has been in existence.

The Unity Day pledge and distribution of purple ribbons in the cafeteria last month served only as the beginning of the long road towards diversity and equality in the student body.

"I hope students didn't just wear a ribbon because everyone else was wearing one, but because of the symbolic representation it had of their beliefs," Ms. King said.

Dimensions could be the answer to the task of dissolving racial tensions.

Source: Pottsville Area High School, Pottsville, Penn., *Tide Lines*, October 15, 1998.

E Would the final paragraph be better as a direct quote from someone to avoid editorializing?

❸ Profiles and Human Interest Features

Because people are inherently interested in the lives of those around them, one of the most popular features is the *profile*. As Chapter 5 discussed, a profile typically focuses on someone who has made a notable impact on the lives of others, someone from the community who has become unusually prominent, or simply someone with a unique hobby or talent.

Profiles and human interest stories are popular among newspaper readers because of their focus on individuals. By recounting stories about people, feature writers can uplift, inspire, and motivate readers.

Profiles are fun to read—a good profile can organize a great deal of information in a lively, interesting package. Again, research must be scrupulously accurate. Here are some questions to ask yourself when writing a profile:

* Have basic biographical information and spelling been verified?
* What is it that makes the source particularly interesting?
* If interviewing a source on location, what is the atmosphere like?
* What props and objects are on hand?
* What do those closest to the source have to say?
* Where has this person, the source, lived or spent time?
* Has the person been profiled in other publications, and if so, did any interesting facts emerge?
* What does the person plan to do in the future?
* Has the person had to overcome any sort of adversity in life? If so, what?

"Backed by 'brothers'" on the next page is a strong example of a high school newspaper profile.

The Profile

A The lead sets the scene and puts Brandon in an environment, although we aren't quite sure what the angle is yet.

Model

Backed by 'brothers'

by Lauren Roederer

Walking down the halls, he hears shouts of "Hey B!" The same sound is audible at the Carmel Ice Skadium as the Ice Hounds skate past him. With a smile, Brandon Hudson, special services student, manager of the varsity hockey team and junior, waves and shouts back.

"Brandon would always watch the Carmel A and B team practice, and one day a couple years ago, one of the players told Brandon if he came to the game, he would bring him home. From then on, he'd go to the games," Mrs. Teresa Hudson, Brandon's mother, said.

Mr. Peter Driscoll, head varsity hockey coach, said, "He started coming to the games and ended up being here all the time, so this year, we made him team manager. The kids had talked about it. I think all the kids decided that was the thing to do. Every year, somebody seems to take over [taking care of Brandon], this year it's the whole bunch of them. It's great because it does something for Brandon, and it does something for these kids, too."

After winning the league championship two years ago, the hockey team invited Brandon to celebrate with them. "We gave him a medal (which the players also received), and it really meant a lot to him," Driscoll said. "We've carried on from there and wanted him to be a part of the team and a part of the organization."

At the end of that season, the coaches invited Brandon to the team's banquet at the Ritz Charles. "[The coaches] gave him a shirt with all the players' names on it that all the players got too, and then they gave him a hockey letter for a jacket as if he had participated in that sport," Mrs. Hudson, said. "He had to get up and give a speech, and he got a standing ovation."

B Quotes from others—his mother, the coach, hockey players—broadens our impression and enriches the detail.

Hudson said, "[Receiving the letter] was cool. I was really happy and excited [about going to the banquet]. [Giving the speech] felt good, but I wanted to get it over with. It was like giving a speech at school."

Mrs. Hudson said, "None of this really impresses him. He just kind of goes with the flow. I think it means more to him than he lets on."

Adam Knott, varsity hockey player and junior said, "I think that [after he received the letter], he was smiling for about an hour straight. He was happy. Everyone was happy for him."

Although Brandon's official title is manager, he doesn't perform all the tasks that might normally be associated with that job. "He really doesn't have any duties," Driscoll said. "It's more of an honorary thing. I don't know if he could fully commit to it. He's here all the time, and I think his Number-1 job is just to be here and just to be who he is.

"He comes to all our games at home, and he's here at just about every practice after school. He gets the guys drinks and just kind of helps them out, and in return they show him great respect."

Brandon said, "I just chill with the hockey players. It's real fun. It's like a family, I guess. [The hockey team] is like a group of brothers."

Knott said, "I consider him a friend. It's kind of cool that somebody wants to come and be part of the team even though he can't play. He's more than a fan. He feels like part of the team. He's always happy. I don't think I've ever seen him sad or upset about anything. I think it cheers us up if we're having a rough game."

Driscoll said, "I think that for Brandon to be here, it makes the kids feel good inside, and I know it does for Brandon; it makes Brandon feel great to be able to hang around with the

continues ▶

The Profile *(continued)*

C We aren't sure Brandon is mentally handicapped until nearly the end of the story when his mother discusses it. The mild suspense is effective.

Model

players and the coaches. His relationship [with the team] is close. He can go up to any one of those guys, and they'll stop and give him the time of day, no matter what. In certain situations, that doesn't always happen for guys like Brandon, but they give him the time of day.

"I've never seen one of them turn him away.

"[To have Brandon around] gave me a respect for the kids on the team. [The coaches] respect the kids on the hockey club when they reach out to a guy like Brandon and make him part of their group when they don't have to. It makes you feel better inside. It showed me that these kids aren't just hockey players—they're people."

Overcoming obstacles

Mrs. Hudson said, "Mildly mentally retarded is his title, and we were always kind of worried that kids would make fun of him. We have three other boys (Gavin and Garrett, 13 and Nolan, 8), and they're so involved in sports. We've always had him in sports, but my husband and I were always under the impression from what other people had told us that the older he got, the worse things would get.

"We thought maybe he'd be an outcast and do nothing, and so it really means a lot to us how accepted he is and how genuine it is. That isn't the norm, but I think with his personality, he knows no stranger."

Driscoll said, "I don't think it takes a lot to keep Brandon happy, and for him to be involved with our organization the way he is, it really does something for him. I don't know how to explain it, but I know it does a lot for him, and it does a lot for us to have him around.

"He's a good inspiration. He's there whether we win or lose. It's an opportunity for him to be involved with a team that he normally wouldn't be involved in. I'd say it's an all around good situation for everyone. It does something for Brandon, and it really does something for those kids, more than they know it. It teaches them to respect people."

Source: Carmel High School, Carmel, Ind., *HiLite*, December 17, 1998.

D Numerous direct quotes let the reader figure out gradually what's going on. It's a sensitive way to handle the story.

❹ Personal Experience and Accomplishment Features

Drawing on the journalist's personal experience, these stories address many subjects, from injuries and adversity to personal triumphs and professional rewards. One article might chronicle a week in an abusive household, while another might focus on a serious injury and how it was overcome. Journalists have chronicled their travels to exotic locales and written of turning points in their lives, all the while informing and inspiring readers.

Here are **three** related ideas to consider with personal experience features:

1. **Modesty.** You as the writer must pay special attention to staying modest. An "I-did-this-and-I-did-that" approach tends to bore readers and makes the writer seem boastful and dull.

2. **Newsworthiness.** A strong personal experience story touches on something greater than the writer. It uncovers a subject readers identify with, placing them right "within" the story. People have experiences every day—so what? To be worth a feature, to be worth the involvement of readers, a story needs to be unusual or compelling.

3. **Honesty.** When you are writing about something that happened to you, remember that readers appreciate honesty from a writer. Above all else, tell the truth.

Feature Writer Steve Lynch

"Over the past few years, I've been a stock-broker, an actor, a chemist—all through interviews and writing," says Steve Lynch, 26, feature writer for the *Orange County Register* in Santa Ana, Calif. "Some people find comfort in a regular beat, getting very in-depth. Me, I prefer variety."

Lynch gets that variety by covering pop culture at the *Register*, where "I'm expected to write about trends, cultural issues, and entertainment, with an eye on the younger generation," he explains. "I wrote recently about how Generation X refuses to grow up and is playing video games in their 30s. I went naked to a nudist colony; mulled over the return of professional wrestling; talked about whether, by limiting children with zero-tolerance laws and curfews, we're taking away childhood."

Lynch generates his own story ideas. "My editor is a great brainstormer, though, and we often begin the week throwing out things that are happening in the world," he says. He writes about one story a week—"they're usually longer pieces, 50-80 column inches"—and does occasional concert or band reviews as part of his pop culture coverage.

Like many feature writers, Lynch came into his specialty through a long apprenticeship in news. He wrote for his school newspaper at Thomas Jefferson High School in Bloomington, Minn., where he decided he wanted to be a journalist. In college at Northwestern University, he spent most of his time at the campus newspaper, ending as editor-in-chief his final year.

The summer following his sophomore year at college, Lynch snagged two internships in the Twin Cities, a paid one at a broadcast news organization and an unpaid one at the *Twin Cities Reader,* an alternative weekly. "I learned to hate TV news that summer," he says, "but the *Reader* was the job I credit with any success I have today."

His editor would assign Lynch a story way above his head, then push him toward sources. " 'Why didn't you ask this question?' he'd demand. 'Why didn't you talk to this guy? Don't snivel, write!'"

It paid off. "At the *Reader* I learned to write long researched copy with attitude," Lynch says. For one story he followed a chief judge around for a month and wrote a piece about how the judge's courtroom dealt with the growth of crime and over-crowding of jails in Minnesota. That story won first prize in the in-depth category in the Hearst Awards Competition, the "Pulitzer Prize" awards for college journalists. As a first-prize winner, Lynch was eligible to compete for the Hearst sweepstakes award in San Francisco, where he won the national championship.

On his next internship Lynch worked at the *Orange County Register* during his junior year and returned there the following summer as a general assignment reporter. "I was there to fill in the gaps, and in 1994 the gap was computers," he says. "So I was able to pitch stories about a strange thing called *America Online* and CD-ROMs called *Myst.*"

After his graduation a year later, the *Register* hired Lynch to start a new beat—cyberspace reporter. "It was my good fortune to arrive the year the World Wide Web and Windows 95 captured the imagination, and Netscape captured one of the largest stock market premieres on record," he says. "I wrote for a weekly technology section the paper started and threw stories to as many other parts of the paper as I could."

After Lynch covered cyberspace for two years, the *Register* began a new Saturday feature section, and he transferred to that.

"The section was light and fluffy—fun but cotton candy," he says. "But it was a change of pace and a way to build up a supply of clips that showed range."

A year later, again ready for something new, Lynch took a job in Hungary as a technology reporter for the *Budapest Business Journal.* "I'd always dreamed of being a foreign correspondent," he says. "I traveled to as many places as I could, covered the war in Kosovo peripherally, and realized that being a foreign correspondent isn't all it's cracked up to be. Perhaps someday I'll go back overseas, but hopefully on my own terms."

So Lynch returned to the *Register*, this time as a full-time feature writer, "the job I was working up to, and I enjoy it immensely," he says.

Advice for high school journalists? "Supreme arrogance is often an asset in this business. You have to be willing to barge right into offices and ask a million questions and call up the family whose son has just been arrested for making crack. And it's a job you learn by doing. 'Work for your school paper' is the best advice any journalism professor can give. In other words, if you want to be a journalist, be a journalist. What will matter in the long term is how well you write, and that only comes from practice."

Organizing Material

Defining a subject, identifying a message, deciding how to present your message, putting the story together, and finishing the story are the **five** steps to creating the feature article.

❶ Define a Subject

One thousand words—that's the average length of a newspaper feature. How do you narrow a topic down to that length? Beginning writers sometimes experience difficulty in focusing on a subject clearly enough to cover it sufficiently in only one thousand words. Consider, for example, the following topics:

* The U.S. Army
* Major league baseball
* The music industry
* Hollywood
* Government

Clearly, each topic above is much too broad for one feature story. But look what happens when each topic is broken down for one story.

* How a one-year tour of duty changed the life of a person just 14 months out of high school
* How quickly fans returned to baseball following the last strike
* How band producers are organizing free concerts to end hunger

* How the politicization of AIDS by the Hollywood community has increased awareness of the disease among teenagers
* How major contributors to a local congressional campaign may have affected a voting decision in the U.S. House of Representatives

These topics are much more specific and allow for precise investigations. Readers come away with increased knowledge about one aspect of a subject instead of having to search for meaning in an extremely broad article.

❷ Identify a Message

While feature stories should not be saturated with opinion, a writer does need to consider the message he or she wishes to convey.

Find It Through Research

Research—be it interviewing, investigating documents, or simply observing—is the key to identifying an underlying message. When you research a subject thoroughly, you may be surprised how a message often emerges as the article comes together. It's almost like it "reveals itself" to you. Thorough research brings on a true feel for a subject. You may find that your "gut feelings" are good ones.

In contrast, when your research is lacking, you often leave important questions unanswered. Readers ultimately question whether you really know what you're writing about.

Be Flexible

Let's say your research reveals that a successful basketball coach has a history of verbally abusing his players in private; a feature story about him may be less than glowing. Perhaps you quickly find that there are many aspects to this story.

* Are you obligated to point out the coach's shortcomings?
* Does his behavior hurt the morale of the team?
* Worse, has it hurt individual players?
* Or is the coach's behavior within the realm of motivation?
* Do players understand that he really cares for their well-being under his gruff exterior?
* What's the line between motivation and abuse?
* What's going to be your message out of all of this?

To answer many of these questions, you need to go past rumor and into the stories of the players as well as the coach. What they think and feel about the coach is at the heart of the story. Did you know you'd have to go this far when you started out? The moral of the story: Be prepared, be open, and be ready to go in another direction as you research your feature stories.

❸ Present Your Message

How do you develop and present a cohesive theme for your message?

Let's say you are assigned to profile a local millionaire and real estate tycoon. In recent years, this person has donated thousands of dollars to your high school,

helping to build a new gym and several classrooms. But he was not always that generous. In his early years, he would have scoffed at the notion of giving money away, wondering what kind of person could be so foolish. Something about him changed a few years back .

Does this sound familiar?

Yes, the character is similar to Scrooge, the cantankerous old man from *A Christmas Carol* by Charles Dickens. Just as Scrooge changed as he visited with the ghosts of Christmas Past, Present, and Future, this old man may have experienced a profound moment in his life that caused him to share his wealth with those around him. What theme or concepts will you emphasize in your story? You might want the ideas of "change," "growth," or "a fresh start" to underlie your story.

You could do this through several approaches:

* Start by describing the Scrooge-like personality of the subject before his transformation.
* Use a neutral tone as you build up to revealing the subject's contributions. Guide the reader from a description of an ordinary rich person to someone who has given tremendous amounts of money back to the community.
* Keep it uplifting for readers. Remember what you like to read. Wouldn't you rather read about those who give, as opposed to those who take?
* Alternatively, you could flip this approach around, beginning by describing your character's recent donations.

Then show how, in the past, the money for the gym and classrooms would not have been available. While the reader might be perplexed for a moment, when he or she gets wind of the experiences that profoundly changed this wealthy person, your story will hit the right note. In fact, a profile is often about the changes a person experiences in life; human change and resolution of conflict are central to almost any story.

❹ Steps to Putting It Together

The best feature writers blend their creative talent with traditional journalistic standards of objectivity, accuracy, and fairness.

Read Up on Your Subject

When first assigned a feature story, explore what, if anything, has been written about the person, place, or thing. If a story on the subject already exists, check it out. What kind of perspective does this story take? Is there anything in it that's quote-worthy?

On the high school and local levels, you can explore a newspaper morgue and ask veterans of the area about the topic. Reporters for professional daily papers have access to **databases** such as Nexis, Totalnews.com and Newspapers.com. They can plug in a key term and thousands of articles are scanned for them in seconds. Subscriptions to these database research services are quite expensive. See Chapter 4 for more information on the kinds of research you as a high school journalist can easily do.

Contact the Main Characters

Once you've completed the initial research, contact the people most central to the story. If, for example, the story addresses the financial costs of athletics versus other extracurricular activities, talk to the athletic director, the speech or forensics director, the school principal, and one or two student leaders. By conducting careful interviews with each source, you'll see patterns emerge. Ask for written documents outlining costs. Check the statements of each source against the statements of others. What contrasts emerge? This "meat and potatoes" research can generate a wealth of information, and from it, some central issues will surface.

Prepare an Outline

After key issues have been identified, construct a rough outline of the story. Of course, the most pressing issues will drive the story, but what information will help fill in the cracks and make the story as complete as possible? Consider the following **three** questions:

1. How will the story begin and how will it build?
2. Are facts present that facilitate writing the story a certain way?
3. What significant changes has the subject experienced?

Use Strong Quotes

Strong quotes are an integral part of a good feature story. If a source says something controversial, sensitive, or highly insightful, put it to use in a quote where you can. A good quote adds punch to the story and lets the reader know that an issue really does exist. In a standard newspaper feature story, five to seven quotes can turn a dull piece into a compelling article. The key is to use the most striking and insightful quotes.

Tell a Good Story

Good feature writing, ultimately, is about good storytelling. The writer provides a comfortable narrative, using facts, quotes, and observations to craft a compelling tale.

The piece should flow from one paragraph to the next and not wander aimlessly. Again, rely on your outline to determine where to begin, where to go with it, and where to end your story.

❺ Finish It Up

After you complete the first draft of an article, let it sit overnight before you proof or "polish" it. Hard-news reporters couldn't hope for such a luxury, but feature writers can usually get away with some delay.

Checklist

How to Polish

Some tips for putting the final touches on a feature story:

- ✓ *Always wait a day,* if possible.
- ✓ *Edit a hard copy* of the story; it will look different than it does on the computer monitor.
- ✓ *Check the overall structure* of the story. Have the key issues been covered?
- ✓ *Check the lead.* Is it descriptive and enticing, keeping the reader interested?
- ✓ *Always check spelling and grammar* and double-check proper nouns.
- ✓ *Check the word count* to make sure the story fits within the space allotted.
- ✓ *Review the story for consistency in tone.* Does it flow?

- ✓ *Comb the article and remove unnecessary words.*
- ✓ *Make sure nouns and verbs tell the story.* Avoid "flowery" adjectives and adverbs, which slow down the reader and put you, the writer, in the article.
- ✓ *Verify* all factual assertions.
- ✓ *Check quotes* for accuracy. Do they reflect what the source said, and do they reflect the context in which he or she said it?
- ✓ *Make sure the quotes selected are those most central to the topic at hand.*
- ✓ *Check the article* for potentially libelous remarks.
- ✓ *Check the ending.* Does it leave the reader with something to think about?

Feature writers have flexibility because features have an element of timelessness that news reports do not. Feature stories often are pegged to a news event—features appear adjacent to news stories. News features, informative features, profiles and human interest features, and stories of personal accomplishment are four types of feature writing. As a feature writer, you still have to define a subject, identify a message, and present the message to the audience. Do careful research before you begin to write and be sure to sketch a rough outline of the story. Once done, let it sit for a day if you can. Go over it again to polish it, not only correcting errors but making sure you've told a truly interesting, useful, and ethical story.

Journalism

WORDS TO KNOW

active verb—a verb unaccompanied by a "to be" verb. Active: "Rick wrote the story." Passive: "The story was written by Rick." Passive verbs obscure the "doer" of an action.

database—in journalism, an electronic system that indexes and manages articles from academic journals and the popular press.

hook—a piece of information that attracts and keeps the reader interested.

Editorials

While great orators make their points using the spoken word, newspaper opinion writers use the editorial page to advance an argument or discuss important issues of the day. Editorialists play a major role in stimulating debate and discussion. The high school editorialist, in particular, can raise issues that concern students and heighten awareness among faculty and administrators. He or she has the power to change attitudes—and even policies.

Types of Editorials

The opinions of journalists are usually presented on a single editorial page. **Three** common types of editorials are interpretation, criticism and persuasion, and entertainment. In high school papers, the staff-written editorial is a powerful journalistic tool and can be interpretive, persuasive, or entertaining.

❶ Interpretation

By taking a complex topic, breaking it down, and crafting a coherent editorial, writers provide a valuable service to readers.

Say, for instance, your school's administrator has decided to decrease the number of student parking spaces on campus. Lately there has been more overcrowding than ever, as well as a series of accidents and minor injuries. The new parking policy is complex, and students, even faculty, do not understand it. In an editorial of interpretation, you might ask:

* Why decrease space instead of increase it?
* Will there be alternative parking? Where? Who can use it?
* Will there be "anti-parking" incentives, such as discounted bus passes or vouchers?

By analyzing the policy and explaining what it really means, you, the editorialist, assist readers, your fellow students.

In another example, your school is about to add more computers for student use. As an opinion writer, you learn of the impending purchase and of the two proposals administrators are considering. Two computer companies have given school officials financial bids. One of the bids is far lower than the other, so it seems the decision will be an easy one—at least until you hear *why* one bid was much lower.

You discover that the company with the "best" deal wants to unload some units that will be antiquated within six months. While the school cannot afford to do business with the other firm—at least not for another semester, when funds may become available—you suspect that purchasing the less expensive units would be similar to buying a fancy car with no engine. You make a list of reasons to wait:

1. Software manufactured in the future may not work on the units for sale.

2. Warranties on the units are suspect because companies get rid of old parts to make room for the new.

3. It will be difficult to locate someone who can maintain computers with antiquated hardware.

4. The less expensive units will make it impossible for students to save documents at home and print them at school, creating headaches for everyone involved.

5. Computers cannot be sold "used" the way cars can. Once technology advances, older units become worthless, collecting more dust than beta tapes and typewriters.

With this list of arguments in your article, school administrators would have to take notice and consider your points. You have identified and interpreted a problem for your readers, and your work may prompt some action.

Chances are that you are not the only staff member with an opinion on issues that affect the entire school. It's important that you discuss important issues with the staff, adviser, and perhaps members of an **editorial board.** By creating an editorial board, you can evaluate the positions of editorialists and discuss how an issue will be written about on the editorial page.

❷ Criticism and Persuasion

In 1998 and 1999, editorialists expressed strong opinions about the private life of President Bill Clinton, just as they routinely do with volatile national issues such as gun control. These issues and many others generate emotion, and often the writers who address them have strong personal opinions. Most newspaper readers do not get upset when a columnist proposes that a local sales tax needs to be raised by one one-hundredth of one percent, but they may become very angry when a writer suggests that laws affecting students' freedom of speech either be made or amended.

Anytime an editorialist attempts to persuade readers about a sensitive issue, the writer can expect a vocal response from the opposing camp. Not everyone sees the world the same way.

Persuasive Editorial

A The writer's byline makes it clear that this is her opinion, not that of the newspaper.

B This opinion piece presents a strong case for the continuation of affirmative action.

Model

Seeing beyond black and white

by Miriam Armendariz, Opinion Assistant

At our age, we all know that racial discrimination is a big no-no. Because bigots are mainly thought of as being Caucasian, many think that only Caucasians can discriminate against minorities.

Caucasians are being discriminated against, but we never hear about it. There's the occasional white trash joke, but nothing very serious. Looking through books on discrimination, there's no chapter called "Caucasian, discrimination against," perhaps because it doesn't happen often and hasn't had the long history of lynchings, slavery, and abuse. Whites have always gotten the jobs, the money, and the respect, so any discrimination is minor.

But it is the 90s, and many Caucasians are screaming "Racism!" because suddenly they aren't getting all of the opportunities as quickly as before, because first priority to many scholarships and college admittance privileges go to minority students.

Affirmative action guarantees that minorities have an equal chance against Caucasians. Colleges and universities are no exception. Many have tried to do the right thing by accepting more minorities. College admissions officers may even choose minorities over Caucasians, even if they are both equally qualified.

In the case of the University of Michigan at Ann Arbor, African-Americans and Hispanic-Americans have a greater chance of getting in than a Caucasian if they are both middle rank in academics and standardized testing results. This alone has angered many people to the point of lawsuits going all the way to the

C The writer offers plenty of background in support of her opinion.

D The editorial closes with several strong, impassioned statements.

Supreme Court. But this is not the first time a Caucasian has felt discriminated against and gone public with it.

It started perhaps 20 years ago, about the time that minorities were becoming acknowledged as Americans. This was the first time minorities were allowed an ounce of hope that they were going to get an equal chance, that they were not going to be turned away because they had dark skin, different hair or almond-shaped eyes. As time has passed, minorities have had more opportunities. There are Asian-American sport heroes, Hispanic-American college students, African-American celebrities and Native American bank presidents. For once, there are rules that make bigots stop their prejudiced ways.

Minorities, however, are still being discriminated against. Whenever they are allowed the smallest advantage, they get pulled back because people complain of reverse discrimination, as if minorities have never been oppressed because of their race, as if they have never felt the hate and hurt of discrimination.

Yet when thousands of undocumented immigrants from another country are enslaved to work for mere dollars a day, nobody cares.

Minorities today are nowhere near where they would like to be and without laws like affirmative action, there is no way they can be.

Minorities who have suffered so much need small things like this now to help them achieve their goals.

Caucasians have had so many opportunities for so many years, now it is time for minorities to claim their share of the pie.

Source: South Eugene High School, Eugene, Ore., *The Axe*, January 22, 1999.

E The newspaper is obliged to publish letters to the editor from writers who want to comment on the writer's premise.

Interpretive Editorials

A Note the headline error: Should be "Are the media taking their rights . . ."

B The forum approach—sometimes called point/counterpoint—gives equal space to both sides of the question.

Model

Is the media taking its rights under the first amendment too far?

PRO—by Jason Moser, Editor-in-Chief

In 1789, the United States Constitution, perhaps this country's single most important document, laid forth the ground rules that have been followed ever since.

In the first addition to this document, or as it is aptly called, the First Amendment, the founding fathers laid down five specific freedoms. One of these was the freedom of the press. This freedom, as it should be clear, granted that the press was free to print what it wanted as long as it doesn't involve slander or libel. This means a news story cannot publicly demean a person intentionally. Before this amendment was ratified, that wasn't the case.

In recent years, the press has been bashed for reporting too much and digging too much. There is no better example than the Princess Diana car accident. The paparazzi (a group of independent photo journalists who chase after famous people to take photographs for profit) were blamed for her accident. Shortly thereafter it was said that the press has too much freedom. But does it really?

If the paparazzi caused the accident from which Princess Diana would later die, then they are guilty of specific crimes. They are not, however, guilty of abusing their freedom. In order to abuse their freedom, the press would have to slander someone. For example, they'd have to print "Mr. X is a lousy, no good disgrace to civilization." That is intentional destruction of a person's name and reputation. It's illegal and it's an example of abuse of freedom of the press.

Now the people are faced with the Clinton scandal and how he has stated over and over again that this matter is private between him, his family and Monica Lewinsky and that the press is infringing on his right to privacy, thus abusing their freedom. This is one of the biggest arguments for people who say the press has too much freedom. This isn't a bad point but had it been held in as high regard by the founding fathers as so many people try to hold it today, there would be six freedoms granted to the people in the First Amendment, rather than five. Freedom of the press has been deemed much more important than the freedom to absolute privacy.

People who break the law are not free to a private trial because there's this little thing which says that all criminal proceedings are public matters because crimes are not committed against a single person but they are, rather, committed against society (civil cases are for one-on-one confrontations, in criminal trials the defendant is charged with crimes against society).

With this new light shed, it is clearly seen that the press is simply reporting facts and information to the members of society that may have missed a thing or two. The press is not abusing its freedom by reporting facts and that's what people must remember. No matter how insignificant or how much a person doesn't want to hear it, the press can report it.

That isn't to say the press HAS to report everything that it does but rather that it is within the legal guidelines set forth by the Constitution that what they report is done so legally.

continues ▶

X 76007

Interpretive Editorials

(continued)

C Both writers are identified, implying that the opinions are theirs, not the newspaper's. The effect is one of neutrality.

Model

CON—by Barry Weiss, Editor-in-Chief

When people feel that they are victims, and that it is necessary to resort to violence or other unacceptable actions, something is wrong.

In our country, certain rights are promised to the press by the Constitution. Members of the different media have a freedom to obtain the truth and to report it to the people. But just how far can these messengers go to uncover such facts?

Last month, Luzerne County Police Commissioner Frank Crossin was arrested for driving under the influence of alcohol. The press jumped on the opportunity to report the truth, and everything it entailed. They interviewed people of the area, police officers, and of course, hounded the commish himself. Now,

how much can one man take? How much does this news have to be repeated until it is not news anymore?

Apparently, the line was crossed by the press, and the commissioner felt that he had been the victim of all this "truth-seeking" long enough. About two weeks after his incident, the commissioner was leaving a press conference when a reporter felt inclined to continue on with old news. The commissioner was fed up and attacked the reporter, shoving him onto a chair. They pressed too hard.

Of course, the topic of our nation's most recent scandal must be discussed. Yes, our President lied. Yes, he withheld evidence. Yes, he cracked when placed under pressure. But it was our beloved press who drove Mr. Clinton into the ground. The press decided the nation

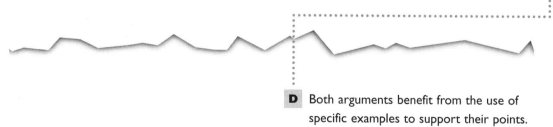

D Both arguments benefit from the use of specific examples to support their points.

should know the truth, that the President was involved in a sexual affair.

However, they didn't stop there. The media reported what the people wanted to know, not what they needed to know. Newspapers turned into tabloids as the purpose of journalism was no longer to inform, but to entertain and sell papers. Our fearless leader's integrity was crippled all because the press, in its frenzied blindness, took a freedom and not only took advantage of it, but abused it.

The early years of our country, the era of the Constitution, brought forth some wonderful rights for which Americans had only dreamed when they had broad restrictions under their former British monarchy. The press was included in all this, as without such a means of communication the masses would be gravely uninformed. However, when other free constituents believe that the press is invading their privacy, something must be done.

Due to separate interpretations of the Constitution, this country is faced with a paradox. While the press is guaranteed the right to report the truth, the people are granted freedom to privacy. A line must be drawn between how deep the press can dig and how far into darkness Americans can recede. This demarcation should result in a comfortable equilibrium where the different media can know that their rights are intact, while the people can rest easy knowing their privacy remains private. Right now, the press is crowding the line, and because of this, some people feel violated.

Source: Pottsville Area High School, Pottsville, Penn., *Tide Lines*, October 15, 1998.

E Both writers finish with strong restatements of their premise.

❸ Entertainment

Some of the best opinion writers use humor to make a point. Molly Ivins of the *Ft. Worth Star Telegram*, for example, has written so many humor columns that she's been able to compile many of them into best-selling books. Funnier than most comedians, Ivins speaks her mind, but does not offend. Ivins has the ability to reach readers who disagree with her political ideology, primarily because she avoids the militant tone common to some opinion writing.

Another strategy for entertainment writing—or any type of editorial writing, for that matter—is the use of numbers or lists. Comedian David Letterman became famous for his "top-ten" lists, and editorialists, to some extent, have followed suit. Lists can be quite compelling when the writer gets the facts straight and organizes them in a logical manner. The example earlier in this chapter about a school's computer purchase uses a list to make a point.

The Staff Editorial

One of the most controversial pieces on the **editorial page** is the staff, or staff-written, editorial. The assertions in this type of editorial are meant to represent the newspaper as a whole, even though everyone at the newspaper may not agree.

For example, in the gun-control debate after the tragic shootings at Columbine High School, many newspapers across America suggested stricter gun-control laws for the betterment of the country. While not everyone employed by those newspapers would have agreed, the "company line" nevertheless prevailed. Individuals who supported the rights of citizens to own and carry firearms had to do so privately.

The staff editorial does not contain a byline and often contains a first-person, plural voice (for example, "We feel that it is wrong to increase the local sales tax"). Those mentioned on the editorial page **masthead** assume responsibility for these editorials.

The model on the next page is a good example of this type of editorial. A staff of 30 takes on the administration on the issue of mandatory expulsions for weapons possession at school. Do you agree?

A Staff Editorial

A Note the clever headline— the double meaning of the word *automatic*.

Model

Weapons expulsions shouldn't be automatic

Another day, another recommendation for expulsion.

Bringing a knife to school results in an automatic 10-day suspension, and a mandatory recommendation for expulsion. Same goes for any other weapon. Sounds normal, right?

Not always.

Anisha Greene, a freshman at Lake Braddock Secondary School, accidentally brought a knife to school, according to her mother. A sexual assault had occurred in the area where Greene lives, so she carries a knife for protection while going to and coming back from work.

One morning, she forgot to take it out of her jacket. She realized this during an assembly, and did what she thought was the right thing: She turned it in to a principal.

For doing the right thing, Greene received a 10-day suspension, and an automatic recommendation for expulsion.

Greene isn't alone. Earlier in the school year, a nine-year-old brought a green toy gun to a Loudoun County school–he was recommended for expulsion. At McLean High School last month, a senior accidentally left an unloaded pellet gun (that didn't work) in the back of his car–he was recommended for expulsion.

According to a 1995 state law, if a student brings a weapon to school, principals have to recommend that student for expulsion. Circumstances don't matter. It's mandatory.

continues ▶

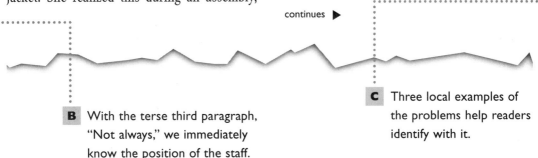

B With the terse third paragraph, "Not always," we immediately know the position of the staff.

C Three local examples of the problems help readers identify with it.

A Staff Editorial *(continued)*

D Paragraphs 8, 9, and 10 explain the drawback of the automatic expulsion rule and argue that expulsion should be handled on a case-by-case basis.

It's automatic. It's zero tolerance. Prior to 1995, Fairfax had its own policy that stated the possession of a gun would result in a recommendation for expulsion, but for first-time offenses, the punishment could be lessened.

When questions about cases such as these arise we revert back to the rule. Not "The student was deemed a danger to the population," but "Here's the rule, look at what it says, we have to follow it." Principals' hands are tied. They are prevented from using their own personal discretion—something for which they were hired. Violence in schools has become a hot-button issue in recent years, but these cases weren't *violent*.

A recommendation for expulsion is the first step in the most severe action that can be taken against a student. It should never be automatic. Each incident should be considered by administrators on an individual basis. Determining factors should be the student's intent, who or how many were hurt, in what way they were hurt, and the student's disciplinary record. Only using one factor—they brought a weapon to school—simply isn't enough. Students can be recommended for expulsion for actions that weren't intentional, and harmed no one.

A recommendation for expulsion should be just that: a principal's suggestion that a particular student should be expelled. But when the "recommendation" is automatic, a rule book is making that suggestion.

Source: Annandale High School, Annandale, Va., *The A-Blast*, March 26, 1999. Artwork by Christina Rodriguez.

E The last part of the editorial offers a solution: let the principal decide.

F Anonymous by definition, this staff editorial wisely included a box (not shown here) citing the staff vote so readers know how much in agreement the staff is.

G The artwork reinforces the message, saying visually what the editorial has said in words.

Writing the Editorial

In an effective editorial the writer uses documented, credible information to voice an informed opinion. The editorial is written in a way similar to newswriting.

Opinion writers sometimes make the mistake of using big words, figuring that readers will be impressed and consider the writer intelligent and credible. Usually, the opposite occurs. Readers get frustrated and move on to another article.

Just as a boring topic can cause readers to skip an editorial, so too can the writing style. It should be direct and should flow from sentence to sentence. Use varying sentence lengths to prevent the article from reading like a police report. Also, be sure to set a professional tone—not a patronizing, all-knowing one.

Ideally, the editorial will generate reaction from readers. Readers who respond to editorials are usually those with the most interest in the topic, and they can be quite passionate when it comes to voicing dissent. Every editorialist can tell of personal encounters with profanity, name-calling, and in some cases, threats of physical violence. After a while, it simply becomes part of the job, though beginning editorialists can feel "shell-shocked" by their first few letters. (See the On the Job profile on the next page.)

Ultimately, as long as you have checked and double-checked factual assertions and made sure the opinions you offered were reasonable and well conceived, you can consider offensive letters and personal insults little more than background noise.

As with newswriting, then, accuracy cannot be over-emphasized. Editorialists—and all who practice **subjective writing**—must get the facts straight.

Columnist/Political Writer Eric Stern

When the *Waterloo Courier* gets angry letters to the editor about its political column, Eric Stern hangs them above his desk.

"There's no bigger rush for me than motivating someone to think," says Stern, 25, who writes a political column every Sunday for the *Courier,* a 50,000-circulation afternoon paper in Iowa.

Stern began working at the *Courier* after graduating from college in 1997. He gathers ammunition for his column by reporting on the Iowa Legislature from Des Moines, the state capital, for four months every winter. He also covers statewide legislative and congressional elections and writes about Iowa's first-in-the-nation presidential caucuses, following the candidates on the campaign trail.

Because the national political press corps focuses so much attention on the early nominating states of Iowa and New Hampshire, Stern finds his column quoted regularly in Washington, D.C., political gossip newsletters. The self-promotional perks of column writing have also landed him seats on live-radio debate panels during the election season.

"Iowa may not be heaven, but this is my dream job," says Stern, who grew up in Mesa, Arizona, and aspires to write eventually for a major metropolitan newspaper.

Stern says he uses his weekly column to offer more insight into his daily nuts-and-bolts government news stories. His job "isn't to tell a farmer how to vote," he says, but to provide big-picture analysis and behind-the-scenes stories about politics in order to excite more people about government.

"The column also gives me a chance to use more voice in my writing by experimenting with expressive language in the tradition of H. L. Mencken and Hunter S. Thompson," Stern says.

Stern enjoys shaking up his readers, and the column has become a must-read for Iowa political junkies. "I like to catch a politician with his pants down," Stern says about his political point of view. "Or pull them down and run away pointing and laughing."

He also prides himself on following in the *Courier* mold of "cocky, upstart columnists." In 1908, recent Yale graduate Sinclair Lewis, who went on to win the Nobel Prize for Literature, was fired from the *Courier* after 10 weeks for writing editorials that clashed with the publisher's political ideology.

Stern began his journalism career in fourth grade when he wrote a letter to the

continues ▶

editor of his hometown newspaper, the *Arizona Republic,* about the national debt. He served as editor-in-chief of his junior high and high school newspapers and was a columnist and editorial page editor for his college daily newspaper.

Stern held several internships during college, including the *Arizona Capitol Times,* a weekly newspaper about state government; the *Tucson (Arizona) Citizen;* and the *Chicago Tribune,* where he worked for the editorial board, attending daily board meetings, writing editorials, and editing nationally syndicated columnists.

Checklist

How to Write Opinion

Eric Stern, political columnist for the *Waterloo (Iowa) Courier,* offers these tips:

☑ ***Don't use the word I.*** Your life is not interesting. Your personal experiences are tiresome. Using the first person also sounds preachy and righteous, which alienates readers. Strive for humility— your mug shot on the column should provide enough of an ego boost.

☑ ***Avoid sarcasm.*** The odds are you aren't very funny, despite what your lunch table says. Too much sarcasm comes off as immature and can ruin your credibility.

☑ ***The sky is not falling—don't exaggerate.*** It makes you seem too emotional and irrational. You can effectively motivate or inspire your readers without a call-to-arms hyperbole and three exclamation points.

☑ ***Challenge authority, not personality.*** Attacking the principal or the coach simply to generate letters to the editor is reckless. But attacking their ideas, policies, or actions is terrific fodder for a column.

☑ ***Don't put away your reporter's notebook—interview.*** It's obvious if you pull a 500-word column out of the air. A column is not a venue to spout off what you think about the issue of the day. So avoid clichéd topics. You are not going to convince someone to change their stance on abortion. Tell a story. Use quotes.

☑ ***Think big picture.*** Use the column to get into the gray analysis between the black and white. Compare apples and oranges.

The Editorial Page Also Contains . . .

Four other elements often share the editorial page: letters to the editor, political cartoons, a statement of editorial policy, and a paper's masthead.

❶ Letters to the Editor

Given the robust debate that many issues generate, it's important to give readers a chance to respond to editorials or to express an opinion about a separate matter. Sometimes the most insightful content on the editorial page appears in the letters section.

Thanks to e-mail, competition to get a letter published has increased dramatically. Because not all letters can be published, editors try to strike a balance and allot column space for all sides of an issue. If, for example, 20 readers write letters blasting over-complicated procedures for using the learning resource center, an editor might publish the one that really epitomizes the issue and is representative of the other letters.

Usually, the letters that get published contain well-reasoned arguments, are not vulgar, and do not contain potentially libelous assertions. Most editors expect letter writers to sign their messages and do not publish unsigned letters.

What policy does your publication have about editors' responses to letters? Who gets the last word?

❷ Cartoons

If a picture can speak a thousand words, can a cartoon? Certainly it can.

Sometimes, a political cartoon can make a powerful statement without containing a single word. In politics, for instance, Republicans are symbolized as elephants while Democrats are symbolized as donkeys. Naturally, political cartoonists and satirists pick up on these symbols, and they often use them to make statements about political issues.

As with satire, cartoons can have a bite, and not all readers will agree with what is presented. Political cartoons are quite personal, coming largely from the imagination of an artist, and the artist's ability to affect readers depends on cleverness, deadlines, and artistic ability.

❸ Statement of Editorial Policy

Readers need to know how an editorial page is assembled. A statement of editorial policy informs readers that letters to the editor are welcome, that space is limited, and that the newspaper reserves the right to edit letters for grammar and space. Readers then know what to expect if they decide to submit a letter.

In addition, editorial policies sometimes indicate that the opinions of columnists do not necessarily reflect the overall position

Political Cartoon

by Adam Howard

Source: South Eugene High School, Eugene, Ore., *The Axe*, January 22, 1999.

of the newspaper. Again, an idea, while vital to the marketplace, is just that: an idea. No idea is presumed to be the ultimate solution for all of the world's problems, but it can be an important contributor. See Chapter 2 for more on editorial policy statements and some samples.

❹ Masthead

The masthead is a box or short section that lists the publisher of the newspaper, the editor, and the editorial page editor. The masthead is important for credibility, as it informs readers how long the paper has been in existence and who founded it. It may be combined with the statement of editorial policy.

Free speech is central to a healthy society. A newspaper's editorial page facilitates the open exchange of ideas and debate that important issues require. Most editorials focus on interpretation, criticism, and entertainment; all are written in a manner consistent with newspaper style. In a high school paper, the editorial is less frequent but important. Good editorials make concise, thoughtful arguments and do not frustrate readers with complexity. Sometimes readers become so involved they respond with letters, and this response becomes an integral part of the process. The mission of the editorial page is to trigger an exchange of thoughtful opinions.

Journalism

editorial board—group of journalists who evaluate the positions of editorialists and decide how an issue will be discussed on the editorial page.

editorial page—part of the newspaper where the opinions of journalists and commentators appear.

masthead—lists the newspaper's publisher, the editor, and the editorial page editor; it is important for credibility, as it informs readers how old the paper is and who founded it.

subjective writing—opposite of objective reporting, this type of writing contains opinion.

Columns and Reviews

In this chapter, you will learn:

- **about personal or interpretive, humorous, and lifestyle columns**
- **what makes columns and reviews interesting and readable**
- **how to ask and answer the right questions to write reviews**

Columns and reviews can be the most interesting articles in the newspaper, but they also can be the most simple-minded. How well has the writer researched the topic? Has he or she really listened to that CD? As a reader, do you feel you've really been reached? Do you laugh, cry, or think? Do you want to see that play? Or are you, as they say, a trifle underwhelmed? In opinion pieces, yes, writers do have more flexibility—a license to use that great sense of humor, to lay out some sharp insights, to take people down a literary memory lane. Just remember that any opinion isn't inherently interesting, outrageous, unique, or thought-provoking in itself. You have to work at making your opinions interesting and readable.

Inside Columns

In hard news, the reporter is simply a provider of facts and quotes from news sources. In a column, the writer's opinion, along with supportive facts, forms the story.

In high school newspapers, columnists write weekly or monthly articles about subjects such as:

* New school policies
* Things that need improvement
* Things well done
* Daily life in the school

Columnists develop a following among fellow students, and often students may approach you with story ideas. A good columnist keeps alert to potential stories to write about and knows what's going on around school.

Personal or Interpretive Columns

One of the most important types of columns in high school papers *observes and interprets* life at school from the perspective of an insightful writer. The personal or interpretive column takes clear and sometimes poignant meaning from everything from everyday events to tragedies. See the model on reaction to the loss of a beloved former student on the next page.

Humorous Columns

Sometimes the best way to heighten consciousness about an issue is through the use of humor. For example, let's say a student columnist can't get a parking permit. In fact, several people she knows can't get permits, despite repeated efforts. She might turn this predicament into a humorous story, relating the frustrating student experiences with sharp wit. She may poke fun at the circumstances, but in the end, the message will be clear: Students need to know why they are having such problems and what can be done about it.

Using humor can be tricky business. What you find funny may be far less amusing to readers. Humor can be a great tool, but first:

* Think seriously about the appropriateness of humor to your subject.
* Try out your humorous scenarios with fellow staff members first.
* Be willing to take a hint and revise, or try something else next time.

Personal or Interpretive Column

A An anecdotal beginning gently introduces the subject.

Model

Setting an example for all

by Stephanie Hales

"Does anybody have any funny Allan stories?"

The question was not expected, but it was probably the best thing he could have said. As the more than 60 past and present Ambassadors wept over the loss of their friend, Allan Chyba, their director, Mr. Ron Hellems, had found a way to allow us all to remember and celebrate the wonderful life Allan led.

After fighting a six-day battle at St. Vincent Hospital in Indianapolis, Purdue University sophomore Allan Chyba, who graduated from this school in 1997, died Oct. 21. While here, Allan was a member of the Ambassadors show choir. At the request of his family, this year's Ambassadors, as well as the group's alumni, met twice over fall break to rehearse an arrangement of "Amazing Grace," which we sang at Allan's funeral Oct. 26.

During the latter of these two meetings, we had just finished a run-through of the song. Tears streamed down our faces as a result of the immense emotional impact of the beautiful piece of music and the tragic occasion for which we were singing it.

As the Ambassadors of today sat among those of yesterday in the blue chairs to which we all have grown so accustomed, the stifled sounds of weeping were the only noises to be heard. As senior Jody Platt put a comforting arm around my shoulder, Mr. Hellems initiated the sharing of our memories of Allan.

In immediate response to his request for stories, the hand of Erin Rogers '98 shot into the air.

"I've got one," she said.

Erin proceeded to tell her memory of Allan. She recalled how Mr. Hellems used to make the Ambassadors do heinous amounts of crunches (sit-ups) on the stage. As they struggled to complete the ab-wrenching exercises, complaints could be heard from all members of the group. All members save one, that is. As Erin told the story, the faces in the room lit up as people recalled the positive encouragement that Allan consistently had offered while everyone else complained.

continues ▶

Personal or Interpretive
Column *(continued)*

B Strong eyewitness observation is evident throughout the column.

Model

Though I perhaps did not know Allan quite as well as many of the people surrounding me, I, too, had a story to share. Although I was merely a freshman during Allan's senior year, I fortunately became acquainted with him through my experiences in the spring musical, "Damn Yankees." As a freshman in the musical, I did not know many people at first. However, Allan was a friend of my sister, Allison Hales '97, and he always made it a point to come over and talk to me whenever I was by myself. Although it may seem like an insignificant act, it really made a difference to me then, and I always have remembered Allan as the one who made an effort to make me feel comfortable in a potentially awkward and lonely situation.

As we continued to share our memories of Allan, one unmistakable theme emerged. No matter where he was or what the circumstances were, Allan Chyba always had a smile on his face and was doing something for someone else. With the telling of each story, we laughed between our tears as we celebrated Allan's positive attitude, endless generosity and indisputable selflessness.

Such thoughts continued to float through my head as I sat on the upper level of the Carmel Lutheran Church Oct. 26. As I gazed over the rail at the assembly on the main level, the number of people who Allan had positively impacted was evident, for the attendance at the funeral was overwhelming. In addition to the almost 70 Ambassadors who occupied the upper level, the church was filled nearly to capacity, and I couldn't help but feel a warmth in my heart as I saw the members of Allan's fraternity, Alpha Chi Rho, file into the pews.

The service was gorgeous, and although we have received many compliments on our singing, I must extend the utmost respect to Allan's brother, sophomore Mark Chyba. I do not know of anything that has touched my heart more than when Mark addressed the entire congregation in tribute to his brother.

As I listened to Mark tell how his mother used to say he and Allan would grow to love each other some day, I couldn't help but hear

those exact words coming from the mouth of my own mother. As Mark recalled the good times he'd had with Allan, I wanted nothing more than to wrap my arms around my sister. For as I wept for Allan and his family, I also did so for the fear I felt within myself. At that moment, each person in the church was confronted with the fragility of life as we realized how easily a similar tragedy could occur in our own families.

Once Mark finished speaking, we fought the tears flooding our eyes and the sobs welling up in our throats and somehow found the ability to communicate our feelings through the beautiful arrangement of "Amazing Grace."

At the conclusion of the service, I descended the stairs and found my mother waiting for me. As mascara-soiled tears poured from my eyes, we embraced with an intensity of emotion that I did not know a hug could produce. As I wept, she clung to me and said, "I'm so glad I have you here to hold." I felt the same way, and I told her such was true. I never will forget that moment.

As I returned to school after the service, my heart remained with Allan and his family.

I extend my prayers and sympathies to Mark and his parents, and to Allan, I offer my sincere gratitude. I thank him for the wonderful example he set for us all. A positive attitude, generosity and selflessness are qualities that we should all aspire to possess.

As I sat in class, unable to focus on Spanish, I could not help but remember the story that Matt Branic '97 had shared the previous evening at our rehearsal. He had recalled a date not too long ago when he and Allan had been playing basketball. As their conversation led to the topic of high school reunions, Matt and Allan debated upon whether or not the Ambassadors ever would reunite and sing together again.

While Matt adamantly opposed his optimism, Allan was convinced that this would happen. I remember looking at all the faces in the room as Matt told his story. At that moment, we all realized that Allan was right. Unfortunately, it was his absence that brought us all together.

Source: Carmel High School, Carmel, Ind., *HiLite*,
November 5, 1998.

Lifestyle Columns

National newspapers sometimes employ columnists who specialize in popular culture. Topics range from music to fashion, fads to television programs. These columns tend to be more light-hearted than most and simply inform readers of popular trends. Below are some subjects you might find in a lifestyle article. (Even these may be outdated by the time you read this!)

* The return of "hip-hugger" and "bell bottom" jeans
* The new popularity of swing or big-band music
* Lava lamps salvaged from the 1970s
* The comeback of vinyl record albums
* Extreme sports

In metropolitan papers, **lifestyle** or **trend columns** often focus on evening hot spots, new activities, entertainment events that pass through town—generally what's going on socially in a community over a given time period. In a high school setting, an **in-the-clubs column** covers what's up in forensics club, chess club, and so on. Ultimately, trend stories are written mostly for entertainment, and they tend to be quite popular among readers.

AT ISSUE

"Guess who I saw . . ."

Gossip columns focus on prominent people in a certain community, most often a large city.

For years, Jerry Berger has written his column for the *St. Louis Post Dispatch*. Berger spends a lot of time out in the community, at functions and fund raisers, taking notes on who is on hand and what is transpiring. He attends several events each week and spends a good deal of time on the telephone, catching up with the "movers and shakers."

Gossip columns are pure entertainment, and their presence in the newspaper reflects our interest in knowing what those around us are doing. Above anything else, people are interested in people, and tidbits of gossip help keep us in tune with others.

But just how much should we expect to know about the private lives of others? Some journalists have hounded people to the point where a physical confrontation has ensued. Media law holds that if a person is in a public place, that person can be photographed. But what happens once the picture is taken or once a gossip columnist disrupts a dinner to ask about a person's private life? The situation can become volatile, which is one of many reasons journalists should exercise good judgment and treat others with respect.

What Makes a Column Interesting?

A column should be written to attract a broad cross-section of readers. Columnists must come up with ideas that are unique and appealing, entertaining and insightful. A good column "speaks" to readers in a manner they appreciate. In most cases, the tone is conversational, as though writer and reader were chatting over a cup of coffee. An ace columnist never patronizes readers or makes ill-informed assumptions about their levels of education or capacity to understand.

How should a columnist *not* do it? A surefire way to alienate readers is to write a column filled with big words and long sentences. Simple and direct is best. Readers don't respect a long-winded writer; they either don't read the column or deem the columnist arrogant and pretentious. A thesaurus can be an important book on a columnist's shelf, but only when it's used to locate the one word that precisely describes something.

As a columnist, then, you relate to your readers and share their concerns and interests. You shed light on issues and provoke thought and discussion. In some cases, readers respond with letters and e-mail to the editor. Whether the readers agree or disagree, you will have succeeded at heightening awareness. After reading a well-done column, the reader goes away knowing something he or she didn't know before.

Capturing Attention

Like a strong news lead, the first few words written in a column must capture a reader's attention and lead the reader into the heart of the article. Columnists have an advantage over hard-news writers in that they can take more liberty with their leads. Sometimes one or two words can be more powerful than 20 or 30.

Consider a columnist responding to baseball slugger Mark McGwire's final home run in his record-breaking 1998 season. The column might begin with nothing more than "Seventy!" in the first paragraph. The readers gets an instant picture of what the column will be about. It captures as much or more interest as a 30-word paragraph.

Another way to begin a column is with an **anecdote,** or very brief story. "So I was sitting at a stoplight on Sunset Boulevard when I spotted a very familiar face . . ." begins the story, building a transition to the heart of the article.

At the Heart of It

The middle, or heart, of a column contains all the supporting material for the overriding point you are trying to make. This information can include statistics, quotes from news sources, or simply well-reasoned arguments.

One of the first lessons a debate student learns is to debate one side of an issue just as well as the other, and the same applies for the columnist.

To write an informed column, you need a feel for all sides of an issue. One of the

Leaving a Tip

Comedian Billy Crystal once received an excellent piece of advice from an older entertainer, who had seen Crystal perform. After the show, in which Crystal drew many laughs for his outstanding impressions of famous people, the older man took a charged-up Crystal to the side and told him that he really didn't care for Crystal's act.

At the time, of course, Crystal was dumbfounded by the criticism—he had just left audience members laughing and applauding his hilarity—but as he recalled years later, the older comedian was encouraging Crystal to leave the audience a "tip."

In other words, leave them a little something by which to remember the performer. The impressions were funny, but where was Billy Crystal in all of this? What were his own thoughts and observations about the world that would make for good comedy? Needless to say, Crystal went on to be a terrific comedian.

The newspaper columnist can operate under the same principle. At the end of every column, or somewhere near the end, leave a tip for readers to take with them. Ideally, a reader will leave the article thinking, "That was really insightful," or "She really nailed down that issue."

---

most effective ways to make a point is to give one side and then demonstrate why the opposite may not hold true. Do this in a professional manner, of course, without leveling personal attacks.

Among the abilities of an effective columnist is a knack for making well-reasoned arguments in as few words as possible, then moving directly to the next point. Dwelling on one point tends to bore the reader, but moving from point to point in a tight, straightforward style keeps the reader engaged and wondering what's coming next.

Parsimony

Sometimes there is a misconception among beginning journalists that the longer the story, the better it will be. One of the most important words you need to know as a columnist is **parsimony.** In a journalistic context, this refers to a fundamental but nevertheless complete discussion of an issue. Going overboard, or rambling, leaves the reader wondering what point the columnist is attempting to make. The verbose columnist sometimes makes arguments that actually undercut the original message.

Ending with Style

The ending is an important part of the column, as it determines, in large part, what the reader will take from the article. It should leave the reader thinking about the topic.

Inside Reviews

On the most basic level, reviews are simply opinions. Whether a review appears in your high school newspaper, a local newspaper, or on national television, it is simply one person's reaction to a book, CD, film, television series, or other entertainment. A good review not only describes content, but also goes a step further and provides a thoughtful analysis of the subject matter. Have you ever read something that bordered on a rant—a **polemic?** This is angry rambling about a subject that never really makes a substantive point and provides no real insight. The best reviews address a subject on a professional level and provide comments specific to content.

Reviewing Background

In most cases a reviewer should have more than a passing familiarity with a subject before reviewing it. On the professional level, for example, movie reviewers will have studied film in college, or they may have had experience within the film industry. Some excellent reviewers have educated themselves by reading extensively about the creation of film and watching hundreds, even thousands, of films. A solid background establishes a foundation and a point at which to begin.

While professional reviewers often have extensive backgrounds, high school journalism students seldom have huge amounts of experience. After all, where are you going to get experience if you don't just start reviewing? What follows are some things to look for when reviewing.

Film Reviews

In film reviews, one of the most important considerations is **character development**. In great films, the central characters tend to undergo change, which of course helps to take the film from point A to point B.

When characters don't develop or change over time, the film's story doesn't develop. It's your job as a reviewer, then, to be fairly critical. Give the film a **holistic evaluation**—that is, consider its overall success as a film. Here are some questions to pose when reviewing a movie:

* What did the film aspire to do?
* How effective were the dialogue and script?
* Did the central characters develop throughout the film?
* Were the actors immersed in their roles, or did they appear to "walk through" the film?
* How were the transitions from one scene to the next?
* What about the cinematography—how visually appealing was the film?
* Did the film contain unnecessary levels of violence or sexual content?

* Was the film's length appropriate?
* Was the plot somewhat original, or was it a Hollywood formula movie?
* Did the musical score enhance the power, or drama, of the film?
* If the film was a sequel, how did it compare to the original?
* Did the film have artistic merit, or did it seem made primarily to showcase a major actor or actress and generate huge profits?

Character Development

In *Rain Man,* the character Tom Cruise played began as a slick car salesman concerned mostly with himself and the money he stands to inherit. Early in the film, he travels east, where he comes face to face with his brother, Raymond, an autistic savant played by Dustin Hoffman. The two take a long drive back west, and as they do, humanistic elements begin to appear in the Cruise character. He comes to know his brother through situations that develop on the road. By the end of the film, he has clearly established some perspective on the differences between material items and genuine feelings toward others. In short, his character developed, and accordingly the movie succeeded in telling a powerful story.

Film Review

A Note the first- and second-person point of view.

Model

The Phantom Menace blasts into theaters

by Loryn Elizares, Editor-in-Chief

It was just like waiting in line for a roller coaster. We arrived at the theater two hours early and began standing in the designated area. Thirty minutes before the show started, we were ushered in through a side door and led down a dark hallway. Our procession continued through numerous ticket checks and finally into the theater. We took our seats and anxiously waited for the 6:30 p.m. showing of "Star Wars: The Phantom Menace" to begin.

As the infamous "Star Wars" theme began to play, accompanied by the words "A long time ago in a galaxy far, far away," the audience, smaller than I'd anticipated, began to cheer. "The Phantom Menace" takes you on a ride through the beginnings of the "Star Wars" saga, when Darth Vader was an innocent nine year old named Anakin Skywalker (Jake Lloyd). The plot revolves around the corrupt Trade Federation, which, at the urging of the Dark Lord of the Sith Darth Sidious, has placed a trade blockade on the peaceful planet of Naboo. The blockade's main purpose is to force Queen Amidala (Natalie Portman), the young matriarch of the planet, into a treaty she doesn't want to sign. As the Federation steps up the process and begins invading Naboo, two Jedi–Qui-Gon Jinn (Liam Neeson) and Jinn's apprentice, Obi-Wan Kenobi (EwanMcGregor) –arrive to protect the queen at the urging of the Jedi Council. The plot spirals from there, introducing you to amazingly detailed landscapes and alien species that could only spring from the mind of George Lucas.

The computer animation, which supposedly affects about 95 percent of the movie's scenes, is astonishing. The backgrounds, characters and action sequences, which are computer animated, are beautifully crafted. The computer characters seem very real and are complemented well by the "real" actors. The only complaint here is Jar-Jar Binks, a member of the aquatic Gungan species from Naboo. He is

Film Review *(continued)*

B The reviewer focuses on animation, acting, and music.

clearly in the story as comic relief, and at times this becomes redundant and—well—stupid.

The performance of the human actors was adequate. Neeson does a fine job in his portrayal as Jinn, and Lloyd isn't the "Mannequin Skywalker" critics made him out to be. The best physical performance was from Ray Park, who plays Darth Maul, the apprentice to Darth Sidious. Park is a master of the martial arts who was picked for the role by Lucas for his amazing abilities. Park delivers a fantastic job of choreographing and performing the fighting scenes. Again, only one complaint: he deserved far more screen time.

John Williams composed another score that was perfectly complementary to the action of the movie. As with the previous "Star Wars" trilogy, Williams has managed to work the various themes of the characters so that they wind through the whole story, intermingling and adding yet another medium to the movie that deserves close attention. Staying through the credits to listen to the closing theme pays off: at the conclusion of the song, the last thing you hear is the breathing of Darth Vader, which is a direct foreshadowing of the plots of the next two prequels.

If it's not obvious, I thought that this movie was well worth the time and money it took to see opening night. I may be a little biased, though; I've seen the original trilogy about 300 times and I can answer (almost) any trivia thrown at me. A person who wasn't familiar with Episodes IV, V and VI and was going to the "The Phantom Menace" as their first "Star Wars" experience may be a little disappointed. Many of the character's developments in latter episodes are alluded to here, and there is subtle irony that would be missed by those unfamiliar with the first three installments. My advice would be to ignore the hype and watch the first three before viewing "The Phantom Menace." Chances are that if you don't enjoy the original movies, you won't like this one either. If you do, see the movie, and may the force be with you, always.

Source: McQueen High School, Reno, Nev., *The Excalibur*, May 26, 1999.

C The writer saves the thesis of the review for the final paragraph.

Mark Caro, Film Critic

Mark Caro writes a weekly movie column, "Behind the Screen," for the *Chicago Tribune*, where he also serves as the paper's number two film critic. But his background is not in film, and he didn't join the paper intending to specialize in it. "I consider myself first a reporter who by following his instincts, developed a beat about the movie world," he says.

Caro, 35, took a journalism course and a college workshop during his high school years in Evanston, Illinois, but that's the only journalism he's ever studied. He was editor-in-chief of his high school newspaper before attending the University of Pennsylvania, where he majored in English.

At Penn he was involved in the campus paper, the *Daily Pennsylvanian*, from his first week on campus, becoming executive editor, the top position, during his junior year. Graduating in 1986, he moved to Boston and began to work as a freelance writer for the *Boston Phoenix*, an alternative weekly. "When I realized no one was covering Boston's rich cultural scene, I drifted to the arts and entertainment section," he says.

At the *Phoenix*, Caro wrote mostly news-features and trend stories (see Chapter 8), although his natural interest in rock music and film led him to submit reviews in both areas. After two and one half years of free-lancing—"at one point I made ends meet by serving pastries at a neighborhood bakery"—Caro returned to Chicago to write for the *Tribune*, again as a freelancer.

He pitched ideas to many sections of the paper, and his work included a three-part front-page investigative series on ticket scalping. But most of his work was in features. In 1992 the *Tribune* hired Caro as the first writer for its new KidNews section, and two years later he moved to the metro desk at the southwest bureau in Orland Park. In 1995 he joined the Tempo/Arts and Entertainment staff, where he splits his time between reporting and reviewing.

Much of the reporting part of Caro's job is covering the film industry. He profiles film-makers and actors; covers film festivals such as Toronto, Sundance, and Cannes; and he reports from Los Angeles on Oscar night. He also reviews two or three movies a week and writes non-entertainment-related features.

"I believe my reporting skills remain my most important asset," Caro says. "Reviewing isn't a matter of just sitting down and spouting off an opinion. It requires analysis and a willingness to dig beneath the surface. And I wouldn't be writing about film if I didn't have a life-long passion for the subject."

Caro has always gone to lots of movies and enjoyed arguing about them after-wards. "I'm happy to have a job that matches my journalistic training to a subject close to my heart," he says.

Book Reviews

Here are some questions to ask when reviewing a book:

* Is the writing clear and concise?
* Is the writing modest or does it draw attention to itself, thereby making it difficult for the reader to comprehend?
* Does the book move logically through chapters?
* Are the characters well drawn and developed?
* Are factual assertions documented?
* Is the author credible?
* Is the content original?
* Is the topic important enough to keep the reader interested?
* Does the author treat the subject matter in a complete manner?
* Is the tone of the book professional or highly emotional?
* Does the writing smack of hyperbole (overstating things)?
* On the whole, is the book worth reading?

CD Reviews

Here are some questions to ask when reviewing a CD:

* How is the overall sound?
* How are the transitions from one song to the next?
* How many songs are on the CD— enough to warrant its cost?
* Does the CD show originality and distinctiveness?
* What about song lyrics—are they funny, silly, irrelevant, irreverent, stupid, uplifting, poetic, profound?
* Is it better or worse than previous work by the group?
* How does it fit within the genre?
* Has the band made any recent changes in personnel?
* How does this CD compare to other work by these same artists or to other similar bands?

Wrap-up

Newspapers offer three types of columns: interpretive or personal, humor, and lifestyle. To capture readers' attention, columnists must address topics that are unique and appealing, entertaining and insightful. The writing should draw attention only to the subject matter. Columnists should have a feel for all sides of an issue before addressing it in print. Reviewers also have a responsibility to their subject matter. They must look at subjects with a critical eye and consider whether creative projects succeed on a holistic basis. Columnists and reviewers alike must exercise professionalism and good judgment in preparing articles.

Journalism

anecdote—brief story that introduces a topic.

character development—manner in which characters change throughout the course of a book or film.

holistic evaluation—analysis of the overall merit of a creative project.

in-the-clubs columns—columns that focus on school clubs, such as Spanish and speech.

lifestyle columns (trend columns)— cover quality of life and recent events in a community.

parsimony—expedient yet complete treatment of a topic.

polemic—emotional rant that lacks substantive points.

Sportswriting

In this chapter, you will learn:

- **how sportswriting is different from newswriting**
- **about pre-game, game, and post-game stories**
- **about sports features and other sports-page content**

We love sports. We watch our favorite football and basketball teams on television, listen to baseball on the radio, attend the games, and check highlights and final scores on the Internet. We went crazy for the United States Women's Soccer team after they won the World Cup. We hike, mountain bike, and water-ski. Sports are so popular, in fact, that new ones are being invented—witness the popularity of the X-Games. It isn't just the major revenue sports generate that people are paying attention to and reading about. Lots of attention is also focused on high school sports for men and women.

Sports and Your School

Baseball, volleyball, basketball, tennis, swimming, football, track and field, hockey—there's a sport for everyone. New high school sports also have emerged, and today women play many sports that used to be played only by men. For the past decade or so, high schools have fielded women's soccer teams, and women athletes continue to excel. Some schools offer sports such as field hockey or lacrosse for both genders, while still others have club sports, in which teams from different schools compete unofficially, or on a non-conference basis. Some students bowl, some play water polo, some wrestle.

In an atmosphere like this, the sports page of a high school newspaper should be literally packed with information. In any given season, teams from at least four sports will take to the field or court, providing opportunities for news and feature stories, editorial commentary, and photojournalism projects.

Is Sportswriting Different?

While hard-news stories may deal with administration and school policy, crimes and calamities, sports stories usually deal with matters less, well, serious. Sports, after all, is entertainment. As such, sports stories can be reported less rigidly than hard-news stories.

Sportswriters are known for putting some flare in their reports, playing off words, using **irony** and humor, and generally taking a step back from the just-the-facts approach. For example, while reporters write hard-news stories in the inverted pyramid style, with the lead paragraph explaining what happened, sportswriters often begin with an anecdote or clever phrase. Readers have little patience with "fluff" in hard news, but they usually tolerate a bit of fun from sportswriters. Also, when it comes to opinion, readers may disagree with a sports columnist, but they tend not to write the kind of angry letters they write over a controversial topic such as gun control.

Sports Reporter Sean Jensen

When Sean Jensen moved from Massachusetts to Alexandria, Virginia, in 1991, he and his mother went to Mt. Vernon High School to fill out his sophomore schedule. He needed one more class, so his mother suggested he take a journalism course because of his ability to write.

"I didn't like journalism at first, but a classmate invited me to join her at a minority program at Howard University," Jensen said. "I met writers from the *Washington Post, USA Today,* and various magazines. They said they saw potential in me, and they steered me toward other opportunities."

Jensen continued to write for his high school newspaper, but he also spent several days a week at *Young D.C.,* an alternative paper for high school students. He was a staff writer for two years and started a sports section.

The summer after sophomore year, Jensen applied for 25 journalism internships. "I got only one offer, from *Black Issues in Higher Education,* but that's all I needed," he said. "They hadn't realized I wasn't in college."

The following summer, Jensen interned at the Freedom Forum in Arlington, Virginia, where he was part of a team that designed the Newseum. He returned there the first summer after his freshman year at Northwestern University.

In college, Jensen wrote sports for the daily newspaper and interned after his sophomore year at the sports section of the *Tennessean* in Nashville. Another internship, this time in news, at the *Charlotte (N.C.) Observer,* persuaded him to stick to sports. "At Charlotte I did general assignment and was the Sunday cops reporter," he said. "I decided I didn't enjoy straight news."

Between his junior and senior years of college, Jensen interned in sports at the *Boston Globe,* and following graduation in 1998 he spent the summer at the sports desk of the *Washington Post.* Then he took his first full-time job with the *Milwaukee Journal–Sentinel,* covering the Green Bay Packers for their entire season, including the Super Bowl. He continued to cover the Packers through training camp of 1999, when he took a job covering the Minnesota Vikings for the *St. Paul (Minn.) Pioneer Press.*

Basics of Sports Coverage

Sports can be covered chronologically in **three** stages, beginning with a preview of an event or game to come, coverage of the actual event, and follow-up analyses. Besides coverage of events, news, features, and opinion pieces also shape the sports pages.

❶ The Preview or Advance Story

Check out a Thursday evening or Friday morning newspaper, and you'll likely see previews of the top high school contests in a given area. Prep football games, for instance, are played on Friday nights, with the exception of homecoming and state playoffs, and preview or advance stories get fans excited and build up the games.

The key to a good preview article is excellent **backgrounding.** This means that you, the reporter, talk to coaches from both teams and talk to some of the players. Do some research: Get and use statistics from athletic departments. Check your paper's files to compare this year's data with data from previous years. Include the information listed in the checklist of sports story essentials.

❷ The Game Story

Backgrounding helps a sportswriter tremendously when the time comes to compose a game story. If you are prepared, you will know who made a big play and can summarize it quickly in one paragraph, instead of having to search frantically through the game program every time a big play is made.

Checklist

Sports Story Essentials

Be sure to include this information in your preview story:

☑ **When and where** the contest will take place.

☑ **Conference and overall records** of both teams.

☑ **Brief review** of how both teams have performed in recent weeks.

☑ **Quotes** from coaches about the performances and what to expect.

☑ **Examples** for any assertions.

☑ **Review of key players** and players injured.

☑ **What the outcome of the game will mean** in terms of post-season play.

☑ **Discussion of whether the teams are ahead or behind** the previous season's pace.

☑ **Anticipation** of the atmosphere at game-time.

Essentially, game stories recap the most meaningful plays and explain why the game turned out as it did. Usually, writers begin by discussing the biggest plays of the game and then move to a **chronological recap** of how the scoring went. In fact, a good sportswriter will take notes in such a way that half the story is written by the end of the contest. By writing down exactly what happened, in chronological order, you are set to complete the rest of the story by writing a strong lead and filling in some gaps.

Quotes help fill gaps, and they also supplement the recap by adding context and emotion to the piece. Get quotes before a game, at practice, and in the locker room after a game.

While the winning coach and players might be ecstatic, players from the losing team may be somewhat down. Respect both sides. If someone does not wish to speak or wants to say only a few words, comply with those wishes. Meaningful contests can prove very disappointing for those not on the winning team, and pushing coaches and players for detailed comments can backfire; tempers may flare, and choice words may be directed at the writer. This advice is certainly not to suggest that you back away from getting the complete story, only that you exercise good judgment and gain a feel for the atmosphere. Be sure your game story answers these questions:

* What was the final score and what made the difference?
* Was the game an offensive or defensive struggle?

* Who made the big plays or scored important points?
* How much time remained in the period or game when the big plays were made?
* Were there any serious injuries?
* What did the coaches and players have to say about the contest?
* Was the crowd large, and if so, what kind of atmosphere did the crowd create?

❸ Writing the Post-Game Story

Follow-up stories address many subjects:

* How a team is preparing for its next game, given its last
* How a team is dealing with injured players
* What a team plans to do with the impact of players who emerged in the last game
* Whether a team will continue to go with players who performed well below average
* How the fans reacted to the previous game

You can write follow-up stories in advance of the actual contest. Gather as much background information as possible, compose a story based on patterns that background data demonstrate, and use the most recent contest to put the article in perspective. Usually, patterns emerge, and it will really help you to gather information beforehand and write at least part of the story.

Sports News

A A simple, effective summary lead begins this post-game story.

Model

Men's basketball remains undefeated on state play

by **Katy Polansky**, Sports Editor

The No. 1 ranked 4A men's basketball team has continued its unbeaten streak in league with recent victories over Marshfield, North, Churchill and Thurston.

In a matchup of the preseason favorites, South defeated Marshfield 69-55 in the Purple Pit on Feb. 5. The Axemen's four leading scorers all finished in double figures. Leading the way was senior Matt Long with 15 points, followed by senior Cogan McCarthy and junior Blake Stepp, who each had 14. Senior Mike Roberts also pitched in 13.

"I thought it was a really good team effort," said Long. "The team gave a balanced effort [in terms of scoring distribution]. Our intensity was also really strong."

Senior Norio Mold also gave a solid performance off the bench, scoring eight points, including the first five points of a 13-2 run in the middle of the second quarter.

"Marshfield is a good team," said Roberts. "It was a tough game, but we pulled it out in the end."

The Axemen then went on to face the North Eugene Highlanders on Feb. 9 in the second game of a three-game home stand. South defeated the Highlanders 68-42. McCarthy led all scorers with 21 points.

"In the first half our shots just weren't falling," said McCarthy. "But the team came out strong in the third and fourth quarters and turned the game around."

continues ▶

B Strong quotes are used throughout.

Model

Roberts contributed 15 points, and Stepp followed him with 12.

In one of the most impressive victories of the year, the Axemen destroyed the Churchill Lancers 63-35. "It felt really good to beat Churchill by a lot in one of the last home games of my senior year," said Roberts.

Stepp led all scorers with 21, while Long and McCarthy each tossed in 11. "I think that the team came out really focused. Nobody had a bad game and that was the kind of effort we needed," said Stepp. "And the crowd did a good job supplying the home court advantage."

"The Churchill game was one that I will remember for a long time," said senior Sean Ritchie. "The way we played and the crowd support helped to make it the most fun game that I have ever played in."

"We played really good defense in the second half," added Roberts. "We were really focused. They couldn't score."

In the Axemen's most recent league victory, they defeated Thurston on the road on Feb. 16.

Stepp led all scorers with 23 points on a night when the Axemen were having trouble completing shots from the field. He was followed by McCarthy with 10 and then Roberts with 8.

"I think that we came out overconfident," said Mold, "but we stuck it out and got the job done."

The Axemen play their final home game tonight against Sheldon at 7:15 p.m.

Source: South Eugene High School, Eugene, Ore., *The Axe*, February 19, 1999.

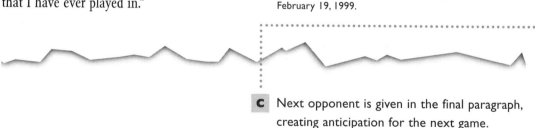

C Next opponent is given in the final paragraph, creating anticipation for the next game.

On-the-Scene Reporting

Perks to working as a sportswriter include going behind the scenes before and after games and viewing games from the best seats in the house. At professional basketball games, reporters commonly sit at tables surrounding the court. Sitting on **press row,** reporters not only see the game up close, they also hear talk among players and intense instructions from the coaches.

Football writers, in contrast, often sit in the **press box,** where they get a bird's-eye view of the game. They may receive periodic statistics and enjoy refreshments courtesy of the home team. Press boxes also have televisions so that key plays can be seen on replay and reviewed from different angles.

At the high school level, working behind the scenes can provide a preview of the excitement of a professional career in sports reporting.

The Sports Feature

Sports features are similar to other features in that they address subjects that readers would not be exposed to in basic news coverage. Examples include:

* How a coach or player overcame a serious illness and came back stronger than ever
* How members of a player's family have excelled in several sports
* How several players excel, not only on the field or court, but in the classroom
* What special memories an announcer has after 30 years on the job

Possible feature subjects are everywhere. For every player on a given team, at least one interesting feature could be written, as everyone has unique qualities and experiences. When you have a sports feature assignment, your task is to discover those qualities and experiences and put them into a well-written article.

In addition to the tips covered in "Features" in Chapter 10, here are some ideas to consider when pursuing a sports feature:

* How the feature relates to current sports news
* Why the topic is unique or interesting
* Whether unusual statistics or background information exists
* What coaches, players, and family members have to say about the person or subject
* What characteristic or trait helps make the athlete seem human to readers

Sports Feature

A Comprehensive lead sets up the topic.

B Baseball section of the story is signalled by a head.

`Model`

Female athletes in a league of their own

by Wei-ying Wang

The phrase "you play like a girl!" doesn't hold any negative connotations to juniors Anne Mabasa and Catherine Tweedie and sophomore Michelle Ng. As female athletes playing in male-dominated sports, they are forging a path for girls in sports everywhere.

A Level Playing Field

Mabasa and Ng are the only two female baseball players currently on the Lowell baseball team. Mabasa, who joined in her freshman year and now plays second base on the varsity team, is the first female baseball player in AAA history.

Teammate Isaac Zones, who has known Mabasa since they played together in Little League, said: "It [Mabasa joining the team] wasn't a big surprise. I thought it was ironic that Anne is the first girl to play baseball in like a hundred years of AAA history, and the next year Michelle joins the team."

Both Mabasa and Ng have been playing baseball since they were young. Ng, the second baseman/shortstop for the JV baseball team, practices most Sundays with her father and younger brothers. Likewise, Mabasa practices with her brother, who plays for George Washington High School, and his friends. Their baseball backgrounds led them to try out for the baseball team, not the softball team.

"I've never played softball before," Mabasa said. "I don't particularly like softball. I don't like the fact that they [softball team members] wear shorts. How can you slide? And I don't like the ribbons they wear. I just don't like ribbons."

Ng never even considered playing softball for Lowell. "Baseball is something I've always been doing," she said. "I didn't want to switch."

On tryout day, Ng said, "Some of the guys were like, 'I think softball tryouts are over

C Baseball and wrestling sections are handled separately.

D Each segment ends with a strong quote from the athletes.

there.' But other than that, no one gives me a hard time."

Mabasa agreed the team adjusted well to her presence. "They [the guys on the team] cut out the vulgar remarks, the guy talk," she said.

Zones said, "Everybody's supportive. It was a little awkward, but we treated her like just another player."

Varsity baseball coach John Donohue said that the team respects Mabasa because of her skill. "She is not on this team because she's female; it's because she's a good player," he said.

Unfortunately, according to Mabasa, other teams are not as tolerant. "A lot of teams think, 'It's a girl, bring the outfielders in' [when Mabasa is up to bat]," she said. "Once a coach of another team said something like, 'We'll never let the pitcher live it down' after I hit a home run. A lot of people don't have respect for me as a ballplayer."

Despite their lack of support from other teams, Mabasa and Ng receive encouragement from the audience. "Sometimes the guys' moms cheer us on," Ng said.

Zones agrees: "The parents are supportive. Moms admire her [Mabasa] for her courage, my mom in particular. She is tougher than most other guys on the team. She works as hard as everybody else, and people respect her for that. The thing that works against her is her size because she's small."

Despite whatever physical disadvantages Mabasa may have compared to her male teammates, Mabasa believes girls should get involved in sports. "I would encourage girls playing for the team, not because it's cool, but because they love the sport," she said.

Her advice to girls interested in playing so-called boy's sports? "Stay strong. Don't be discouraged if you don't get things, it takes time to develop skills. Don't give up."

Mean, Lean, Wrestling Machine

Guys fear junior Catherine Tweedie. And they have good reason to: She has the distinction of being the first female in San Francisco to pin a male wrestler.

continues ▶

E Quotes are used generously throughout.

Model

Although she isn't afraid of facing her male counterparts, Tweedie says that some of the male wrestlers are intimidated by her. "When they [male opponents] are faced with the possibility that they might be beaten by a girl, they'll try their hardest," Tweedie said.

Although she may be the only girl hitting the wrestling mats at Lowell, Tweedie doesn't feel alienated. "It's like having 20 brothers," she said. "A lot of people think the guys give me trouble, but I get a lot of support."

Fellow wrestler junior Colin Ikeda admitted that he felt some uneasiness when Tweedie first joined the team. "There was some awkwardness, but now she's just another member," he said.

Ikeda also feels that Tweedie is a good addition to the team. "She is very good; she has very good techniques," he said. "She always boosts morale."

Tweedie did not have any previous wrestling experience before she joined the team. She said that she learns wrestling techniques as she goes along.

Although it is a relatively new experience for her, Tweedie doesn't feel strange about wrestling boys.

"It's not a big deal," she said. "It's a sport and when you're wrestling, you don't think, 'Oh, it's a guy!' You think 'I've got to win.'"

Tweedie has not wrestled against female opponents until recently, when she went to an all-girls tournament. "Wrestling them [girls] was not that much different from wrestling guys," she said. "There were some amazing girls there [at the tournament]."

She encourages other females to join the wrestling team. "I wouldn't say I'm a feminist," Tweedie said. "If you're in good shape, then you should join the wrestling team."

Aside from wrestling, Tweedie has participated in many sports, including track, softball, swimming, tennis, basketball, soccer, gymnastics, and tai kwon do since an early age. "They [sports] give me a physical outlet for releasing stress," she said. "Wrestling seems to do this better than anything else I've tried so far."

Source: Lowell High School, San Francisco, Calif., *The Lowell*, February 12, 1999.

F Each segment ends with a strong quote from the athletes.

What Else Is on the Sports Page?

Besides news reports about games and meets, the sports page contains several items that make it unique.

Columns

In high school newspapers, the first page of the sports section often includes a column by the sports editor. This column usually addresses the performances of one or more teams from the school, focusing on winning and losing streaks, outstanding or poor play, funding issues, school spirit, and support. The best columns are timely and well conceived. They focus on up-to-date issues and use a positive, upbeat tone. A columnist's job is to share insight, helping readers become better informed about subjects they may not have considered.

News-in-Brief

Sometimes a series of news items appears, but they are not significant enough to stand alone as stories. News-in-Brief sections typically take the form of a column and provide a series of news blurbs separated by asterisks or horizontal lines.

Scorecard

This section of the sports page provides bits of information such as box scores, team rosters and statistics, league standings, and transactions. The key to a good scorecard section is stellar layout. Columns of information should stay perfectly vertical, leaving no uncertainty as to where one box score ends and another begins. Each section should have a small heading (for example, "League standings"), and the information should not be crammed together, which often confuses readers.

Special Features

Some high school newspapers showcase athletes of the month, providing statistics of their performances and, if possible, a few quotes from the athletes and their coaches. Some newspapers highlight athletes who excel at sports and academics.

Special features also may focus on faculty members who have donated significant amounts of time to coaching, keeping score, tabulating statistics, and simply getting involved in extracurricular activities.

Filler

Sometimes a couple of inches of **white space**—an area containing no copy, photos, or graphics—will appear in the bottom corner of a page, and filler material is needed. In this context, filler might be a famous quote, a question involving a famous athlete or sport, or a small graphic. Filler keeps the page from having glaring holes and makes it appear complete and appealing to the eye.

Sports Column

Model

Pro athletes are today's role models

Brett McWethy, Sports Editor

It bothers me that we, as a society, are focusing on the wrong athletes as the people we look up to. Athletes' statistics draw fans' attention, but it is what they do off the court or field that portrays athletes as role models.

People in the public eye have the duty of being role models to youth and other fans. It is the sacrifice they make, and some athletes and celebrities accept that responsibility better than others. Chicago Bulls veteran Dennis Rodman has won numerous rebounding titles along with four championship rings and is one of the best players in the NBA, but his acts during games and off the court are ridiculous. Someone who kicks a cameraman after a missed play or someone who spits in an umpire's face after a questionable call, such as Baltimore Oriole Roberto Alomar, are not figures we should admire.

In the July 1997 issue of *Sports Illustrated,* an author expressed his feelings about how we look at our "admirable" athletes. He writes: "Sadly, the apple of the public's eye is rarely an admirable champion like Pete Sampras." Figures like Sampras, Mark McGwire, Sammy Sosa and the ever important Michael Jordan, the one and only person who can save the NBA right now, should be the apple of the public's eye. It's also interesting that these great sports figures also put up great numbers, with Sampras dominating tennis the last seven years, and Jordan just doing what he does.

It seems that the acts of public figures are getting worse. Sports, even at the collegiate level, are turning from a mere game into a competitive business. Usually every year we, as fans, hear two or three stories of college athletes and teams breaking NCAA rules to either win more games, or in most cases, get more money. The programs that get caught are the unlucky ones because the odds are that it happens all over the country.

Source: Portage Central High School, Portage, Mich., *Central Stampede,* November 13, 1998.

News-In-Brief Column

faLL rewiND

Volleyball
Record: MVC 8-0, Overall 44-1-1
Coach: Diane Delozier
Wrap up: Only one loss in its season, the girl's team won the first volleyball state title in school history.
First Team All Conference: Tanya Hammes '99, Kelli Chesnut '99.
Second Team All Conference: Stacy Moss '99, Megan Recker '99.
Honorable Mention All Conference: Teesa Price '99, Emily Rowat '99
Conference Athlete of the Year: Chesnut
All State Tournament Team for 3A: Moss, Hammes
First Team All State: Chesnut
Second Team All State: Moss, Price
Third Team All State: Hammes
Honorable Mention: Recker
Elite All State Team: Chesnut
All Team All Area: Chesnut, Moss, Hammes
Second Team All Area: Hammes
All Stars Team: Moss, Chesnut

Emily Rowat '99, pumps the volleyball over the net during a game against Dubuque Senior

Boys Cross Country
Record: 8-4
Wrap Up: The team finished second behind Dubuque Senior at the state meet. Earlier in the season the team had lost twice to Senior.
First Team All Conference: Quincy Ely-Cate '01, John Farlinger '99, Bob Moreno '00
Second Team All Conference: Paul Kresowik '00, Eric Mittman '00, Jeff Spence '01, Jacob Smith '99
Elite All State Academic: Smith

Bob Moreno '00, races in the state meet October 31. The team finished second.

Girls Swimming
Record: 3-11
Coach: Keith Branstetter
Wrap Up: Despite finishing 32nd at the state meet, the girls finished

Nina Lohman '99' stretches

A A briefs column enables schools to give some coverage to all sports.

B Sports take turns getting full coverage.

C Pictures add interest to the column and draw the eye down the page.

D The column records team performance as a matter of record.

E Brief stories are highly enticing for readers because they are so quick and easy to read.

Sportswriting differs from hard news in that it focuses on a form of entertainment. Sports writers thus have some "wiggle room" in the topics they choose as well as the way they write. Good sports reporters do thorough backgrounding and prepare themselves for any contests they are assigned to cover. They answer the basic questions and let their sources deliver intensity and emotion through quotes. The sports page also contains columns and feature stories, as well as news-in-brief, a scorecard, special features, and filler material.

Journalism

backgrounding—gathering information prior to a contest to observe and communicate how a team or athlete is performing.

chronological recap—telling a story sequentially; reporting events in the order in which they occurred.

irony—feeling that occurs when words and their literal meanings run opposite.

press box—located near the top of a stadium; houses journalists, league officials, and other important personnel.

press row—area next to the court reserved for journalists covering an event.

white space—place on a page that contains no copy, photos, or graphics.

Photojournalism

In this chapter, you will learn:

- how photography staff members work
- about planning assignments and photo shoots
- what makes a good picture
- how to take a good picture
- how to select and use photos in a publication

You've probably heard that a picture is worth a thousand words. This old adage is not meant to downplay the importance of the written word—especially in journalism. Rather it emphasizes the importance of photographs in telling the story. Good photographs can make the difference in the reader's decision to read a story. Each of us can think of images that have shown the heart of a big story. We remember the photo of the fireman holding a baby after the Oklahoma Federal Building bombing. We remember Columbine students pouring out of their school building with their hands in the air on April 20, 1999. These photos demonstrate the purpose of **_photojournalism_**—getting to the heart of the story, instantly, in a visual way.

People Who Make It Happen

It would be wonderful if all members of your publication staff carried cameras with them and thought like photojournalists when life happened around them—taking well-composed, well-exposed photographs. Since that isn't likely to happen, high school papers have photography staffers whose jobs are to get quality, storytelling photographs.

Photo Editor

The photo editor's job is broad and important. Not only must the editor be on top of what's going on, he or she must work with the rest of the staff as a liaison, or go-between, who keeps the lines of communication and understanding open between photographers and editors. A big part of the job is interacting with both the editorial staff and the photographers, providing ideas, and **photo editing** (making sure that photos are displayed and cropped properly).

Here's how a photo editor and photographer begin work on a story about unusual student jobs:

* First, they brainstorm about how to tell the story.
* The photo editor then provides the photographer with a list of students the staff wants "shot" (jargon for photographed) and when and where they work.

* The two discuss possible difficulties of the assignment. (Will they let the photographer shoot there? What will the lighting be like? Is it okay to have non-students in the photo?)
* They determine the amount of film and the speed of the film needed. (Film speed has to do with how much light is required to expose it.)
* Together they set a deadline for shooting, processing, and providing the **contact sheet** (a direct print of **negatives** onto photographic paper) to the photo editor.

The photo editor's job has its necessary but mundane tasks as well: record-keeping and making sure that assignments are done on deadline, to specification, and with creativity.

Job Description: Photo Editor
Teaches shooting, processing, and printing.
Coaches photographers.
Works as a lab technician.
Administrates.
Acts as liaison for the photo staff and the editorial staff.
Provides creative ideas and suggestions.
Critiques the staff photographers' work.
Acts as watchdog over technical quality and deadlines.

Job Description: Staff Photographer
Keeps up with photo assignments.
Has camera and film always ready to shoot.
Gets film and prints processed in a timely manner.
Keeps negatives and contact sheets in an easily retrievable format.
Provides creative ideas for photographic coverage and feature photos.
Works as part of the team to make deadlines.

Staff Photographer

Slinging cameras filled with different films and sporting various lenses and straps, the staff photographer lopes through the staff room, ready for action. Later he or she emerges from the darkroom, squinty-eyed, clutching a handful of prints to give to the photo editor.

The staff photographer is the workhorse of the photo staff. He or she must keep a calendar of events to be shot, while constantly being on the lookout for **enterprise shots**—unassigned photo opportunities that flesh out coverage. The staff photographer ideally carries a loaded camera at all times and is constantly thinking about visual images that will help tell the story of the school.

Planning Assignments and Photo Shoots

Photographers won't automatically shoot the photos the editors need. The reality is that they don't know what staff members need unless they're told.

Good Photo Shoots

Preparation is the key to taking good photos. It starts with a meeting between the photo editor and the editor and staff member in charge of writing and designing the story. Discussing the possibilities for photographs helps clarify exactly what the photographer is to shoot while encouraging other creative ideas.

Making the Assignment

Once the photo editor understands what's needed, he or she must assign a photographer. Clear photo assignments are essential. Ideally, the assignment should come in **two** parts:

1. A discussion with the photographer
2. A clearly written assignment of how the photos will be used

Vague assignments are the bane of every photographer's life. The assignment to "shoot a pep rally" may result in lovely photos of the cheerleaders, band, and drill team, when what the writer and editor wanted was fan reaction and close-ups of the drummer's hands in action.

PHOTO ORDER   3502

Circle one: Yearbook   Newspaper   Magazine   Ordered by_____
Date ordered:_____   Class Period_____
Date needed:_____   Phone_____
Time and date to be taken:_____

Location: _____

Contact Person:_____ PHONE_____
Number of photos planned_____ #Vert_____ #Horiz_____
_____
_____

Specific suggestions for photo content (angle, essential things that must be included. Is the photo going
a dominant? Does it need to face a certain direction? Don't expect the photographers to be mind reade
_____
_____
_____

PHOTO EDITOR/ADVISOR USE ONLY
Photographer(s) assigned_____
Date shot_____   Date completed _____
Photos given to:_____   Grade on overall photo assignment_____

Top copy to photographer • 2nd copy to Babb • Bottom copy to Publication adviser (except yearbook—give to person ordering the

---

Checklist

What Makes Clear Photo Assignments?

✓ Name of the person ordering photos and his or her phone number

✓ Contact person and phone numbers

✓ Specifics about time and place the photos should be taken

✓ What the story is about

✓ How the photos will be used

✓ How many photos are needed; whether they should be verticals, horizontals, or both

✓ Deadline for the contact sheet

✓ Deadline for prints

CAPTION FORM

One of these forms must be attached to each photo submitted for use i
publications. Fold this portion over the front of the photo, leaving the lon
side on the back. The photo should be facing out so that we can see the
photo and flip over and read the information. Staple the form on the whi
edge. DO NOT STAPLE IN THE IMAGE AREA.

Photographer's name: First_____ Last_____
Assignment/picture topic:_____
Date turned in:_____
Enlarger information: f-stop_____ timer_____ enlarger height_____
                filter_____ Burning/dodging_____

Be as specific as possible on the following. You are graded on your capt
information.

Who:

What:

Where:

When:

Answer Why/How only if it adds to the caption info:
Why:

How:

Additional information:

Printed by (if not the person who took the photo)_____

Caption info grade:_____ Photo grade:_____

How to Prepare for a Photo Shoot

Before the shoot, the photographer should:

✓ Determine exactly **where to go** and **what time to be there,** get directions and parking instructions if necessary, and set up a meeting place if there needs to be a rendezvous with anyone.

✓ **Be there early.** The best "mood" or human interest shots often happen outside the time of the actual event. (The rule to remember, actually, is "go early and stay late.")

✓ Evaluate the **lighting situation** and the kind of film needed.

✓ Determine the **number of rolls** of film needed (always have extra).

✓ **Pack extra batteries,** a reporter's notebook, masking tape, and a pen.

✓ **Have extra equipment:** filters, a tripod, a telephoto lens for sports, and a flash.

During the shoot, the photographer should:

✓ Make sure to **get the photos** that were specifically assigned.

✓ Look for **opportunities for feature** photos that could enhance the story and tell the story in a better way.

✓ Look for the **human interest element.**

✓ **Mark each roll of film** with a number and film speed; record in a notebook what is on each roll.

✓ **Stay for the entire event;** if possible, stay after. Hasty shootings of homecoming, a sporting event, or a play rarely result in the best photos.

✓ **Get full names,** title, grade, and other relevant information about the people photographed. Spelling counts! (You wouldn't want your name misspelled or to be misidentified in the paper.)

After the shoot, the photographer should:

✓ Immediately **record information** about the event or people that might provide good caption or story information.

✓ **Process the film promptly**. Storing it and allowing it to age will not improve it and could result in loss or damage. Don't store film anywhere you wouldn't put a candy bar—for example, in the sun or on the dashboard of your car.

✓ **Make a contact sheet** and get it to the photo editor with suggestions for which photos to select.

✓ **Print the selected photos promptly** and attach a sheet with <u>captions</u> or <u>cutlines</u>—written explanations of photographs (more on captions later in the chapter).

Photography Time Line

Italian painter and engineer Leonardo da Vinci diagrammed the workings of a camera in his famous Notebooks.

Frenchman Louis Daguerre, in partnership with Niepce, produced the first successful daguerreotype, a photograph made on a metal or glass plate.

350 B.C. EARLY 1500s A.D. 1600–1700s 1827 1837 1841 1860–1865

Greek philosopher Aristotle described the process of the "camera obscura" (literally meaning dark room). Aristotle observed that when a beam of light was allowed to enter a darkened room through a small hole, an image was formed.

Frenchman J. N. Niepce made the first permanent photograph, the result of bitumen process on a pewter plate.

Mathew Brady took photo equipment to American Civil War battles, becoming one of the first photographers of active combat.

Several people began experimenting with chemicals that were sensitive to light.

W. H. Fox Talbot worked out the positive/negative process.

—

J. Petzval designed the first fast camera lens.

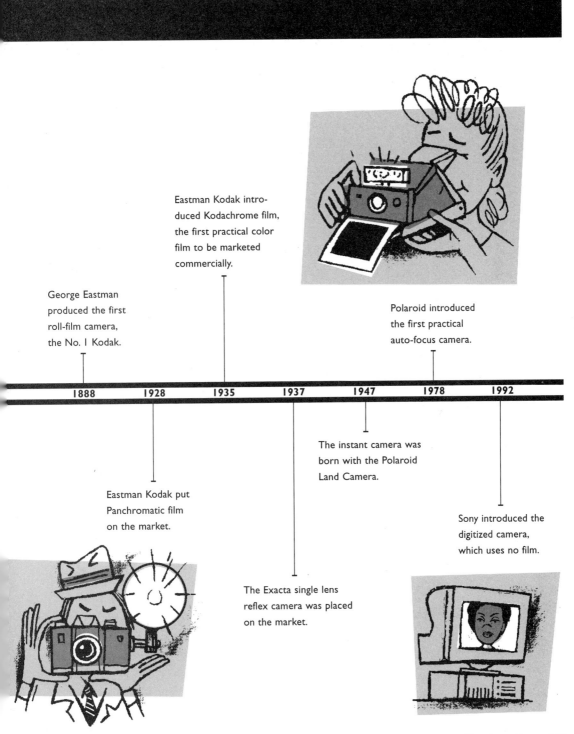

Eastman Kodak introduced Kodachrome film, the first practical color film to be marketed commercially.

George Eastman produced the first roll-film camera, the No. 1 Kodak.

Polaroid introduced the first practical auto-focus camera.

| 1888 | 1928 | 1935 | 1937 | 1947 | 1978 | 1992 |

The instant camera was born with the Polaroid Land Camera.

Eastman Kodak put Panchromatic film on the market.

Sony introduced the digitized camera, which uses no film.

The Exacta single lens reflex camera was placed on the market.

Mike McLean, Photographer

Photographer Mike McLean, 35, started his career at the *Tiger Rag* newspaper and the *Lair* yearbook at Irving (Texas) High School. "There I discovered the power of images," he says. "I saw the impact my photos had with other kids in school."

After a photojournalism career at the *Dallas Times-Herald,* McLean became a freelance photographer who shoots magazine and corporate assignments. "I really love the fact that I get paid to do something I would do for free," he says. "What a concept!"

McLean still appreciates his high school photo teacher's requirement that students clip photos from area newspapers and write details about what made them good. "It really helped us to learn how to cover assignments like the big guys," he says.

He began hanging around the professional photographers who covered Friday night high school football games. "All the pros were eager to help out," he says. "One even let us use some of his gear. I think it's important to use your local resources. Even small newspapers have a few photographers who would be happy to help out if they knew there was a need."

During high school summers, McLean worked as a freelancer for the *Irving Daily News* and then studied photography in junior college with a photographer from the *Dallas Times-Herald.* "He gave some of my work to a photo editor, and I was offered a job as a lab technician," he says. "I worked nights in the lab, and during the days I went with the photographers to learn how they were able to bring back such great photos."

McLean spent nearly two years in the lab before he started shooting pictures full-time at the *Times-Herald.* He was on the staff for only a year when he helped cover a plane crash at the Dallas airport that earned his team a Pulitzer Prize nomination.

Teamwork is essential in photojournalism, McLean explains. "The important thing is to bring together all the key team members to talk about story ideas, to get input from the reporters, editors and layout folks, anyone who's got a hand in the process," he says. "I take notes at these meetings, then try to think about what may happen visually. It's good to have a few ideas, but learn to be open if something better comes along."

McLean still uses this approach when he has an assignment. "My clients really like the fact that I'm serious about getting photos that are not just good, but great, images that tell a story," he says.

What Makes a Good Picture?

You've seen photos you know are good. And you've probably seen photos that would do. Still, ascertaining what makes a good photo is not a guessing game. There are differences between the photos we take of our vacations or for our scrapbooks and the photos we take for story-telling purposes in publications.

The difference is in what you are trying to communicate. While your personal photos might merely be saying "We were here" or "These are my friends," *photojournalistic photos* need to tell a story. This story is communicated by capturing a specific moment. The photographer should look for *action*, *reaction*, and *emotion*—the story-tellers of photography.

Photojournalistic Photos

The photographer should be looking for a relationship between the subject and something else in the photo. If a teacher is teaching or a speaker is speaking, participants should be included in some way. If a student is working on a project, the project should be in the photo as well. Relationships are vital in photojournalistic photos.

Action Two soccer players keep their eyes on the ball as they vie for control. ▶

Action

Whether it means waiting for the instant when the soccer player heads the ball, the second when the student body president corners a volunteer for a job, or the "eureka!" when an idea is suddenly understood, a good photographer learns to look for the right moment to shoot in order to capture the perfect photograph.

Reaction

Sometimes the best photos come after something has happened. That isn't to say the photographer doesn't shoot the action but rather that he or she learns to anticipate what might happen next. Sideline shots at the big game can show some wonderful moments—prayers, tears, exultation may tell the whole story.

Emotion

Often coupled with reaction, emotion photos show joy, anger, sadness, love, or any of a myriad of emotional responses.

Emotion Instead of showing the play that won the game, this photo tells the story of exultation as a player and a cheerleader share their happiness.

▼

Reaction The expression on this young woman's face tells the story of what many think about giving blood.

▼

Quality and Composition

A good photo is also technically good. A number of criteria are used to determine the quality and composition of photos.

Photo Quality

This means:

* Black and white photos should have **photo blacks** (true blacks, not charcoal gray colors that pretend to be black), **photo whites** (white areas that are not just white blobs but rather have some detail), and a full range of grays.
* Details should be clear. A muddy gray photo or a photo that has excessive **contrast** is not a good photo, whether or not it tells a story. (Contrast is the tonality in a photo and should run the full range from the blackest blacks to whites with detail.)
* Colors in color photos should be true, and definition of details should be clear (not underexposed).
* Prints should be free of scratches, fingerprints, and lint.

Cropping

Far too many wonderful photos have been damaged by poor cropping. On the other hand, a good crop can save a photo from mediocrity. **Cropping** involves making a decision about what part of the photograph will be included on the printed page. There are **three** opportunities to crop a photo:

1. The photographer makes the first crop when looking through the camera lens, taking a certain position, and moving in or out—either physically or with a zoom lens—before taking the photo.
2. The second crop could be made in the darkroom if the photo editor and photographer decide to edit out more of the photo through enlargement.
3. The final crop is made when the editor places crop marks on the photos to indicate to the printer the portion of the photo to be scanned and printed.

Cropping is only one part of **photo composition,** the technique of capturing a photo that draws the reader's eye to the subject. Photographers and editors alike should know the rules of photo composition.

Rules of Composition

Fill the Frame. Get close to your subject. Edit out all excess, or "dead," space around the subject that doesn't add to the photo. New photographers tend to use the focusing circle in a camera to place their subject in the center, a choice that leaves dead space over heads and around the subject. Instead, it's ideal to focus and then recompose the photo to use all the space in the frame.

Follow the Rule of Thirds. Consider this the tic-tac-toe rule of photography, dividing your photo both horizontally and vertically into thirds. Placing your subject dead center kills the dynamics of a photo. Instead, envision an invisible tic-tac-toe board on the photo and place your subject so that he or she is on one of the intersections of that board. The subject should be looking or moving toward the open parts of the photo.

Use Leading Lines. Often the photographer can find a way to lead viewers to what he or she wants them to see. A line—either visible or invisible—can help do this. A group of people looking one way leads the viewer to look that way. A table top, a hallway, or a line of lockers can provide a leading line to a subject.

▲
Leading Lines The bench and the boy's leg both set up lines that lead the viewer to his face.

◀ **Rule of Thirds** Note that if you drew an imaginary tic-tac-toe board on the print that the television would fall in one intersection and the boy watching it in another.

Use Repetition or Patterns. The repetition of shapes or of people doing the same thing can pull the viewer into a photo. A photo of standard subject matter—a classroom scene for example—can become interesting with the addition of shadow stripes from blinds or the repetition of three students in a row sitting at their desks with their heads resting on their hands.

Avoid Busy Backgrounds and Mergers. There are ways to avoid both busy backgrounds that distract from content and **mergers,** intersecting objects that look as if they were merged together (for example, things growing out of or intersecting with a person's head). Move to a different position or lower your f-stop to reduce the area in focus and remove clutter and mergers.

◀ **Repetition** The repetition—a row of girls with their arms raised—pulls the viewer into this photo.

Avoiding a Merger This picture could have been a perfect example of a photo with bad mergers had the photographer not used a low f-stop number. Notice the tree and swing set pole that would be growing out of the child's head.

▼

Getting Great Pictures

Often photographers miss the best photos because they are not prepared. They need to look for photo opportunities. Photographers also need to add an artistic touch.

Photo Ops

Before you go to shoot an event, you need to think about what will be happening. What's an unusual way to tell the story? Could the best photo of the homecoming court be of the girls getting ready before they are presented? Could the best photo of the football game be the offensive line huddled around the coach as he shows them the strategy? Here are **three** basic rules for photo ops:

1. Think before going to a shoot.
2. Watch for the moment that may best tell the story.
3. Be prepared to shoot.

An Artistic Touch

Photography is an art. Rules of composition are based on artistic principles, and the artistic eye is the one that will take the extraordinary photo of an ordinary situation. That means looking for lighting that will isolate your subject and finding a way to frame your subject or an unusual angle from which to take a photo.

Contrast

Contrast comes in two forms:

1. **Contrast of light and dark.** Since the viewer's eye is drawn to the lightest part of the photo, you can use light and dark contrast to emphasize your subject. A person sitting in a pool of light surrounded by shadow is visually appealing.

2. **Contrast of action.** This contrast works to pull the viewer's eye to a certain part of the photo. If you have a class full of students with their heads down taking a test and one student standing up looking around the room, the viewer's eye will automatically be drawn to the one doing something different.

◄ **Contrast** The contrast of the light background with the girl silhouetted in the photo adds interest, as does the texture of the blinds in the background.

◀ **Camera Angle** Taken from a bird's-eye view, this photo illustrates the concept of using parts of the whole

Selective Focus and Framing How does this photo demonstrate selective focus? Framing?

▼

Camera Angle

Beginning photographers tend to shoot everything from a standing position, giving readers the same view they always see. Think in terms of bird's-eye view and worm's-eye view. Avoid "lock-knee"; look for a vantage point that makes the ordinary look different.

Selective Focus

You can create a shallow area of focus by using a low **f-stop** number. By blurring the background and/or foreground, the reader's eye is pulled to the area in focus. This can also help get rid of busy backgrounds.

Framing

Framing a shot can be as simple as shooting the subject through the shoulders of two people sitting opposite or through the fork of a tree. A frame might be something the photographer finds or creates to outline the subject. For example, shooting through a mail slot into a classroom or through the legs of a chair can provide a frame.

Natural Diagonals and Curves

Look for groups of people who are stair-stepped rather than all the same height or in the same placement, and look for natural curves and S-shapes.

Three-dimensionality

Provide a foreground, middle-ground, and background in your photos. Instead of shooting a group of people from straight on, move toward the side to show them on different planes. If your subject is a single person working on a project, look for ways to include something in the foreground and background as well.

Another way to think of this is to envision a clock. If you are photographing a group of people standing in a more-or-less flat line at 12 o'clock, consider shooting them from 3 or 9 o'clock rather than from 6 o'clock, which would be a flat, one-dimensional way of looking at them.

Selecting and Using Photos

When a story is turned in to an editor, he or she reads it for content, choice of words, grammar, completeness, tone, and more. When a photographer turns in a contact sheet from a photo assignment, the photo editor must evaluate it in a similar way. The photo editor looks at the individual images, or **frames,** on the contact sheet and decides which image best tells the story and which has the best focus. He or she evaluates each frame with the rules of composition in mind, looking for clean, crisp images. This process is an important part of photo editing.

Working with the Layout

You've heard the saying that you can't put a square peg in a round hole. Many publications staffs try to do just that when they work with photos. The editor and the photographer should have discussed whether horizontal or vertical shots were needed; ideally the photos will fit the space. If the best photo is not the right shape, it's better not to force it. Consider redesigning to make it work.

◀ **Natural Diagonal and 3D Look** This photo shows a diagonal created by the pyramid and a three-dimensional look created by shooting from the side.

Cropping and Sizing

It's a good idea to print the photo as close as possible to the actual size it will be used. Enlarging a photo affects the way it reproduces, and photos can be over-enlarged. Once the editor has the photo, he or she will have to crop and size it. Often this means marking the photo with a non-reproducing pen or a grease pencil. It's a good idea to lay four sheets of white paper around the crop marks to get a clearer idea of what remains.

<u>Sizing</u> a photo means indicating at what percentage of its size the photo will be reproduced. If the photo is smaller than the picture window planned, the number will be over 100 percent. If the photo has to be reduced, it will be a number less than 100 percent. Consider reprinting closer to actual size if your percentage is more than 150 percent.

Writing Captions

Your picture may be worth a thousand words, but don't assume that it doesn't need a verbal explainer—a **cutline** or a caption. While yearbook and newspaper captions differ, both publications need good captions—sentences that tell the *who,*

Sidebar

How to Write a Good Caption

Lead-In. This should be a punchy, one- to three-word phrase that is clever and catchy, without being cliched or trite. Steer clear of a lead-in for a school drama production, for example, of "Lights, Camera, Action!" It's been done to death. Humor is fine, but be sparing with puns and Batman (onomatopoetic) words like "pow," "zap," and "zowie." Alliteration—beginning each word with the same letter—is also fine for a lead-in. Set off your lead-in typographically. (See "Publication Design" in Chapter 15.)

First Sentence. Use present tense and a complete subject and verb. This sentence talks about the content and action of the photo—usually several of the 5Ws and 1H appear here. Also, be sure to identify all the people in the photo. Make sure that those who are photographed have their first and last names included, as well as a title (principal, 200m hurdler, senior, and so forth). If the person pictured is running track and is also the student council president, list the title that most corresponds to what he or she is doing in the photo.

Second Sentence. Use past tense and discuss some actions outside of what is happening in the photo. For example, if the photo is of a carwash fundraiser for the band, the second sentence might say how much money the band members raised overall. This part of the caption is the point of entry from the caption back into the body of the story, so it should contain interesting information that makes the reader want to find out more.

what, where, when, and sometimes, why and how. Captions should tell more than the obvious.

Yearbooks often expand the basic caption to give background information, to explain what happened next, or to add statistical information or even a quote. Newspaper cutlines will do these same things when the cutline takes the form of a **stand-alone,** a caption that must be a mini-story because it goes with a photo that is not specifically related to a story on the page.

Cutlines should stand out from the rest of the content on the page. It's a good idea to put them in a different type face, perhaps in a bold version of the text type. Starting them with a visual lead-in is also a good idea. Consider an all-cap or boldface phrase to help pull the reader in.

The Photo Essay

Your photographers have captured the essence of the big game with wonderful shots of the fans at tailgate parties, the players stretching on the field, the coaches priming the players for play, the cheerleaders, the dance team and band performing, the big plays, and the victory scene.

You've got what you need to do a **photo essay**—a story told through photos and captions, sometimes supplemented with a little bit of text. While many school newspapers will take the back page or the center spread for a photo essay, you can run one anywhere and on any subject. It's a good idea to make one of the photos large so that it becomes a dominant element on the page or spread and to vary the size and shape of the other photos for visual variety.

Digital Photography

In **digital photography,** photos are taken with a special camera that records the image to memory, which in turn can be immediately translated into a photographic image in a computer. This process made immediate and permanent changes to journalism. Digital imagery involves **three** technologies:

1. **Digital camera:** a camera that bypasses the darkroom by recording the image on a memory chip or disk, allowing the image to be downloaded and used.

2. **Photo CD:** a CD to which images can be saved and then downloaded directly to a page.

3. **Scanner:** a device that "reads" images from one printed surface and translates them into a digital image that can then be printed on another page or surface; can be a flatbed (for scanning photographic prints) or a negative scanner (for scanning negatives).

Digital photography has several advantages:

* Cuts costs (after the initial expense for the camera) because no film is needed.
* Allows an immediate preview of results.
* Allows storage of images on a computer for later use.
* Good for identification photos, such as mug shots.

Unless you are using a high-end camera with additional digital technology (which is very expensive), digital photography has its disadvantages as well:

* Requires the photographer to be close to the subject to shoot.
* Film speed cannot be varied to shoot in difficult lighting situations.
* Generally not good for shooting action sports.
* Requires a lot of storage space on computer hard drive.
* If not shot at a high resolution, photos cannot be enlarged as needed.

Digital cameras are changing the face of publications mostly because they provide immediacy that regular cameras cannot. On the other hand, most have a very limited lens length and do not have the capability of operating in low-light situations (there is no film to push). You have to balance the pros and the cons and use a digital camera only when it fits the situation.

The Ethics of Photography

Do you need permission to use a photo? The answer is both yes and no. Generally, photos shot in public places for publications don't require permission from the person or persons in the photos. Some states and schools require permission from parents before photos of children under 18 can be used.

You may not use photos taken in private places without permission. A private place is a home, public restroom, and the like. That isn't to say you can't take pictures at someone's home, but that the people you are shooting need to know that you are shooting for publication.

Technology has made changing photo content very easy and very possible. (See Chapters 15 and 17.) It is, however, unethical and should not be done. Your publications should have a **photo policy,**

a written statement about what you consider allowable and not allowable when manipulating photos. (See the example on the National Press Photographers Association Code of Ethics on the next page.) You should not add or subtract people from a photo, remove distracting elements simply because they are distracting, or do anything else that couldn't be done in the darkroom. You can crop a photo closer, but you cannot erase or replace someone or something in a photo. You can clean up scratches or dirt, improve contrast, and dodge or burn (lighten or darken an area).

The general rule is: If you can make the same changes in the darkroom that you can with today's technology, you are following ethical guidelines and are not altering the true nature or meaning of the photo.

National Press Photographers Association
Code of Ethics

The National Press Photographers Association, a professional society dedicated to the advancement of photojournalism, acknowledges concern and respect for the public's natural-law right to freedom in searching for the truth and the right to be informed truthfully and completely about public events and the world in which we live. We believe that no report can be complete if it is not possible to enhance and clarify the meaning of words. We believe that pictures, whether used to depict news events as they actually happen, illustrate news that has happened or to help explain anything of public interest, are an indispensable means of keeping people accurately informed; that they help all people, young and old, to better understand any subject in the public domain. Believing the foregoing we recognize and acknowledge that photojournalists should at all times maintain the highest standards of ethical conduct in serving the public interest. To that end the National Press Photographers Association sets forth the following *Code of Ethics*, which is subscribed to by all of its members:

The practice of photojournalism, both as a science and art, is worthy of the very best thought and effort of those who enter into it as a profession.

Photojournalism affords an opportunity to serve the public that is equaled by few other vocations and all members of the profession should strive by example and influence to maintain high standards of ethical conduct free of mercenary considerations of any kind.

It is the individual responsibility of every photojournalist at all times to strive for pictures that report truthfully, honestly and objectively.

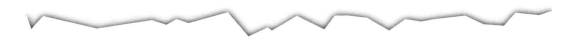

As journalists, we believe that credibility is our greatest asset. In documentary photojournalism, it is wrong to alter the content of a photograph in any way (electronically or in the darkroom) that deceives the public. We believe the guidelines for fair and accurate reporting should be the criteria for judging what may be done electronically to a photograph.

Business promotion in its many forms is essential, but untrue statements of any nature are not worthy of a professional photojournalist and we condemn any such practice.

It is our duty to encourage and assist all members of our profession, individually and collectively, so that the quality of photojournalism may constantly be raised to higher standards.

It is the duty of every photojournalist to work to preserve all freedom-of-the-press rights recognized by law and to work to protect and expand freedom-of-access to all sources of news and visual information.

Our standards of business dealings, ambitions and relations shall have in them a note of sympathy for our common humanity and shall always require us to take into consideration our highest duties as members of society. In every situation in our business life, in every responsibility that comes before us, our chief thought shall be to fulfill that responsibility and discharge that duty so that when each of us is finished we shall have endeavored to lift the level of human ideals and achievement higher than we found it.

No Code of Ethics can prejudge every situation, thus common sense and good judgment are required in applying ethical principles.

Source: National Press Photographers Association Code of Ethics. Printed with permission of Bradley Wilson, Executive Director, NPPA.

Photojournalism is an art and a science. It is essentially a way of telling a story through pictures that helps people understand what is going on around them. Photos are a means of quickly transferring information. In a publication, photos grab readers and entice them into the story. Whether a stand-alone photo or an image in an essay or package, photos give information, provide insight, and tell a story through action, reaction, and emotion. Journalists respect photos. Make sure you give your readers the best story-telling photos that you possibly can.

Journalism

caption (cutline)—a written explanation of a photograph.

contact sheet—the result when negatives that are pressed against a sheet of photographic paper, exposed to light, and developed into a positive photo.

contrast—tonality in a photo; should have a full range, from the blackest blacks to whites with detail.

cropping—determining what part of the photograph to include on a printed page.

cutlines—another term for caption.

digital photography—process of taking photos with a special camera that records the images as data that can be stored in computer memory; data can be immediately translated to a photographic image in a computer.

enterprise shots—photographs that are not assigned but rather are the feature photos that flesh out coverage; generally these have a human interest angle.

frames—individual photos on a roll of negatives.

f-stop (aperture)—size of the lens opening; affects the amount of light that comes through the lens.

mergers—points in a photo at which objects wrongly appear to be a part of other objects.

negatives—term used for film once it is processed because it is in reverse image; blacks appear transparent and whites look black.

photo blacks—true blacks, not charcoal grays that pretend to be black.

photo composition—techniques to draw a reader's eye to a photo's subject.

photo editing—making sure that photos are selected, displayed, and cropped properly.

photo essay—a story told through photos and captions, sometimes supplemented with a brief text.

photojournalism—journalism that uses photographs to get to the heart of the story in a visual way.

photo policy—a written statement about what is allowable and not allowable when manipulating photos.

photo whites—white areas that are not burned out (blobs), but rather have detail.

sizing—telling at what percentage a photo will be reproduced when published.

stand-alone—a photo and its caption that serve as a mini-story; not related to a specific story on the page.

Publication Design

The graphic designer's job is not only to get the reader to look at the majority of the elements on the page before moving on, but also to get the reader to read the copy. Studies have shown that a reader only skims a page for three seconds before deciding whether to read further. Three seconds! One current professional trend is to include lots of visual "bytes" for the newspaper reader—things that are visual, colorful, and easy to read in short periods of time. High school publications have limited budgets, however, and most cannot afford color. They must find a middle ground where good writing and good design work in tandem to get the information to the reader in the easiest, cleanest fashion.

Size, Shape, and Systems

Before you learn about design principles, here's a brief run-through of *what* is to be designed as well as the basic systems used in publication design.

Sizing Up School Publications

Size matters in design. School publications come in different sizes. Here are the most common ones:

* Some schools print papers by **offset press** on white, bonded paper; usually offset papers are 11 x 17 inches, folded in half to make an 8.5-x-11-inch individual page size.
* Others use a larger format and print by **web press** on **newsprint**. Most professional daily papers are printed on newsprint and on web presses in **broadsheet** format. More colleges and high schools have gone to a broadsheet format, allowing them to publish more information on fewer pages.
* Still other schools publish a **tabloid**-size newspaper, which is the size, for example, of the infamous tabloid the *National Enquirer,* or the slightly smaller **mini-tab**.
* High school literary magazines are usually one of two sizes: 11 x 17 inches folded in half to 8.5 x 11 inches or 8.5 x 11 inches folded in half. Binding may be saddle stitched (stapled) or perfect bound (glued).
* Yearbooks come in two standard sizes: 8.5 x 11 inches and 9 x 12 inches. Costs vary according to page size.

Measuring Systems

Page measurement is critical to understanding design as well.

* The **pica**, at 1/6 inch, is the standard unit of measure for journalists.
* Type is measured in **point size,** which refers to the height of a letter. There are 12 points in a pica and 6 picas in an inch.
* The advent of computer technology and options in desktop software to use inches or decimal inches *has not lessened the need for points and picas at all.* It is important to know how all these measurements fit together.

Using a Grid System

While most newspapers use columns to arrange and organize the information on the page, **grids** are being used more and more, not only for newspapers, but for yearbooks and magazines as well.

A grid acts as the underlying structure of the designed page, forming the framework in which all the graphic elements will be aligned. It is formed per page or spread by a prescribed number of columns of a prescribed width, measured in picas.

A grid system uses more "compartments" in which to work; this makes the design more flexible. For example, if the page has 12 columns or grids, they're going to be narrow but offer many possibilities of how wide to make text and artwork. In contrast, if your design employs a five-column system, you're limited in what you can do with text and white space—you can make text one- or two-columns wide, and that's about it.

Many high school papers use 12 columns per page as their grid basis, knowing that it can be divided by 2, 3, 4, and 6; division by the "evens" can yield lots of options for varying a design while still providing an underlying consistent grid pattern.

But what would happen if we thought "oddly"? What if our grid was 9, 11, or 13 columns? Then, we'd be forced to do some creative things with the "leftover" single column. Think about that after reading this chapter.

The Page Dummy

No, a dummy isn't the staff member who is the last to catch on to points, picas, and the grid system. The **dummy,** or **thumbnail sketch,** is the design equivalent of taking a notebook to an interview and putting film in the camera. For the designer or layout artist, it's the very first step.

The best dummy sheets or thumbnails are miniatures of the layout sheet. If your publication uses five-column pages, your dummy should have five columns. Or, if you're on a grid system, the dummy sheet should follow the grid as well. The same goes for yearbook thumbnails.

Dummies can be done on notebook paper or the back of an envelope, depending when the idea hits you. Ideally, dummies or thumbnails are as detailed as possible, and they include as many graphic elements as can be foreseen in the early stages of the design process.

Typography and Design

Choice of **type fonts,** or styles of type, is integral to the overall look of a publication. Is yours a traditional-style school or publication? Or is your student body more cutting edge and modern?

When redesigning your publication, think about things such as fonts for the body copy and headlines. Fonts can be **serif** (with little "feet") or **sans serif** (plain strokes with no "feet").

For a clean design, stick with three **font families** (three fonts with all their different styles: **bold,** *italics,* and condensed). Choose one serif font for the text and captions.

Choose a bolder, simple sans serif for your headlines, subheads, caption lead-ins, or initial letters. A third, more decorative font, for "display" and artistic uses **(pulled quotes,** bylines) may be added. In choosing fonts from the enormous variety available, the most important thing to remember is to use fonts that are readable and clear, not overly trendy or wild.

Leading (pronounced "ledding") is the "air" between the lines of type. Leading can be used as a design element as much as a typographic consideration. In a story's lead, for example, extra leading can draw the reader's eye into the story. (See the model on the next page.)

Example

Examples of Serif Type Fonts

Bookman

Cochin

Garamond

Memphis

New Century

Palatino

Times Roman

Veljovic

Examples of Sans Serif Type Fonts

Helvetica

Arial

Avant Garde

Examples of Decorative Fonts

Impact

Postino

Egbert

Comic Sans

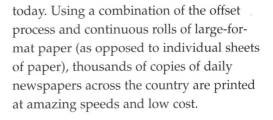

A Case of Type

Some of the printing terminology that we use today is at least 300 years old. Type for newspapers was first painstakingly set by hand, the typesetter slowly arranging the type by individual letters. Newspapers were actually constructed with hot metal type and printed one sheet at a time. Leading got its name from the actual hot lead that was used to separate lines of type.

Typesetters stored their metal letters in trays organized into little compartments to help them set the type into the press faster. The capital letters were in the case on the top, and the smaller letters were in the case on the bottom. Hence, the terms "uppercase" and "lowercase" letters.

A great advance in printing came with the offset printing process, which used film and metal plates for printing more copies at a much faster rate. After offset came the web press, which is how many professional papers are printed on newsprint today. Using a combination of the offset process and continuous rolls of large-format paper (as opposed to individual sheets of paper), thousands of copies of daily newspapers across the country are printed at amazing speeds and low cost.

Model

Type as a Design Element

A Extra leading draws in the reader's eye.

Source: From *The Face of Generation Next* by Sue Lackey. Reprinted by permission of the author.

Modular Design

The best design is **modular,** with rectangular elements. Just like bricks in a wall, all the elements fit together neatly and help guide the reader through the page.

* The reader's eye is first drawn to the **dominant element,** usually artwork of some kind, then probably to the caption, the headline, and the story. The dominant element captures the reader's attention, and the **subordinate elements** are structured around the layout so that the reader is actually *guided* around the page.

* The invisible "trail" that the reader's eye follows around the page is a planned part of the design called the **eyeline.** The reader is usually not aware that he or she is looking at things in any particular order, but the designer has planned this process by placing graphic elements in a desired and pre-planned pattern or sequence.

* Throughout the story, visual tidbits (**drop caps**—the oversized letters that begin the first word of a story—pulled quotes, and so on) keep the reader interested. Remember that "form follows function"—*content* should help determine your design format.

Elements on the page should have **unity,** or look like they belong together. A good eyeline will help accomplish unity. Clustering the larger elements close to the top and center of the layout and putting the smaller elements (such as captions) toward the outer edges also helps unify the layout.

Just as the triangle is the strongest shape for building things from bridges to roofs, it's also the strongest shape to design with. Consider a page with a bold headline and initial letter in one area, a large dominant graphic in another, and a pulled quote elsewhere on the page. If you drew an imaginary line from one element to the other, you'd get a triangle. The best part about keeping a triangular shape in mind

Example

Triangle Layout

Source: From *They're Not Safe* by Gary West. Reprinted by permission of the author.

as you design is that it will help keep you designing all the way to the bottom of the page. Putting one point of your triangle down at the bottom helps create **balance** in the design.

Standing Elements

Standing elements are the bylines, headers and footers, captions, and other graphics that your publication uses consistently. Many design elements that you'll work with in journalistic publications have several names. Here are some basic standing elements:

* The **logo** of your school newspaper that appears on the front page, can also be called the **nameplate** or the **flag.** Is that confusing? Usually, a flag runs across all the columns on the page (a **banner**), while a logo or nameplate can be less than a full banner.
* The spot in the paper where the staff's names and positions, editorial policy, and so on are mentioned can be called either a "masthead" or "staffbox." In yearbooks, it's called a "colophon," and it also includes information about the printing company, the fonts and paper stock used, and so forth.
* A **jumpline** is the "to be continued" line that comes at the end of the first part of a story, before it is continued, or jumped, to a page further back in the publication. Usually, the jumpline appears in the same font as the body copy or headlines, perhaps in bold or otherwise distinguished

to stand out. Jumpline style varies from the polite: "Please see 'Sinkhole,' page 9, column 5" to the simple "Continued on page 12."

* The **refer** is a short statement, usually set off in a box and some textwrap, located somewhere near the beginning of the story. Its purpose is to literally refer the reader to other articles on related topics elsewhere in the publication.
* Another standing element is the **column bug.** On the sports, feature, or opinion pages, certain members of your staff will have personal columns. Graphically, these need to look a bit different than a regular story (often they are boxed in). You also may want to attach a face to the writer's name and column. The column bug contains the writer's **mugshot** (a head-and-shoulders shot), the title of the column, the writer's staff position, and perhaps some simple artwork that sets the column apart from another similar element, the pulled quote.
* A good design can use **white space** within it—holes on the page where there is no element. The eye is drawn to white space, just as it is to any other element. (White space, then, becomes an element.) "Trapped white space" is a vacuum between other graphic elements that has a distracting effect. Relieve trapped white space with art or a pulled

quote. The result is that the *whole* shape is a rectangle with perhaps a U-shaped or L-shaped copy flow within the larger rectangle. Text wrapped around a photo or other art is called a **textwrap** or **runaround**.

Example

L-Shaped Textwrap

FEATURE: Dueling Grounds

You, Sir, are a drunkard, a worthless scoundrel, and a coward.

64 • *the* BACKSTRETCH • September/October 1997

Source: From *You, Sir, are a drunkard, a worthless scoundrel and a coward* by Bill Mooney. Reprinted by permission of the author.

Rules for Rules

Lines, or **rules,** are used in a variety of ways in a publication. They should not exceed one point in width. Conservatively designed publications sometimes use "hairlines" (very thin rules) between columns of type. Below are some of the other ways you can use rule lines in your publication:

* To set off captions, bylines, pulled quotes, and other text-oriented graphic elements.
* To border photographs for better contrast against the page.
* To box in sidebars, infographics, and so on. (Note: Sometimes a light tint box or **tintblock** of 5 to 20 percent gray is a nice addition to the box, to set the story off from the rest of the layout.)
* To guide the eye across the page and join the elements of the **folio line** (the page number, section heading, date of publication, and name of the publication that runs across the top or bottom of each page).

Life in the Gutter

The **gutter**—the large space splitting the column between the two pages on a newspaper center spread or a yearbook design—is definitely an entity to be contended with. A photo subject's face or other integral body part should never appear in the gutter. Headlines and other type should stay out of the gutter, too, especially in yearbook design, where words there may be totally unreadable. To unify the two-page spread in a modular design, some element should cross the gutter, however, so that it's evident that both pages function in tandem.

Even when you're doing a single-page design in a newspaper, the gutter still comes into play. Photo subjects on the page should look as if they are moving or looking toward the gutter, or "in" toward the story. This practice guides the eye of the reader into the story, not off the page.

Nut Graf, Extra Leading, Tintblock, Folio

Source: From *The Dip* by Jennie Rees. Reprinted by permission of the author.

Test Your Layout

See if your layout can pass these tests. If not, review the basic design principles.

The dollar bill test. You should be able to lay down a dollar bill anywhere on the page (horizontally, vertically, or diagonally) and have it touch something in addition to text.

The five finger test. When you lay your hand down on the page with your fingers spread out, you should be touching at least three or four graphic elements or **points of entry** other than the text.

Squint scrutiny. When you've finished the layout, print it out full size and tape it to the wall. Back up and squint. Can you still see the dominant artwork? Can you still trace the other elements on the page in the order that you had wanted the reader to see them (for example, first dominant art, then subordinate art, then headline, then drop cap)? If not, it's time to fine-tune some more.

Stay Organized as You Work

Handling Standing Elements Onscreen

One good way to standardize your graphic elements is to set up each page document on your computer as if you were working on a master page (sports, for example). Then use an "extra" page in that computer file on which you've saved a sample byline, caption, pulled quote, bulleted list, folio line, column bug, and so on. When you're using your dummy to drop in those elements, all you have to do is go to the second page of your computer document, lasso the element you want, copy it, then go back to the master file. That way you don't have to reinvent everything each time you want to drop in a pulled quote. Not only is it easier to copy and paste, but you won't run the risk of having three pulled quotes in one publication that are all just a little bit different.

Using a Spec Sheet. Another graphic design necessity that will help your consistency is a **spec sheet,** where all your type and design specifications are written down with actual examples. Let's say you want all your bylines to have the word "by" in 10-point Helvetica bold, 80 percent width, and the name of the writer in 10-point Palatino italic, 80 percent width. Just think what would happen if all the section and page editors on your staff tried typing the byline out each time, then setting those type specs in each one. You probably wouldn't end up with a consistent byline. The same goes for trying to re-create a pulled quote with a textwrap each time one would be used. While the copy-and-paste method is a good one, it's also important to have the type and design specs written down for quick reference in the publications staff room.

Image Control

Artwork

Artwork refers to photos, drawings or illustrations, infographics, pulled quotes, initial letters—that is, anything other than the text of a story. Artwork is what hooks a reader into a story about 80 percent of the time. The dominant art should be about 20 to 30 percent larger than any other element on the page, and the page should be at least 50 percent art. That's a lot of math to keep in mind when laying out a page, but the formulas reflect how *visual* we are in this society. Here are **four** rules of thumb for artwork:

1. Don't be afraid to run it big!
2. Don't use a bad photo just to have some art. There are a lot of other options.
3. Make sure your design can pass the "dollar bill" or "five finger" test. (See "Stay Organized as You Work" on the previous page.)
4. Check to see how your layout withstands "squint scrutiny."

   What do you do when you have a news page with *no* photos or illustrations at all? That's where design creativity really comes in. You'll have to use type as a design element. Be careful not to butt headlines; you'll need to box some sidebars and make good use of tints in order to pull this off.

Icons

Icons are small bits of art that communicate an idea or topic instantly—they "represent" the concepts. You see them every day, in the newspaper, in news broadcasts, on road signs, in shopping malls, and on restaurant menus. These little snippets of art communicate almost metaphorically.

In student publications, we see icons on yearbook contents pages, indexes, and dividers; in newspapers, they're on the front page and all throughout the publication. There are icons for news, sports, reviews, and club news. Icons are in wide use in both professional and high school magazines.

Icons overrun the Internet, and people in general are becoming more and more accustomed to knowing where to click, where to look, and how to interact with media because of them.

Example

Icons

Source: Jefferson High School, Corydon, Ind., *The Hyphen*, Oct. 6, 1995.

Sidebar

Making Icons

Icons are relatively simple to make. Clip art can provide a wonderful starting ground for icons, but it is an absolute must to *adapt* the clip art to your specific use. From a design perspective, it is best not to use clip art as filler when there's not enough copy or to plug a hole of white space that somehow got trapped in the middle of the spread.

Make sure that the clip art you use in conjunction with your icons is:

* Legally procured (not scanned out of a magazine or downloaded off someone's Web site).
* Pertinent to the icon it is accompanying. Clear and recognizable even when run very small; most icons are less than an inch square.

Infographics

Infographics, or infographs (short for informational graphic, first discussed in Chapter 8), are visuals and art that quickly present key or supporting information. They can be maps, bulleted lists, pie charts, bar or fever graphs, tables, bios and time lines, opinion polls and quotes, checklists and glossaries, Q & As and quizzes, and so on. Infographs present quite a bit of information in a quick and creative way. Follow these guidelines for infographics:

* Make the graphic for information not decoration.
* Be scrupulously accurate: Mathematically calculate data in graphs and pie charts before enhancing it.
* Use a short, punchy, one- to three-word title, not a headline with complete subject and verb.

Example

Michael Jackson Infographic

Source: Reprinted with permission of Glenn W. Murphy, Jr.

* Match your format to your purpose. For example, if you're dealing with percentages of a whole, a pie chart might be the best form for the infographic.
* Take another step artistically and tie the information to a visual theme. Let's say you're doing an infographic about standardized test scores in your school, comparing their results over a period of the last five years with the results of other area schools. Get creative with the bars of the graph—make them pencils or rulers. But remember: Less is more.
* Use a **graduated fill,** a tinted shape (elongated rectangle if you're doing a bar graph or a circle if you're doing a pie chart) that goes from 100 percent of 1 to 100 percent of another.
* Include an explainer paragraph. Usually, the reader needs a little bit of background information, not only to make sense of the information presented in the infograph, but to understand how it relates to the story's content.
* Cite your source. To lend credibility to your information (and subsequently your publication as a whole), make sure your sources are valid and documented in the graphic.
* Credit the creator of the infographic.
* Enclose your infographic in a simple box so that they don't appear to be "floating" around the page.

Using Full Color and Spot Color

If your publication's budget allows for it, you may be able to add a splash of **spot color** or even full color to your newspaper or yearbook. Most yearbooks have sections of spot color with black, and some have full-color pages, which are printed with a **four-color process.** In four-color printing, all colors of the spectrum are created through varying tints of cyan (blue), red, yellow, and black. When planning a newspaper issue or a yearbook, color is a major consideration. One reason is the cost, but the other more important reason is that color often dictates which stories get read and which art gets looked at first. Plan for your use of color carefully.

Do you need a rule of thumb for planning color for the cover of your yearbook or the inside pages of your literary magazine? Don't design in colors that you wouldn't wear on a date or paint your room.

Sidebar

Ideas for Color Combinations

Look for inspiring color combinations in these ordinary places:

* **Cars:** Notice basic exterior car colors, then the contrasting interior colors.
* **Men's ties, sweaters, shirts:** Wander around a nice men's store and look at, for example, how many complementary colors are in one paisley tie.
* **Menus:** Restaurants spend a lot of time and money on their eye-catching menus.
* **Magazines:** See how car and fashion magazines, hobbyist periodicals, and publications aimed at teens use color.
* **Other high school and college yearbooks:** Keep these in your staff room to refer to any time fresh ideas seem to be in short supply.
* **Business and college brochures, annual reports:** These expensive publications for organizations take a lot of planning.
* **Advertisements:** Note color combinations on billboards, in magazine ads, and even on television.

* **Gift-wrapping paper:** This one seems weird until you really start noticing the colors that are used together.
* **Book jackets and covers:** Colors help distinguish books on a shelf.
* **Catalogs:** Does a pleasing palette help to sell merchandise?
* **Clothing and fashion accessories:** Does everyone in your school seem to be wearing at least one article of clothing that is lime green? Maybe it should appear somewhere in your yearbook.
* **Old houses:** Homes in historic districts that have a lot of "gingerbread" or wood carving will show you that hunter green, burgundy, dark teal, and plum all look sensational with taupe.
* **The Internet:** What are the colors of your favorite Web sites?
* **Wallpaper and paint samples:** Paint stores stock a whole library of books with wallpaper samples.

Glenn W. Murphy, Jr., Graphic Designer

Working with people is the greatest lesson from high school journalism, according to Glenn W. Murphy Jr., 25, art director for The proMedia Group in New Albany, Indiana.

"Whether you're 14, 24, or 40, people still act like babies sometimes," Murphy says. "To be an editor of a high school publication is a small lesson in life. You learn about setting an example. If you miss deadlines, if you skip work sessions, if you don't take your job seriously, your staff won't take you seriously. When you learn that, you've just learned management."

Murphy credits the foundation for his current job to his high school journalism days in Jeffersonville, Indiana.

"Understanding the basic principles of design and having the opportunity to have my work published put me miles ahead of my peers in college," he says. "I excelled faster, becoming the design editor of my college paper my first year. By the time I was finished with college, I had so many examples of my published designs that I had five different portfolios for different styles of design. And let me tell you, an employer cares more about your portfolio than anything else."

After graduating from Indiana University, Murphy worked as a marketing director for a bank, an interactive designer for an advertising agency, and an assistant art director before taking his current job with proMedia, which specializes in design work for audio, video, and interactive media clients, including animation, web sites, and print graphics.

One benefit of a high school journalism background was teamwork, according to Murphy. "We really had to work together to get our newspaper out every two weeks," he recalls. "If one person didn't accomplish a task, it hurt everyone. And if all went well, there was a product to show off your hard work. It was a tangible group accomplishment."

What is the advice from Murphy? "Get published, maintain a portfolio, and compete," he says. "Get as many of your good design clips as possible and put them in a big design book. Your college publication will want to see what you can do. Encourage your adviser to let you compete in publication design contests. A large part of design is observing and making better. If you do those things, you'll be well on your way to a great graphic career."

Creating the Layout

Visuals that are *not* symmetrical are more interesting to look at than those that are symmetrical. That's where the concept of contrast comes in. In creating a basic two-page spread, whether for a yearbook or newspaper center spread or photo essay layout, contrasting sizes and shapes are used alternately to provide visual contrast.

Building a Design

Follow these **six** basic steps as you begin to build a design:

Design Steps
Step 1—Place the dominant
Step 2—Contrast dominant
Step 3—Repeat dominant
Step 4—Cluster remaining photo(s)
Step 5—Add captions
Step 6—Add copy and headline(s)

1. **Place the dominant.** The dominant image can be vertical or horizontal, depending on the best photo you have. Skip squares (too boring) and stick with rectangles for modularity and visual interest. This photo or artwork should be about 30 percent larger than any other element on the page. It's a good idea to cross the gutter with the dominant to unify the spread. To promote a basic L-shaped layout, the dominant will fall somewhere in the upper right quadrant of the layout. You can use the principles of modular design and put the dominant elsewhere in the layout. It's perfectly acceptable to bend the rules from time to time for visual appeal.

2. **Contrast the dominant.** If your dominant is horizontal, as the mast head and photo are in our example on page 282, make the second visual in the layout a vertical. Because it's a subordinate element, the second image needs to be smaller than the dominant. In the example, notice how on the righthand page the second photo aligns with the bottom of the dominant, rather than being a few picas higher or lower. This sets the stage for an organized and unified spread when the rest of the elements are added in.

3. **Repeat the dominant.** Now add another photo, graphic, or piece of art (such as a small map, quote box, or the like) that is more or less the same shape as your dominant, only smaller. Again, it should also align on one side with the dominant. In our example, we chose to attach this photo to the bottom margin, to "anchor" the bottom of the layout. It's important to do this because usually some graphic elements touch the top and both sides of the layout, but sometimes the bottom is "ragged"—the elements are not all the same depth. One element needs to touch the bottom margin to complete visually the whole rectangle of the page. (In modular design, even the layout page itself is a rectangle.)

4. **Cluster the remaining photos.** Make sure to keep your internal margins (the space between all of the inside elements on the page) consistent. The standard unit for these internal margins is one pica. The smaller subordinate photos should also align in some fashion with the dominant. The placement of these photos helps create the spread's eyeline. In the example on page 283, one of the photos **bleeds** off the bottom, meaning that it goes past the margin of the page and is cut off at the edge of the paper. Our eyes are attracted to breaks in the repetition of the design, which is what happens when one photo on the layout bleeds.

5. **Add captions.** Notice how the photos fit together to form triangular spots in the layout. Those V-shaped "holes" are where the captions snug in. Try this: Think of the layout as a splotch of paint in the middle of a wheel. When the wheel starts spinning, the dominant would stay close to the middle, the other subordinate photos would cluster around it a bit farther out, and the captions and white space would get hurled to the outside. A good rule of thumb is that, on one side or another, the caption should "touch" (with a margin of one pica or 1/6 inch) the photo with which it goes. And whatever white space is left over should fall to the outer borders of the layout. (We'll discuss planning for white space and using it as a design element a bit later.)

6. **Add copy and headlines.** In this final step, you fit the copy and write the headline, subhead, or kicker. (See more about headlines in Chapter 16.) The headline would probably be a **bullet head,** in that it is short, punchy, and attention-getting, instead of the usual subject-verb construction. Design trends are currently getting away from long stories, relying instead on longer, narrative captions to tell the story with the photos. To complete the modular design, the copy block also needs to lay out in a rectangle, L shape, or U shape (textwrapped around a quote, artwork, or mugshot).

Making It Fit

Copy fitting is the process of working the type and graphic elements to fit the pages as laid out in the dummy. There are some tricks to copy fitting, and some practices to avoid absolutely. One trick to adjusting copy up or down is to look for **widows** and **orphans.** Widows are the last few words in a paragraph that run over to the top of the next column. Similarly, orphans are the last couple of words in a paragraph that don't extend at least halfway across the column.

Tracking is another way to alter the copy to expand or contract its length. Tracking is the space between the letters of the text. Usually, headlines are tracked tightly, and your body copy may have no tracking, normal tracking, or tight tracking if you're trying to fit in a lot of text.

What should be avoided in copy fitting? Maybe the rule of thumb is that subtle alterations are okay, but obvious squeezing in or stretching out copy is to be avoided. Changing the point size to something different from all the other stories, changing the leading of the body copy, varying the **horizontal scaling**—adjusting the width of a letter—are not good choices. For consistency of design, the type elements must remain the same from story to story and from page to page.

Walk Through the Paper

Page One

The saying, "You can't judge a book by its cover" doesn't really apply here. Your newspaper's visual appeal on page one will affect whether readers go inside to read other articles as well as how they judge the paper as a whole. Remember the three-second rule: A reader decides in three seconds whether to read further.

Not only is consistency important throughout the whole publication, but consistency within the elements on the front page is also key. Start with the logo. It should occupy no more than 20 percent of the front page. Type, the dateline (with school name, date, issue, and so forth), and any rule lines or **bullets** should all be consistent. These elements of the design need to be consistent, not only with each other, but also with the other standing elements in the publication.

On the next page are two examples of design that carry consistent elements from page one to an inside page. The highlighted parts are the standing elements that are most consistent with the logo. Also highlighted are the icons that appear on the front page and that are then used in their corresponding sections.

Inside Pages

The Double Truck

A newspaper spread, commonly called a **double truck,** is a great deal like a yearbook spread. The main difference is that where your yearbook design would primarily contain photos, the newspaper double truck would have considerably more space allotted for text. Also, in place of some of the photos, you'd want to include some sidebar stories and perhaps an infographic or boxed-in bulleted list.

When dummying up your double truck, think about how much text you have for the main story, what sidebar stories there might be, what graphic element is going to be your dominant, and what information in the story would best lend itself to a graphic. In designing a double-truck on a delicate topic, your dominant element might not be a photograph. Instead, it might be an illustration or infographic.

Consistent Elements

A Logo is placed prominently at the top of the page.

C Headlines are consistently horizontal in this design.

Source: Assumption High School, Louisville, Ky., *Rosecall*, Sept. 1997.

B Icons introduced on first page are used on other pages.

D These pages reflect traditional design styles.

Double Truck

A Two pages side-by-side designed as one unified spread.

B Headline runs across both pages.

Model

How a 45-year run began with a walk ...

Source: Reprinted with permission of Melissa McIntosh, Our Lady of Providence High School, Clarksville, Ind.

C The large, dominant photo with light copy reflects a new, more magazine-like design.

Editorial and Op-Ed Pages

A newspaper's editorial section is its signature. Not only should it be an open forum for student opinion, it should also be a place where your newspaper can show its leadership within the school community as a whole. Because the opinion section gets so much attention from your readers, it should have a consistent and readable design. Do your readers know where to look for the main editorial in every issue? Is there a personal opinion column that appears all the time? What about editorial cartoons—do they accompany the main opinion article, or do they stand alone? Where can a reader find information about how to go about writing a letter to the editor? Even though these questions deal with content and the written word, the answers are design oriented.

The main editorial page should begin your opinion section. On it should appear your staff editorial (a collective opinion not signed by one person) and a dominant graphic. If there is a sidebar to this main editorial, or a point-counterpoint of opinions on the same topic, it should also appear on this page.

The op-ed page, opposite the editorial page, is a kind of catch-all for other opinion-related articles that you won't have room for on the main editorial page. You might put a standing opinion column here, or maybe a graphic with opinion poll statistical data every issue. The thing to remember on both the op-ed and the editorial pages is to be consistent. If you're going to lean one way with the design, lean toward being conservative.

Layout for Multiple Stories

In the event that you have several stories and elements on a page where space is at a premium, graphics can be used to separate multiple stories. Boxes, graphics, and differing **decks** in headlines (lines in a headline or subhead; a two-line headline would have two decks) can also help to avoid running the headlines of separate stories together.

What's New in Design

Many school newspapers across the country are switching to a more "magazine style" design approach. This type of design is a bit more flexible than the traditional newspaper layout. A magazine style allows for more contrast by making use of more white space along the outside of the layout. Here, the outer columns of an odd-numbered, multicolumned layout are called **rails**. This exaggerated use of white space is that it increases the contrast of the design of the page and calls attention to exactly what the designer wants to emphasize. For example, it's great to use one large, dominant photo as the visual center of interest, then very little copy and lots of white space. It's not traditional newspaper design, but it would work well for a single-theme page, a center spread, or in magazine and yearbook design.

Design elements are only as good as the basic journalism fundamental—writing. Yet there are so many creative design options available to student journalism staffs. Though good designing involves much precision and detail work, your imagination within the boundaries of modular design is virtually limitless. What's even better is that the design style you decide on this year or next year will be unique. Just as the best writers are always looking for new stories and great photographers always have an eye out for that perfect human interest shot, as a designer, you also need to be on the lookout for design ideas that you can implement in your publication. Since your publication's design will evolve from year to year (and staff tastes will also vary), it's a good idea to keep a clips book of good design ideas that can be adapted for your use. This will serve as a springboard to stop "designer's block" and get you moving in the right direction. The important thing to remember when using other sources for your ideas is don't steal. Borrow. Change. Take a basic idea from a newspaper across the country and adapt it to fit your needs.

Journalism

artwork—photos, drawings or illustrations, infographics, pulled quotes, initial letters; anything other than the text of a story.

balance—visual appeal of a page achieved not through symmetry, but by even distribution of design elements over the entire area of the page or spread.

bleed—a photo that is run beyond the margin of a page.

broadsheet—the standard size of professional newspapers.

bullet head—sometimes called a "hammer"; a punchy, one-word headline.

bullets—also called "dingbats"; tiny symbols or icons that appear in front of items in a list or in an infographic.

clip art—artwork available on CD or from books that can be used without violating a copyright.

column bug—photo and name of the person writing a regular column; sometimes contains the name of the column as well.

copy fitting—the process of making the type and graphic elements fit the pages as laid out in the dummy.

decks—lines in a headline or subhead; a two-line headline has two decks.

dominant element—the most eye-catching element on the page, should generally be artwork and should be at least 30 percent larger than any other element on the page.

continues ▶

double truck—a two-page spread of facing pages that is seen as one horizontal unit, rather than two separate vertical pages.

drop cap—the oversized letter that begins the first word of a story.

dummy (thumbnail sketch)—a rough outline of what a page will look like when designed; indicates where headlines, photos, art, and text will go.

eyeline—the visual pattern a reader makes when viewing all the elements on a page, in the order that the page designer intended, from dominant to all the other subordinate elements.

flag (banner)—the logo of the publication that runs across all columns.

folio line—information at the top of a newspaper page, or the bottom of a yearbook page, that gives the page number, date of publication, section, and sometimes the name of the publication.

font families—fonts that belong to the same general typeface but may have different attributes or styles; for example, Avant Garde is a typeface, and Avant Garde Condensed Bold is in the same font family.

four-color process—full color, a process where all colors of the spectrum are created through varying tints of cyan (blue), magenta, yellow, and black.

graduated fill—a tintblock that has two colors, ranging from 100 percent of the first color, through a smooth progressive blend of the two, to 100 percent of the second color.

grids—multiple, thin columns on a page.

gutter— the middle margin of a two-page spread, where the fold or spine would be in a newspaper or yearbook.

horizontal scaling—adjusting the narrowness of a letter so that it is more visually pleasing and fits better horizontally in the space allotted.

icons—small, photolike artwork representative of larger concepts; for example, a computer icon that looks like a printer stands for "to print."

infographic (infograph)—a blend of artwork and statistical information that is put together so that the reader is able to digest a large amount of data in a visually pleasing format.

internal margins—the amount of space between all the graphic elements on a page; usually 1/6 inch or one pica.

jumpline—a line of type at the bottom of the last column of a story that tells the reader the page where the story is continued.

leading—the amount of white space between individual lines of type.

logo (nameplate)—the name of the newspaper, prominently displayed on the front page, not to be more than 20 percent of the page area.

modular design—the style of design where all graphic elements are rectangular in shape and fit together cleanly and concisely.

mugshot—head-and-shoulders portrait of a person.

newsprint—type of porous, grayish paper on which most news publications are printed.

offset press—press that uses a process in which the image is stamped onto paper from a rubber blanket on the press around a drum; the inked blanket is stamped against the metal plate onto which the ink adheres.

pica—a standard measurement in journalism; 1/6 inch.

point size—a way of keeping track of how large or small type is; there are 12 points in a pica.

points of entry—graphic elements whose purpose is to catch the reader's eye and guide attention back into the story; examples are initial letter, pulled quote, artwork, photos.

pulled quotes—direct quotes or other concise statements that are lifted out of a story and set off in larger, bolder type; always accompanied by a source.

rails—the outside margins of a two-page spread, usually narrower than a regular column width; used for special information.

refer—small statement boxed off in a story that will refer the reader to a related story elsewhere in the publication.

rules—lines that box in elements or separate elements on a page; should be no greater than one point wide.

sans serif/serif—serif fonts have marks at the endpoints to help the reader track the lines of type across a column, and should be used for body copy; sans serif fonts have no extra marks and are used for headlines and other display type.

spec sheet—a form that ensures consistency in a publication's design elements; should contain font family, size, style information on all the standing elements, as well as line width, screen percentages, and so on.

spot color—use of one color on an otherwise black and white page.

standing elements—graphic elements that stay the same from issue to issue or within a yearbook section, such as bylines, pulled quotes, column bugs, and captions.

subordinate elements—smaller graphic elements that surround and support the dominant in a layout.

tabloid/mini-tab—shorter than a standard broadsheet-size newspaper; got its name from the editorialized London papers that sell at newsstands and checkout counters. The mini-tab is as wide as a tabloid, but shorter in length.

textwrap or **runaround**—text shaped to fit around a graphic.

tintblock—a section of spot color or screened down color (or shade of gray) used to set off a sidebar, graphic, or other boxed item for visual effect.

tracking—the spacing between letters in a story; should never be very loose or very tight.

type font—a style of type.

unity—visually pleasing package of graphics that function as a whole.

web press—prints paper (usually newsprint) on a continuous roll that is threaded all through different areas of the press before being folded and cut into customary newspaper sizes.

white space—areas on a page that have no graphic element.

widows/orphans—single lines of type that appear odd to the eye because they are not at least half the length of a regular line in a column of type; a widow is a few words at the end of a paragraph at the top of a column; an orphan is a short line at the end of a paragraph at the bottom of a column.

Headlines

In this chapter, you will learn:

- about the purpose and qualities of an effective headline
- sizes and styles of headlines
- how to write headlines

"We sell stories," says a copyeditor/headline writer for the Chicago Tribune. Headlines advertise a story to readers. Each competes with all the others for the reader's attention, so without an effective one, chances are the writer's days of research, writing, and rewriting will be wasted because few people, if any, will stop to read the story. Headline writing is one of the most important, if not the most difficult, of the journalist's jobs, one done all too often up against the inevitable pressure of a final deadline.

The Story at a Glance

Effective headlines draw the reader into the story. What else do they do? To be effective, a headline must:

* Retell the story accurately or be a truthful and ethical representation of at least part of the story.
* Reflect the tone of the story—serious for news stories and perhaps lighter for feature stories.
* Follow generally accepted rules for headline writing.
* Follow the publication's rules for design (covered in Chapter 15).

Ironically, on most publications—professional and scholastic alike—the writer of the story does not get a chance to compose his or her own headline. That important task is often completed by a copyeditor or a page design specialist. To help the headline writer create the most effective presentation for a story, the reporter may want to suggest a headline angle when submitting the story for publication. Some publications even have a special form for this purpose.

For those using the maestro, or team, approach to coverage of a single topic, the writer, photographer, designer, and artist work together to create a total package, including the headlines. (See a description of the maestro system in Chapter 8.)

Case Study
Comparing Headlines

Friday, July, 2, 1999: A lone gunman goes on a shooting spree in the Chicago area.

In West Rogers Park, a northwest side Chicago community, six Orthodox Jews in traditional Sabbath clothing are wounded. In suburban Skokie, an African-American ex-basketball coach for Northwestern University is dead. In suburban Northbrook, an Asian couple is uninjured but terrified. By Sunday, July 4, Chicago police continued their investigation, calling the incident a potential hate crime but not yet able to identify the gunman or his motive.

"Manhunt follows trail of bullets" read a banner headline on the front page of the July 4 Chicago Tribune. The second deck of the headline continued, "Byrdsong slain, 6 Jews shot in spree tinged by hate."

This is a local story for the *Tribune*, but it is not the only newspaper to run the story on its front page. Coverage by the Associated Press and the *New York Times* News Service enabled Sunday newspaper readers across the country and in at least one other part of the world to awaken on this Independence Day to front-page stories of violence and heartbreak in these unlikely Chicago locations.

Which of these would make you stop and read the story? Why?

Headlines

Police hunt man in shooting spree

Black man slain, 6 Jews wounded in Chicago area

Courier-Journal, Louisville, Ky.

Ex-coach killed; six Jews wounded

White gunman sought in Illinois

Richmond Times-Dispatch, Richmond, Va.

One killed, 6 wounded in Ill. drive-bys

Boston Sunday Globe, Boston, Mass.

Man kills one, wounds six in 10-mile Chicago shooting spree

Great Falls Tribune, Great Falls, Mont.

Hate crimes suspected in Chicago shooting rampage

Statesman Journal, Salem, Ore.

Chicago shooter kills black man, wounds 6 Jews

Clarion-Ledger, Jackson, Miss.

7 shot around Chicago

Dallas Morning News, Dallas, Tex.

Gunman sprays bullets at Chicago minorities

Sunday News & Observer, Raleigh, N.C.

Chicago-area gunman kills 1 and wounds 6

Philadelphia Inquirer, Philadelphia, Pa.

Ex-coach killed, Jews injured as gunman stalks Chicago

Atlanta Journal-Constitution, Atlanta, Ga.

Gunman Fires at Minorities in Illinois
Black Ex-Coach Dies, 6 Orthodox Jews Are Wounded in Spree

Washington Post, Washington, D.C.

Chicago drive-by gunman kills ex-coach, wounds six

The State, Columbia, S.C.

Orthodox Jews, black man shot in Chicago

Jackson Sun, Jackson, Tenn.

Minorities Targeted in Chicago Area Drivebys

Los Angeles Times, Los Angeles, Calif.

Chicago rampage may be hate act
One killed, 6 wounded in late-night shootings

Oakland Tribune, Oakland, Calif.

Ex-UA coach slain in Chicago drive-by
6 Orthodox Jews hurt in spree

Arizona Republic, Phoenix, Ariz. [Note the localization to the University of Arizona.]

One man dead, 6 Jews hurt in Chicago hate shootings

The Jerusalem Post

Headlines—
Then and Now

Technology in the mid-1800s dictated that stories be run down the length of a vertical column with headlines only one column wide. (See on the next page the *New York Times*, Nov. 20, 1863.) As a result, headlines of the time typically consisted of several different decks, or sections—sometimes as many as 15—often using all capital letters and mixing a wide variety of typefaces. These **multi-deck headlines** told the reader important bits and pieces of the story. By 1912, with the sinking of the *Titanic*, the *New York Times* used a three-line, all caps banner headline above the multi-deck one-column heads to signal the importance of this event.

Today, designers have virtually abandoned all-caps heads with some exceptions, such as tabloids like the *New York Post*. Readership studies have found all-caps heads hard for the reader to understand quickly. First, designers favored upstyle headlines, and more recently downstyle. In **upstyle headlines**, all words may be capitalized or all important words may be capitalized, leaving prepositions and other less important words in lower case. In **downstyle headlines,** only the first word and proper nouns are capitalized.

Examples of upstyle headlines can still be found in some of the most respected newspapers today, including the *Wall Street Journal, New York Times, Washington Post,* *Los Angeles Times*, and the *International Herald Tribune* (published with the *New York Times* and the *Washington Post*). However, most professional and student newspapers use downstyle headlines because of their more modern look and readability.

Example

This Type Illustrates Upstyle Headlines

This type illustrates downstyle headlines

New York Times, Nov. 20, 1863

Civil War News

This front page illustrates the accepted style at the time of the Civil War—stories running down the length of a vertical column with headlines only one-column wide. Civil War news is reported in multi-deck heads; Lincoln's Gettysburg Address appears in column 3.

1912 With the sinking of the *Titanic,* the *New York Times* incorporated a three-line, all caps banner headline above the multi-deck one-column heads to signal the importance of the loss of the huge passenger ship on its first voyage.

As technology evolved, so did the use of multiple columns to lay out a story more horizontally. This made the same story appear shorter and thus more inviting to the reader. Along with multi-column stories came multi-column headlines to cover all columns, or **legs,** of the story.

Example

The New York Times.

"All the News That's Fit to Print."

THE WEATHER.

NEW YORK, TUESDAY, APRIL 16, 1912—TWENTY-FOUR PAGES.   ONE CENT   TWO CENTS

TITANIC SINKS FOUR HOURS AFTER HITTING ICEBERG; 866 RESCUED BY CARPATHIA, PROBABLY 1250 PERISH; ISMAY SAFE, MRS. ASTOR MAYBE, NOTED NAMES MISSING

Col. Astor and Bride, Isidor Straus and Wife, and Maj. Butt Aboard.

"RULE OF SEA" FOLLOWED

Biggest Liner Plunges to the Bottom at 2:20 A. M.

RESCUERS THERE TOO LATE

New York Times, April 16, 1912

1940 The *New York Herald Tribune* used a caps and lower case three-line banner above multi-deck one-column and two-column heads to signal the importance of the Nazi blitzkrieg in Europe.

Example

NEW YORK

Herald Tribune EXTRA
LATE CITY EDITION

THE WEATHER

FRIDAY, MAY 10, 1940

Germans Bomb Holland, Belgium, France And Switzerland in Invasion by Air Fleets; 'The Hour Has Come,' Hitler Tells His Troops

Fair Weather Forecast for

Queen Wilhelmina Says Holland Will Do Its Duty

Chamberlain Clings to Job; Roar as Nazis

Belgian Guns

Planes Bomb Dutch Cities,

New York Herald Tribune, May 10, 1940

1942 American involvement in World War II screamed at readers from front pages across the country. The *Bangor (Maine) Daily News* used a variety of approaches in heads—from a multi-deck banner to multi-column decks combining roman and italic type—in its front-page coverage on November 9, 1942.

Example

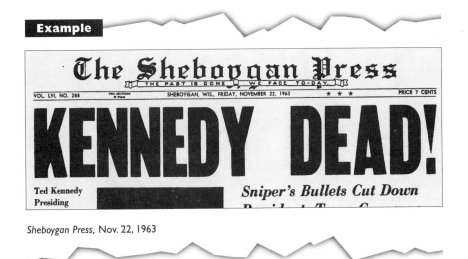

Paid Circulation OF THE NEWS Saturday 49,109

Weatherman Says: COLDER Forecast for Maine: Colder today.

Bangor Daily News

VOL. 53   BANGOR, ME., MONDAY, NOVEMBER 9, 1942   PISCATAQUIS   FIVE CENTS

Puppet France Breaks With U.S.
Roosevelt Explains America's Motives
Second Front Opened In Africa
Americans Push Way Into Vichy Colonies

The *Bangor Daily News,* Nov. 9, 1942

1963 By the time of President John F. Kennedy's nation-stunning assassination in 1963, the approach to a major story became stark. A single all-caps one-line head proclaiming "KENNEDY DEAD!" could be found on front pages across the country—and the world. *The Sheboygan (Wis.) Press* from November 22 illustrates this direction in headline writing.

Example

The Sheboygan Press
THE PAST IS GONE — WE FACE TO-DAY.

VOL. LVI, NO. 288   TWO SECTIONS 24 Pages   SHEBOYGAN, WIS., FRIDAY, NOVEMBER 22, 1963   ★ ★ ★   PRICE 7 CENTS

KENNEDY DEAD!

Ted Kennedy
Presiding

Sniper's Bullets Cut Down

Sheboygan Press, Nov. 22, 1963

Point Sizes

Although today's computer technology allows the page designer to choose from an infinite number of point sizes, for the sake of consistency most stick to the traditional sizes ranging from 14 to 72 point. (In printer's language, 72 points equal 1 inch.) Here is a range of traditional type sizes:

Example

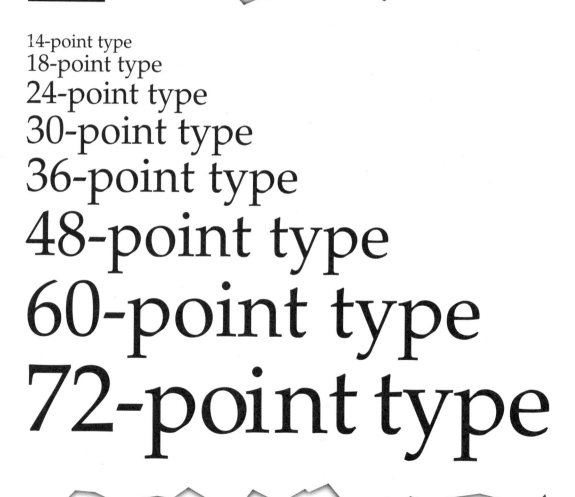

14-point type
18-point type
24-point type
30-point type
36-point type
48-point type
60-point type
72-point type

Of course, exceptions to these traditional point sizes are always possible, especially with a creative headline style.

Over 72 Points

VIOLENCE: coming closer to home

Abuse leaves terror in path of destruction

Source: Peninsula High School, Gig Harbor, Wash., *Peninsula Outlook*, Vol. 43, No. 8, April 6, 1999., p. 12.

Headline Styles

By far, the most common headline found in today's publications, especially for traditional news stories, is **multi-column** and **flush left**, starting at the left margin of the story and running fully, or nearly fully, to the right margin of the story. This style is most easily read and understood. On occasion a **centered** headline, one that is centered horizontally in the space available for the headline with white space on each side, may be appropriate. Likewise, there are a few times when it's appropriate to use a **flush-right** headline, with each line of a deck starting at the right margin of the story, or the right margin of one column of the story, and running less than the full width of the story or column.

This represents flush-left headline style

This represents centered headline style

This represents flush-right headline style

A variety of headline styles is available for the page designer to choose. If reporters are to suggest appropriate headlines for their stories, the reporters must also know and understand their options. Some headline styles include:

* **Banner**—one deck running all the way across the page; avoid overuse since overemphasis results in no emphasis.
* **Multi-line**—one deck with two or more lines running all the way across the story, usually set flush left.
* **Multi-deck**—more than one deck with at least one deck running all the way across the story; decks contrast in size and weight within a font family, with the largest and boldest first, usually set flush left.
* **Kicker**—two decks with a creative key word or phrase above the main headline and half the size of the main headline; has contrast within the font family (italic with regular or regular with bold); kicker is set flush left; main head may be flush left or indented.
* **Hammer**—two decks with a big, bold phrase above a smaller main head, twice the size of the main head, set flush left or centered; has contrast within font family, may have contrast across font families; main head may be flush left or indented; good for features.
* **Slammer**—one deck with two parts, both the same point size, with a bold word or phrase followed by a colon leading into a regular main headline; good for features.

* **Tripod**—three parts with a big, bold word or phrase (which may be all caps) followed by a colon and two lines of smaller main headline leading from it; twice the size of the main headline; good for features.
* **Wicket**—two-part with a bold main head under two or more lines of secondary headline that are half the size and contrasting weight of the main head; main head may read out of or stand alone from the secondary head; good for features.

Most headlines, including those described above, cover all legs of a story. These (shown on page 301) don't:

* **Raw wrap**—multi-line headline that does not cover all columns of the story; reserve for use with a boxed or screened story or when a tool line will make the story area clear; set flush left; use sparingly.
* **Sidesaddle**—multi-line headline set beside the story in its own column; reserve for use with a boxed or screened story; set flush left, centered, or flush right; use sparingly.
* **Jump**—smaller version of or a one-word association with the original story headline; jumpline at the bottom of the original story should indicate the content of the jump head; may vary in size but should be consistent throughout the publication.

Example

Banner headline:

Multicultural group hosts event

Multi-line headline:

Multicultural group
hosts diversity event
to educate students

Multi-deck headline:

Multicultural group hosts event

Annual Display of Cultures
aims to educate students
about clothing, dances
in 15 different countries

Main headline with kicker:

Hoping to educate fellow students

Multicultural group hosts event

Hammer headline:

Celebrate Diversity!

Multicultural group gears up for annual Display of Cultures on May 28

Slammer headline:

Let's Celebrate: Display of Culture

Tripod headline:

DIVERSITY DAY: Multicultural celebration focuses on understanding

---

Wicket headline:

*Annual Display of Cultures
uses fashion, dances, food
to focus on understanding*

SHADES gears up for May 28

Raw wrap headline:

Annual Display of Cultures uses fashion, dances, food to focus on understanding

An example of a raw wrap headline is shown with the head on the left "Annual Display of Cultures uses fashion, dances, food to focus on understanding." An example of a raw wrap headline is shown with the head on the left "Annual Display of Cultures uses fashion, dances, food to focus on understanding." An example of a raw wrap headline is shown with the head on the left "Annual Display of Cultures uses

Sidesaddle head:

An example of a sidesaddle headline is shown with the head in the center "Annual Display of Cultures uses fashion, dances, food to focus on understanding." An example of a sidesaddle headline is shown with the

Annual Display of Cultures uses fashion, dances, food to focus on understanding

head in the center "Annual Display of Cultures uses fashion, dances, food to focus on understanding."

An example of a sidesaddle headline is shown with the head in the center "Annual Display of Cultures uses fashion, dances, food to focus on understanding." An example of a sidesaddle headline is shown with the

Jump headline:

Multicultural group
(continued from p. 1)

Trends in Headlines

C Titles are used (rather than full headlines) to grab the reader's attention; a more traditional subhead underneath follows up.

D More magazine-style heads, especially in feature sections; decorative type picks up on the tone of the story.

A Nut graf boldly set out on the left.

Model

Non-Traditional Headline with Nut Graf

'Ride With the Devil': Jeffrey Wright, left, Tobey Maguire and Jewel in a Civil War tale

By John Clifford, Universal Studios

Big little movie season

Offbeat inspirations — such as 'Being John Malkovich' — from independent filmmakers will be competing for screen space this fall and giving big studio releases a run for their money.

By Mark Horton, Sony Pictures Classics

'American Movie': Pal Mike Schank, left, with director Mark Borchardt in the documentary about the Wisconsin filmmaker

By Harlan Jacobson
Special for USA TODAY

Maybe you're not sure how you feel about seeing *Fight Club.* Seem a bit too tame?

Well, in the coming months you can try a film about some folks who set up a thriving business diving into a famous actor's life (*Being John Malkovich*).

Or one with Harvey Keitel reclaiming every bit of Kate Winslet in a shack in the Aussie desert (*Holy Smoke*).

Or one about mothers, daughters, women and men who wish they could be women (*All About My Mother*).

This fall's alternative movies promise to be the richest in years. More than 60 films made outside the studio system and hailing from offbeat sources will gradually make their way across the country. Many are

Season's highlights, 2E
A ★★½ 'Malkovich,' 4E
Movie reviews, 8E

"I gave only three or four 4-star reviews in the first nine months of the year," says megacritic Roger Ebert. "Suddenly there are one or two every weekend. The year started slow and is ending like gangbusters."

Smaller art-house films are now mandatory viewing for any movie fan — not just the cinema elite.

"We have passed through an evolutionary phase from the black-and-white days of studios making teen comedies and Fellini or Bergman making art films and almost nothing in between," says Amir Malin, president of Artisan Entertainment, the company that made indie history with *The Blair Witch Project* (at $140.3 million and counting since summer). "To-

Source: *USA Today,* Friday, Oct. 29, 1999, Section E, p. 1.

B Multiple decks are used for the headline.

Real Headlines

Numerous Web sites list actual unintentional wacky headlines that have made it into publication:

* Kids make nutritious snacks
* Grandmother of eight makes hole in one
* Deaf mute gets new hearing in killing
* Police begin campaign to run down jaywalkers
* Stiff opposition expected to casketless funeral plan
* Two convicts evade noose, jury hung
* Farmer bill dies in house
* Iraqi head seeks arms

Some headlines become unintentionally suggestive:

* Queen Mary having bottom scraped
* NJ judge to rule on nude beach
* Child's stool great for use in garden

Bad syntax often goofs up headlines:

* Eye drops off shelf
* Squad helps dog bite victim
* Dealers will hear car talk at noon
* Enraged cow injures farmer with ax
* Lawmen from Mexico barbecue guests

* Two Soviet ships collide—one dies
* Two sisters reunite after eighteen years at checkout counter
* Miners refuse to work after death.

Once in a while, a botched headline takes on a meaning opposite from the one intended:

* Never withhold herpes from loved one
* Nicaragua sets goal to wipe out literacy
* Drunk drivers paid $1,000 in 1984
* Autos killing 110 a day—let's resolve to do better

Sometimes newspaper editors create a comic headline because they state the obvious:

* If strike isn't settled quickly it may last a while
* War dims hope for peace
* Cold wave linked to temperatures
* Child's death ruins couple's holiday
* Blind woman gets new kidney from dad she hasn't seen in years
* Man is fatally slain
* Something went wrong in jet crash, experts say
* Death causes loneliness, feeling of isolation

Sidebar

Jay Leno on Headlines

* Screwdrivers were made to tighten, loosen screws
* Researchers call murder a threat to public health
* Bush gets briefing on drought; says rain needed to end it
* Tribal council to hold June meeting in June
* Death ends fun
* City outlaws giving out phone numbers, addresses of police
* Engine falls off plane, lands safely at O'Hare
* Family catches fire just in time, chief says
* CRIME: Sheriff asks for 13.7% increase
* When it comes to student achievement, how high is your school?
* Blow to head is common cause of brain injury
* Low pay reason for poverty, study says
* Smaller families require less food
* Jail crowding caused by increase in criminals, new study concludes

Source: Complied from Jay Leno. Jay Leno's Real But Ridiculous Headlines from America's Newspapers, Books I, II, III. New York: Wings Books, N.Y., 1992.

Writing Headlines

Traditional news headlines follow time-honored rules, while more contemporary feature headlines often break at least some of the rules. **Two** rules, however, should never be broken:

1. **Be honest.** Headlines must be written ethically. You should never think of a clever headline just to trick readers into stopping at your story. "Elvis lives in Traverse City" may draw readers to your story—until they read far enough to discover you're writing about Elvis Jones, not Elvis Presley. If readers fall for such a trick once, they aren't likely to again. Worse yet—they may suspect your entire publication of having no credibility.

2. **Read the story.** Before you can possibly write an accurate and effective headline to attract the reader, you need to read the entire story. Waiting until deadline time to write headlines makes the job infinitely more difficult. While you might assume a news or sports story is written correctly, with the key ideas in the lead, that is not always the case.

Top 10 Rules

The 10 top traditional rules for headline writing are:

✓ Use subject-verb-object or phrase order with active voice verbs. Avoid "to be" verbs and label headlines that simply name something.

✓ Be sure to write a headline specific to one story, not a general headline that could apply to several stories.

✓ Use present tense for past and present events; use future tense ("to" or "will") for future events.

✓ In the interest of saving space, omit "a," "an," "the"; use a comma in place of "and"; use single quotation marks when this punctuation is needed; do not place a period at the end of a headline.

✓ Keep associated thoughts together in multi-line headlines. Do not split verb phrases, prepositional phrases, adjectives and their nouns, hyphenated words, or proper nouns between lines.

✓ Use only widely known abbreviations and omit periods.

✓ Avoid using the school name or abbreviation, or the mascot name; your readers know articles in your school publications are about your school.

✓ Avoid repeating the same word or another form of the word; also try to avoid repeating words in different headlines on the same page or spread.

✓ Attribute opinion; avoid including the writer's opinion, except in opinion pieces (for example, editorials, reviews, or columns) when opinion should be included in the headline.

✓ For a news or sports head and some feature heads, use facts from the lead of a well-written story; for many feature stories, use facts from anywhere in the story.

Sidebar

Writer Fails to Read

Imagine the embarrassment of a suburban Chicago headline writer for a boys' basketball story who wrote "Wheeling trounces Warren," assuming the "Wildcats" mentioned in the lead and early paragraphs of the story were the Wheeling High School Wildcats. In reality, Wheeling didn't play Warren the previous night. It was the Libertyville High School Wildcats who "trounced" Warren, which the headline writer would have discovered had he or she taken the time or had the time to read the entire story.

What's Wrong with These Headlines?

Using the checklist of top 10 headline writing rules, cite one or more weaknesses of each of the following and suggest improvements:

Strict security appreciated by former student, parent

A fond farewell

"The Mummy" unwrapped

Long and winding road ends with record performances for varsity baseball team

Student Council makes plans

Special Olympians strike gold again; track competitors win 30 gold medals

PSAE to replace IGAP/ISAT as standard measure of learning

Injuries plague Pirate line-up as basketball season continues

HHS to host good competition Election held to elect class officers

Forensics team on to state

Speech and debate going state and national meets

Girls tennis team completed goals of the season

District outlines policy on equity and diversity in the schools

ACHS promotes drug abuse prevention with red ribbons

Society & media have made violence the "norm"

Man hit by car in intensive care

Breaking the Rules

Since writers of feature headlines have more freedom, they may break some of the rules. Consider the following feature headlines:

* *Back in the swing*—for a story about professional golfer Fred Couples's comeback on the PGA tour, in *Partners*, March/April 1999.
* *Bye-Bye Birdie*—for a story about golf courses using border collies to deal with the problem of geese, in *Golf Journal*, May 1999.
* *Lynx to the Past*—for a story about trying to return lynx to their natural habitat in Colorado, in *Newsweek*, February 15, 1999.
* *Getting Her Kicks*—for a story about a female kicker on the all-male high school football team, in *Sports Illustrated for Women*, Spring 1999.
* *Star Track: The Next Generation*—for a story about plans for a new track, in the York High School, Elmhurst, Ill., *York Hi*, September 23, 1998.
* *No way to park at Parkway*—for a story about parking lot woes at Parkway Central High School, Chesterfield, Mo., *Corral*, November 13, 1998.
* *They're not trash; they're Garbage*—for a story about the rock band Garbage, in the South Lake High School, St. Clair Shores, Mich., *The Lancer*, December 1998.
* *A 'Boo'dacious experience*—for a story about haunted houses, in the Kirkwood, Mo., Kirkwood High School *Call*, September 18, 1998.

* **Teacher's retirement takes Toll on students**—for a story about the retirement of Dennis Toll, a popular teacher, in the Wheeling, Ill., Wheeling High School *Spokesman*, April 23, 1999.
* **Snow day sends communication aflurry**—for an editorial about miscommunication related to snow days, in the Darien, Ill., Hinsdale South High School *Stinger*, January 29, 1999.
* **Taking Care of Business**—for a story about using assignment notebooks and daily planners successfully, in the LaGrange, Ill., Lyons Township High School *Lion*, April 23, 1999.
* **Cleaning house**—for a behind-the-scenes story about a custodian, in the Naperville, Ill., Central High School *Central Times*, December 18, 1998.
* **She takes the cake**—for a story about a freshman with a hobby of cake decorating, in the Hinsdale, Ill., Central High School Devil's *Advocate*, February 25, 1999.
* **Health food stores 'sprout' up everywhere**—for a story about rapid growth of health food stores in the area surrounding Live Oak High School, Morgan Hill, Calif., in the *Oak Leaf*, March 11, 1999.
* **At the head of the class**—for a story reporting results of a survey to find students' favorite classes at Peninsula High School, Gig Harbor, Wash., in the *Peninsula Outlook*, March 23, 1999.

Headline Construction

Page designers determine headline size based on story importance and placement on the page. They assign a copyeditor to write a headline with a shorthand method. For example, if the designer needs a two-line, 36-point headline running across three columns, he or she assigns a 2-36-3 headline to be written.

Example

Shorthand Method

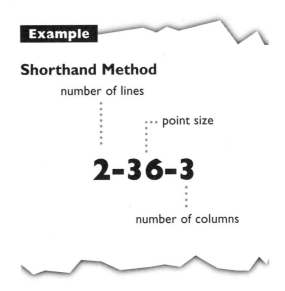

number of lines

point size

2-36-3

number of columns

Headline writers, usually copyeditors, work from a **headline schedule**, a chart that includes all the fonts available for the publication in all of their sizes. Using the **unit count system**, the writer can tell at a glance how many "counts" a headline of a specific size must contain to cover a specific number of columns. Because all letters set in type do not take up the same amount of space, the unit count system (see box) has become an accepted standard.

Let's say the 2-36-3 headline has a count of 30. The headline writer must come within one count of 30 in each line when writing the headline. For example, using the unit count system (and counting lowercase *r* as 1/2), the following headline

School Board votes to increase fees for activity card, graduation, driver ed

counts 30 for the first line and 30 for the second line. It would be acceptable as a straight news headline and would fit the 2-36-3 assignment given above.

The headline writer can experiment with writing a headline manually or on the computer screen. The same steps should be used when working with headlines on the computer. Ideally, the page designer assigns a point size and style of headline. However, the publication staff should establish specific guidelines about manipulating headlines to fit in order to retain consistency in appearance from page to page and section to section.

Generally, the finished headline should not be expanded or condensed enough to distort the type noticeably from its assigned size. Likewise, the finished headline should not deviate more than one or two points up or down from the size assigned by the page designer. These guidelines are especially true for straight news, sports, opinion, and feature heads. More creative styles may allow the writer to deviate from these guidelines.

The Unit Count System
Most lower case letters = 1 count.
Lower case *m, w* = 1-1/2 counts.
Lower case *f, l, i, t, j* (and *r* in some fonts) = 1/2 count.
Most upper case letters = 1-1/2 counts.
Upper case *M, W* = 2 counts.
Upper case *I* (and *J* in some fonts) = 1 count.
Spaces between words = 1/2 count.
Most punctuation = 1/2 count
?, $ = 1 count.

PRESS PASS
ON THE
JOB

Michelle Pendleton, Journalism Teacher

"For the most part, I have a great job," says Michelle Pendleton, who teaches journalism and advises the newspaper and yearbook at Episcopal High School in Houston, Texas. "I get to work with media and journalism all day. I teach only four classes. With the school's commitment to technology, I get to try the latest things, like digital imaging."

Pendleton, 29, is in her fourth year at Episcopal, her first teaching job. She teaches media literacy, introduction to journalism, yearbook, and newspaper. "When I first got here I had one student in intro, four in newspaper, and 13 in yearbook," she says. "We had to rebuild from scratch, which in a way was good because I could set the standards."

At first that rebuilding required Pendleton to act as both editor and adviser. "With the yearbook the first year I created all of the section templates," she explains. "The next year the students did this, but I made the templates on PageMaker. The following year they did that, but I did all of the digital imaging using Photoshop."

As Pendleton has gradually handed over more responsibility to her students, her numbers have grown to 13 on the newspaper staff and 27 in yearbook. "This is the first year I've felt really confident that the students will be able to take the lead, especially on the yearbook," she says.

As for censorship, "We are in a private school, so the administration could be really hard on us," Pendleton says. "In the time I've been here we've been told only once that a story could not go in the newspaper." No adult besides Pendleton reads newspaper or yearbook copy for content.

The job has some downsides, Pendleton acknowledged. "Once the deadlines start I am often here from 6:30 a.m. to 6:30 p.m. or later," she says. "And there are traditions at the school that are detrimental, such as the expectation of giving each senior a full yearbook page—that's 144 pages of the book. But on the plus side, I've been able to get rid of junk like horoscopes and senior superlatives."

As a student herself, Pendleton was active in publications in junior high at Parker, Colorado, and at Ponderosa High School there. "I took yearbook instead of going to lunch," she says. A summer journalism workshop during high school motivated her further.

"When I got to college, I knew that I wanted to learn how to be a journalist but

continues ▶

also that I wanted to teach high school kids what journalistic writing was really like," she says.

First she earned bachelor's and master's degrees in journalism at Northwestern University, interning at the *Roanoke* (Va.) *Times* and as a Washington correspondent for the *Huntsville* (Ala.) *News*. She also worked in a graduate magazine publishing program, helping to develop a magazine for the catering industry, and she taught in summer high school publications workshops.

After marrying her college boyfriend and moving with him to Houston, Pendleton attended the University of Houston for two years to earn a teaching certificate. She spent half that time in an internship at La Marque High School in Houston, working half the day with an English teacher and the other half with journalism. She is certified in Texas to teach English, journalism, and speech.

"My future goals are to develop the introduction to journalism class more and to get students more self-sufficient in the production classes," Pendleton says. "I'd love to get to the point where they can earn some recognition at either the state or national level, and my final goal would be to have a student actually go into journalism—then I would feel like I'd really done what I'd set out to do."

Wrap-up

A headline can make or break the story. Without an effective headline to draw the reader into the story, the writer's days of research, writing, and rewriting are wasted. Headlines must be accurate, truthful, and ethical, and they must reflect the story's tone. They should follow generally accepted rules for effective headlines, deviating from these only for good reason and usually only for feature stories. While desktop publishing programs allow for nearly unlimited point sizes and scaling of type to fit a certain space, the publication staff should establish guidelines for deviations from standard point sizes and for expanding or condensing type.

banner headline—one deck running all the way across the page, usually one line.

centered—placing a headline or line of body copy in the midpoint of a given space with white space on either side.

downstyle headline—headlines in which only the first word of a deck and proper nouns are capitalized.

flush left—positioning each line of a headline or copy block beginning at the left-hand margin of a page or story box.

flush right—positioning each line of a headline or copy block at the right-hand margin of a page or story box.

hammer—two decks consisting of a big, bold phrase above the smaller main headline and set twice its size.

headline schedule—chart that includes all the fonts available for a publication in all sizes.

jump headline—smaller version of original story headline, or a portion of it, used on the page to indicate where the story continues.

kicker—two decks consisting of a creative key word or phrase above the main headline and set half its size.

leg—vertical column of type in a story.

multi-column headline—headline running horizontally across more than one column of a page.

multi-deck headline—headline consisting of more than one section; at least one deck runs all the way across the story.

multi-line headline—one deck with two or more lines running all the way across the story, usually flush left.

raw wrap—multi-line headline that does not cover all columns of a story, must be boxed or separated from other copy with a tool line to avoid confusion for the reader, usually flush left.

sidesaddle—multi-line headline set beside the story in its own column, can be flush left, centered, flush right.

slammer—one-deck, two-part headline with a bold word or phrase followed by a colon leading into the second part of the headline that is not bold but is the same point size.

tripod—three-part headline with a big, bold word or phrase followed by a colon and two lines of smaller main headline leading from it; twice the size of the main headline.

unit count system—way of measuring letter size used by headline writers to create a headline to fit a given horizontal space.

upstyle headline—headlines in which all words or all important words are capitalized.

wicket—two-part headline with a bold main head under two or more lines of secondary headline that are half its size.

Copyediting and Production

In this chapter, you will learn:

- about copy formatting
- about the importance of coaching in the copyediting process
- how to edit copy efficiently and effectively
- the role of the proofreader
- some guidelines for organizing your newspaper production process
- what desktop publishing can offer
- how to evaluate your staff's need for hardware and software

Once the stories are written, the photographs taken, the cartoons drawn, the advertising sold, and the pages designed, what happens next? The staff begins the task of putting it all together. Copy must be edited for consistency and to correspond to your publication's journalistic style. Proofreading must be done. Captions and headlines must be edited and arranged to fit the page designs. Photos, artwork, and cartoons must be sized and cropped. All of this material must be produced, with a reasonable understanding of computer technology, to achieve pages that are ready to go to press. At this point in the journalism process, the skills of teamwork really begin to pay off.

Formatting Copy

Copy is the typed version of any story, headline, caption, ad, sidebar, blurb, and so on, which is intended for publication. Historically, the writer created this version on a typewriter, and a typesetter set it in type. Today, with desktop publishing, things are different, and the process goes something like this:

* In some cases, reporters keyboard their stories directly into a box on a page layout. This is not the recommended procedure, because changes are more difficult to make once the copy is in its final place on the page.
* Usually reporters word process their stories using a program compatible with the publication's desktop publishing program.
* Once the writer makes all her or his own initial corrections to the story, a **hard copy**, or paper copy (as opposed to on-screen copy), of each story can be printed.
* Hard copies facilitate copyediting; with a hard copy in hand, it is easier to discuss stories and changes with more than one person on the staff before the original writer makes final corrections.
* Writers, especially student writers, keep their hard copies, to show each major rewrite from start to finish. Filed in a **portfolio**, a complete file of all work for each student, these sequential versions of each story help writers learn from their mistakes and allow their instructors to assess their progress.

Identifying Parts of Copy

Because typesetters often took pages of one story apart so that several of them could work on typesetting the same story at the same time, several helpful ways of identifying copy were developed.

* All these practices are still a good idea today to give staff members who are editing copy ample room to make corrections and suggestions, to write comments, and to ensure that all the pages of a story are returned together.
* Writers put **slug information**, also called the **guideline**, at the top left-hand corner of each page and the word "more" at the end of each page until the second-to-last page.
* At the end, writers put # or -30- so there would be no doubt where the story ended.

Understanding Slug Information

Slug information consists of:

* A few words indicating the subject of the story—called the **slug**
* The reporter's name—also known as the **byline**
* The number of words in the story
* The actual page number or "add one" for the second page, "add two" for the third page, and so on
* In addition to the number of words in your story, you should also indicate the number of characters if your staff's page designers use that number to determine how much space to leave for a story. Your staff may also decide on other information to add to the slug information, such as the publication date or issue number.

* Sample slug information is placed in the upper left corner of the page:

  Security Cameras
  Tamica Jones
  491 words/2746 characters
  for Issue #3

* All copy should be typed double- or even triple-spaced with at least a one-inch margin all around the page to allow plenty of space for handwritten corrections. Editors make these corrections with a sharp, very soft, black lead pencil. Reporters typically leave the top one-third to one-half of the first page blank for the editor's use. Here, the editor may write comments or questions about the story or may use the space to write instructions about the headline.

* If the story is written in a location other than where the newspaper is published, the reporter starts the opening paragraph with a **dateline**, including the city and state or country where the story originated.

Sidebar

Datelines

Most likely, your stories will not have datelines, but exceptions could occur. Someone from your school could be an exchange student in another country and send a story for your newspaper to publish. A teacher from your school may change places with a teacher in another state or country and send you a story. Your staff may decide to pick up stories from exchange newspapers to publish. One of your staff members may write a story during a visit to a college campus, from a trip to Disney World, or from a national forensics competition. The dateline is followed by a dash. All these examples require a dateline, such as ORLANDO, Fla.— (for a story written at Disney World).

Copyediting

Copyediting is the process of reviewing copy intended for publication. A good copyeditor checks for adherence to style rules, grammar, usage, mechanics, accuracy, effective communication and organization, clarity, and completeness. Even professionals routinely submit their writing to copyeditors.

Reporters should submit their stories for editing as early in the publication cycle as possible. Copyediting and rewriting can be much more effective without final deadline pressure.

The job of copyeditor may seem overwhelming. If you're thinking it is one of the most important jobs on the publication staff, you're absolutely right. To help ease the burden on one or two staff members, effective copyediting should begin with reporters themselves. After completing their stories, writers should always run their word processing program's spelling and grammar checkers. While these will not catch every error, they are an excellent starting point. Next, reporters should read their stories aloud—either from the computer screen or from a hard copy—following the editing checklist on page 321. In addition, ask yourself **three** basic questions about your story:

1. Have I said what I meant to say?
2. Have I said it as clearly and concisely as possible?
3. Is my story well organized?

Answering these three questions and performing all the other steps in the editing checklist are likely to take at least three thoughtful readings. You make the initial changes, then print a hard copy to pass along to the next person in the editing process. Depending on how your staff is organized, the next person may be a department editor or copyeditor or someone else. Be sure to staple all versions together for a complete record of your progress on the story to place in your portfolio.

Copyediting Toolbox

Anyone who reads copy—and that includes every writer on the staff—must develop a keen grasp of details. The better the story is originally, the fewer changes will need to be made as deadline approaches.

Of course, all staff members should learn and use style rules—both general ones and those applicable only to their own publication. Those who are designated as copyeditors must:

* Have a firm knowledge of style.
* Know what makes a sentence or paragraph or story communicate well to readers.
* Be an excellent speller.
* Be aware of details about school life to be able to spot inaccuracies quickly.

Few copyeditors, even professional ones, carry every detail in their heads. Copyeditors must also know where to go to find information. To help all writers do a better job of producing accurate copy that communicates well, the staff room should contain at least the following for instant reference:

* The local stylebook
* *The Associated Press Stylebook and Libel Manual*, which also contains excellent sections on sports guidelines, punctuation, and writing photo captions or cutlines
* *The Word: An Associated Press Guide to Good News Writing*
* A dictionary that everyone uses, for consistency
* A thesaurus
* Lists of all staff and student names
* A school calendar
* The student handbook containing school rules and regulations
* A local telephone directory

Notes from the Pros on Coaching

Roy Peter Clark and Don Fry discuss the mentoring, or coaching, approach in *Coaching Writers: Editors and Reporters Working Together* (1992). Although they talk about coaching in the professional newsroom, everything they say applies to the scholastic journalism room as well. Think about how your staff can apply this approach as you read this excerpt from the book's introduction:

"Coaching writers is the human side of editing. Coaching involves nothing more than talking with writers, in certain ways. A city editor can help a reporter plan a story. A copyeditor can help a colleague write a headline. A reporter can respond to the story of a friend.

"Even people with junior status can coach. A copy clerk can coach the ace columnist. A student can coach a teacher.

All you need are some basic reporting skills: Can you ask good questions? Can you get people talking? Can you listen? Can you observe and see patterns? Can you read with curiosity? Do you like stories? If you answered 'yes' to these questions, you can coach. If you also have a sympathetic nature, so much the better."

When copyeditors receive stories to edit, first they need to ask writers what they think works best and where they think the problems are with each story. Answers to these questions guide copyeditors in judging the overall story. Once copyeditors have finished reading a story, they go back to the writer with an overall evaluation of the piece. They may agree or disagree with the writer's assessment. This is the place for discussion to begin. Editors should be sure to ask writers for their ideas about revising so the writers retain ownership of their work.

A Coaching Attitude

The goal of copyediting is twofold: to make stories the best they can be and to prevent inaccuracies. Helping reporters learn to write effectively and correctly pays off in better stories for later issues.

The Right Attitude

Most of all, copyeditors need patience. Instead of ripping a new writer's copy to shreds, try to develop a mentoring approach. Be thoughtful and ethical about suggestions and corrections. Be sensitive to the feelings of the reporters whose work you are reading. Improving stories needs to be a collaborative effort between the copyeditor and the writer.

Copyediting Symbols

In the days of typewriters in newsrooms, reporters typed their stories on 8-1/2-x-11-inch sheets of newsprint. They reorganized stories by literally cutting and pasting instead of performing a computer function. **Copyediting symbols** indicated changes required or emphasized punctuation marks, such as periods and commas, that were sometimes difficult to see on the newsprint. (See copyediting symbols on the next page.) These symbols are standard worldwide and are still used everywhere copyediting is not performed directly on the computer screen.

The Copyediting Process

Even accomplished copyeditors read each story more than once to perform all the required functions. This system suggests at least three readings; however, more may be necessary.

1. **First reading.** In a coaching approach, your first reading of a story focuses on gaining a general understanding of the story and on what the writer has told you works best and what needs work. After noting comments to discuss with the writer about these areas, move to a second reading.

2. **Second reading.** Consider overall effective communication and organization along with clarity and completeness. Does this story make sense? Is it well organized? Do transitions exist and are they effective? Has the writer answered all the news questions (5Ws and 1H)? Do you still have questions after reading the story? For non-opinion pieces, are any opinions expressed in the story that seem to be the writer's rather than from a documented source? Note any ethical or legal problems the story might have (see Chapter 2). Note suggestions for improving communication with the reader, organization, clarity, and completeness.

3. **Third reading.** Use copyediting symbols to make changes and check for adherence to style rules and proper grammar, usage, and mechanics—capitalization, spelling, punctuation. This is a good time to check spelling of names, to note facts that don't seem right, to edit wordiness and check for other word choice problems, and to check for active versus passive voice. Is there a quote by the third paragraph, if possible? Are quotes and attributions handled according to the publication's style?

Once these three steps and their sub-steps are complete, get together with the writer for a conference. Discuss the strengths and weaknesses of the story. Remember to ask writers for ideas about improving their stories in the areas being discussed so they retain control of their own story. After the conference, ask the writer to make improvements before resubmitting the story.

Depending on how your staff is organized, the story may go to your editor-in-chief or your adviser—or both—for another careful reading. Again, before beginning to

---

Example

Standard Copyediting and Proofreading Symbols

SAMPLE COPYREADING SYMBOLS

USES	MEANINGS	PRINTER'S PROOF
into the room. She	New paragraph here.	into the room. She . . .
into the room. No ¶ She told the	No paragraph.	into the room. She told the . . .
into the room.	Take out letter.	into the room.
into the room.	Close up space.	into the room.
into the room. stet into the room.	Let the word stay as it is.	into the room.
into the room.	Insert letter or word.	into the room
to study Eng. and Fr.	Spell out.	to study English and French.
Professor Pengloss	Abbreviate.	Prof. Pengloss
five students	Use numeral.	5 students
5 students	Spell out.	five students
into the room. She the teacher told . . .	Transpose letters or words.	into the room. She told the teacher . . .
into the room	Put space between letters or words.	into the room
Weekly Bugle.	Use italics.	*Weekly Bugle.*
By Jim Sparks	Use bold face.	**By Jim Sparks**
By jim Sparks	Capitalize.	By Jim Sparks
By Jim Sparks	Use lower case letter.	by Jim Sparks
into the the room.	Delete.	into the room.
Sam Mary and George	Insert comma.	Sam, Mary and George
into the room	Insert period.	into the room.
is called Big John	Insert quotation marks.	is called "Big John"
more	The story isn't complete.	
30 or #	End of story.	

SAMPLE PROOFREADING SYMBOLS

SYMBOLS	MEANINGS	EXAMPLES
¶	Start a new paragraph here.	came into the room. She told the teacher her
#	Space needed as indicated.	toldthe teacher her
ℐ	Take out letter, letters or word.	told teacher her name
∧	Insert letter or word.	the told teacher her name
lc	Set in lower case type.	told the teacher her
×	Broken or burred letter; clean or replace.	told the teacher her
stet	Let it stand. Correction made by mistake.	stet told the teacher her
⌒	Draw the letters closer together.	told the teacher her
tr	Transpose letters or words as indicated.	told teacher the her
ital	Reset word in italic type.	*ital* told the teacher her
rom	Reset in roman (regular) type.	rom told the teacher her
[or]	Move over to the point indicated.	came into the room. She told the teacher her
⌐⌐	Lower to the point indicated.	came into the room. She told the teacher
⌐	Raise to the point indicated.	came into the room. She told the teacher
∧	Insert comma here.	told the teacher her name and then she went
∨	Insert apostrophe here.	asked the teachers name
⌄⌄	Use quotation marks around this word.	pretended to teach the class
No ¶	This should not be a separate paragraph.	asked the teacher's name. Then she started to
spell out	Spell out the encircled word(s).	will teach Eng. and Fr.
bf	Reset in bold face type.	told the teacher her name
see copy	Something is left out here or there are numerous error; refer to the original copy.	asked the name. Then to work in the book.
⊥	Type has worked up; push it down.	told the teacher her

Source: From School of Journalism and Mass Communication, University of Iowa, *Quill and Scroll Stylebook*, Iowa City, Iowa, 1997.

read the story, according to the coaching approach, the next person should ask the writer to describe the most and least successful parts of the story. If the copyeditor and writer have done their jobs well at the previous checkpoint, few errors should remain.

Checking for Accuracy

If the facts in a publication are not accurate, both the writer and the publication lose credibility. Writers first, and then copy editors, must be certain everything in the story is accurate. If a writer has done a careless job of reporting, the last place an error is likely to be caught and corrected is in the copyediting process.

An accuracy check includes confirming details such as:

* Spelling of names
* Faculty identifications
* Students' years in school
* Whether the football game is really October 9 instead of October 10
* In a list of five National Merit Semifinalists, five names are listed— not four or six

Above all, pay special attention to stories involving potentially unethical or libelous information. (See Chapter 2 for more on ethical and legal issues.) Read quotes thoughtfully, perhaps to protect sources from embarrassment or worse when the newspaper or yearbook is published. For example, in a story about cheating, does that freshman who is identified by name really want to tell the world how she cheated on her biology test?

Example

Common Errors

Staff members involved in the copyediting process should make a list of the frequent errors they find, especially those in style, grammar, usage, and mechanics. The lists can then be combined into what Roy Peter Clark calls a "Yucky List" in *Free to Write: A Journalist Teaches Young Writers* (1987). The errors should then be posted in the staff room. Seeing this list of errors each day should help writers prevent them in future stories.

Common errors in scholastic publications include:

* Writing "alot" instead of "a lot"
* Confusing *it's* and *its*
* Writing *advisor* instead of *adviser*
* Confusing *to, two,* and *too*
* Confusing *here* and *hear*
* Confusing *then* and *than*
* Confusing *there, their,* and *they're*
* Misspelling names
* Faulty subject-verb agreement
* Faulty noun-pronoun agreement
* Misplaced and dangling modifiers
* Passive voice instead of active voice
* Violations of style rules

What other errors can you add?

Andrea Passalacqua, Copyeditor

With the initials AP (for Associated Press) and the letters CQ (the copyediting symbol for "correct as written") in her name, Andrea Passalacqua was born to be a copyeditor. It just took awhile for her to figure it out.

After two years at Northwestern University, where she worked as a reporter for the campus daily, including the police beat, Passalacqua took her first crack at copyediting in a summer internship at the *Florida Times-Union* in Jacksonville. Although she'd been editor-in-chief of her high school newspaper in Titusville, Florida, the majority of her experience had been reporting. "With no intentions of leaving reporting permanently, I thought copyediting for a summer would be a way to test out another area of journalism—and maybe even improve my writing," she says.

Little did Passalacqua know that those 12 weeks would mark the beginning of a new career path. She began to realize that the thrill that comes from editing on a typical night is rarely matched by reporting on even the most exciting days.

"I discovered that being at the end of the production line gives editors a chance to participate in all of the final decision making without having to deal with some of the more mundane tasks that come with reporting, like waiting for sources to call you back," she says.

And she felt that she played a role in more major news stories each day than even the most ambitious reporter ever could. Serving as the last of many filters, copyeditors carry more responsibility than Passalacqua ever imagined. "From the fine points of AP style to the chance to exercise news judgment on a daily basis, I enjoyed so many aspects of the job that I knew this wouldn't be a short-term commitment," she says.

Going on to three-month copyediting internships during college at *Newsday* on Long Island, New York, and at the *Dallas Morning News,* Passalacqua eventually set her sights on editing at the *Chicago Tribune.* A few weeks after she started an internship on the *Tribune's* national/foreign copy desk during her final quarter of college in 1999, a permanent position opened up on the metro desk. Thanks to great timing, she got the job a couple of weeks later.

Planning to remain on the editing track, Passalacqua eventually hopes to become an assignment editor on either the metro or national desk at the *Tribune.* But, at age 22, she says, "I still find it hard to believe that a job I barely knew existed three years ago is now so appealing."

How to Copyedit a Story

Use this as a guide to your three readings of each story.

Performed by _____

First Reading.

✓ Ask the writer: What do you think works best in this story? What do you think needs work in this story?

   As you read, note comments about the above to discuss with the writer.

Second Reading.

Check for and use copyediting symbols to make corrections.

✓ Are all style rules followed?

✓ Are grammar, usage, mechanics—spelling, capitalization, punctuation—correct?

✓ Are all names spelled correctly?

✓ Are all the facts accurate?

✓ Are there word choice problems, including wordiness, jargon, clichés?

✓ Is active voice used rather than passive voice?

✓ Is there a quote by the third paragraph?

✓ Are quotes and attribution handled properly?

Third Reading.

Consider overall effective communication and organization along with clarity and completeness.

✓ Does this story make sense?

✓ Is it well organized, or do I have a suggestion for improvement?

✓ Do transitions exist, and are they effective?

✓ Does the story answer all the 5Ws and 1H questions?

✓ Are there questions left in my mind after reading the story?

✓ Is there any editorializing (opinions expressed in the story that seem to be the writer's rather than coming from a documented source)?

✓ Does the story have potential ethical problems?

✓ Does the story have potential legal problems?

✓ What suggestions do I have for improving the story in terms of overall communication with the reader, overall organization, clarity, or completeness?

   Finally, schedule a time to discuss the story with the writer.

Proofreading

__Proofreading__ is carefully reading and making corrections to typeset copy.

In the past when reporters typed their stories on 8-1/2-x-11-inch sheets of newsprint and sent them to a typesetter, proofreaders read __galley proofs__. Galley proofs are long strips of paper with individual stories printed out in one long column. Proofreaders, usually working in pairs, compared the final version of the typed story to the story as set in type. One member of the team read aloud to the second member, including announcing every capital letter, punctuation mark, and new paragraph. The second member of the team marked errors to be corrected on the galley proof using __proofreading symbols__ by drawing a line from the location of the error to the margin of the galley proof and writing the appropriate symbol. Like copyediting symbols, these symbols are universal.

Today, instead of reading galley proofs, most publications staffs read __page proofs__, entire pages printed just as they will appear in the final publication. Since desktop publishing pages are created by transferring the writer's final story directly into the final page design, there's no need to read in comparison to the original story. However, reading page proofs must be done just as carefully as copyediting, since this is the final opportunity for corrections. The staff member responsible for producing a page should also check it before giving it to a proofreader.

Because proofreading usually occurs under the pressure of a final deadline, staff members should not depend on proofreaders to find major errors. When time permits, each page should be checked by at least two staff members other than the person who produced the page. If the copyediting and rewriting steps have been carried out carefully, few errors should remain at this point. This final step is an opportunity for fine-tuning rather than major revision.

Production

As writers write and copyeditors edit, designers crop, size, and scan photos and art. Ad staff members prepare advertisements, following up on the last detail or tracking down the last missing bit of information. **Production** is coordinated so that all elements come together on the page proof. In essence, production begins when all the parts are ready to assemble.

Staff Management and Organization Tips

Regular staff meetings, tried-and-true guidelines and procedures to follow, and great staff attitudes are the three human elements essential to production success.

Have Regular Staff Meetings

Daily meetings will enhance your production, organization, and morale. They don't have to be long, and they surely shouldn't take up 80 percent of your class period. But you do need to address certain issues on a daily basis: deadlines, content, tough sources, problems, things to praise, assignments, fundraiser information, ads, and so on. A meeting is a great time to recognize staff members who have excelled, as well as to head off any potential flare-ups before they burn the whole deadline up.

Use Your Staff Manual

As first discussed in Chapter 6, a staff manual is an essential for every staff; every staff member should have a copy.

* It includes editorial and advertising policy and design and writing style sheets.

* Often it includes deadlines and job descriptions for every position on staff, including specific responsibilities and deadlines.
* In addition, it includes forms for business and editorial, including ad contracts and rate sheets, photo order forms, and caption forms. If the class is graded, the grading criteria are spelled out.
* It may contain a complete staff listing with addresses, phone numbers and birth dates, a list of deadlines, sample stories and captions, each section's final designs and the specifications for them, and a contact list for various information.
* Consider the staff manual your survival kit for high school journalism. If you knew almost nothing about journalism and wanted to get on your school's newspaper or yearbook staff, the staff manual should be your guide to what you would need to know.

Add Time and Effort

Perhaps the most important elements in the production of your publication are time and *effort*—by you and other staff members.

* Are staff members willing to go the extra mile by staying late if necessary on production nights?
* Are the editors willing to put in extra work on their sections to make them exceptional rather than just acceptable?
* Is there good communication among staff members?
* Do staff members help others in a crunch? Good teamwork will really count in the long run.

The Schedule

A sample Two-Week Newspaper Production Schedule appears below. Each deadline step in the 10-day process must be respected for everything to fall in place before the issue goes to the printer.

Week 1

Monday
Reporters set up interviews today.
Assignments from section editors are due in writing.
Ad sales begin for upcoming issue.
Editors page dummies are due today!
All staff members turn in story ideas.

Tuesday
Class critique of previous issue. Awards (best story, coolest photo, helping hand, and so forth) given out.
Editors make sure you talk to your reporters and work out angle and source problems.
Reporters work on stories.
Ads need to be sold if not finished.
Mortems of the last issue with pros and cons of each page.

Wednesday
Sell ads, if not done.
Editors clean off pages on disk.
Reporters work on stories.
Everyone turn in story ideas.

Thursday
Finish up ad sales.
Reporters work on stories.
Editors start typing in stories that are finished.
Turn in stories by 7:35 tomorrow morning.

Friday
Stories should have been turned in by 7:35 a.m.
Photos printed and turned in by the end of class.
All stories typed on disk.
Everyone turn in story ideas.

Week 2

Monday
Ad templates run out and ads pasted down.
Design starts for new ads.
Editors start working on page designs.
Reporters check with your editors—do you need to add to your story, fix a lead, or make a last-minute change?
Turn in story ideas.
Production Night 1

Tuesday
Check ads.
Editors work on pages.
Reporters do beats and help editors.
Turn in story ideas.
Production Night 2

Wednesday
All ads to be finished.
Editors finish pages and proof everything.
Reporters check your stories for accuracy.
Turn in story ideas.
Production Night 3—the late one

Thursday
Editors make last-minute corrections.
Photos should be finalized.
Paper to print by noon.

Friday
Count and distribute papers.
Editorial board meeting directly after staff meeting.
All assignments made and handed out.
Turn in story ideas.
Clean up staff room.
Notice that "Turn in story ideas" appears almost every day in the schedule. On this paper, it is a requirement that each staff member come up with fresh ideas for upcoming issues on a continuous basis.

Going to Press

The words "Going to press" can evoke quivering fear or jubilation when spoken in a high school publications staff room. Whether it's mailing off a big chunk of the yearbook or sending the twice-monthly newspaper to the printer, so much preparation goes into the final product that going to press is both a relief and cause for a glowing sense of accomplishment. Whatever your in-house production process, how you submit your computer files, your photos, and your layouts to your printer will depend on how your newspaper or yearbook's printer works.

* Does your printer have high-tech output devices so that you can just mail a disk (or a layout disk with the original photos)?
* What about photos—do you scan them, as with a newspaper, or do you send negatives or prints? Does the printer have a higher quality scanning process for the photos, as with a yearbook?
* Do you roll up your sleeves and do paste-up—print out laser-quality parts of the pages, paste them up on larger sheets, and send them off like that?

It all depends on the commercial printer your school uses and on the equipment your school has.

* Do you have a laser printer or an ink jet that shoulders the majority of the workload of your publication's hard copy?
* Do you have light tables to do paste-up?
* Is your printer outputting directly to film or to plate?

You need to answer these questions—and more—in order to know how to prepare your final product for the printer.

From Words to Print

Before desktop publishing, production of school papers was fairly basic and began with **paste-up**. Copy was typewritten into columns, which were then cut and pasted onto layout sheets using rubber cement or wax. Photos were printed conventionally in a darkroom, and the newspaper or yearbook's printer was responsible for taking the cropped and proportioned images from that form to the printed page.

As technology progressed and computers came into more widespread use in the 1960s and 1970s, more and more of the production process of school publications became mechanically digitized. Reporters and editors began to use word processors and servers to enter and edit stories. The photo-reproduction process began to involve phototypesetters that could churn out high-quality type in pre-measured columns. Many school staffs did their own pasting up of pages this way, using large cameras to develop halftone images for photos and artwork. Much of this technology was difficult to learn to use and expensive in terms of a school's investment. Still, the publication's visual quality was enhanced.

It wasn't until the early 1980s that computers and other technology really made it to high school newspapers and yearbooks. With the advent of the Apple Macintosh and affordable PC-compatible personal computers, desktop publishing with professional-looking results became possible for small home offices as well as high schools and colleges. Design and production tasks that previously could only have been done professionally are now in the hands of students, and creative possibilities are blown wide open.

Desktop Publishing

Desktop publishing, the computerized way of designing and laying out publications, can result in high-quality and visually pleasing newspapers, yearbooks, and magazines. But computers and programs don't run themselves.

Evaluating Desktop Software

Pick up any computer catalog or visit a software Web site, and you'll be amazed at all the choices available for desktop publishing. Many school newspaper staffs believe they can't afford all the software that they'd like to use in the production of a newspaper or yearbook. Remember there is a difference between "like to have" and "have to have." Much of the available software really does exceed many needs.

* How many page design programs do you need? Probably just one.
* How many word-processing programs or drawing programs do you need? Probably one of each.

That's not to say that students shouldn't have as much experience as possible with many types of software; in fact, the more versatile a high school graduate is, the easier the transition to a college publications staff may be. But for simplifying the production process of the publication itself, one of each program is all you need.

PageMaker or *QuarkXPress*?

The two most widely used page layout programs are Adobe *PageMaker* and *QuarkXPress*. Which one is better and why? Ask 12 professional designers, and you'll get 12 different answers. Some will say *PageMaker* is better for color management; others will say *Quark* is unmatched for its professional file output options.

Example

A PageMaker Screen

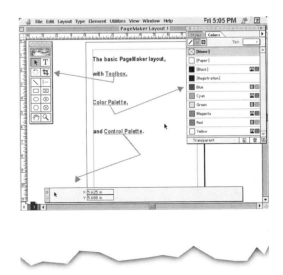

Generally, since Adobe offers price breaks to schools and educators, and since *PageMaker* is a bit less complicated to learn, most publications on the high school level choose this program. But, since many professional ad agencies and marketing or design firms use *Quark,* many colleges choose that program to better prepare their publications graduates.

Ultimately, your choice should come down to the answers to two questions:

1. How easily can the students on staff who need to use the technology use it?
2. What kind of files does our printer prefer?

The good news is that in the most recent versions, the applications are very similar. The authors of the software have combined the best of the two programs' abilities. The result is that once you learn one program fairly thoroughly, it's not a difficult transition to the other one.

Choosing an "Illustrator"

The top drawing programs in the design industry are Macromedia *FreeHand,* Adobe *Illustrator,* and Corel *Draw.* Again, which is "better"? Which should your staff buy and use? The answer depends on how technologically experienced the staff is, who will be doing the work with the programs (the design guru, all the editors, or everyone on staff), cost, and other program attributes.

Each application has pros and cons. For example, for many years, schools used *FreeHand* and professionals used *Illustrator,* because *FreeHand* was simpler and easier to use and *Illustrator* had more versatility and options. Now that both programs have been through several version updates, that's no longer true. And, many professional design firms have both programs for their employees' use, so it comes down to which one you were trained on and are the most comfortable with. While Corel's *Draw* has some features that make it appealing to beginning student designers (lots of textured fills for shapes, for example), some printers are unable to output files as well from that program as they are from *FreeHand* or *Illustrator.* So, as with many decisions in the production process, much depends on the constraints of your commercial printer.

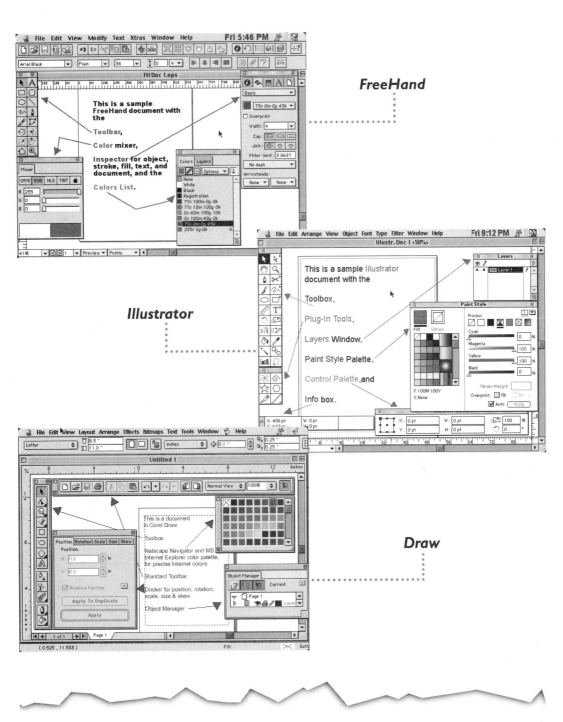

FreeHand

Illustrator

Draw

Using *PhotoShop*

One program that doesn't have many competitors is Adobe *PhotoShop,* which is used for everything related to photos and illustrations, from the scanning process to color separations and output. In many ways, this program and advanced hardware development have revolutionized the professional photo industry as well as student publications.

Now, many professional daily papers and high-end magazines scan their images directly from the photo negative, completely eliminating the need for a conventional black-and-white or color darkroom where prints are made. Scanners are now more affordable than ever, and this scanning process, whether from prints or negatives, has enabled high school publications to improve greatly the look of their photos.

Remember when working with photos that people tend to believe that what they see in photos is the absolute, undoctored truth. Certainly, you'd want to label any really computer-manipulated images as "photo illustrations" rather than as unretouched photos. See Chapter 14 for a discussion on the ethics of photography.

Example

Before

After

Example of a photo with improved crispness and clarity after being enhanced with *Photoshop.*

Two Word-Processing Screens

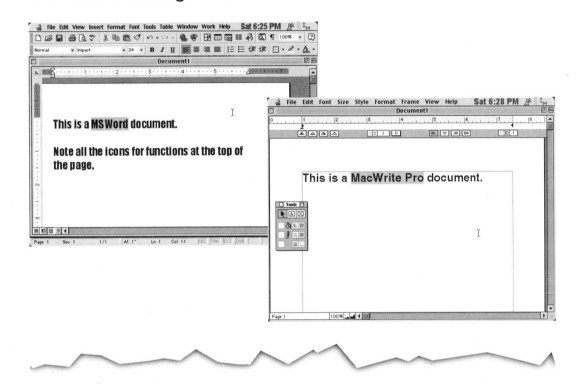

Word Processing

Reporters have to have word-processing applications for writing, and there are a lot of choices out there. You should keep **two** criteria in mind when purchasing a word-processing package:

1. How complicated is it for staff members to use?
2. Is it compatible with the computers you have and the layout program you're using?

Some programs are fairly simple to learn and use, and some are more complicated but have more functions.

Software Suites

Often, these word-processing programs come in a suite with other software, so you get more than just one program for your purchase price. These software suites, also known as integrated programs, can generate documents in a word-processing format, spreadsheet, or database. These can be helpful as a combined way to keep track of document files as well as advertising dollars, student phone numbers, and so on.

Hardware Options

Choosing the right hardware involves answering a number of questions. Imagine you have been asked to recommend upgrades. Where do you start?

* A **hard drive** of at least 4 GB (**gigabytes**) will give you plenty of storage. Hard drives are available up to 30 GB, but that's overkill.
* You'll need at least 128 MB (**megabytes**) of **RAM**, more if you're doing a lot of scanning and photo manipulation. This could go up to a gigabyte, but that money could easily be better spent elsewhere. Also, some older computers aren't expandable, and some newer models have a limited number of slots in the motherboard for expansion.
* Your **micro-processing chip** should run at 300 Mhz (**megahertz**) at least; chips that are more than double this fast are around now. How necessary is that? When your processor is faster than the cabling or the hardware device itself, it's not a good investment of your publication's dollars.
* Options for **network cabling** include **firewire**, **scsi**, **phone cable**, **USB**, or **ethernet**. The faster you can file share, the better.
* Monitors should measure at least 15 inches and be full color. Larger screens are nice for preventing eye strain, but also look for the **dot pitch**.

For example, many monitors have dot pitch of .26mm or smaller. The smaller the dots, the finer the resolution is and the sharper the image.

* For storage, the 1.44 MB 3.5-inch high-density floppy disk may have become extinct, like the dodo bird. Files for page layouts won't fit on disks anymore and wind up cluttering your hard drive if they're not stored elsewhere. Generally, it's a good idea to leave your programs on the hard drives in your publication's staff room but save the files somewhere else.

While diskettes may not hold much else than your text files, there are many options available at a nominal price. The **Zip drive** costs less than $150, reads Zip disks (cost: around $10), which hold 100 to 250 megabytes of information. Another option is a **SuperDrive**, which reads 1.44 MB high-density 3.5-inch floppies, as well as 125 MB disks that are the same size.

* With scanners as well as hard drives, RAM, monitors, and processors, sometimes bigger really is better. The more dots per inch you can scan, the better the resolution will be. Also, the larger the surface area of your flatbed scanner, the better the resolution. Compare costs of various products, because it pays to shop around.

Keeping Up with Technology

Technology is constantly changing. You could spend more than $5,000 for a computer and all the peripherals, only to find that in fewer than three years it's too limited and slow for your needs. Software is the same as hardware in this respect; there's always something new on the horizon.

In the last 10 or 15 years, a software trend has developed: every new version of a program requires more of a computer's RAM (temporary working memory), and the files require more hard drive space (storage on the computer for later retrieval). These large files eat up a lot of memory, and your computer processes them more slowly because of their size. Similarly, older computers with slower microprocessors, smaller hard drives, and little RAM are almost painful—and sometimes impossible—to use with larger layout and photo manipulation programs.

And, in a vicious cycle, often a school will invest in a software upgrade only to find that the new version of the program requires better computers than it owns. Knowing the best time for upgrading your computer is like trying to predict a turn of the stock market.

What's the solution? It's a tough call. Some software is worth the expense; some falls into the "wouldn't it be nice if . . ." category. Probably it is best to go with tried-and-true software packages, and don't believe that any one thing is going to be the panacea for your publication's problems.

No software can get everyone to meet deadlines, but some program packages can help compensate for your design team forgetting the details of a spread. For example, a program called *Flight Check* can ensure that you print your layout file properly.

But what about more nuts and bolts of design? What if you want a precise infographic in a pie chart? There are graphing programs that make sure every pie wedge is exactly the percentage of 100 that it should be. There are scanning programs to help you with photo touch-up, zillions of fonts, clip art, and stock photo CDs, and tons of plug-ins and filters for *PhotoShop.*

Just as with good design, less is more. Get what you really need, and leave the rest in the computer store's demo aisle.

Moving journalism toward the physical product, the publication, takes determination as well as precision and care. From precise copy formatting of finished stories to the perfecting strokes of the copy editor to the computer screen where words and images merge and then on to the printer, production follows a path of a million details. Honor schedules rigorously, for they lead step-by-step to the deadline, the moment of truth in journalism when no matter what happened before, your work has to leave your hands. If it's work you will be proud of, you haven't waited until the last minute. The copyediting and production phases in journalism are teamwork at its best.

Journalism WORDS TO KNOW

byline—reporter's name.

copy—typed version of any story, headline, cutline/caption, ad, sidebar, blurb, and so on intended for publication.

copyediting—process of reviewing copy intended for publication for adherence to style rules, grammar, usage, mechanics, accuracy, effective communication and organization, clarity, and completeness.

copyediting symbols—universal symbols a writer or editor uses to indicate changes in copy.

dateline—location where a story was written if other than where the newspaper was published, including the city and state or country.

desktop publishing—computerized way of designing and laying out publications.

dot pitch—measurement of the color dots that create an image on a computer monitor; the finer the resolution, the sharper the image.

firewire, scsi, phone cable, USB, ethernet—ways to connect computers and printers or to connect peripherals (extra drives) to individual computers.

galley proofs—long strips of paper with individual stories printed in one long column.

gigabyte (GB)—currently the largest increment of computer memory available; equivalent to 1,000 megabytes.

hard copy—printed paper copy of a story or page, as opposed to an on-screen copy.

hard drive—"brain" of the computer where all the system information and programs are stored; files can also be stored here.

megabyte (MB)—unit of measurement for computer memory used to measure both hard drive storage space and RAM; Zip disks hold 100–250 MB, CDs hold 650 MB, 3.5-inch diskettes hold 1.44 MB.

megahertz (Mhz)—speed at which the internal micro-processing chip of a computer runs.

microprocessing chip—chip that controls the internal speed of a computer's hard drive.

network cabling—way a lab of computers is connected to a main server and/or to one or more printers.

page proofs—entire pages printed just as they will appear in the final publication.

paste-up—using wax, rubber cement, glue, or other paper adhesives, the process of affixing stories, photos, lines, and other graphic elements to a page in preparation for printing.

portfolio—complete file of one person's work.

production—coordinated work to put the pieces of a publication together; starts when parts are ready to assemble and ends with delivery of film, disk, or even paste-up to the printer.

proofreading—process of reviewing copy that has been set in type.

proofreading symbols—universal symbols used to indicate changes necessary in stories after they have been set in type.

RAM—random access memory, or the temporary memory that the computer uses while processing information; generally, graphics programs require more RAM than word-processing programs.

slug—words indicating the subject of a story.

slug information (guideline)—information included at the top of each page of a story, including the story's identification (slug), the writer's name, the number of words and characters in the story, and the page number.

SuperDrive—disk drive that reads 1.44 MB high-density 3.5-inch floppies as well as 125 MB disks that are the same size.

Zip drive—disk drive that holds disks containing 100 to 250 MB of information.

Working on the Yearbook

In this chapter, you will learn:

- how to organize a staff for yearbook publication
- how to set a budget and raise funds for your yearbook
- how a yearbook is organized
- about planning the book's content and coverage
- about developing a theme for your yearbook
- about yearbook layout basics

On delivery day, the halls fill with people paging through their yearbooks, flipping from index to page, and then leafing through, smiling at faces and antics of classmates. This first glance tells you one of the things a yearbook is—a look book. But it's more than that. Your yearbook's primary function is to preserve the memories of the year in a journalistic fashion. A yearbook is journalism. A complete yearbook has well-written stories, story-telling photographs, meaningful captions, informative sidebars, and identification photos—including group and team pictures and class photos—all packaged in a well-designed format.

The Yearbook Staff

While the yearbook serves as a memory book for your school, it also gives the staff an opportunity to learn while doing. Every aspect of the process, from collecting information and writing stories to designing and creating the pages, is an educational experience teaching key journalistic concepts.

The Adviser

The adviser has many responsibilities. Usually, the adviser is responsible for teaching writing, design, journalistic standards, photography, and editing.

* The adviser provides the organizational structure for making deadlines, grades the staff members' work if the class is an academic one, makes sure the budget is workable, and handles most of the finances.
* He or she dishes out creative inspiration and encourages students to try new ideas.
* The adviser is also the liaison between the administration and the staff and between the staff and the yearbook printer.

The Editor

The yearbook editor provides student leadership. From setting goals with the group to helping create the design and cover concepts, to editing and proofing, the editor is highly visible.

* The editor pitches in to make sure all goes well and that the staff is working as a team to create the yearbook.
* She or he is often personally responsible for guiding the development of the **theme** or **concept** pages. These pages set the tone or mood, give a book its personality, and tell the year's story in a unified way through content and graphics. (Read more about concept pages later in the chapter.)
* Often the editor is responsible for deadlines and monitoring others in the deadline process. Preferably the editor assigns someone whose sole job is to be sure assignments are completed on time and that work on the yearbook progresses according to schedule.

Section Editors

Depending on the size of the book and the size of the staff, each section could have one or several editors.

* Usually responsible for design and coverage ideas, the section editors work with the staff to ensure that coverage is complete and the design is consistent within the section.
* Often section editors will work with the editor–in-chief to check and correct proofs. **Proofs** are the pages the printer returns to the school that allow the staff to see the photographs in place and all copy, captions, and headlines as they should appear in the book. Proofs allow an opportunity to correct mistakes.

Production Editor

The production editor may be called the managing editor, art director, or design editor. Sometimes the job of the production editor is rolled into the jobs of the section editors and editor–in–chief.

* The production editor oversees the computer-design end of the yearbook, perhaps scanning photos, double-checking to make sure the design is consistent within each section, making sure all graphics, photos, and artwork are sent to the printer, and making proof corrections.
* Sometimes the production editor works with the printer's account representative for the yearbook. She or he checks deadlines and the flow of pages through the printing process and makes sure all graphics and photos have been received and are reading properly.

Photography Editor

The photo editor's job involves a great deal of organization. (See also Chapter 14.)

* It includes making sure photos are taken at all events and photo assignments are done on time, keeping a calendar of what needs to be shot when and who is responsible for it, organizing all the negatives and contact sheets or photos for easy retrieval, and making sure the photos are delivered to the staff member or editor by the time they are needed.
* While the photo editor position does not have to be filled by a photographer, it's a good idea. The photo editor and the photographers must discuss photographic problems and how they can be overcome.

Business Manager

Money is on the mind of the business manager. He or she must be responsible for the book and advertising sales campaigns.

* The business manager keeps track of the cost of the book, what ads have been sold, and where they will be placed in the book.
* Often this person is responsible for the creation of the ad packet, the organization of advertising sales teams, making sure designed ads are shown to the advertiser, and ordering and paying for needed supplies.

Money Pit or Cash Cow?

The yearbook can be either a way to make money or a way to get into debt quickly, depending on the policies and attitudes of the administration, adviser, and staff. Financing a yearbook is no easy matter. Many programs must be self-sufficient, earning all of their funds. Other staffs may receive administrative support, perhaps through student fees or budgeted money, to help offset the cost.

Expensive Extras

Yearbooks can also be loaded with "extras" to create a slicker, glossier—and more expensive—product. Here are a few of them:

* Special covers
* Dies
* Embossing/debossing
* Four colors
* Spot color or varnish
* Pop-ups
* Special tip-ins and extra pages

School Funds

If the yearbook is part of an academic program rather than an extracurricular activity, it may receive school funds. More typically, yearbooks are expected to support themselves at least partially through book sales, advertising sales, patron pages, sales of photographs, or other fundraisers. Basically, when a staff is planning its yearbook, the staff must consider the amount of money it expects to raise or has available when it plans the book.

Selling the Book

Book sales generally are the most obvious and profitable way to raise money to pay for your book. Whether your school has a one-day sale, has a sale that takes place over an extended period, or has an outside company selling the book for you, staffs generally need some sort of sales plan. It will help ensure sales of the book and help you anticipate the number of copies to order. Yearbook companies have to know how many books are needed several months before the book is delivered.

A sales campaign has many stages, with announcements, posters, assemblies and, sometimes, mailings to parents. The more books you sell, the less each one costs. Private schools usually don't have a problem selling books; often, the yearbook is part of the fees the students pay at the beginning of the year.

Outside Money

Advertising, including pages purchased by patrons and sponsors, helps to raise extra money for your yearbook. Journalism students need to raise money in widely varying degrees, depending on what is provided and what is needed or wanted. See Chapter 21 for an in-depth look at raising money through advertising.

Budget Planning

No standard yearbook budget exists because how much a book costs depends on variable factors such as these:

* The number of books ordered
* The number of pages in the book
* The weight of the paper chosen
* The kind of cover selected
* The number of four-color and spot-color pages

Staffs can generate additional funds to help pay for the yearbook, for such extras for the yearbook as embossing or better paper or to upgrade or replace technology. Additionally, personal ads, usually for seniors or groups and organizations, can bring in much of the additional money if the staff will work on marketing the ads.

Checklist

How to Create a Step-by-Step Budget

Project income. (Be conservative so you don't end up in the red.)

✓ Book sales

✓ Advertising money

✓ School funds

✓ Fund-raisers

✓ Money from photographer (percentage from photo packages)

Figure costs.

✓ Office supplies and telephone

✓ Photographic costs

✓ Technology

✓ Software

✓ Special design features (fonts, paper, embossing)

✓ Book critiques by scholastic press organization

✓ Extras such as sending students to workshops and conventions and the cost of food for late-night production sessions

Basics of the Yearbook

Get to know the parts of the yearbook and the order of presentation. Several pages and elements are standard.

Title page. Page one of the yearbook, the title page should repeat the theme or concept (more on the theme later in this chapter) and have a strong photo that reflects that concept. The text provides information including the name of your book and the year, the name of the school and complete school address including zip code, and the volume number in arabic numerals. Additional information could be the school population, phone number, and e-mail and Web site information.

Book Specifications
Book size
Number of pages
Number of pages/flats of color and spot color
Kind of cover
Deadlines for on-time delivery

Endsheets. The endsheets are the heavy paper sheets that connect the cover of the yearbook to the inside of the book. These can be printed or left blank; they come in many colors and paper stocks.

Spine. This part of the cover faces out on a book or stands vertically when the book is on the shelf. It's the stiff part on which the name of the book, name of the school, city, state, and volume number in arabic numerals appear. You can also repeat the logo of the theme on the spine.

Folio/folio tab. The folio is the page number that should appear on every page of the book, generally in the outside bottom corner. The folio tab provides additional information, such as the section and the spread content.

Table of contents. The table of contents generally lists the main sections of the book—including student life, sports, people, clubs and organizations—as well as ads, the index, and community resources. The table of contents need not be labeled as such. It should appear on the endsheet or by pages 2 and 3. It should not take up a spread.

Opening section. Generally a spread or two at the beginning of the book, this section immediately follows the title page. These first spreads introduce the theme or concept in specific terms.

Division spreads. Division spreads divide sections of the book; they introduce each section and continue the theme story in specific copy. These pages should be similar to the opening section in that they use the same fonts and design graphics but should not be identical. They should look like relatives.

Double-page spread. Two facing pages in the yearbook that should be designed as a single unit.

Closing section. This section wraps up the theme or concept of the yearbook, using the same design concept created for the opening section. In addition to completing the theme story, it should also give a feeling of closure to the book.

Colophon. A colophon, usually included at the end of the book, is a section containing printing information, including the yearbook printer and location, the number of books ordered, the cost of the book to the purchaser, and possibly the total cost of the book. The colophon should include design information, such as fonts and colors used in each section. Text could also state who designed the book and the design inspiration. It could include information on student workshops and guest advisers. This is also the place to thank those who have provided special help.

People pages, mug pages, panel pages. These are the portrait panel pages on which individual students, faculty, and staff are pictured, in alphabetical order, usually by grade. Some schools choose to combine the non-seniors in an alphabetical list with the grade indicated behind the students' names. Names should be listed first name first. Class portraits should be placed together in rectangular blocks with the names to the outside next to the row they identify.

Signature. <u>Signatures</u>, or **<u>multiples</u>**, are 16-page units printed together. Every 16 pages of your book is printed on one single sheet of paper and then folded and cut as a consecutive 16 pages in your book. Signature one is pages 1 through 16. Signature two is 17 through 32. Only the two middle pages in a signature are considered natural double-page spreads, the two pages that face each other without a division in the gutter

of the spread. These two pages are actually one piece, so they do not have to be lined up by the yearbook company. Using the natural spread allows you to run a photo through the gutter without worrying whether it will align perfectly.

Flat. A <u>flat</u> is the eight pages that are printed on one side of a signature. It is important that you know what pages are on the same flats and signatures for color and spot-color placement. If you are using color, you will want to limit it to a few flats for cost reasons.

Special Additions

While your book is mostly made up of traditional sections, your staff may decide to do some special things, too.

Tip-Ins

A **tip-in** is an inserted section of pages. Tip-ins can be used to add color or can take the form of a foldout page or pages of different material or size than the rest of the book. A tip-in may be a way to allow your school to put its seniors in color or to add a special news section. A tip-in can also be something special your staff decides to do to handle a section of the book, such as group or team shots and scoreboards.

Mini-magazines

Your school may consider a **mini-mag**— a section of pages devoted to creative handling of a topic or area of your book. A mini-mag does not have to fit into a specific section. It can be a way to cover a part of the year after the final deadline of the book or to add humor to your book. A mini-mag can be just about any concept or topic you wish.

Working with a Company

While your staff is responsible for providing the photographs, copy and captions, design, and creative energy, the yearbook company is responsible for taking those pages and photos and creating the final bound product.

Most often, the adviser and staff will work with a yearbook representative who will call on the staff and set up specifications and pricing for the book. This representative should apprise the staff of extras that would cost the staff money. In many cases, the

representative can help with teaching and training the staff on desktop publishing or specific software design programs.

In the printing plant, the school will have an in-house account representative who follows the progress of the yearbook as it gets printed and bound. The account rep also addresses problems with the school's submission of the pages and suggests how to fix them.

Working with a Theme

A theme is a slogan or concept that helps unify your book. The theme sets the tone or mood for your book, gives it a personality, reports the year in specifics, and unifies your book from beginning to end visually and through specific content. While many themes could be used at many schools, the theme copy should be full of specific anecdotes and details that fit your school. Themes can be serious or playful but should never be negative.

Possibilities

Here are some ideas for yearbook themes:

* **Pride**—based on pride in your school but in a subtle way: *Something to Write Home About, True to Our School, We're So Sure, Change with a Twist of Tradition*

* **Actual event**—based on something happening in your school or to your student body, such as construction, a bond issue, removal or addition of a class, combining of schools, or something like a flood or other natural disaster: *Ripped to Pieces, Laying It on the Line, Final Reduction, Never Quite Like This, Sweating It Out*

* **Anniversary**—based on anniversaries at your school; should be limited to the big ones: *Only a Quarter But Worth a Whole Lot More, A Touch of Silver, The Gold Standard*

* **Fun or double-edge**—based on a slogan that people recognize; must be backed up with specifics that show it fits your school and the school year: *Same Difference, Getting There Is Half the Fun, Now Look What You've Done, Talk's Cheap, What Your Mama Don't Know, Are We Having Fun Yet?*

* **Personal**—themes that make the book personal to the reader by the use of "you" or "we": *Just Your Type, You of All People, Your Book, You Said It, We Made It Happen*
* **Themes to avoid**—song titles, movies, television shows, signs of the times, change, directions, footprints, windows, games, puzzles, circus motifs. With rare exceptions, these are trite—often gimmicks that are forced on books rather than real and specific to your school and year.

Visualizing It

Once your staff has selected a theme, you need to develop a visual for it. Often this is done by choosing typography. A type <u>logo</u> creates a visual to represent your theme and can be combined with other elements to execute a design concept that is continued in a variety of ways and in all the standing elements, such as bylines, section headers, folios, pulled quotes, fact boxes, and captions.

Graphics, which are repeated visuals other than logo type that help the reader recognize a theme or thought, may start on your cover. These might include lines, geometric shapes, type placement or handling, boxes, or special photo techniques.

Remember that you are creating a single book with pages that should look like they belong together. Consistency is important within each section, but you should also look at creating design concepts that unify the whole book.

Three Yearbook Covers

Sources: McKinney High School, McKinney, Tex., *Lion*, 1999; Overland High School, Aurora, Colo., *Trail*, 1999; Kirkwood High School, Kirkwood, Mo., *Pioneer*, 1999.

Planning Content

A yearbook is a 12-month history of your school and its students. The most typical way of organizing such a book is in sections that cover student life, academics, clubs and organizations, sports, and people. While no required order exists for these sections, you should start with a section that is the most interesting. Often this is student life.

Some schools use alternate forms of organizing their yearbooks. Sometimes it may be as simple as combining two sections, such as organizations and academics. Others create an entirely new approach, such as what goes on inside the school and what goes on outside. City High School in Iowa City, Iowa, under the leadership of Jack Kennedy, created a book using a week-by-week structure, newspaper style.

However you structure your book, it is most important to give adequate coverage to a variety of aspects of school life.

Dividing Up the Book

After subtracting theme and ad pages, your book should divide up close to these percentages:

* Student life: 20 to 25 percent
* Academics: 8 to 10 percent
* Sports: 15 to 25 percent
* Organizations: 15 to 20 percent
* People: 20 to 30 percent

Student Life

Students scrape paint from a dilapidated house as they prepare to help a community member. Football fans stand around barbecue grills and have tailgate parties before home games. Drums beat the cadence for the pep rally as students stream in to rev up their teams. Summer activities, back-to-school, working, night life, weekends, dating, transportation, community service, holidays, homecoming—all of these should be part of your student life section.

* Student life should reflect the lives of students in and out of school. You might start by brainstorming a list of things that are important to students at your school and planning coverage around these things.
* Additional coverage would be on specific events and milestones, such as dances and graduation.
* Consider the visual effect of the photos you will be able to get. Sometimes story ideas are good for secondary coverage but do not lend themselves to photographic coverage.

Academics

Costume-clad students play the three witches in Shakespeare's *Macbeth*. Papier-mâché houses recreate a medieval village. A frog becomes a sum of its parts. A choir sees how its parts make a complete sound. Academics is why we have school, yet all too often academics is given too little space in a yearbook. Make sure your academics section is more than awards assemblies and honor clubs.

* The academics section should be about students learning and should show students actively involved in that process through photography and stories.

* Although sometimes faculty is run as a part of the academics page, this definitely is not the faculty section.

* A **topical approach**—grouping content by cross-functional topics and activities—is a good way to avoid the departmental approach where the stories often end up being about what is taught rather than how students learned.

Sidebar

A Topical Approach

Student life

* Summer (spreads on summer vacation, summer jobs, summer school/camps/workshops)
* Getting into the swing of things (spreads on shopping for school, first day of school, change of lifestyle from summer to school, incoming freshmen)
* Just for fun (spreads on pep rallies, tailgate parties before football games, dances, birthday parties, and holidays)
* Freedom (spreads on cars, jobs and spending money, dating)
* Helping others (spreads on community service projects, tutoring, student council projects, the campus clean-up project, the Big Sister Project to bring freshmen into the fold)

Academics

* Labs (home economics, photography, sciences)
* Presentations (English, history, psychology, foreign languages)
* Hands-on (auto mechanics, agriculture, home economics, physical education)
* Performing (choir, dance, speech, and debate)
* Projects (classes that do term papers or science projects)
* Group work (classes that do group exercises)
* Games (classes that use games to learn)

Clubs and Organizations

Service club members talk to children at a day-care center, bringing them holiday cheer, food, and gifts. Cheerleaders prepare skits and make costumes for the next day's pep rally. National Honor Society members hold tutoring sessions in the library after school.

* Clubs and organizations, the people that are in them, and the things that they do should be documented in specific stories.
* While group shots are a part of the clubs section, action photos should show what happened and be the larger elements on the spreads.
* In some books, group shots are placed in the ads and index pages or on separate pages, allowing better coverage of the club on the organization pages.

Sports

The wind howls through the stadium, blowing in the face of the kicker as he sizes up the punt he must make to edge his team into the playoffs. Starters injured in scrimmage games force the would-be state champions to look to the junior varsity team to fill the ranks. An unfortunate placement of course signs causes the cross country team to run out of bounds and be disqualified from the district race.

* The sports section is made up of several parts: the pivotal or important moments in the season—told in copy and captions—the scoreboard and team pictures, and action photos of the games, sidelines, and practices.

* Sidebars can add statistical information, player profiles, fast facts about the season, and more.

People

Also called the classes or album section, this is where individual portraits are placed in panel pages.

* Class portraits should be placed in modular units with the names to the outside, first names first.
* Additional student life coverage should go here as well. Anything from students' activities out of school to profiles about individuals to polls and lists of interesting facts can be part of the people coverage.
* Coverage is limited by the space taken up by the mugs but should be well researched and interesting to the reader.

Laying Out the Book

Once you've divided the book according to the recommended percentages, you need to decide what will be covered and where.

* Start by making a list of events, groups, and teams that you know must be covered.
* Then brainstorm topics that your school, your student body, and your community are interested in and see how they fit into the section plan.
* Generally, you want to assign topics in double-page spreads rather than one topic or group to a page.

The Ladder Diagram

A **ladder diagram** is the way you get your book organized. A ladder diagram is a spread-by-spread plan of the book, laid out in 16 signatures. It can help you organize your book's content, plan when the work can and should be done, and keep track of work completed.

* Indicate on the ladder what coverage is going to go where, on what deadline it should be turned in, and if the spread or page uses spot or full color.

* Once a spread is sent to the printer, highlight the numbers of those pages on the ladder diagram in a color that indicates the pages have been sent.
* Use a different color for each deadline. Color coding helps you see when something is due and when it was turned in.

Signatures are made up of back-to-back flats. The white "pages" represented here are one side of the flat, and the gray are the other side of the flat. To use four-color and spot color the least expensive way, plan color to fall (1) on one side of the flat and (2) on one signature, not partially on one and partially on another.

Example

Ladder Diagram
Signature #1

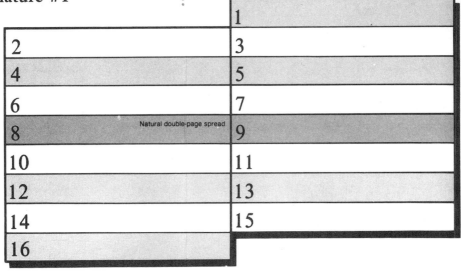

	1
2	3
4	5
6	7
8 _Natural double-page spread_	9
10	11
12	13
14	15
16	

One Adviser's Plan for Meeting the Deadline

DAY by Day — The Schedule

Each of the day listed is a school day. Understand that while it only lists school day deadlines and activities, you will be expected to work on your own time to insure that all deadlines are met. It is your responsibility as a staff member or an editor to keep up with and meet all deadlines. Report immediately if you encounter problems that would keep you from making a deadline. Highlight each day as completed so you know you are on schedule.

Name_____ Pages_____ Deadline_____

How to
SURVEYS are a way for people to discover how they compare to other groups of people. (How typical am I). They usually have to be reworked several times before they are completed. Think what information you want. Survey template is found under the apple under templates. Be sure to save it to YOUR DISK.

Re-do survey daily until it is finaled. These have to be turned in as sets. None can be turned in til all are done.

How to
CHANGE FOLIO information in the bar to correct information. REMEMBER, left side ALWAYS says the page number, then the section name. If it is a classes spread, the alphabetical spread of people is in the folio. If it is another section, it probably also contains a mini-theme.

Day 1 Story is assigned. Open spread and check out requirements of the spread. Sit down with editor/photographer and discuss story, angles, picture possibilities.
- Figure what you will need in the way of photographs (how many etc.). Write photo orders. FIND OUT to whom they are assigned. You are responsible for following up.
- See how the story is to be written (a single story with transitions or anecdotes connected by subheads within the story. Plan interviews. Begin interviewing.
- Note the design of the headline/subhead. Look for sidebars and determine what they will require of you.
- Determine if you need a survey and if you need information/ stats that should be gleaned from library/source/internet research.

Day 2 Continue interviews, collect anecdotes, quotes (with signatures). Get background information to flesh out story, fact bars etc. First draft of survey, if you have one, due today. Make an manila envelope with your page numbers on the outside to place inside the hanging folder. Keep all your photos, disk etc. in this folder.

Day 3 First rough draft due. Write date and your page numbers on it. Begin working on spread design.
- Place spread on your disk and IMMEDIATELY rename it your three digit page numbers (i.e. 008-9).
- Go to left/right pages and change page numbers in Josten's information area. Make sure job number, school name, page number are correct and are tagged registration (in color palette).
- Determine what things can and cannot be changed. Begin working on rearranging. MAKE SURE YOU STAY ON GRID AND KEEP INNER SPACING TO ONE PICA Checking this is easiest at 200 or 400% view.
- Make corrections to survey and turn in again. DO SO DAILY UNTIL FINALED.

Day 4 Second draft of rough draft is due on Day 5. Make sure you do ALL the things that are indicated by your editor. Initial each correction as you make it.

Day 5 Type and staple re-write on top of original draft. Write the date on top of the re-write. YOU WILL BE EXPECTED TO TURN IN A Re-Write EVERY TWO DAYS until you are finaled. Each rewrite is to be radically improved. DO NOT turn in one where you corrected typos and did nothing else that was asked.

Day 6 Follow up on photo orders. Refine them if necessary to get what you still need. Begin working on your third draft. Continue working

How to
CAPTION WRITING: Vary beginnings. Avoid captions starting with name, grade or -ing beginnings. Captions should give information not provided anywhere else on the spread. No general information. Good captions are usually several sentences and may contain a quote.

Hot tip
AVOID INTERVIEWING YEARBOOKERS or using people in more than one story. Goal: make this a book for the whole school, not just for yearbookers and their friends.

Hot tip
INTERVIEWING: Remember, you don't want to tell the reader what they already know. That kind of stuff will go in a fact box. Remember always to ask for detail, specifics, ask why and how. Those are the most interesting parts. Get out of your comfort zone of friends and look for people who can tell their stories. Ask if people know other people who your might add to or expand your story. Get a variety of grades and sexes.

Hot tip
SAVE WORK DAILY: Remember to save your work to your disk AND to the section folder. To do this, go to the 1998 yearbook folder on the desktop and double click on your section name and then save. This will put it loose in the folder. THIS IS YOUR BACKUP. Failure to have a backup is no reason for not making deadline. MAKE SURE EVERYTHING IS NAMED YOUR PAGE NUMBERS.

How to
CROPPING: Place the cropper upper left and bottom right and square it off on picture window. Without touching cropper arms, reduce or enlarge on your photo. Mark it on the photo with the cropping pencil. I'm the cherk

LAY paper around the crop marks to see if this is the best crop. Redesign or move photos around if crop doesn't work.

How to
SETTING STORY INDENTIONS: Highlight over copy block with text tool. Under the type menu, pull down to indents and tabs, click on the ruler and drag the arrow until the number in the box says 1.

How to
GUTTER FORMULA: Measure width from edge of picture window to gutter. Divide that by the total with of the picture window. This gives you a percentage. Measure the full width of the cropped area of the photo and multiply that number by the percentage. The number you get is the point where the gutter will fall on the photo. Make sure the faces or action are not lost in the gutter. Do this before ordering and 8X10. Be sure to show cropped area and to write your page numbers on the xerox.

on redesigning your spread. If you have any of your photographs, begin working on captions. YOU MUST INTERVIEW FOR YOUR CAPTIONS. Do not assume the information given you by the photographer is correct.

Day 7 Third re-write is due. Attach it to the previous ones. Date it. Make sure all errors on previous version have been changed and initialed.

Day 8 Have design checked and okayed by your editor.
- Begin cropping pictures. Make sure photos face in rather than off the spread.
- Begin typing captions AFTER THEY HAVE BEEN APPROVED.
- Begin working on the headline/subhead.
- Your survey should be FINALED by now. Check on its distribution and when you might expect to begin compiling responses.

Day 9 Fourth re-write is due. You should be getting there or really close.

Day 10 Sidebar information should be on your spread.

Day 11 Fifth re-write is due. Hopefully your last. But if not, keep them coming every other day until you are finaled.

Day 12 Report to your editor and the photo editor on your photo situation. Both should help you in getting the photos you still need. Put photo stickers on the photos you are sure you will be using. Put the page number on the back so that if they are left out, maybe, just maybe someone will put them up for you.

Day 13 Keep working on captions and sidebars. Flow in story if it is finaled. Make sure to set it in the correct size and leading.

Day 14 If your story is too long and needs to be edited, get assistance from an approved editor. We try to edit so that the story remains and excess verbiage or irrelevant material is removed.

Day 15 Dominant should be selected and gutter crops should be checked. After you have cropped and checked the gutter, photo copy the photo and the attached caption sheet. Make sure crop marks show. Write your page numbers on the sheet and attach it to the door frame with instructions to the photographer to print CROPPED area on 8X10 sheet.

Day 16-20 Place picture stickers on the bottom of the photos. Remove caption forms and staples. Fill out envelopes. Print out pages for checking. Continue making corrections until you are told you are finaled. Print out color separations. You must be finaled in this four day period unless you are told otherwise.

You are responsible for keeping up with all your materials: your photos, your disk, your backup, your final envelopes. Do not leave things laying around the room. Generally when things are lost, it is because of carelessness on the part of the person doing the spread. We really *don't* have marauding herds looking to steal your disk and photos.

Finaled? Place caption forms, surveys, signed quotes etc. in manila envelope for filing.

Hot tip
WE USE AP STYLE: Use your style sheet to see how we handle punctuation, spelling, numbers, abbreviations, capitalizations and more. Check the spelling of all names.

Hot tip
GET EVERYTHING APPROVED: Every caption, sidebar, headline must be approved for your spread. They must be approved so that they fit the design concept and to make sure they are complete and accurate.

How to
Placing your story: Once your story is finaled, change it to 9 point Stone Serif, delete your name and heading. Open your spread move original story off to the side. Place story (file placed) and make it the same grid width as the original. Click into the original story and look at the control panel to determine size and leading. Most are in 9 on 10.5 leading. If the leading is 10.8, change yours to 10.5 regardless. Look to see if the story has subheads. Make sure you do them exactly as they are in the original story. Consistency in design is essential. YOU MUST CHECK.

How to
SPELL CHECK AND SPACE CHECK: When you think you are through, run spell check (click into story, edit/ edit story, utilities/spell check. Click in the box that says ALL STORIES. Check every name as well. Space check: Go under utilities to change. In the FIND box, type a period and hit the space bar twice. In the change box, type a period and one space. Click on all stories and start.

Source: Highland Park High School, *Day-by-Day*, Highland Park, Ill.

Yearbook Design Primer

Yearbook design is composed of a number of pieces called the "elements of design." The elements include photos, captions, headline, copy, white space, and additional infographics or sidebar features. These elements can be arranged in one of two overall ways:

1. **Modular design** is designing in rectangular units. This means that each photo is a rectangle, and the copy and headline are one rectangular unit. Think of the design as you would a house with all the rooms placed next to each other. Just as you would not place a bedroom off from the rest of the house, all photos and the headline and copy unit should be placed directly next to each other as well, generally separated by only one pica, a printer's measurement equaling 1/6 of an inch.

2. **Mosaic design** is a form of modular design in which rectangles of varying sizes and shapes are placed adjacent to each other to provide a pleasing pattern.

On the Spread

A yearbook spread is made up of any combination of elements of design.

Photos

In a yearbook, photographs are generally your most important and most used element. A yearbook spread may contain only a few photos (some theme pages may contain as few as one to three) or many more (some panel page spreads may contain more than a hundred mugshots as well as other coverage). Most non-panel page spreads will contain between five and seven photos, although this number is not a hard and fast rule.

Captions

All pictures need identification, and that identification comes in the form of a caption. A caption, in its simplest form, is the sentence that describes what is going on in the photo. Captions should have some sort of graphic device to start them, such as a boldface **lead-in**, which is basically a headline, or a graphic that helps the reader see the caption.

Captions should be placed so they are above, below, or adjacent to the photo.

Example

Yearbook Photo and Caption

Source: Kirkwood High School, Kirkwood, Mo., *Pioneer*, 1999.

Headlines

Headlines are the "now read me" for the copy. They serve several functions. They should grab the reader's attention both by what they say and by how they look. Often the primary headline should be followed by a secondary headline or subhead that tells the reader what the story is about. The primary headline doesn't have to contain a verb, but the secondary headline should use a verb in the present tense. Headlines should be placed with the copy, generally above it. (See Chapter 16 for more on headlines.)

Example

"Now Read Me" Headlines

Sources: "Weekend Fun," Highland Park High School, Dallas, Tex., *Highlander*, 1998; "Overcoming the Worst," Hillcrest High School, Dallas, Tex., *Panther*, 1999.

Sidebar

See It on Video

A number of schools throughout the country are supplementing their print yearbooks with other products that help document the year. Video yearbooks and CD-ROM yearbooks can be sold as a part of a package or separately.

Video yearbooks generally run about an hour in length and contain both camcorder footage and still photos documenting special events, concerts, games, and more. They may capture the sounds of the year along with the events through voice-over narration and sound bytes from students and staff. Often these videos are edited by outside companies and given to the students after the yearbook has been delivered.

CD-ROM yearbooks are another way of bringing sound and moving visuals to your yearbook. Because they are played on a computer, the user can select what he or she wants to see or hear and in what order. The CD can also include other visuals, such as maps, charts, or even interactive games.

While both the video yearbook and the CD-ROM provide additional coverage for the reader in a fresh and even exciting way, the staff has a number of things to consider before deciding to add these: cost, time, and whether or not students will have compatible technology. Another consideration is whether technological advances will soon make the CD yearbooks obsolete.

The Write Stuff

A yearbook isn't just about photographic coverage. It's important that the story of the year be told in carefully written, accurate articles. These stories should not be general ones that are true every year, but should tell the specific stories of the people in your school in that specific year.

Checklist

How to Write a Yearbook Story

Here are 15 tips for the yearbook reporter:

1. Interview and get information while the story is still fresh.

2. If you are reporting about an event, attend it and take notes about things you can describe. You want to be able to paint pictures with words.

3. Interview for factual information and listen for good quotes—something no one else could say. Get at least three good quotes from three different sources. Look for diversity in those you interview.

4. Be conversational when you interview. If you are interested, you will get more and better information. Have a list of questions but listen for things that may take you to better stories.

5. Ask for specific stories and information. Avoid general words: "most," "some," "few," "others," "several," "many." All are cues you are writing too generally.

6. Use specific words and visual images. Show, don't tell.

7. Get out of your comfort zone. Interview people who aren't your friends.

8. Be fair. Talk to a variety of people. Tell all sides of the story. Never make up anything.

9. Be accurate. Verify information and have sources sign their quotes. Keep your notes.

10. Be prepared to rewrite. A good story is rarely the first draft. More likely it's the fifth or sixth rewrite if you really want it to be good. Allow yourself plenty of time for rewrites.

11. Write stories in past tense and active voice.

12. Don't summarize or conclude. Let the story end naturally.

13. Keep paragraphs short. Rarely should a paragraph exceed 40 words. A one-sentence paragraph is acceptable in journalistic writing.

14. Quotes should stand as their own para-graphs. Attribution should follow the quote if it is one sentence, or fall in between sentences if it is two or more sentences. Use the word "said" for attribution. It is neutral and invisible.

15. Have fun.

Ideas for Great Leads

A lead is the introduction to your story. Not only should it set the mood or tone for your story, it should entice the reader in. Here are some ideas for leads.

* Use an *anecdote,* a specific story that represents the whole story. Here we tell the story of an individual student's vacation, providing detail and quotes.

   The mountain path took a twisting route through the Alaskan wild for sophomore Adam Corinth and his family as they followed the forest ranger up the path into the woods. Corinth wrinkled his nose at a foul smell and came to a sudden stop as he bumped into the back of his guide.
   "Don't move," the Ranger said.
   Corinth peered around the Ranger's shoulder and saw the source of the smell, a huge black bear standing in the trail, placidly chomping on berries.
   "We were fortunate to be downwind," Corinth said. "He couldn't smell us but we could sure smell him."

* Craft a *description,* employ detail that allows the reader to see, smell, hear, and feel what the story was about.

   The rusted brick red El Camino shuddered on the shoulder of the two-lane highway as white smoke belched out of the windows from an emission system that no longer vented through the tail pipe.

* Give characters a *face* by showing insight into a person through description of appearance or behavior.

   Everything about him said "coach"—from the top of his head, covered with a baseball cap, to the sweat-stained team shirt with the nickel whistle hanging from a chain, to the red coach's shorts that strained at their seams as he stomped up and down the sidelines, yelling orders.

* Start with a *good quote,* which should be something no one else could say.

   "I looked down at my arm and saw the bone sticking out and my hand hanging at an angle I couldn't imagine," senior Clay Parle said. "The amazing thing to me was it didn't hurt."

* Use a *startling statement,* an irony or unexpected teaser, that pulls the reader into a story. Often these are short and pointed.

   It was no longer dark.
   The light from the flashlight pierced the darkness, ruining the intimacy of the moment and blinding the young couple caught in the bright light of the policeman's beacon.
   "It was the first and last time I would go parking," sophomore Jennifer Jackson said.

Wrap-up

A yearbook is a powerful way to provide your school's student body with a permanent memory of the school year. When a staff undertakes this huge job, members need to remember the power of the printed word and photograph and use them in a responsible way. The yearbook should show the life and excitement of your school. It should show the fun and joy of being a teenager. It should also show the stress, the problems that have to be overcome, and the reality of teenage life within the confines of your community's standards. Your yearbook should be a well-constructed piece of journalism, demonstrating the same high standards as the newspaper in your school. And in fact, of the two, the yearbook is the more permanent.

Journalism — WORDS TO KNOW

flat—eight pages printed on one side of a signature.

ladder diagram—spread-by-spread plan of the book, laid out in 16-page segments called signatures or multiples.

lead-in—basically a headline for your caption, which often provides a written link to the photo; or a graphic that helps the reader see the caption.

logo—visual, often done with type, that becomes an icon for a theme, a section, or an idea.

mini-mag—section of pages devoted to creative handling of a topic or area of your book.

modular design—designing in rectangular units.

mosaic design—form of modular design placing rectangles of various sizes and shapes together to form a pattern.

proofs—pages the printer returns to the school that allow the staff to see the photographs in place and all copy, captions, and headlines as they should appear in the book.

quick reads—items presented in non-traditional story form that allow the reader to quickly access information.

rails—vertical columns of white space, often used to set off an element; may contain quick reads.

signature (multiple)—16 pages of the book that are printed together, folded, and then trimmed to fit.

theme (concept)—overall idea that sets a mood or tone for your book, helps give a book its personality, provides specifics about the year, and unifies your book from beginning to end through content and graphics.

tip-in—special section that is glue stripped into a book; may be a way to add color or a foldout page or pages that are of different material or size.

topical approach—grouping content by shared activities.

Magazines

In this chapter, you will learn:

- about a quick overview of the popular magazine business
- how publishing a literary magazine might work at your school
- about the support a literary magazine project needs

Think of a topic. Most likely you can find a popular magazine today that covers it. Mainstay magazines such as Time, Life, *and* Sports Illustrated *compete with hundreds of other publications at the newsstand. Magazines have gone from very general to quite specific and highly specialized. Does your school publish a literary magazine? What does it take to do it right, to make it worth all the time and effort students and advisers invest? This chapter is about magazines, but from two very different angles. First, it presents an overview of the magazine business; then it discusses the high school literary magazine and how it may work for your school.*

Commercial and Trade Magazines

<u>Commercial magazines</u> are those you find in grocery and drugstores, bookstores, and newsstands. <u>Trade magazines</u> usually focus on an industry and are written for a specific audience—those who understand the jargon and have a vested interest in new developments.

Like most industries, the magazine business is based on competition and what appeals to mass audiences. Glancing across a large magazine rack, one can see the interests of middle Americans. Entertainment magazines such as *People, Us,* and *Entertainment Weekly* keep us in tune with our favorite celebrities. Health and fitness magazines, such as *Muscle & Fitness* and *Shape,* outnumber magazines that focus on public policy issues by a margin of at least six to one.

Comparatively few people go rushing to the bookstore to see what the latest edition of *The Nation* contains, but they go charging to newsstands in droves when a celebrity is involved in a scandal. That's simply the way it works. Today's magazines reflect popular culture. Here are the **five** most common types of magazines.

❶ News Magazines

These magazines usually appear on a weekly basis and explore important issues and events in-depth. They seldom are able to compete with newspapers when it comes to reporting the daily news, but they can surround and nail down a topic.

This list of news magazines begins with the most general publications and moves to those that address political issues and the American social climate in specific terms, often from a specific political vantage point (such as conservative or liberal).

General News Magazines
Time
Newsweek
U.S. News & World Report
News Magazines with a Political Bent
The American Spectator (conservative viewpoint)
The Progressive (liberal viewpoint)

❷ Literary Magazines

While news magazines appeal to a broad, national audience, literary magazines appeal to a more specific readership. These magazines publish fiction as well as poetry, nonfiction, and political satire. As opposed to highly commercial magazines, literary publications contain little advertising and consequently can be thin in terms of page count. The writing, however, is generally excellent, and for readers who appreciate great prose, these magazines are regulars on the nightstand.

Literary Publications
The Atlantic Monthly
The New Yorker
The Iowa Review

❸ Entertainment Magazines

Just as we like to be entertained by television, music, films, and the Internet, we also like to read about the people who entertain us and what goes on "behind the scenes." No matter what the subject, at least one magazine will be devoted to covering it. Some of these magazines, such as *Rolling Stone,* often go beyond entertainment and into public affairs issues.

Popular Entertainment Magazines
Music
Rolling Stone
Spin
Film and Television
Entertainment Weekly
TV Guide
Premiere
Soap Opera Digest
Performing Arts Magazine

❹ General Interest Magazines

General interest magazines appeal to a broad audience, and like entertainment publications, they often contain stories about celebrities and the latest events in popular culture. Some are more gossip oriented than others, but all aspire to entertain as well as inform readers. Standing in the grocery line, it's hard to avoid glancing at the cover of *People* or *Us.* Publishers hope a certain cover will lead you to look inside. While not everyone will be prompted to buy, one or two interesting stories can lead thousands of people to purchase weekly.

Some general interest magazines are geared to either men or women. These magazines are not written exclusively for a certain sex, as you are free to read whatever you like. However, content in gender-specific general interest magazines does, by and large, reflect the interests of a certain audience.

Gender-specific Magazines
Men's
Details
Esquire
GQ
Men's Journal
Women's
Cosmopolitan
Glamour
Jane
Self

General interest magazines may also appear as inserts in a newspaper. For many years, Sunday newspapers across the United States have contained *Parade,* a national magazine that explores the lives of prominent people and the overall quality of life. *Parade,* or in some papers, *USA Weekend,* makes an informative supplement. Both publications have question-and-answer sections inside the front cover, and both have a column toward the end in which the career of an established person is reviewed. Focus on people keeps the Sunday supplements popular.

❺ Special Interest Magazines

As magazines become more and more content specific, special interest publications continue to pack magazine stands. One area, health and fitness, has so many magazines in print that one has to ask how all of them manage to stay afloat.

Health and Fitness Magazines	
American Fitness	Muscle & Fitness
American Health for Women	Muscle Media
Better Health	MuscleMag International
Better Nutrition	Muscular Development
Diet & Exercise	Natural Bodybuilding
Exercise & Health	Natural Health
Exercise for Men Only	Oxygen
Fit	Prime Health & Fitness
Fitness	Pump
Flex	Runner's World
Gym	Shape
Health	The Walking Magazine
Ironman	Weight Watchers Magazine
Let's Live Magazine	Women's Fitness
Men's Exercise	The Yoga Journal
Men's Fitness	Your Health
Men's Health	Your Health & Fitness
Ms. Fitness	

Inside the Magazine Business

Magazines operate on one of **two** levels:

1. Major publications, such as *Time* and *Sports Illustrated*, have large and established staffs to do the writing and research.

2. Smaller, more specialized magazines typically have just a few key employees—publisher, editor, advertising manager, graphic designer, and administrative assistants—and rely on freelance contributors for much of their copy. Established freelancers are most in demand by specialized magazines, while those with no experience have a bit more trouble breaking in.

Sidebar

A Writer's-Eye View

Publishing an article in a national magazine can be a tremendous thrill for a freelance writer. This explains, in part, why some writers are willing to compose articles for little more pay than an author's copy of the magazine. It also explains why competition is fierce among freelancers. In short, there are thousands of talented people who crave the thrill of publication, but only a few who satisfy these cravings.

Articles often are rejected not because they're poorly written, but because they don't quite fit with the direction of the magazine or because they resemble other articles recently published. If you're an aspiring magazine writer who gets a rejection slip, don't take it personally. Rather, look over your article, make some revisions if necessary, and send it right back out to another publication.

In addition, aspiring magazine writers should come to know the *Writer's Market*, a book produced every year for freelancers. The *Writer's Market* contains information on thousands of magazines where authors can submit their work. Included in the information that accompanies each entry are a contact name, address, and phone number; the percent of content that comes from freelancers; pay rates; and the types of articles the magazine publishes. The *Writer's Market* is a useful resource and merits study by anyone who is serious about writing for magazines.

Kristen Kemp, Magazine Editor

Once high school features editor, now associate editor of *Cosmopolitan* magazine, Kristen Kemp, 25, sees a lot of similarities between the two jobs.

"I knew what I wanted to be at age 15," says Kemp. "As a result, I've been working toward a career in writing for 10 years now. That gives me a huge advantage over people who are 23 – or even 25—who have just decided they want to become writers."

Kemp says her journalism experience at Jeffersonville High School in Indiana gave her career a solid foundation. "I really practiced my interviewing skills while I was on the school newspaper staff," she says. "It gave me a huge edge when I got my first job at a small daily in Indiana. I was able to beat out other writers who hadn't had early experience getting good information out of their sources."

Writing experience helped as well. "In high school I wrote two or three articles per issue," Kemp recalled. "The mere quantity of journalistic writing I was able to do as a teenager put me way ahead of other people when I was competing for jobs. I learned the basics of writing in high school, so I was able to concentrate on perfecting my skills in college."

Kemp majored in journalism at Indiana University, where she was news editor of the daily newspaper. She worked as an assistant editor for two East Coast magazines, *Girls' Life* and *Twist*, before joining the *Cosmopolitan* staff in New York City.

The deadline pressures haven't changed much since high school, says Kemp, "but the better you get at nailing them, the more prepared you'll be for your future job. I remember being in my high school's newspaper office until 11 p.m.—at *Cosmo*, the same thing happens."

The real point is that everything in journalism gets better with practice, Kemp says. "The best part for me was becoming a speedy writer. Articles that used to take two days now take me two hours. You'll get faster at everything you do—whether it's writing, designing, or taking pictures."

Working with others on a publication has changed a bit since high school, according to Kemp. "In high school, emotions run high," she says. "When you get into a professional job, the interactions can be the same—it depends on the tone your boss sets. I've worked at places where we screamed at each other, but where I am now is much more professional. All interactions happen via memo."

continues ▶

Her ability to accept criticism of her work has improved since high school too, Kemp says. "I used to lash out against editors and friends when they criticized my work. Of course I would still have to rewrite the pieces. I've really learned that being even-tempered—or at least waiting until I was alone to blow up—is much more productive and less upsetting for me."

Kemp advises students pursuing a magazine career to "write all you can right now. Your clips from the school newspaper, local papers, and arts magazines will get you your first jobs. After awhile you'll notice that the places where you get published have bigger and bigger circulations—that's how I got to *Cosmo*.

"Offer to write for free if you can't get a certain publication to accept your work," she advised. "And eventually you'll collect enough clips to convince the next place to publish you."

What's Behind High School Magazines?

While most high schools have a newspaper, many are unable to produce a magazine. It takes a strong commitment and work ethic from students and an appreciation for the arts and creative projects by administrators, who must allocate the financial resources.

Producing a news magazine in addition to a student newspaper may not be possible for many school budgets. But a school magazine that showcases art, creative writing, or topical coverage and analysis may receive support. The high school magazine offers students who enjoy creative work the opportunity to focus on good writing and illustration. As such, the high school magazine can be an interdisciplinary project for journalism, English, and art students. See "A Newspaper Spinoff" on the next page for a look at a topical, or thematic, high school magazine.

Unlike electronic media, high school magazines, particularly literary magazines, tend to be short on explosions and debris—just what serious readers want. Readers who enjoy magazines crave a great story but prefer that it be told in a subtle, thoughtful manner. They want to use their imagination to visualize characters or setting. The written word can paint a picture for the reader that movies and television programs cannot.

Questions to Ask

✓ What will this cost to get up and running?

✓ What are possible sources of revenue beyond school funding (for example, advertising)?

✓ Who will be in charge of maintaining a tight business budget?

✓ How many people will it take to produce a quality publication?

✓ What types of articles will the magazine's audience be interested in reading?

✓ How can the magazine differentiate itself from the look and content of the school paper?

✓ Is there an individual willing to serve as faculty adviser?

✓ Will the content of the magazine come primarily from staff members, or will the magazine depend, to some extent, on articles from students?

✓ If freelance material is sought, what kinds of strategies can be put in place to spark interest?

✓ Does the school have software to assist with layout and design?

✓ Are any staff members proficient with the software?

✓ Does the school have sufficient facilities to produce the magazine?

✓ Should the magazine appear on a bi-monthly, quarterly, or semi-annual basis?

✓ Could or should the magazine appear online?

Case Study

A Newspaper Spinoff

Just as major daily newspapers such as the *New York Times, Washington Post,* and *Los Angeles Times* have their Sunday magazines, a high school newspaper can produce its own magazine as a spin-off from the regular publication.

The *New Trier News,* published since 1919 by New Trier High School in Winnetka, Illinois, did just that in the fall of 1999 with the *New Trier Examiner,* a four-page tabloid format scheduled for production 10 times during 1999–2000, compared to 25 issues of the *News.* The *Examiner* focuses on a new theme each issue; it doesn't try to cover breaking news or sports, nor does it publish creative writing.

The *Examiner* began because New Trier enrollment is increasing, and more students taking journalism needed an outlet for their writing. Instead of simply enlarging the *News*, its staff set up the *Examiner* with separate co-editors and nine reporters to add a new dimension to journalism at New Trier. The school provided additional funds, and nearly 2,000 copies of each *Examiner* will be printed.

At first the *Examiner* editors planned to model the new publication on the British magazine the *Economist,* said co-editor Craig Segall, "but we soon realized our readers wouldn't be as enthusiastic about all things British as we are." So the new publication evolved into a thematic one.

School violence was the topic of the first *Examiner*. The center spread reviewed the recent history of violence in U.S. high schools, from Columbine to earlier incidents. One story reported the psychological element, interviewing social workers, the police, violence interventionists, and Anti-Defamation League officials. Another story probed whether school officials' reactions to the threat of violence are interfering with student rights. A survey polled student opinions about school violence, noting the paradox of students wanting to feel safe in school but resenting authorities' rules to ensure safety.

The second edition of the *Examiner* looked at successful New Trier alumni and whether their high school days helped them succeed. Subsequent issues for the first year have focused on sex, a guide to arts and entertainment in nearby Chicago, and a day in the life of a New Trier student.

So far student and faculty response to the *Examiner* has been solid, and the staff plans to expand the number of pages. Although the *Examiner* could have been set up as an insert to the *News*, it wasn't, which has provided it with its own identity. "But they're not dueling newspapers," said Andrew Pacelli, co-editor. "*The New York Times* magazine doesn't compete with the *New York Times* newspaper."

Example

The *New Trier Examiner*

Source: New Trier High School, Winnetka, Ill., *New Trier Examiner*, Oct. 15, 1999.

The Literary Magazine

One of the most important tasks for those beginning a literary magazine is to establish a well-conceived philosophy that guides editorial content and business practices. From there, goals, roles and organization, and procedures for review of submissions can be developed.

Generating a Philosophy

As Ann Edgerly Klaiman explains in her book, *Publishing the Literary Magazine,* "A literary magazine assumes the reader's interest and desire to dive into the literature offered. . . . The purpose of such a publication is to offer readers, without distraction, an intense, distilled interaction with the printed word. A literary-art magazine does not assume the reader's interest in reading every item, which is also true of most magazines found on any newsstand." In short, magazines containing photography and art create images for readers, many of whom may wish to create their own images by way of the written word.

Before putting together a magazine, then, editors must decide whether to pursue a *literary* or a *literary-art* publication. At the high school level, visual arts may be necessary to produce a complete volume. Creative writers can be scarce, and therefore the contributions of talented artists can strengthen the publication and let administrators know that many artists, writers, and readers will benefit from the publication.

Setting Goals

Klaiman also advises that literary magazine staffs establish a set of goals for the publication, and she provides **four** examples:

1. To provide recognition of the high-quality art and good writing produced by student authors and artists.

2. To promote interest in literature and art at school and to a wider audience.

3. To gain experience in magazine journalism, including publicity, design, and content development.

4. To encourage readers to enjoy and better understand literature and the visual arts.

Roles and Organization

In working on a magazine, each student must have a clear understanding of what his or her role is, as Klaiman discusses. Some students may be interested in the management aspects, while others may be interested solely in the creative components. Either way, the adviser and staff may want to design an organizational flowchart. Klaiman offers **three** models.

1. **The All-Staff Plan.** The first of the models is an all-staff plan. It does not contain a hierarchy and is useful when a small group of people produces the magazine. Because so few people must carry out so many tasks, a formal structure is not necessary.

2. **The Delegation Approach.** When more people are involved, a plan with a more traditional hierarchy may be required. Here an editor takes charge of the operation and delegates responsibilities to staff members, who may work at generating publicity and selling advertising, keeping financial records for all transactions, and teaming with the editor to evaluate written and visual projects.

3. **The Committee Model.** Finally, a more advanced approach may be taken. See the graphic below to picture how a staff with standing committees might appear.

When a lot of people are involved in a creative production, especially a production featuring both written and visual works, it sometimes is best to establish committees. Instead of one person making all of the decisions, committees vote on proposed content and procedures.

Ultimately, organizational structure rests on the number of people involved, their experience levels, and the experience and observations of a faculty adviser, who may have observed successes and failures in previous years.

Example

Literary Magazine Standing Committees

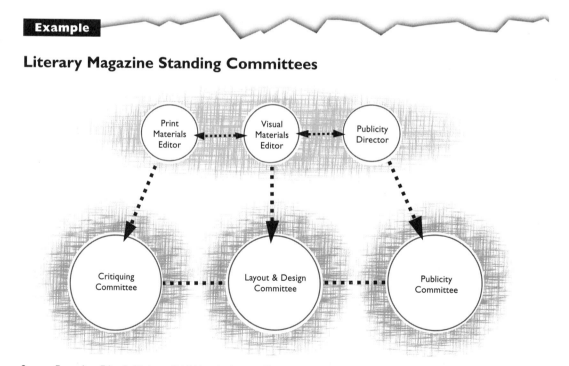

Source: From Ann Edgerly Klaiman, *Publishing the Literary Magazine*, National Textbook Company, Lincolnwood, Ill., 1991.

Generating Materials

The decision to publish a literary magazine is one thing; producing quality content on time is quite another.

Need for Publicity

Ideally, all members of a student body who enjoy drawing and creative writing will be aware that a publication exists and that its deadline for submissions is, say, February 1 for a spring edition. In reality, good publicity for the magazine is essential. Many students either will not know about the magazine at all or be unaware of deadlines for submission.

Guidelines for Submission

Klaiman also mentions the importance of repetition and the need to inform prospective contributors of the kinds of materials sought and who may contribute. Most commonly, current members of the student body may submit creative works, although in some cases faculty and staff also submit. Submission guidelines should be based on and be consistent with the general philosophy of the magazine. If it is to be called a student magazine, then it may be best to limit the publication to student content.

Using Surveys

One of the best ways to gain a feel for what students look for in a publication is to conduct a survey. Magazine staffers can distribute in classes a survey that asks several key questions. (See example below.) While surveys may elicit some less-than-serious responses, they also can generate a great deal of useful information, which ultimately will help improve both the business and creative dimensions of the magazine.

Writers' Guidelines

The literary magazine staff should follow or establish a set of **writers' guidelines**, which indicate, for instance, the maximum number of words allowed for a short story or the number of lines permitted for a poem. Magazines also may require entry forms to let the contributor know exactly what is expected and what rights the magazine reserves.

Literary Magazine Student Survey

Source: From Ann Edgerly Klaiman, *Publishing the Literary Magazine*. National Textbook Company, Lincolnwood, Ill., 1991.

Sample Entry Form

THE SEED Manuscript and Art Entry Form

Please fill out an entry form for each manuscript or artwork, attaching it to your work with staples or paperclips provided. If you have a work too large or fragile for our entry box, please hand it directly to Mr. Vincetti. THE SEED staff thanks you for your submissions.

Name _____
Class _____
Phone _____
Title of work * _____

If you have already filled out one class schedule for THE SEED, you do not need to fill out another.

Class Schedule

_____
_____
_____
_____
_____

Signature   Date

Your signature verifies that your art or literary entry is completely original and done solely by you.

Notes:
a. All works must be done by a JHS student or faculty member.
b. THE SEED staff reserves the right to make minor changes to manuscripts.
c. Maximum entry: Any combination of ten manuscripts or works of art per person.
* A title must accompany each entry.

Source: From Ann Edgerly Klaiman, *Publishing the Literary Magazine*. National Textbook Company, Lincolnwood, Ill., 1991.

Evaluating Submissions

In *Publishing the Literary Magazine*, Klaiman suggests **four** strategies for selecting manuscripts for publication. Based on the editorial structure of the magazine, the strategies can be combined to generate the best content.

1. **Select a top work from every author.** Using this strategy, editors request that authors submit a series of works, and then the best work is chosen. "When this strategy works," Klaiman notes, "the student body sees their magazine as a forum for their peer group and a smorgasbord of reading choices."

2. **Develop a creative writing club.** Here a group of writers meets periodically to discuss one another's efforts. This strategy works well for turning average manuscripts into excellent ones. It should be noted, however, that when all content comes from members of a club, the content can be somewhat "inbred," in that editors and writers choose their own projects.

3. **Engage an independent panel of judges to periodically judge potential articles.** Klaiman mentions retired teachers, alumni, journalists, and authors as examples of judges. This may be the most impartial approach; when respected critics assess the relative worth of creative projects, magazine staff members are not caught contesting and judging their own materials.

4. **Solicit manuscripts from the entire student body and then evaluate all items themselves.** This strategy is beneficial in that students determine content and that content goes beyond that created by staff members.

Whichever strategy—or combination of strategies—is used, editors should take care to log every manuscript that comes in and make sure the author's name is deleted from the paper when it is reviewed. "Blind" reviews ensure that everyone gets a fair chance.

Klaiman also notes that a routing system should be established, so that editors can inform contributors where a manuscript stands. Typically a manuscript is received, reviewed (by one or more people), accepted or rejected, edited, and slated for publication. Manuscripts can get lost in this process if care is not taken. Editors should treat every manuscript as though it was their own.

Following a checklist will ensure that every manuscript is reviewed as objectively as possible.

Raising Funds

While high school administrators allocate money for publications, often more funds are needed to produce a quality newspaper, yearbook, or magazine. This is where fund-raising projects enter the picture. Ads with catchy graphics often appear throughout newspapers, yearbooks, and commercial magazines. In literary magazines, bold ads do not appear until the end of the magazine. This preserves the tone of the creative work.

Grants and sponsors are still other ways to help fund a school magazine.

Commercial magazines have become highly specialized. Competition for advertising dollars is fierce, as is competition among freelance writers to get published. To a large degree, popular magazines reflect popular culture, with celebrities and events at the heart of coverage. While most coverage in magazines such as Time *and* Sports Illustrated *comes from staff members, freelancers contribute most of the copy in more specific, highly specialized magazines. High school magazines are not as common as high school newspapers, but with the right leadership and sufficient interest, quality literary and other types of magazines can be produced. Having a philosophy, goals, and an efficient staff is critical to success.*

Journalism

commercial magazines—magazines widely distributed and sold to a broad audience.

trade magazines—magazines that target a specific group of people and contain information on a specific industry.

writers' guidelines—list informing writers of article expectations.

Broadcast Journalism

Broadcast journalism is news that's carried on radio, television, and the Internet. It's a powerful medium, for its images can shape public opinion. Broadcast images can touch your heart—who could fail to react to the image of John F. Kennedy, Jr., saluting his father's coffin as a three-year-old, flashed repeatedly on television after his own death in 1999? Images can inspire—as when Neil Armstrong walked on the moon. Images can influence—after the war in Vietnam started to be televised, opposition to the fighting grew. Images can transport you to the scene of major news events. How else would you be able to celebrate with Mark McGwire when he hit his 70th home run?

How Broadcast
Is Different

Think about what television can do that print cannot do. Imagine still photographs of Michael Jordan running down the court, leaping into the air, and stuffing the ball in the basket. The same holds true for radio. Imagine reading a quote from a woman who lost everything in a tornado. Now imagine hearing the heartbreak in her voice as she describes losing her wedding pictures. This emotional element is the difference between print and broadcast.

Yet the foundation of journalism is still print. That's partly because print preceded broadcast in the historical development of journalism. Even though in broadcast we hear and see news stories instead of reading them, someone has to create a printed script. As a broadcast journalist, that script writer is you. So you don't need to start over to learn how to write broadcast news. Instead you can build on what you've already learned about thorough, accurate reporting, solid news judgment, and strong writing.

Broadcast
Writing Steps

Keep it simple. Remember, broadcast is a spoken medium. Viewers have only one chance to hear the news and understand it. In print, readers can go back and reread paragraphs if they don't understand the first time. In broadcast, you have just one shot to get the facts across.

Keep it conversational. Write your stories as you speak, only better. Imagine you're telling the story to your mom or best friend. Start with the most interesting facts. Don't try to impress listeners with your vocabulary. It's more important that they understand. For example:

Don't say: "Citing inflationary increases, the school board has authorized an increase of 20 percent in parking permit fees for next year." *Instead, try:* "Central students will pay $120 for a parking sticker next year. That's $20 more than it costs to park this year." *Changing it this way puts the focus on the students—your listeners, who perk up and pay attention the second the words "Central students will pay" hit their ears.*

Use present tense. One of the most valuable aspects of broadcast—one that separates it from print—is that it's immediate. Your audience does not have to wait until the next morning to find out about the story. You can go into their homes immediately. That's why TV programs promote "breaking news" or "eyewitness news." So start with the newest information and make it feel as "now" as possible. If a house fire happened last night, why start off by telling viewers there was a fire? That's old news. Start with the clean-up effort, what residents are doing for housing today, how the victims are doing at the hospital. Then you can follow up with a nut graf. For example:

"Central sophomore Bud Jones slept in a church basement last night, and this morning he ate breakfast at Burger King. No, he hasn't run away from home. Bud and his family are living temporarily at the Methodist church because their house was partly destroyed by fire yesterday morning. Voiceover from Bud: "It's kind of rough—the only clothes I have left are what I was wearing yesterday. But everyone's been really helpful."

Try something besides the who, what, when, where, why, *and* how *in your lead.* That would be the whole story! Use a sentence for each idea. You should be able to read each sentence aloud in just one breath. A good rule of thumb is if you have to use a comma or a semicolon in your sentence (like this one), it's probably too long for you to read and listeners to follow.

Boil your story down to the most essential elements. Broadcast news is constrained by time. The simplest stories tend to run just 30 seconds.

Use the differences between print and broadcast to your advantage. If "a picture is worth a thousand words," think about all the words you can save when you write for television news! Instead of trying to describe a parade with words, you can show the colorful floats and the cheering crowds. Your script should work with the video to explain to viewers what they're seeing and provide additional information. (See script writing information on page 380.) In radio, you can use sound—the blare of a brass band or the emotion in a lottery winner's voice—to transport viewers to the scene.

Try to transition from one story to another so the one following seems a logical next step. Stories appear in an order called a **rundown**. With a newspaper, readers can pick the order themselves. If they want to read the comics before the front page, they can. In broadcast, producers decide the order of the stories. It should be done in a way that makes sense to viewers, starting with the most important news, then going to the least. If you can make the stories flow—for example, going from one business story to another—you're doing your job.

Radio Journalism

The main difference between radio and TV is obvious: With radio you hear images but you don't see them. Sound helps to tell the story. Radio is a great way to start learning about broadcast. All you really need to get started is a tape recorder for interviews and a place to broadcast, which can be as basic as your school's public address system.

Jobs in Radio

News and sports directors as well as newscasters and reporters are four of the jobs in radio. All **four** jobs are available at the high school level.

1. **News Director.** In charge of news programming for the radio station, the news director schedules the newscasts, chooses stories, assigns reporters to them, and supervises the mix of studio reporting, live reporting, and audio during the newscast.

2. **Sports Director.** As many high school newscasts include a large sports component, the sports director specializes in determining the sports format, including the decision of which sports events will get play-by-play coverage. The director also assigns reporters and announcers and oversees equipment to be used in sportscasts.

3. **Newscaster.** A newscaster's job is just as it sounds. He or she reads, and often writes, the news on the air. This is different from a disc jockey (or DJ). Disc jockeys host music programs, not news.

They aren't journalists. Talk-show hosts aren't really journalists either. But they come close because their topics are often newsworthy. They don't report the news; instead they comment on it and encourage their guests to do the same.

4. **Reporter.** Armed with tape recorders, reporters go out into the field and interview people. They then write a story based on what they've learned and deliver it on the air. That delivery can be done from the studio or while the reporter is still live at the scene of the news event. For live reports, a telephone at the scene is needed to call in your report.

Radio Terminology

As with many other aspects of journalism, radio has its own terminology.

A reader is the most basic story. It's simply read aloud by the newscaster.

Nat sound means natural sound. It's the sound you would hear at a news event; nat sound could be protesters chanting, bagpipes playing, or the NASA announcer counting down before the space shuttle lifts off. In radio, nat sound is woven into reports every three or four sentences. For example:

"Southeast High School is kicking off its homecoming celebrations. (Nat sound of chanting: "S-O-U-T-H-E-A-S-T . . . SOUTHEAST!) 15-hundred Southeast students showed their school spirit at a pep rally this morning. Tonight, the Golden Buffaloes football team will take on the North Wranglers. If the Buffaloes win, they'll be undefeated in the league. Kickoff is at seven this evening at Southeast."

Nat sound separates radio from print. You can actually transport listeners to the event.

A _soundbite_ *is equivalent to a quote in print.* But in broadcast, viewers can hear it directly from the source. That means listeners can hear the joy in a lottery winner's voice or the sadness in the voice of a tornado victim. Once you've tape-recorded an interview, you can use a portion (or bite) of it in your news report. Soundbites can't stand alone. They need context. So the story might start out as a reader, then go to a soundbite, then continue as a reader. Go easy on such clichéd soundbites as "I can't believe I won" from the contest winner or "We're really up for this one" from the sports fan.

A _package_ *is a more complex story*. It is narrated by a reporter or newscaster. It often has multiple soundbites and natural sound in it, so it is tape-recorded in advance. Packages are introduced with a lead read by the newscaster and followed with a tag to provide additional information and help the flow of the newscast. It doesn't make sense to listeners to hear a reporter's voice all of a sudden without knowing who it is or what she or he is talking about.

Television Journalism

Television is similar to radio in terms of conversational writing, up-to-the-minute coverage, and the use of sound from the scene of news events. But television adds sight or video images from the scene, so that you see as well as hear portions of the event.

Jobs in Television

Some of the key jobs in television are people you'll never see when you turn on the news. They work with the on-air people (also called talent) to create a seamless end product. Meet **twelve** of them here.

1. **News Director.** This is the highest ranking job in a television newsroom. The news director is responsible for budgets, staffing, and overall direction of the station's news.

2. **Assignment Editor.** This editor coordinates coverage. He or she sends crews to news events, keeps track of story ideas, and is responsible for making sure the station doesn't miss any big news stories. Assignment editors often listen to police and emergency scanners and make beat calls to police stations. The editor works with producers and news directors to decide what stories to cover.

3. **Producer.** The producer is in charge of a newscast. She or he decides the rundown—the order of stories in the newscast, how they will be handled, and how long each should run. The producer also assigns stories to writers and reporters and oversees the show.

Producers often approve the scripts in their shows. They also watch the timing. The 6 o'clock news can't start at 6:01, and it can't run too long. It has to time out perfectly, and that's the producer's job.

4. **Anchor.** Anchors sit in front of the camera and read the news to viewers. That means they have to look good, sound good, and have a way with storytelling. Many anchors write their own scripts. During breaking news coverage, anchors have to be able to think on their feet and ad lib.

5. **Reporters.** Like their counterparts in print, reporters go out and conduct interviews, gather facts, and put together a story.

6. **Writers.** Generally writers stay in the newsroom and write many of the shorter stories that the anchor reads.

7. **Photographers.** They videotape news events. This job requires technical know-how: If the video you shoot at a rally is blurry or the sound isn't recorded, the video is useless. The job also requires an eye for visual elements and a talent for being in the right place at the right time.

8. **Editors.** These technicians edit together video and/or audio pieces. This job requires a keen eye for detail, particularly visual elements.

9. **Director.** The director's job is to decide which camera to go to and when, to make sure the video is rolling when it's supposed to, and to monitor a technically smooth newscast.

10. **Floor Director.** He or she makes sure things run smoothly in the studio during the newscast, ensuring the anchors are looking at the right camera, indicating to the anchors when they're on the air, letting them know if things change during the show (for example, if a story needs to be dropped because of time limits or if it has to be stretched).

11. **Audio Engineer.** Responsible for all the sound that goes out over the air, she or he watches levels of microphones and tape elements and adjusts them as needed.

12. **Graphic Designer.** He or she designs maps and other visual elements for use during the show. This job is all done on computers.

Television Terminology

Terminology specific to television includes the following:

Just as in radio, a reader is the simplest form of story. It has no video or soundbites. It's delivered by a "talking head"—the viewer sees only the anchor reading on camera.

VO *stands for voiceover,* which means the anchor is talking while the viewer sees video. It usually starts with the anchor on camera, then goes to video.

An SOT is sound on tape. It's similar to a soundbite in radio, but now we're not only hearing from the sources, we're also seeing them. Someone involved in the story is talking on camera. Just as with a quote, SOTs don't make sense if they stand alone. They need context. The story might start as a reader, then go to SOT.

VOSOT *means the broadcast starts with the anchor talking over video,* then goes to an SOT from the scene.

The package story format is similar to its counterpart in radio, but in television you also work with video to tell a more complex story. It can include a **standup**, which is recorded in advance; we see and hear the reporter talking into the camera, providing more information. A good time to use a standup is when you have numbers or background information and no video to cover. A package in television can also be introduced with a lead read by the anchor and followed with an anchor tag to balance it out.

In television, nat sound is often used at the start of a VO. The anchor reads a sentence on camera to set up the story. Next the anchor pauses when the tape starts rolling, and viewers hear something directly from the scene. The video continues, and the anchor talks over the rest of it.

Example

Sample Rundown for a Broadcast

Use a variety of story types and techniques in your television show to keep it interesting and make the most of your time limits. Here's a sample rundown.

Slug	Anchor	Form	Reporter	TRT
New Principal Lead	Dana	ONCAM	Mike	:15
New Principal	Matt	PKG	AP	1:30
New Principal Tag	Dana	ONCAM		:10
Teachers Reaction	Matt	VO/SOT		:45
Sports Budget	Dana	READER		:25

Joie Chen, TV Anchor

"My career in journalism is the product of a series of well-thought-out, well-executed accidents," says CNN anchor Joie Chen. Chen says her immigrant parents worried their only child would have trouble learning proper English. They suspected that cartoon characters on television would not be suitable role models for the toddler. "So they kept the TV off during the afternoons—and made me watch Walter Cronkite every evening," she explains. "Now they credit themselves with launching my career."

But the 38-year-old Chicago native recalls her early ambitions a little differently. In the summer before eighth grade, she attended a preview seminar designed to show students what to expect in high school. "The one thing that stood out was an option offered for juniors—a journalism class that trained you to write for the school newspaper," Chen remembers. "I came home and told my mother I wanted to take that class and become a newspaper reporter."

Chen did report and later helped edit the newspaper at Evanston (Illinois) Township High School. In 1978 she enrolled at Northwestern University's Medill School of Journalism. "I was determined to be a good writer and a great newspaper reporter," she says. In those days, Woodward and Bernstein, the *Washington Post* reporters who chronicled

the Watergate scandal, were popular icons for young journalists. "I didn't care about television at all," Chen says. "I just wanted to be a great newspaper reporter."

But just a year earlier, one of Chicago's great newspapers, the *Chicago Daily News*, had folded, as had several other big city papers. "My adviser told me to read the handwriting on the wall," Chen says. "He convinced me to get into television."

Chen wrote news copy for the campus radio station, but there wasn't much opportunity for broadcast experience outside the classroom. "I did have one terrific newspaper internship, at the *Wilmington News-Journal* in Delaware," Chen says. "I wish I had the kinds of opportunities students have today, but TV internships were practically unheard of when I was in college."

Certain she didn't have the skills to get a job in television, Chen entered the graduate school program. "I'd never seen a TV camera before, much less an editing deck," she says. "But I had learned how to write news copy, and that was the most important skill."

Graduate school also gave her an internship opportunity in Washington, D.C., feeding reports to WTOL-TV in Toledo, Ohio. Chen's reports for that station became the foundation for her résumé tape. After applying to about 20 stations in

1983, Chen was offered her first job at WCIV-TV in Charleston, South Carolina.

"It paid only $10,000 a year, practically minimum wage," Chen says. "But I would be given an opportunity to report in the afternoon and then produce the late evening newscast. My long-range goal was to be a show producer, not an on-air type, so I figured this was the best way to learn."

But her producing career got off to a rocky start. "My first show began with two minutes of extra promotional spots because I wasn't ready," she says. "At the end of the newscast, my boss told me it was the worst show he'd ever seen. And all I could say was, "You're absolutely right; that was the worst show I've ever seen too."

After that, Chen was assigned to full-time reporting. "I was disappointed that I wasn't any good as a producer, but as my reporting improved, I began to realize that maybe I wasn't cut out to produce," she says.

Nearly three years later Chen moved to Atlanta and WXIA-TV. In six years at that station, she won a number of awards and grew more confident in her writing and reporting skills. "I was the police beat reporter, and I loved the work," she says. "I developed a lot of great sources, got to see the 'seamy' side of life, and loved to get great scoops."

But Chen began to suspect that the new management didn't like her work, so she began to look for a new job. "As it turned out, my new boss grew to really like my reports and was ready to promote me to a better position," she recalls. "When he called me in to tell me that, I had to interrupt to say that I was leaving for CNN."

In December 1990, Chen started as an anchor for CNN International, which is seen in 210 countries outside North America. "I never wanted to be an anchor—I thought they were just news readers," she says. "But our newscasts were fascinating. We included reports about Yemen, Congo, Tajikistan—places I had never even thought of before. I learned a lot."

After three years, Chen was asked to move to the domestic CNN network. "I didn't want to leave CNN International, but I realized it was a great opportunity," she says. "And besides, my parents would be able to watch me on TV."

In her current position, Chen has covered the NATO air strikes against Yugoslavia, President Clinton's impeachment hearings, the Oklahoma City bombing, hurricanes, tornadoes, and other disasters. She contributes long-form, magazine-style reports, has hosted CNN interview programs, and now anchors the network's flagship newscast, "The World Today."

"But the job remains the same," she says. "I always compare being a reporter, or a news anchor, to being a third-grade student. It's an opportunity to come in every day, study, ask questions, learn new things, write about them, and tell the story. It's an ongoing education."

Setting Up Scripts

Because broadcast scripts are meant to be read aloud, a script will look different from a print story. The following are specific prescriptions for broadcast scripts.

A Broadcast Script

Write scripts entirely in capital letters. Each sentence is a new paragraph. That's easier for anchors to read, particularly if they don't have time to practice reading the story before show time.

Use a narrow margin on your script, one that's about three words long. If the reader, the anchor on the air, has to "eyeball" the copy all the way across the page and then back to the start of a new line, it's easy to get lost. And anchors whose eye movements go from side to side tend to look shifty.

Instead, use a margin that's about three words long.

Indent each new sentence by two spaces.

Isn't that easier to read?

Write the story so it's easy for the anchor to read and easy for viewers to quickly understand. An example of this is the special style used for numbers and abbreviations. In print you could write $200,146,967.72. But that's unwieldy for broadcast. For numbers over 999, use a combination of numerals and words:

12-thousand or 964-million. And if possible, round the number off: "Just over 200-million dollars" is still accurate and easy to follow. Remember to write numbers out just the way you want the anchor to say it. Years before 2000 are still written in numerals because that's how they're said: 19-99. But starting in January 2000, use a combination of numerals and words: 2-thousand, 2-thousand-1.

Handle attribution differently than in print, where it's no problem to attribute with a full name and title: "The fire was started by a child playing with matches," said Sedgwick County Fire Dept. Lt. Bob T. Baker, Jr.

But that gets a little long when you try to read it aloud. So for broadcast, you simplify: "The fire was started by a child playing with matches," a fire investigator said.

There's another problem with that sentence. The statement has different credibility if it was said by a fire official or by a neighbor or by someone who's been arrested for arson. So begin the sentence with the attribution, telling your reader right away how much weight to give to the facts: "A fire investigator said the fire was started by a child playing with matches."

Now, tighten the sentence and get rid of that dead "was." Turn it around and put part of it in the present tense: "A fire investigator says a child playing with matches started the blaze." That's simpler, stronger, and more direct.

Something else your script may need is pronouncers. Remember, this is a spoken medium. If you have a tricky name, you need to indicate to the anchor how it should be said. Put the pronouncer in parentheses directly after the word in question: "Polar Cola is based in Worcester (WUH-ster), Massachusetts." "Jennifer Bachus (BAH-cuss) won the election for student body president by one vote."

Make your script organized and easy to follow. Each story has a slug, usually one or two key words to identify it. The slug should be in the upper-left corner, along with the time the newscast will air. Each story should be on an individual page, and before the newscast, each page should be numbered according to the rundown.

Indicate production elements on your script. For example, in radio you need to make clear when you want a soundbite or nat sound to be played. These are on tapes called **carts**. You need to indicate the **incue** (the first three words on the cart), **outcue** (the last three words on the cart), and the total run time (**TRT**) of the cart on your script. That way the anchor knows when to stop reading and when to start again.

Example

Sample Radio Script

Driver's Ed
3 p.m.
(Bob)
A NEW DRIVER'S EDUCATION PROGRAM AT DEERING HIGH SCHOOL IS GETTING A GREEN LIGHT. FOR THE FIRST TIME, DEERING SENIORS WILL BE ALLOWED TO GET BEHIND THE WHEEL OF A CAR . . . INSTEAD OF A COMPUTER SIMULATOR. THE BOARD OF EDUCATION APPROVED THE NEW PROGRAM TODAY. SOME STUDENTS SAY IT'S ABOUT TIME.
(CART 1—TRT :30)
INCUE: I can't wait to get out . . .
OUTCUE: It will be more educational

THE PROGRAM WILL COST 40-THOUSAND DOLLARS. PRINCIPAL KUPETZ PLANS TO TAKE THE MONEY OUT OF THE BUDGET FOR NEW BAND UNIFORMS.

A Television Script

A television script requires different information than a radio script, such as when to start video, when to take SOT full, and so on. You will also want to include **supers**. Super is short for superimpose. These are words that go across the bottom third of the screen to help add to viewers' understanding. It can be the location where the video was shot or the name and title of the speaker in a SOT. That saves time during your script because the anchor doesn't have to say it aloud.

Example

Sample Television Script

Driver's Ed

3 p.m.

page 1

BOB ON CAM	(BOB ON CAM) A NEW DRIVERS EDUCATION PROGRAM AT DEERING HIGH IS GETTING A GREEN LIGHT.
TAKE VO SUPER: Deering High School	DEERING SENIORS WON'T HAVE TO USE THESE COMPUTER SIMULATORS ANYMORE. TODAY, THE BOARD OF EDUCATION DECIDED STUDENTS CAN DRIVE CARS FOR PRACTICE DURING CLASS. SOME STUDENTS SAY IT'S ABOUT TIME.

When writing your script, divide your page into two. This makes it clear for the anchor to read and the technical staff to follow. The left side is for technical instruction. The right side is for the anchor. Be sure you write out SOTs verbatim. That way, you can make sure you lead into them well—and if you have closed captioning, it will make it on the air. Remember to write to video, use short sentences, and keep the story in present tense when possible. Study the sample TV script that follows.

TAKE SOT FULL
TRT: :30

page 2
SUPER: Matt Strauss
Student

    (TAKE SOT FULL)
    "I can't wait to get out
    and drive during class.
    A computer just isn't
    the same as being
    on the road."

SUPER: Emily Williamson
Student

    "I'm really looking forward
    to drivers ed now. It will be
    so much more educational."

OUT: MUCH MORE EDUCATIONAL
CONTINUE VO

    THE PROGRAM WILL COST
    40-THOUSAND DOLLARS.
    PRINCIPAL KUPETZ PLANS
    TO TAKE THE MONEY
    OUT OF THE BUDGET
    FOR NEW BAND UNIFORMS.

Sample Package Script

A package (PKG) script builds on the same elements. Here's a sample package script.

Spring Break
3 p.m.

page 3

BOB ON CAM	(BOB ON CAM) YOU MIGHT DREAM OF SPENDING SPRING BREAK RELAXING ON A BEACH . . . OR HITTING THE SKI SLOPES. BUT FOR THREE SPRINGFIELD HIGH SCHOOL SENIORS, SPRING BREAK BRINGS A CHANCE TO IMPROVE THE COMMUNITY. S-H-S REPORTER GAIL SMELTZER SHOWS US HOW THEY'RE BUILDING A HOME WITH A HEART.
TAKE PKG	(TAKE PKG) (nat sound hammering) ANNE QUADE HAD NEVER SWUNG A HAMMER BEFORE LAST WEEK. NOW THE 17-YEAR-OLD IS BUILDING A HOUSE! ANNE, SHELBY CARMICHAEL, AND DYLAN BENDELL (ben-DELL) ARE VOLUNTEERS FOR HOME WITH A HEART THIS SPRING BREAK.
SUPER: Anne Quade SHS Volunteer	((sot: We wanted to give something back to the community. It would be easy to hang out on a beach somewhere, but we thought this would have a more lasting impact.)) 15 STUDENTS FROM ACROSS THE CITY ARE WORKING ON THE HOUSE. THE VOLUNTEERS SAY IT'S NOT ALL WORK AND NO PLAY.

Spring Break
3 p.m.

page 4

SUPER: Shelby Carmichael Student	((sot: We're having a great time. We're meeting cool people and we've had an amazing response from the community.))
SUPER: Gail Smeltzer SHS News	((standup: In fact, community stores have donated 15-thousand dollars worth of supplies for this two-story house. This is the seventh Home with a Heart built in northwest Springfield.))
SUPER: Joyce Lee Home with a Heart president	((sot: These houses are for low-income families who just need a good start. We couldn't do it without the volunteers.))
BOB ONCAM	(BOB ONCAM) THIS HOUSE IS BEING BUILT FOR THE SMITH FAMILY – A MOM, DAD AND THREE KIDS. FIVE-YEAR-OLD HANNAH SMITH SAYS SHE CAN'T WAIT TO MOVE IN.
SUPER: Hannah Smith	((sot: It's so beautiful. I love it!))
SUPER: Dylan Bendell SHS Volunteer	((sot: That's all the thanks I need. Seeing the Smiths makes all the hard work worthwhile.))
BOB ONCAM	(BOB ONCAM) THE SMITHS ARE SCHEDULED TO MOVE IN NEXT WEEK. YOU DON'T HAVE TO WAIT FOR NEXT SPRING BREAK TO VOLUNTEER FOR HOME WITH A HEART. THE GROUP BUILDS HOUSES YEAR ROUND. IF YOU WANT TO VOLUNTEER, CALL 555-1234. THAT'S 555-1234.

Wrap-up

Broadcast journalism builds on the same principles as print journalism—careful reporting, accuracy and objectivity, and smooth writing. The difference lies in the imagery that can be included—sound in radio, both sound and sight in television. Because of these added dimensions, broadcast techniques are somewhat different than they are in print. But a solid understanding of print journalism is the best preparation you can develop for experience in radio and television news.

Journalism — WORDS TO KNOW

cart—radio or videotape that contains soundbites and nat sound for a newscast.

incue—first three words of a soundbite recorded on a cart; printed in the script.

nat sound—natural sound, such as band music, recorded for a broadcast.

outcue—last three words on a soundbite on a cart, printed in the script.

package—complex radio or TV story that includes narration, soundbites, and nat sound.

reader—basic story for broadcast, simply read aloud by the newscaster.

rundown—list of the order of stories in a newscast, usually from most important to least important.

SOT—sound on tape in video, in which we see as well as hear the source talk on camera.

soundbite—direct quote from a source used in a newscast.

standup—appearance of the reporter on camera to deliver information for the story.

super—words across the bottom of the TV screen that help explain the video.

TRT—total run time of a cart; printed in the script of the story.

VO—voiceover, the newscaster's voice reading aloud as the video plays.

VOSOT—voiceover that moves into an SOT during the story.

CHAPTER 21

Advertising

In this chapter, you will learn:

- about the role of advertising in scholastic publications
- how the staff works together to manage advertising
- guidelines for good advertising
- how advertising sales are made
- how to prepare ads for publication

Your publication's budgeted income comes from a variety of sources—the school, student fees, fundraisers, and perhaps donations from parents or community groups. Funding mixes vary considerably from school to school. It is common for publications staffs to find, no matter what the circumstances, that they need additional funds. You may need updated equipment— cameras, scanners, or software. You may have the talent to produce a video yearbook but not the funds. You may want to go with a four-color cover for the newspaper; color signatures, additional pages or tip-ins for the yearbook; or a yearbook cover that has embossing or foil stamping. All of these things cost your publication money. Advertising can be an answer.

Why Advertising?

There are **three** main reasons for your publication to carry advertising:

1. To generate funds.
2. To give students information about products and services they want and will use.
3. To improve your advertisers' business by expanding their markets to your student body.

Selling ads for your publication should be a team effort. Just as everyone would participate in a fund-raising event, everyone should sell ads. (It may be part of your publication grade.)

Everyone should also benefit from the advertising dollars. Whether the money buys computer peripherals, darkroom equipment, or even office supplies for the reporters, if everyone benefits, everyone will work harder to sell the ads.

Advertising Management

Although teamwork is involved, usually some staff members have the specific responsibility of generating advertising revenue. How many people this should be depends on the budget, the estimated need for ad dollars, and the size of the staff.

The **advertising manager** is a staff member on the same level as a page or section editor. This person is responsible for ad sales, revenues, overseeing design, billing, and a host of other ad-related responsibilities.

Financial Considerations

How much ad revenue do you need for a year? How does the advertising manager come up with the figure? Serious thought goes into preparing an ad campaign for the publication's school year. Consider these **three** criteria:

1. How much, if any, is left over from the previous year?
2. What funds are available from the school or from the student fees that started up your account?
3. How much additional money do you need for a full year of quality publications?

The first thing you need to do, probably during the summer before the school year begins, is a cost analysis.

A **cost analysis** is a breakdown of the expenses you know you will face during the year compared to your expected income. Most likely, these figures will fluctuate as the year progresses.

Start with Last Year

Start estimating by looking at last year's books, following **three** steps:

1. Total up the money you took in from ads, the school, donations, fees, and other sources.
2. Total the expenses of printing, office supplies, postage, darkroom supplies, computer equipment, photo equipment and cameras, graphics supplies, software, and so on.

3. Evaluate which expenses and income streams are going to be consistent from year to year and which were one-year-only expenses or sources of income. This information will give you a solid jumping-off point for creating your budget.

Look at This Year

The next phase is to figure in the items for the upcoming year that are not listed, both on the expense side and the revenue side.

1. **Get the bottom line.** When both columns are totaled, what's the difference between them?
2. **Make some decisions.** Is the figure one that can be realistically achieved through advertising sales? If achieving everything on your wish list means all staff members would have to sell $4,500 in ads, and that's not going to happen, you need to look at either scaling back your expenses or investigating additional ways to generate funds.

Work with Your Printer

Working closely with your printer is also important to a sound budget. Your yearbook account representative or commercial newspaper printer should meet with you and your adviser before the start of school to work out the estimated printing costs for the year.

Ad Records Sheet

Advertising Record Sheet
Newspaper: Issue 4, Nov. 16, 1999

	Business	Address/Phone	Contact Person/Title	Sold By	Size	Price	Date Billed	Date Paid	Check No.
1.	T and L Printing	1214 Court Ave./944-9922	Al Thompson, Owner	Daniel T.	1/2 pg	$85	11/18	11/23	#1214
2.	Bahama Bronze								
3.	LNB Bank								
4.	Larry Wilder								
5.	Shades of Summer								
6.	Bales Automotive								

Record Keeping

Some people are born to be in sales. If you have staff members like that, they will happily do what they do best: contacting businesses that could advertise in your publication. But a detail-oriented member of the staff, usually the ad manager, needs to keep track of all the paperwork. Nothing will make your publication look worse to a local business than sending them a duplicate bill when it has already paid in full. And nothing will be less motivating than trying to sell ads to a business that has already turned away another staff member.

How do you solve this problem? Develop and use a potential advertiser list and keep good records.

Building an Advertiser List

Here are **three** guidelines for composing a list each year:

1. Start with the companies that have traditionally advertised with your school's publications or athletic department in the past.

2. Look at local newspapers to see what businesses advertise there. Go through the Yellow Pages of your local phone book.

3. Check out what other schools in your area have done.

Using an Advertiser List

Once you have a list of potential advertisers, how do you use it?

1. Your ad manager may ask all staff members to sign up for businesses to call on.

2. After making sales calls, staff members can mark the list with pertinent information: to whom they spoke, the outcome of the visit, notes on the reaction of the business owner or manager. This information will be important in future years when staffs are considering prospective advertising clients.

Tracking sales

After sales have been made, it's important to keep track of the ads scheduled to appear in a particular issue as well as the ad sales force's **commissions.** Generate easy grids to help you keep this information organized.

* **Ad records sheet.** You need to know what ads have been sold for each issue. Fill out a form that includes the advertiser's name, address, and phone; the size of the ad; the cost of the ad; the date billed; the date paid and check number; and the salesperson's name. That way, when you're planning for Issue 4, you only have to look at the sheet to see how many ads have to be worked into the design of the issue. And, when checks come in, you'll be able to accurately keep track of them.
* **Commission sheet.** Because grades or commissions may be riding on sales, you need to record who sold which ads.

Generate a form for each member of your staff, with a column for the name of the business, issue number, size of the ad, and prices. In that way, you can tell at a glance if someone has met his or her sales quota for the grading period or has been paid a commission each grading period, quarter, or semester.

Fill out both of these forms as soon as the staff member comes back with a signed **advertising contract** in hand. This way you always have a current, accurate record of the ads sold, issue-by-issue, and how much each person sold.

Client Paperwork

Using the proper business forms to manage your ad accounts is also the mark of a well-organized and professional student publication. Here are **five** of the most important aspects of advertising paperwork:

Commissions Sheet

Ad Commissions Sheet

Staffer Name	Advertiser/Business	Issue #	Size	Price
Roxanne P.	Water Energizers	1	1/8	$25
	Bo's Video	6	1/4	$40
	Glenn's Carry-Outta	15	1/2	$70
	T & L Printing	4	full	$125
	Gray & Wells Body Shop	10	1/16	$15

1. **Ad contracts.** When making a sales call, take a blank contract that includes space for the name and address of the company, the size of the ad, the number of newspaper issues in which the ad is to appear, the dates of publication, the logo of the business, other elements to appear in the ad, and signatures of both the staff salesperson and the businessperson. A sample ad contract is shown here. When you sell an ad, it is very important to get the agreement in writing, with a signature. A signed contract is part of any businesslike agreement and protects you. Each party should keep a copy, so you may want to use duplicate forms.

2. **Ad form.** You will also need a standardized form for the statement or ad. This form should contain the name, address, and phone number of both the school publication and the business, as well as the name of the contact persons for each (the business owner and staff ad manager). There should also be spots for the issue number, date of publication, size of the ad, cost of the ad, and a time frame for paying the amount owed.

3. **Thank-you note.** It's also a good idea to write a short thank-you for the company's patronage of your publication. Personal touches are the mark of a detail-oriented ad campaign.

4. **Ad statement.** When you send the bill, or statement, you need to include a **tearsheet,** or an actual sample, of the ad as it appeared in your newspaper or yearbook. An advertiser should receive

Example

Sample Ad Contract

proof that the ad really ran when the bill says it did, as well as see how the ad looked. If there's a mistake in a newspaper ad, it should be corrected before the next issue.

5. **Receipt.** After the advertiser has paid, send a receipt. A book of generic receipts can be inexpensively purchased at an office supply store. Do this promptly and be sure to keep a copy.

Complimentary Copies

Don't forget to "comp" your paid advertisers. A **comp** is a free, or complimentary, copy of your publication. You'll find that this practice is also good public relations for your newspaper or yearbook because often the publication will be placed on the front counter or on the coffee table in the lobby of the company's business, giving your school and community added exposure.

General Paperwork

What do you do with all the paperwork generated for each business's ad account? For each advertiser, you'll probably have a copy of the ad contract (sometimes for several years with repeat advertisers), various receipts for payment, copies of bills, business cards, tearsheets, and maybe some of the design materials used in generating the actual ad.

Be organized. Keep alphabetical file folders, one for each company, in a cabinet in the staff room. The files should provide quick answers to questions that either the business staff or ad staff might have. For example, once an ad is sold and the yearbook is in production, the ad designer will need to know what exactly goes in the ad. All he or she should have to do is pull the advertiser's file and find the contract; all the information should be there.

Good Advertising

What kinds of ads work best—for both the publication and the advertiser? Should you print business cards in the yearbook? Should staff members sell ads to relatives who live out of town? Keep in mind the **three** purposes of an ad campaign:

1. To inform students of products and services of interest to them.
2. To generate money for your publication's budget.
3. To help companies and stores in your community get more student business.

Sales Tips

Practice is the key. The first few times you go out to sell an ad, you may be a bit unsure of how to talk easily with business-people in your community. Don't be surprised if your first selling attempts aren't successful. The usual success rate for sales is 1 out of 10 sales calls. But while salespeople need to get used to being told no, there are several things you can do to improve your percentage of "getting a yes."

Training

Training is integral to the success of any project, whether it's reporting, design, photography, or ad sales. The more you know about what to expect during a sales call, the better you'll be able to think on your feet.

1. **Use the buddy system.** A good way for an inexperienced staff member to benefit from the knowledge of those more experienced is to sell ads in teams of two. Just as with swimming, there's safety in numbers. You'll find that the two salespeople will play off of each other when speaking with the advertiser and complement each other's strengths and weaknesses.

2. **Be businesslike on sales calls.** Do your homework, find out who is in charge of advertising for the business, identify yourself and the school, respect the client's time and schedule, dress appropriately, and practice.

Information

After you've been trained in how to speak with a businessperson on an ad sales call and you've got your list of potential advertisers, are you ready to hit the streets? You're probably not ready just yet. You still need to get information about the local businesses on your list.

You need to know which businesses advertise with other student or professional publications or in athletic or fine arts programs around town. Which businesses generally don't have much of a budget for advertising?

Before the ad sales call, find out:

* Directions to the business.
* Name of the contact person who is authorized to buy the ad (manager or owner).
* The products and services that would most interest students at your school.
* A good way to attract students to the business with an ad.
* Where else the business advertises.

Advertising Surveys

Where do the students at your school eat? Work? Buy clothes? Shop for music? Buy accessories for their cars? Go for entertainment? Teenagers do have discretionary funds (available spending money). If they're aware of what a business has to offer them, they're more likely to patronize that business.

A great tool for gathering information is the student **advertising survey**. Students spend billions of dollars annually on clothes, accessories, cars, cosmetics, insurance, computer supplies, music, entertainment, and more. Why not find the companies close to your school that have products or services that fit the needs and tastes of your student body? Not only will students notice and use the ads in your publication, you'll be establishing a credible relationship with the local business community as well.

Sidebar

Instead of Money, Try . . .

You've investigated the business, and you were brilliant in your sales call. But the client just can't spend the money. Not all ads need to be paid in cash. Often, the business's product can be quite valuable. Some ideas:

* Offer an ad to a restaurant in exchange for food to be delivered during busy production times.
* Offer an office supply store an ad in exchange for a specified amount of supplies that you need.
* Offer a silk-screening company an ad in exchange for printed T-shirts.

Sometimes it may not be an even trade (or it may be hard to tell what's even), but discounts on things you need can add up. Receiving payment in kind for as much as 25 percent of your ads can provide a budget boost as you generate goodwill with businesses in your community.

Your homework might well include using the products and services the client has to offer. If it's an ice-cream store, buy a cone. If it's a barbershop, get a haircut. Not only will the store owner remember you and view your return as an ad salesperson in a more favorable light, you'll also have firsthand knowledge of whether the company offers anything your readers want.

Sales Call

Just as with an interview, you want to be completely prepared for a sales call. First, know why businesses should advertise with your publication. Back up reasons with facts. Also, be sure to:

* *Show your publication*. If the advertiser asks about the overall look of your publication, be sure to have one to show. If it's a newspaper or literary magazine, leave a copy. If it's a yearbook, show it there or offer to leave it temporarily and come back for it later.
* *Leave a business card.* What if the advertiser wants to think about your pitch and call you later? Leave a business card with the name of the publication, your name, your adviser's name, the school's phone number, and the best times to call.
* *Have a sales kit.* The checklist on this page details other items a sales kit should include.

Checklist

Inside a Sales Kit

In addition to copies of your publications and business cards, be sure to have the following:

✓ *A spec ad or mock-up of what the business's ad would look like if your staff designed it.* A <u>mock-up</u> helps business people visualize what their ad would look like in your newspaper or yearbook.

✓ *A <u>rate sheet.</u>* A rate sheet, or <u>fee schedule,</u> is a list of sizes, prices, discounts, deadlines, and any extra charges for advertisements.

✓ *A blank ad contract.* You'll need two copies if you're not using carbon.

✓ *A sample statement.* The advertiser may want to see a <u>statement,</u> or form that shows what they'll be getting, in the mail when it's time to remit payment.

✓ *The results from your student spending survey.* Try to dress up the statistics with some infographics so the advertiser can see at a glance what students at your school spend on various items.

Alternative Ad Options

In addition to straightforward ads, several alternative advertising options exist:

Parent-sponsored yearbook ads. Yearbook ads that feature baby pictures of graduating seniors along with a blurb from the parents are popular in many parts of the country. However, some publication staffs feel this type of ad cheapens a yearbook or newspaper. What does your staff think? How would the parents in your school's community respond? Would this type of ad make your publication appear less professional?

Patron ad. Generally, these types of ads appear in literary magazines more than newspapers and yearbooks. A **patron ad** could be a listing of businesses or parents who have contributed to the publication but who don't necessarily want a display advertisement. Often, levels of patrons are listed according to the amount of their donation.

Some people or businesses would rather be patrons of your publication and have their names (or messages to graduating seniors or staff members) listed for a nominal fee than purchase a more expensive display ad.

Discounts. What if an advertiser does business with your newspaper for an entire semester—for an entire year, every issue? Is there something you can do to say, "Thanks for your business"? If advertisers appear in every other issue, you might give them 10 percent off each ad. If they are in every issue, you might give them

20 percent off. They get a deal, and you get a longer contract for their ads. But make sure to change the design of the ad slightly each time, perhaps by adding a different coupon or spotlighting a different product so that readers don't start ignoring a too-familiar ad.

Coupons. Advertisers might find that another way to get readers to notice their ads is with coupons. When students think they're going to get a bargain on the things they buy most, your advertisers might be pleasantly surprised at the amount of student traffic they get. With coupons, businesses have proof-in-hand of how many students are coming into their stores.

Sidebar

Yearbook Ad Discounts

How do you handle a multiple ad sale in the yearbook? Instead of discounting for multiple ads within the same year, give discounts for larger sizes. For example, if an 1/8-page ad costs $25, an ad twice as large should not cost twice as much. A 1/4-page ad in the same yearbook might cost $40 instead of $50, thereby giving the ad client twice as much space for less than twice the cost.

Advocacy ads. Some ads may provide a message to your readers rather than provide money to your publication. **Advocacy ads,** or ads that reflect a service, provide information that might help readers live safer or more well-rounded lives. Some of these clients have budgets and will pay the regular rates. Even if they don't, you may want to run some of these ads. Sometimes being a reader-oriented publication isn't just about making money. Possible sources for advocacy ads include:

* Funeral homes
* Adoption agencies
* Alternative lifestyle organizations
* Counseling services
* Environmental organizations

Example

Advocacy Ad

Buy recycled. It would mean the world to them.

Thanks to you, all sorts of everyday products are being made from materials you've recycled. But to keep recycling working, you need to buy those products. For a free brochure, write *Buy Recycled*, Environmental Defense Fund, 257 Park Avenue South, New York, NY 10010, or call 1-800-CALL-EDF.

AT ISSUE

The Advertising Policy

What happens when your most enthusiastic and successful ad salesperson comes gleefully back to the publications room, waving a signed contract for a repeating half-page ad . . . for a local restaurant and bar? Everyone is jubilant until someone realizes that maybe the school administration won't want the publication to run an ad that even remotely promotes a business that sells alcohol. But, you say, food and alcoholic beverages are in separate parts of the establishment, and many students eat dinner at the restaurant with their families (and don't order alcohol). It's confusing, and to avoid a **conflict of interest**, some guidelines are needed on what is acceptable and what isn't. Your publication needs an **advertising policy**.

Will your school accept ads that advise on options for unplanned pregnancies, whether abortion or adoption? Divorce counseling services? Support for students with nontraditional sexual orientation? Certainly things that are illegal for people under age 18 (smoking, drinking, and so on) should be off-limits, but your staff must have rules that govern ad sales and publication. Policies for small schools in rural areas, private or religious schools, and large urban schools will differ, as each reflects its community's values.

Sample Advertising Policy

(as it would appear on the advertising rates sheet and on the contract)

The Newspaper/Yearbook has the right to accept, reject, edit, or cancel any advertisement at any time. If the business pays for the advertising in advance of publication and the staff decides to cancel the ad, money will be promptly refunded for remaining ads. Ads should not contain statements, illustrations, or implications which could be considered offensive to good taste based on the opinion of the staff. Advertising shall offer merchandise or service on its merits, and refrain from attacking competitors unfairly or degrading their products, services, or business practices. The staff may run regular paid political advertisements and ads that could be considered controversial due to their sensitive nature. Staff may reject ads that promote objectionable goods or services, or products illegal for purchase or use by minors/high school students. The staff will not accept ads that are racist, sexist, or which violate other standard journalistic principles (libel, obscenity, invasion of privacy, disruption of the educational process).

Ads which the staff does accept are not an endorsement from the staff, the adviser, the faculty/administration, or the Greater Clark County Schools board of education. Advertiser agrees to pay within 10 business days of receiving invoices, which are mailed within three days of publication and contain tearsheets of published ad. Liability does not extend beyond purchase price of ad space.

Preparing Ads for Publication

Design and production of advertising is similar to design and production of other areas of your publication: It seems as if you need to keep straight a million details. An additional factor in advertising is your responsibility to clients.

Ad Components

Most ads should contain the following information:

* Headline
* Body copy
* Slogan or jingle
* Phone number
* Address
* Contact person
* E-mail or Web site address
* Artwork

Information Needed

Staff members may be tempted to create an ad with just a company's logo and maybe a short, punchy slogan. Most of your clients, however, won't have that kind of instant product recognition. Generally, ads need to carry a lot of information. If you omit information, make sure you have the advertiser's permission. If not, you may have to make a refund.

Policy on Using Color

Probably most of the ads you design will be in black-and-white, at least in a yearbook. If advertisers request color, here are **four** things to keep in mind:

1. In a newspaper, you may have occasion to use spot color on the same page, such as a single feature layout, where you also have ads. If you give your advertising clients the option of using spot color or four-color ads, request a 10 to 25 percent surcharge for these ads.

2. Some newspapers have full-color covers, and for these the printer could supply color on the back cover for a nominal fee. You may be able to accept an ad for the back cover at a nice fee.

3. In a yearbook, your use of color depends on what section the pages fall in. Literary magazines are often custom-made and vary from issue to issue.

4. For black-and-white-only pages, you can use tint blocks and screened type in your ads. This sometimes draws attention to an ad almost as well as spot color.

In general, check with your printer to determine where color can go and apply this information not only to your designs but to your ads as well.

Ad Copy

Eye-catching graphics are important in an ad, but text is a huge part of whether the ad motivates anyone to purchase the product or service. If businesses need ideas for what to say in their ads, provide some samples of ads with brief, clear advertising copy.

Ad copy should do **two** things:

1. Create a need for the product or service.
2. Stir readers to buy.

As with design, "less is more" is a good rule when it comes to ad copy. Busy, copy-heavy ads usually don't get noticed. In most instances, ads with less copy look better.

Designing Pages with Ads

The design editor hates nothing more than having to work a new layout idea around several ads that just came in at the last moment. Yet those last-minute ads produce just as much revenue as the early ones. You can do a couple of things to encourage both the acceptance of last-minute ads and the sanity of the designer.

Design with Modularity

If you use a modular design, adhere to the same standard for your ads and make them modular.

Use standard sizes. Sell ads in the following sizes:

* full page
* 1/2-page
* 1/4-page
* 1/8-page
* 1/16-page (business card size)
* In this way, you can easily combine the ads at the bottom of the page.

For example, let's say you have a half-page story to run in the sports section. No problem. You can also run a 1/4-page ad, along with an 1/8-page and two 1/16-page ads on the same page. They all fit together like pieces in a puzzle. Or, if you have a longer story in the news or feature section, you can run two 1/8-page ads horizontally across the bottom and still have 3/4 of the page for editorial.

Design without Modularity

Some schools sell ads per column inch to give advertisers flexibility in the shape of their ads and how much they cost. If your ad manager won't go for modular ads and wants the flexibility of selling space in column inches, **two** ways exist to create an attractive page.

1. **Smokestack.** One way to get the ads to the bottom and outside edges of the page and the editorial content to the top is called the **smokestack design**. In this design, the horizontal ads go at the bottom of the page, and the long, narrow, vertical ads go toward the outside edge of the page, with the tallest of these ads on the very outside. If you look at the ads with "squint scrutiny" (see Chapter 15), you'll see that they do, in fact, look like smokestacks rising from the bottom of the page. The copy then works around the ads.

2. **Skyline.** The **skyline design** approach places ads at the bottom of the page, regardless of their height. When you squint at the page, the irregular shape of the ads looks like a city skyline at night, with irregularities in the heights of the buildings. The other design options are preferred over the skyline.

Wrap-up

Just as a reporter needs to get the feel for what's happening in your school, the advertising staff member has to understand what's going on in the business community. Selling ads is a good way to generate funds for your publication's expenses, and it's also a great way to gain communication and people skills. When all staff members are taking part in the earning and spending of publication funds, a real atmosphere of teamwork exists within a publication. From crunching budget numbers to pounding the pavement, it's a challenge to come out in the black every year. But just as writers and designers enjoy seeing their story packages come to life in print, you'll also enjoy seeing an ad that you sold and organized the paperwork for get published and delivered to a satisfied client.

advertising contract—signed agreement between an advertiser and a publication that specifically outlines the content of the ad, the price, any discounts, the size, the number of issues, and other pertinent information.

advertising manager—staff member who oversees the ad sales and design staff; is responsible for many business transactions (billings and payments of ads) for the publication.

advertising policy—written statement adopted by the publication specifically outlining what kinds of ads are and are not acceptable for print; may include deadlines, how payments are to be handled, and so on.

advertising survey—list of specific questions designed to generate statistics on how students earn and spend their money; helpful information for ad sales calls.

advocacy ads—ads that supply information in order to help non-profit groups or charities.

commission—bonus paid to ad sales representatives.

comp—complimentary copy of the publication given to advertisers or other patrons.

conflict of interest—situation created when a school publication publishes articles or advertisements that are fundamentally against school or publication policy, or accepts them for a financial benefit outside of journalism ethics.

cost analysis—process of breaking down the publication's cost, issue by issue and page by page, to determine the amount of advertising a publication must run to keep the account in the black.

mock-up—sample ad taken by the publication sales representative to a sales call; used to show the business owner how the company's ad may look.

patron ad—advertisement funded or sponsored by parents or businesses in the community for the express purpose of funding the publication, not necessarily for furthering the image or income of the company; found more often in literary magazines and yearbooks than newspapers.

rate sheet (fee schedule)—list of sizes, prices, discounts, deadlines, and extra charges for advertisements in a publication.

skyline design—non-modular page design in which ads are mostly vertical and are aligned with the bottom of the page so that the outline looks like a cityscape.

smokestack design—non-modular page design in which vertical ads are arranged to look like a series of chimneys; sometimes called "pyramid" design when the ads ascend or descend from largest to smallest.

statement—bill sent to the advertiser after the publication comes out detailing the type and size of ad purchased, the amount due, and the date due; may also include other account information such as any outstanding debts.

tearsheet—sample page of the yearbook or newspaper on which the ad was published; offered as proof of publication and to show how the ad looked.

Credits

9 Reprinted from *Warp Speed* by Bill Kovach and Tom Rosenstiel with permission from The Century Foundation, Inc. © 1999 New York. 28 "High School Newspaper Policy Statement" from *Times*. Lakewood High School, Lakewood, Ohio. Used by permission of *The Lakewood Times* Student Editorial Board. 39 "Campus Clipboard" from *The Lance*, September 21, 1998. Omaha Westside High School, Omaha NE. Reprinted by permission. 64 From *Interviews that Work, 2nd edition*, by S. Biagi. © 1992. Reprinted with permission of Wadsworth, a division of Thompson Learning. Fax 800 730-2215. 72 "Get right outta Stoughton" by Emily A. Winecke from *The Norse Star*, January 29, 1999. Stoughton High School, Stoughton WI. Reprinted by permission. 74 "Hsu scores 1600 on SAT" by Kris Fields from *The Informer*, November 20, 1998. Cerritos High School, Cerritos, CA. Reprinted by permission. 76 "Chicago Tribune editor raps 'politically correct' news" by Justin Evenson from *Johnsburg Weekly News*, December 18, 1998. Courtesy of the *Johnsburg Weekly News*, Johnsburg, IL. Reprinted by permission. 78 "Leaving it behind: Senior Jonathan Fenton" by Juliette Wallack from *HiLite*, August 18, 1998. Carmel High School, Carmel, IN. Reprinted by permission. 90 "Student group to spearhead anti-tobacco use campaign" by Jill Rosenberg from *Trapeze*, March 12, 1999. Oak Park and River Forest High School, Oak Park IL. Reprinted by permission of Jill Rosenberg. 94 "Stolen 'chariot' returned" by Michael H. Ritter from *Flyer*, March 17, 1999. Brentwood School, Los Angeles CA. Reprinted by permisson. 96 "Explosion leads to expulsion" by Kate Tresley from *The Devils' Advocate*, January 25, 1999, Hinsdale Central High School, Hinsdale IL. Reprinted by permission. 99 "Disability: Junior has opportunity to experience handicaps" by Kelly Tibbert, from *The Tower*, March 10, 1999. Grosse Pointe South High School, Grosse Pointe Farms, MI. Reprinted by permission. 118 From *How to Write a News Article* by Michael Kronenwetter. Copyright © 1995 by Michael Kronenwetter. Reprinted by permission. 121 "VTS suspension rates fall below county average" by Kelly Lutzeier from *The Kirkwood Call*, February 22, 1999. Reprinted by permission. 130 "Technology & education: Girls type, boys program. Report reveals widening gap between genders in technology use" by Andrea Haughton, *The Academy Times*, March 30, 1999. Charles Wright Academy, Tacoma, Wash. Used by permission. 136 "Tallying the Troops" from *The Central Times*, May 28, 1999. Naperville Central High School, Naperville, IL. 144 "Fire safety: No way out?" by Jeb Blount from *The Evanstonian*, November 6, 1981. Reprinted by permission. 148 "Reading, writing, and religion" by Dana Lenetz from *Los Angeles Times*, (Orange County Edition), December 23, 1994. Copyright 1994, *Los Angeles Times*. Reprinted by permission. 150 "Cyber Love" by Crystal King from *Lakewood Times*, November 7, 1997. Used by permission of *The Lakewood Times* Student Editorial Board. 162 From *Journalism Education Association Stylebook*. Reprinted by permission. 166 From *The Word: An Associated Press Guide to Good Writing* by Rene J. Cappon. Reprinted by permission. 168 From *The Word: An Associated Press Guide to Good Writing* by Rene J. Cappon. Reprinted by permission. 170 From *Writing and Reporting The News, Second Edition*, by Gerald Lanson and Mitchell Stephens. 181 "Promoting diversity: New club works toward eliminating oppression and hate" by Jennifer L. Hammer, from *Tide Lines*, October 15, 1998. Reprinted by permission. 184 "Backed by 'brothers'" by Lauren Roederer from *HiLite*, December 17, 1998. Carmel High School, Carmel, IN. Reprinted by permission. 198 "Seeing beyond black and white" by Miriam Armendariz, January 22, 1999. Used by permission of *The Axe*, South Eugene High School, Eugene, OR. 200 "Is the media taking rights under the First Amendment too far?" by Jason Moser and Barry Weiss from *Tide Lines*, October 15, 1998, Pottsville Area High School. Reprinted by permission. 205 "Weapons expulsions shouldn't be automatic" from *The A-Blast*, March 26, 1999, Vol. 44, No. 9., Annandale High School. Reprinted by permission. 211 Clinton cartoon, *The Axe*, January 22, 1999. Used by permission of *The Axe*, South Eugene High School, Eugene, OR. 215 "Setting an example for all" by Stephanie Hales from *HiLite*, November 5, 1998. Carmel High School, Carmel, IN. Reprinted by permission. 223 "'The Phantom Menace' blasts into theaters" by Loryn Elizares from *The Excalibur*, May 26, 1999. Robert McQueen High School, Reno NV. Reprinted by permission. 233 "Men's basketball remains undefeated in state play" by Katy Polansky, *The Axe*, February 19, 1999. Used by permission of *The Axe*, South Eugene High School, Eugene, OR. 236 "Female athletes in a league of their own" by Wei-ying Wang from *The Lowell*, February 12, 1999. Reprinted by permission. 240 "Pro athletes are today's role models" by Brett McWethy from *Central Stampede*, November 13, 1998. Portage Central High School, Portage MI. Reprinted by permission. 241 "Fall Rewind" from *The Little Hawk*, December 11, 1998. City High School, Iowa City, Iowa. Reprinted by permission. 262 "Code of Ethics" from *National Press Photographers Association*. Reprinted with permission from the National Press Photographers Association, © 2000. 269 From "The Face of Generation Next" by Sue Lackey. Reprinted by permission of the author. 270 From "They're Not Safe" by Gary West. Reprinted by permission of the author. 272 From "You, Sir, are a drunkard, a worthless scoundrel, and a coward" by Bill Mooney. Reprinted by permission of the author. 273 From "The Dip" by Jennie Rees. Reprinted by permission of the author. 275 "What's Up?" from *The Hyphen*, October 6, 1995, pg. 3, Jeffersonville High School, Jefferson, IN. Reprinted by permission.

276 "Michael Jackson Can't Beat It" by Glenn Murphy from *The Hyphen*, Jeffersonville High School, Jeffersonville, IN. Reprinted by permission. **282** "Program to keep community close" by Emily Scmitt from *The Rosecall*, September, 1997. Assumption High School, Louisville, Kentucky. Reprinted by permission. **282** "Enrollment climbs to all-time high" by Melanie Hampton from *The Rosecall*, September, 1997. Assumption High School, Louisville, Kentucky. Reprinted by permission. **282** "Vargo goes distance on course, in classroom" from *The Rosecall*, September, 1997. Assumption High School, Louisville, Kentucky. Reprinted by permission. **282** "National champs travel to Russia, Europe" from *The Rosecall*, September 1997. Assumption High School, Louisville, Kentucky. Reprinted by permission. **283** "How a 45-year run began with a walk. . ." from Our Lady of Providence High School, Clarksville, IN. Reprinted by permission. **294** *"The New York Herald Tribune,"* May 10th, 1940, from General Research Division, The New York Public Library, Astor, Lenox and Tilden Foundations. Reprinted by permission. **295** "Puppet France Breaks With U.S. Roosevelt, Roosevelt Explains America's Motives," from *Bangor Daily News*, November 9, 1942. Reprinted by permission. **295** "Kennedy Dead!" Page supplied by *The Sheboygan Press*. November 22, 1963. Reprinted by permission. **297** "Violence coming closer to home" by Julia Fox from *The Peninsula Outlook*, April 6, 1999. Peninsula High School. Reprinted by permission. **302** From "Big little movie season" by Harlan Jacobson, *USA TODAY*, October 29, 1999.

Copyright 1999, *USA TODAY*. Reprinted with permission. **316** From *Coaching Writers* by Clark et al. Copyright © 11/91 by Bedford/St. Martin's Press, Inc. Reprinted with permission of Bedford/St. Martin's Press, Inc. **318** Reprinted with permission by Quill and Scroll Society from the *Quill and Scroll Stylebook*. **319** From *Free to Write: A Journalist Teaches Young Writers* by Roy Peter Clark. **345** Yearbook cover from *The Lion, 1999*, from McKinney High School, McKinney, TX. Reprinted by permission. **345** Yearbook cover from *The Trail*, Overland High School, Aurora, Colorado. Reprinted by permission. **345** Yearbook Cover from *1999 Kirkwood Pioneer*, Kirkwood, High School, Kirkwood, MO. Reprinted by permission. **350** "Day by Day - The Schedule" from Judy Babb, SMU Publications adviser. Reprinted by permission. **351** From *1999 Kirkwood Pioneer*, Kirkwood High School, Kirkwood, MO. Reprinted by permission. **352** "The Weekend Fun Begins" from *Highlander 1998*, Highland Park High School, Dallas, TX. Reprinted by permission. **352** From "Overcoming the Worst: A freshman faces her fears about the Homecoming Dance" by Ebony Moore from *The Hillcrest Panther*. Hillcrest High School, Dallas, TX. Reprinted by permission. **364** "Stars of New Trier" from *The Examiner*, October 15, 1999. Courtesy of New Trier Township High School. **366** From *Publishing the Literary Magazine* by Ann Klaiman © 1990. Used with permission from NTC/Contemporary. **368** From *Publishing the Literary Magazine* by Ann Klaiman © 1990. Used with permission from NTC/Contemporary.

Index